The Developm of Criminological Thought

This book focuses on the history and development of criminological thought from the pre-Enlightenment period to the present and offers a detailed and chronological overview of competing theoretical perspectives in criminology in their social and political context. This book covers:

- A discussion of how major theorists came to espouse their ideas and how the social context of the time influenced the development of criminological thought;
- An exploration of the scientific method and the way in which theories are tested;
- Details of the origins of each theory as well as their recent developments in scholarship and research;
- Comparative and international research in theory;
- The empirical support for theory and the relationship between research and policy;
- Biosocial and developmental criminology, including the biosocial underpinnings of criminal behavior and the influence of neuroscience and brain psychology;
- Theoretical applications for explaining different crime types, such as genocide, white-collar crime, and environmental crime;
- A summary of the current state of criminological knowledge and a vision for the future of criminology.

The book includes lists of further reading and chapter summaries, and is supported by timelines of key works and events. This book is essential reading for courses on criminological theory, criminal behavior, criminal psychology, and biosocial criminology.

Chad Posick is Assistant Professor at the Department of Criminal Justice and Criminology, Georgia Southern University, USA.

The Development of Criminological Thought

Context, Theory, and Policy

Chad Posick

Routledge
Taylor & Francis Group

LONDON AND NEW YORK

First published 2018
by Routledge
2 Park Square, Milton Park, Abingdon, Oxon OX14 4RN

and by Routledge
711 Third Avenue, New York, NY 10017

Routledge is an imprint of the Taylor & Francis Group, an informa business

British Library Cataloguing-in-Publication Data

A catalogue record for this book is available from the British Library

Library of Congress Cataloging in Publication Data
Names: Posick, Chad, author.
Title: The development of criminological thought : context, theory and
    policy / Chad Posick.
Description: Abingdon, Oxon ; New York, NY : Routledge, 2018. | Includes
    bibliographical references and index.
Identifiers: LCCN 2017042460| ISBN 9781138190504 (hardback) | ISBN
    9781138190511 (pbk.) | ISBN 9781315640976 (ebook)
Subjects: LCSH: Criminology—History.
Classification: LCC HV6021 .P67 2018 | DDC 364—dc23
LC record available at https://lccn.loc.gov/2017042460

ISBN: 978-1-138-19050-4 (hbk)
ISBN: 978-1-138-19051-1 (pbk)
ISBN: 978-1-315-64097-6 (ebk)

Typeset in Stone Serif and Rockwell
by Apex CoVantage, LLC

To my wife, Sandra, for always supporting me, pushing me, and loving me.

Contents

List of illustrations   xi
Foreword   xii
Preface and special dedication   xv
Acknowledgments   xvii
About the author   xviii

Introduction   1

01 Science, theory, and empirical investigation   3
Introduction   3
Science and theory   4
The scientific method   5
Elements of a theory   7
Micro and macro theory   8
Theory and underlying assumptions of human behavior   9
Theory, science, and paradigms   10
Summary   11

02 Pre-Enlightenment theories   13
Introduction   13
Theory   14
Classical Greek and philosophical perspectives   14
Pagan perspectives   16
Christian and monotheistic perspectives   17
Naturalistic perspectives   19
The Enlightenment and the emergence of contemporary criminology   20
The case of Abigail Williams: the 11-year-old witch   20
Empirical support   22
Remaining questions   22
Policy   22
Summary   23

03 Lombroso and early biological theories   25
Introduction   25
Theory   26
Origins   26

Recent developments | 32
The cases of Carrie Buck and Abdelmalek Bayout: the genetic basis of crime | 35
Empirical support | 36
Remaining questions | 37
Policy | 37
Summary | 38

04 The city and social disorganization theories | **40**
Introduction | 40
Theory | 41
Origins | 41
Recent developments | 45
The case of Rochester, New York: a great city with great problems | 49
Empirical support | 50
Remaining questions | 51
Policy | 52
Summary | 53

05 Anomie and strain theories | **56**
Introduction | 56
Theory | 57
Origins | 57
Recent developments | 60
The case of Tanya Mitchell: the stressed killer | 63
Empirical support | 63
Remaining questions | 64
Policy | 64
Summary | 65

06 Differential association and social learning theories | **68**
Introduction | 68
Theory | 69
Origins | 69
Recent developments | 70
The case of the Boston Marathon bombing: learning crime and terrorism | 73
Empirical support | 74
Remaining questions | 75
Policy | 75
Summary | 76

07 Labeling and critical criminology | **78**
Introduction | 78
Theory | 79
Origins | 80
Marxism | 80
Labeling | 82
Recent developments | 84
Peacemaking | 84
Left realism | 84
Feminist criminology | 85
Green criminology | 87
Queer criminology | 88
The case of Brock Allen Turner: sexual assault and violence against
women at Stanford | 88
Empirical support | 89

	Remaining questions	90
	Policy	90
	Summary	91

08	**Social and self-control theories**	**94**
	Introduction	94
	Theory	94
	Origins	95
	Recent developments	97
	The case of Randy Kraft: the successful serial killer	101
	Empirical support	102
	Remaining questions	102
	Policy	103
	Summary	104

09	**Deterrence and rational choice theories**	**106**
	Introduction	106
	Theory	107
	Origins	107
	Recent developments	110
	The case of John Snow's old maps and new models of policing	114
	Empirical support	115
	Remaining questions	117
	Policy	117
	Summary	118

10	**Developmental criminology**	**121**
	Introduction	121
	Theory	122
	Origins	122
	Recent developments	123
	The case of Stanley "Tookie" Williams, III: from gang leader to children's book author	129
	Empirical support	130
	Remaining questions	131
	Policy	131
	Summary	133

11	**Biosocial criminology**	**135**
	Introduction	135
	Theory	136
	Origins	136
	Recent developments	137
	Crash and crime: the case of stress and genetic susceptibility	143
	Empirical support	143
	Remaining questions	144
	Policy	145
	Summary	146

12	**Criminology in international perspective**	**149**
	Introduction	149
	Theory	150
	Origins	154
	Recent developments	155
	The case of the Super Bowl and sex trafficking	159

Remaining questions 159
Policy 160
Summary 161

13 Theory and various crime types **166**
Introduction 166
Theory 166
Recent developments 167
The case of "Pharmabro" Martin Shkreli and white-collar crime 174
Summary 174

14 Crime and victimization **176**
Criminology and victimology 177
Strain 181
Social interaction 181
Subcultural theories 182
Self- and social control 184
Biosocial victimology 187
Summary 188

15 The future of criminological theory **191**
Developmental and life-course criminology 192
Biosocial criminology 192
Mass murder, terrorism, and genocide 193
Cybercrime 195
Crimes of the powerful and green criminology 195
Evaluation of theory and crime prevention 196
Conclusion 199

Appendices **201**
Appendix I Important criminological works, 1700 to the present day 201
Appendix II Important world events, 1700 to the present day 204

References 207
Index 230

Illustrations

Figures

1.1	Alhazen	6
2.1	Matthew Hopkins the witch-hunter	18
2.2	The Love Potion	19
3.1	Della Porta: Raven, Owl, and Man	27
3.2	The Kallikak family	27
4.1	Burgess's concentric zones	43
4.2	Collective efficacy theory	48
4.3	Rochester, New York	49
6.1	Akers' extensions	71
6.2	Akers' social learning theory	72
9.1	Rational choice framework	109
9.2	Routine activity theory (RAT) framework	111
10.1	Moffitt: Life-course-persistent vs. adolescent-limited offenders	125
10.2	Agnew's life domains	127
10.3	Farrington's Integrated Cognitive Antisocial Potential (ICAP) theory	128
10.4	Domains of maturation	129
14.1	The victim–offender overlap	179
14.2	Theories of victimization	180
14.3	Extension of low self-control to explain victimization	184
15.1	The cost of genome sequencing, 2001 to 2015	193
15.2	Intergenerational transmission of criminality: explanations and prevention	197

Tables

5.1	Merton strategies + The Maximizer	63
12.1	The Geneva Conventions	162
12.2	The Nuremberg Codes	163

Foreword

It was our joint appreciation of theory that prompted my introduction to Chad Posick. Back in early 2015, Chad, along with his colleague and good friend Michael Rocque, asked if I was interested in being a critic for an author-meets-critic session at the upcoming American Society of Criminology meetings in Washington, DC. The book in question was Simon Singer's award-winning *America's Safest City: Delinquency and Modernity in Suburbia*. At the time, I had not read the book but a quick glance through its pages along with Chad and Michael's persuasive email about Singer's theoretical contribution to the field convinced me that this was something I wanted to be a part of. Fast forward a few years. the author-meets-critic session was a big hit, Michael and Chad went on to co-edit a special issue of *Crime, Law and Social Change* that featured our panel's commentary, and I have come to know Chad as an extremely bright, insightful, up-and-coming young scholar. Most of all, I have come to realize that Chad, like me, has a deep appreciation of theory – something of a rarity these days.

Chad's interest in theory is evident in much of his work, including in his first book, *The Criminal Brain*, co-authored with Nicole Rafter and Michael Rocque. Among other things, *The Criminal Brain* provides an up-to-date overview of the newest research in bio-social criminology. Yet Chad's theoretical focus goes well beyond bio-social criminology, spilling into his other research interests such as the intersection of victimization and offending, identity and desistance from crime, and the history of criminology. In a delightful way, Chad's research interests converge in this book, *The Development of Criminological Thought*, a text which traces the construction of ideas that were used to understand crime and criminality from the ancient Greeks up through the contemporary theorists of today. In this book, Chad reviews ideas and theories about why people commit crime and why rates of crime are higher in some areas than in others.

There are several reasons why *The Development of Criminological Thought* stands out from other theory texts one might read. First and foremost, a deliberate focus is placed upon the historical context and social events that influenced how theorists understood – and continue to understand – criminal behavior. Chad's discussion of each perspective highlights theory's embedded and dynamic nature (two descriptors not often paired with the word "theory"), and reveals that theories cannot be separated from history, or from the conditions of the times. As just one example, the chapter on social disorganization theory, concerned with explaining why crime rates vary across neighborhoods in a given city, carefully traces the theory's intellectual history, describing its development during the first part of the twentieth century – a period marked by rapid political, economic and social change that affected virtually all aspects of life. Industrialization, urbanization and immigration were central features of the American landscape in the 1920s and 1930s, something not overlooked by theorists at the time. A clear link between what was happening and the development of social disorganization theory emphasized the challenges of this country's heterogeneous, rapidly changing society and considered the implications for crime. As with all theories in this book, Chad details this historical backdrop. In this way, *The Development of Criminological Thought* is ideal not just for those wanting to learn the content of criminological theories themselves but for anyone curious about the development of ideas. History buffs welcome!

Who better to learn from about this history and development than the theorists themselves? One of the most unique features of *The Development of Criminological Thought* is the inclusion of personal interviews with luminaries in the field. Through responses to a series of interview questions, the reader becomes privy to impromptu reflections by some of the leading architects of criminological theory. Although I enjoyed all of the interviews, my favorite was with Simon Singer, the author of *America's Safest City*, mentioned earlier. His comments about the need for criminological theory to better capture the complexity of modern-day life for youth are spot-on.

Beyond these interviews, Chad also delves into the biographies of key theorists, offering a glimpse into their personal backgrounds and histories. Much of this information was new to me and incredibly fascinating. For example, I learned that one of my all-time favourite theorists and leading criminologist in the field, Robert Sampson, was just a "fairly average student" in college and only went to graduate school after deciding that selling shoes for a living wasn't as "easy" and as "lucrative" as he had originally thought!

Also unique to the book is the broad range of theories covered – from the earliest thoughts on criminality reflecting the perspectives of ancient Greek philosophers and those philosophers closer to the Enlightenment period as well as religious figures throughout history to contemporary theories, which have emerged in the field in the past 50 years and show considerable promise for guiding future theoretical efforts. Beyond the theories themselves, Chad also introduces the reader to critical issues which one must keep in mind as one studies theories of crime and offending. In particular, I found the chapter on crime and victimization, which considers the overlap between offenders and victims, extremely useful. I am not at all surprised by this; Chad's dissertation project involved investigating victim–offender overlap in 30 countries, and he has published extensively in this area. His contributions were recently recognized when he received the New Scholar Award from the Victimology Section of the Academy of Criminal Justice Sciences.

I can honestly say that no other theory text covers such a wide range of criminological theory and identifies so many key issues related to offending, something that is no easy feat. And I say that as someone who routinely teaches courses on criminological theory, has written theoretical articles published in leading journals in the field, and has even written her own theory text, *Researching Theories of Crime and Deviance*, co-authored with Thomas Stucky and Marvin Krohn. Take my word for it; Chad has done a remarkable job here.

After reading *The Development of Criminological Thought*, you will come away with a broader and deeper understanding of criminological theory. You will also gain an appreciation of just how emergent and ever-evolving theory is, as the title of the text itself implies, and as Albert Einstein and Leopold Infeld acknowledged nearly 80 years ago in their book, *The Evolution of Physics: The Growth of Ideas from Early Concepts to Relativity and Quanta*, which traces the development of ideas in physics:

> To use a comparison, we could say that creating a new theory is not like destroying an old barn and erecting a skyscraper in its place. It is rather like climbing a mountain, gaining new and wider views, discovering unexpected connections between our starting-point and its rich environment. But the point from which we started

out still exists and can be seen, although it appears smaller and forms a tiny part of our broad view gained by the mastery of the obstacles on our adventurous way up.

Enjoy the journey!

Charis E. Kubrin, Professor of Criminology,
Law and Society, University of California, Irvine
Irvine, CA

Preface and special dedication

This book is about the development of ideas and theories about why people commit crime and why rates of crime are higher in some areas than in others. The history of criminology is often overlooked and only a few theorists have pressed us to think seriously about the foundations of criminological thought.[1] To this end, I hope this book gives readers insight into the origins of criminology and the progression of thought up until today. I also hope to give due credit and attention to recent theories and ideas in criminology that are "in the works." So much insightful and progressive work has been done and is currently being done in the field of criminology. Not only is this extremely important for the field, but it is very exciting! My intent is to carefully document this progression by discussing classic theories as well as contemporary theories – and/or extensions of theories – in the contexts in which they appear.

At this point, I wish to point to three criminologists who have profoundly impacted the field through their theoretical and empirical contributions as well as their mentorship of several students who have gone on to accomplish great things. Professors Thomas C. Castellano, Nicole H. Rafter and Chester L. Britt III, all colleagues and friends to me and several others, passed away much too soon, leaving a significant hole in the field and in the hearts of many. However, their legacies live on in their scholarly contributions and in the ideas they transmitted to their students.

Dr. Castellano, the professor who gave me my first student research position and introduced me to the field, taught at Southern Illinois University before coming to the Rochester Institute of Technology where I had the pleasure of studying under his mentorship. Tom's work began with attention to neighborhood context and crime. He wrote early articles with State University of New York at Albany colleagues Robert Sampson and John Laub exploring the role of inequality and neighborhood conditions on victimization and offending.[2] Of course, Sampson and Laub both went on to make significant contributions to criminology in that area – and in many others. Throughout the 1990s, Tom's work evaluated the efficacy of boot camps and other intermediate sanctions.[3] These approaches, based on the assumption that structure and discipline will lead to desistance from crime, were popular during this decade. However, his work debunked this assumption and, along with research by others such as Doris MacKenzie, likely led to their fall in popularity to virtual non-existence today. Finally, his most recent work was centered on super-maximum prisons and their negative impacts upon people and society.[4]

Dr. Rafter, who worked closely with me during my graduate studies at Northeastern University where she taught for over 30 years, introduced me to biosocial criminology and co-authored a paper and book with me on the topic.[5] Nicole's (Nicky's) work was in the areas of feminist criminology,[6] the history of criminology,[7] and biosocial criminology,[8] and had a widespread impact. She was responsible for assisting in the development of the Division of Women and Crime through the American Society of Criminology, establishing one of the first courses on biosocial criminology in the country, and she still tops lists of the most productive female scholars in the field of criminology.[9] Always, her work contained a deep appreciation for history and the importance of context in the production of knowledge. Perhaps it is not surprising that I attempt in this book to follow in her footsteps and give attention to the history and development of criminology.

Most recently, Dr. Britt passed away just after taking over as chairperson of the sociology department at Iowa State University. While I never formally took a class with Chet, I did audit his advanced statistical methods course at Northeastern University (I still hear his encouragement, "It's just a little bit of algebra!"). His work was diverse, investigating criminal justice decision-making,[10] victimization[11] and statistical methods.[12] He served as editor of *Justice Quarterly* and, in that capacity, was a disseminator of knowledge in the field at that time. Most importantly, Chet was always there with a word of wisdom, a kind word of support, and a welcoming smile. His scholarly work, in both theory development and statistical methods, advanced the field in countless ways that we will appreciate for decades to come.

We all build upon what our family, friends, teachers, and mentors pass along to us. There is a rich history to knowledge – both worldly and personal – that should be honored. I have no doubt that many who read these pages will go on to do great things with the knowledge accumulated across the generations.

Notes

1. Laub, 2006; Rafter, 2010.
2. Sampson & Castellano, 1982; Sampson, Castellano, & Laub, 1981.
3. Cowles & Castellano, 1996.
4. Briggs, Sundt, & Castellano, 2003.
5. Posick, Rocque, & Rafter, 2014.
6. Rafter, 1995.
7. Rafter, 2004, 2007, 2008, 2010.
8. Rafter, Posick, & Rocque, 2016.
9. Weir & Orrick, 2013.
10. Britt, 2000.
11. Britt, 2001.
12. Weisburd & Britt, 2007.

Acknowledgments

It's hard to know where to start in thanking all those who had a hand in the final product that is this book. First, I must thank friends and colleagues who have read the manuscript in its entirety. That is more than I could ask for – but I did. Michael Rocque, thank you for carefully reading every word of the text. As always, your keen eye and critical approach is always helpful. Thanks for giving the book quite a glance with little to no reward. I also have to thank my department chair and colleague Brenda Blackwell not only for supporting me while I wrote this book but for providing insight and resources to flesh out sections that I could not have done by myself. Two graduate assistants in particular helped envision the material in the book and bring it to fruition. Thank you, MacKenzie McBride and Tyler Edwards, for all your hard work. I really look forward to seeing what you do in the future. Also, thanks to Jeremy Bell for all the insight on the early theories of crime and justice, and to Jared Sexton for encouragement and company during times of stress and doubt. I am really indebted for all the advice and materials from the scholars interviewed for this book. Although there is not room to name each individually here, I am appreciative of every single one. Each person gave their time and efforts to this project with little assurance that their efforts would pay off. I hope they have. A very special thank you goes to Charis Kubrin for reading the text, offering feedback, and agreeing to write the Preface to the book. Charis is the first person I approached to write the Preface, as there is no better person in my mind to start off the journey through the book, and she so graciously agreed to do so. Finally, when writing led to being stir crazy in the house, I want to thank Three Tree Coffee Roasters in Statesboro for providing a nice place to write with caffeinated beverages. And thanks to Gnats Landing across the street for providing something harder to drink when it was called for. Finally, for the sweet sounds of jazz from Keith Barber who serenaded the final revisions of the text at Gee Da's Table.

About the author

Chad Posick is Assistant Professor of Criminal Justice and Criminology at Georgia Southern University. He received his doctorate in Criminology and Criminal Justice from Northeastern University in Boston, Massachusetts. His research interests focus on how biology shapes behavior and how trauma and abuse can shape later biological functioning. Currently, his research is exploring how to intervene in the cycle of violence, comprehensively explain victimization, and improve police–community relations. At Georgia Southern University he currently teaches Criminal Behavior, Statistics, and Inside-Out. Outside of work, Chad likes to watch college sports, go backpacking, birdwatch, and watch movies with his wife Sandra, two dogs Lulu and Silas, and two cats Penny and Hank.

Introduction

Developing and evaluating criminological theory may sound like a very technical and scientific pursuit (which it definitely is to a degree), but it is also something that we do every day. When we hear about a horrible crime in the media like a murder, school shooting, or abduction, we begin to formulate theories. Was the shooter mentally disturbed? Did they have access to a gun? Were they abused as a child or did they have poor parents? Were they pressured into crime by bad friends? All of these are common "theories" people in society have regarding the commission of crime.

The theories covered in this book are similar but have been very carefully formulated by scholars, and have received some level of scientific support (either recently or in the past). There are hundreds of theories of human behavior broadly and of criminal behavior specifically. We cannot cover them all in this book. As the author, I had to consciously choose which theories to discuss. My intent was to cover important foundational work in criminological thought and the most recent theories that have begun to generate scientific support. Theorists from the Enlightenment period to the mid-1900s are considered classical theorists and their work – while setting the foundation for current theories – has largely been disproved or substantially revised in light of evidence that did not support the theory. The contemporary theories are those that have begun to emerge in the field of criminology over the past 50 years and show promise to guide future theoretical efforts.

While the book proceeds in a rough chronological order, it is impossible to progress through the development of criminological thought in a neat way, placing theories in silos across time. Theories and perspectives emerge, transform, and re-emerge throughout time and this should be noted by all readers. That said, I have tried to progress through the book in a way where theories are discussed in the order from when their ideas first emerged onto the criminological scene. Not all would agree on this order, and even who should be credited as the first to come up with certain ideas, but I have used my judgment based on the existing literature.

To reiterate, I had to choose which theories to include in this book. Therefore, it does not cover all theories, but my effort was to include a wide range of ideas regardless of my own personal opinion about those theories. In all science, personal opinions, political orientation, and religious ideology must be left out in favor of objective science (we will talk more about what this means in Chapter 1). The theorists featured and interviewed are the result of efforts to reach out to as many theorists as possible and their willingness to talk to me. Their appearance is not a reflection on my personal opinions of their theories or on them as scholars (although everyone I reached out to was more than nice and agreeable – regardless of their willingness to participate in an interview). Furthermore, it is impossible to cover each theory or set of ideas in their totality. In some respects this means that each discussion of theory is necessarily "watered down." Theory is a wonderful world of deep philosophy, nuance, and intrigue. I only hope to reveal the tip of that iceberg; it is up to you to dig deeper.

Theory is not independent of context. The social and cultural mindset of the time directs how people approach scientific questions and provides the lens with which they view the world. I have attempted to contextualize theory by putting it within the milieu of the time when the theories were developed. I felt that was very important, especially after considering the thoughts and writings of others. For example, in a conversation with criminologist Shadd Maruna, he told me,

> Criminology isn't worth a whole lot if it isn't contextualized. Whatever appeal our field has (and it has been remarkably popular for a good long stretch) derives primarily from the sense of the field being 'alive' and in touch with the 'real world' (in ways that some of the older, better established disciplines are not). So, if the strength of our work is that it is connected to contemporary controversies and issues in society, then it follows that criminology is automatically grounded in the context of the wider society around it.[1]

I couldn't agree more.

Criminology is a science. Therefore, as students and scholars, one must approach the study of behavior with a critical eye. Be suspicious. Question each aspect of a theory. Leave your personal opinions at the door and walk into a room where you can feel free to question other people's opinions and offer your own. In turn, do not take offense at those who disagree with your thoughts. Develop a tough skin to accept criticism, learn, and revise your thoughts. We are all continuing to learn. No one theorist in this book has all the answers – and I certainly don't either. But together, we can all make strides into finding out more about why people commit delinquent and criminal acts and how to address those individuals who take part in those acts. What an exciting and interesting topic! I hope that all of you who read this book go on to expand and revise these theories and apply them in your life's work – whatever that may be.

Note

1   Personal Interview with Shadd Maruna, December 12, 2016.

Science, theory, and empirical investigation

Introduction   3
Science and theory   4
The scientific method   5
Elements of a theory   7
Micro and macro theory   8
Theory and underlying assumptions of human behavior   9
Theory, science, and paradigms   10
Summary   11

Introduction

> The duty of the man who investigates the writings of scientists, if learning the truth is his goal, is to make himself an enemy of all that he reads, and [...] attack it from every side. He should also suspect himself as he performs his critical examination of it, so that he may avoid falling into either prejudice or leniency.
>
> —*Alhazen*[1]

It is expected that this chapter, and several of its sections, will be consulted throughout the reading of the following chapters. Do not be concerned if everything discussed here doesn't stick upon first (or several) readings. The material is dense and comes with many unfamiliar concepts. While the book is structured in a way to reduce unneeded complexity, understanding the foundation of criminological theory is essential when evaluating the theories presented in the subsequent chapters. Again, the idea is to revisit this chapter as you continue and apply the material to the theories as you move along.

Science and theory

A common theme throughout this book is the idea that criminological theory is based on science. Theories include a specific set of ideas that are testable using a systematic method (called the scientific method which will be discussed at length in the following section). This is what makes theories scientific. It is far better to come up with explanations of behavior that are testable and based on observable information than on gut feelings or, worse still, ideology.

Scientific investigation is based on empiricism. For something to be empirical, it has to be observable and measurable. For something to be observable, it must be real. This may sound awkward and you may think: "well, isn't everything real?" Not necessarily, and when we are talking about theories we have to be conscious of epistemology – or the appropriate theoretical orientation and methods by which we believe we should accumulate knowledge. There are three main epistemological frameworks that are important for criminology: (1) objectivism; (2) constructivism; and (3) subjectivism.

Before Socrates, the famous classical Greek philosopher, there lived a man by the name of Parmenides. Parmenides wrote a poem that became the basis of Western philosophy. In his poem, Parmenides argued that there is a real world to be studied and that it exists outside of people's own thoughts. This is exemplified by one line of his poem in which he states, "For never shall this prevail, that things that are not are."[2] In other words, things cannot exist if they are not real.

Objectivism follows from Parmenidean thought and is based on the orientation that there exists a "real world" outside of people's consciousness. In other words, there are universal truths or facts about the world, and it is the scientist's job to uncover and explain these truths. It should be noted that objectivism does not deny individual thoughts, feelings, attitudes, and beliefs. Certainly we all have our own ways of thinking; however, scientists must study these objectively without their own biases. Today we call this objective science of uncovering the realities of the world positivism.

Around the same time Parmenides was developing his ideas of *being*, Heraclitus, another Greek philosopher, was developing an alternative view of *becoming*. Remember how I said that not everything is real? Well, Heraclitus believed that nothing is "real" beyond people's own perceptions of things. There is not one objective reality or one truth that exists.[3] There are multiple realities according to all the views of people in society. These ideas are the foundation of constructivism.

The term *constructivism* is appropriate because people construct or create their own reality. A perfect example of a social construct is the concept of crime or criminality. Crime is not something that exists naturally in the world – it is, quite literally, something we (society) made up. Most people agree that we call rape, robbery, and murder crime because crime is something we condemn and punish. However, it is still the case that we have determined those acts to be criminal as a society of people – and that crime does not exist, say, among chipmunks. This does not mean that chipmunks do not kill one another or steal each another's pine nuts; it just means that they don't have a concept of crime which they formally condemn and prosecute.

We will not discuss subjectivism in much detail in this book but it is worth noting here. Subjectivists also believe that reality is socially constructed but this construction is not done consciously (as constructivism argues) but unconsciously. It is people's thoughts, dreams, and beliefs that construct the world, and people impose these constructs upon others and upon society as a whole. We will come back to this briefly when we discuss postmodernism later in the book.

At this point, it makes sense to introduce what the concept of crime means in terms of this book. Crime, the term, is a social construction. As a society, we decide what it means (or what a crime *is*). Is drinking under the age of 18, or 21, or at all, a crime? Is smoking marijuana? Is it a crime to have multiple wives or wives that are 13 years old?

If you look across history (time) and across geography (different countries), the answers to these questions will vary. In one country it may be totally acceptable to have many wives where in the United States this is illegal. Hundreds of years ago there was no law against drinking, during prohibition it was illegal, and only recently was drinking legal but only for those over the age of 21. Crime changes.

The reason why crime changes is that most definitions of crime include a violation against an act or omission of an act that is against criminal law as defined by the state or case law.[4] What is defined in criminal law changes as society changes. It might have been unthinkable to some generations that marijuana could be legal – think back to movies like *Reefer Madness*, the 1936 movie classic that depicted teenagers high on marijuana as deranged maniacs – but we are seeing today widespread decriminalization and legalization of marijuana use in the United States[5] and across the globe.[6]

Recently, Emory University criminologist Robert Agnew[7] presented an "integrated definition of crime" which incorporates several important elements, or core characteristics, when defining criminal acts, including: (1) harmfulness, (2) blameworthiness, (3) condemnation by the public, and (4) sanctioning by the state. Crime harms a person through direct physical harm, the destruction of their property, and the violation of their human rights. Those who commit the act have a specific amount of blameworthiness which is related to their intent to commit the crime and the extent of harm they wished to cause. These acts are seen as "bad" and worthy of punishment by both the general public and the state. This definition should be kept in mind throughout this book but may also be expanded upon to consider, as Agnew does, other types of harms – such as harms to the environment and human rights – that might fall outside the scope of traditional definitions of crime.

The scientific method

Along the banks of the Nile in Cairo, Egypt lived a man of many talents named Ibn al-Haytham – also known as Alhazen (Figure 1.1). One of his major contributions was a book on optics written in the eleventh century, from 1011 to 1021. In this seven-volume series, Alhazen combined geometry and anatomy to explain how people perceive light. The only way he believed he could argue his points was to conduct a series of experiments using various tools such as lenses and mirrors. He would systematically vary the conditions (the environment) in which he conducted his experiments and carefully note the outcomes. Because of Alhazen's careful experimentation, many credit him with developing the foundation for the scientific method.[8]

The modern understanding of the scientific method is a process. It is not always linear but bounces back and forth between coming up with large ideas, making specific predictions called hypotheses, and testing those hypotheses using systematic experiments. Each experiment might support the hypotheses or put them into question, in which case the researcher must go back to modify or create a new hypothesis. This process can literally go on forever.

To make it easy to conceptualize, usually the method starts with coming up with a broad or general idea (or theory). This is followed by making observations (remember: this is empiricism!). Based on observations, interesting questions emerge which are followed by hypotheses about what the researcher believes to be true. The researcher then develops a way to test his or her ideas and gathers information (called data) to test these predictions. Based on the outcome of the tests, the researcher must decide to either come up with more questions (called refining a theory) or revise hypotheses based on results that do not support their original predictions.

Let us use a relevant criminological example to illustrate this process. In Chapter 8, social bonding theory will be discussed in detail but we can use it as an example here

Figure 1.1 Alhazen

Source: Portrait of Ibn al-Haytham Alhazen (c. 965–1040) [digital image] (2009). Credit: islam.ru. Available at: www2. hao.ucar.edu/Education/FamousSolarPhysicists/ibn-al-haytham-alhazen-ca-965-1040.

to illuminate the scientific method. In his doctoral dissertation, Travis Hirschi[9] wanted to test the broad idea that people are naturally inclined toward self-interest and are predisposed to commit acts that are antisocial or deemed to be delinquent. This idea was contrary to strain theories (discussed in Chapter 5) and cultural deviance theories (discussed in Chapter 6). This idea was based on Hirschi's readings and understanding of human nature derived from Enlightenment thinkers such as Thomas Hobbes. Following this logic, Hirschi predicted, or hypothesized, that it was a person's bond to conventional society that controlled them, ensuring that they would not commit acts of delinquency because these would jeopardize their bonds or relationships to people (parents) and institutions (school).

Hirschi could not stop there – he had to test these ideas systematically using data. He used a sample of adolescents from Western Contra Costa County (the San Francisco/ Oakland metropolitan area) who were surveyed as part of the Richmond Youth Project. Using only the males from this sample, Hirschi ran statistical models on variables related to his ideas on social bonding along with variables related to the other points of view on strain and cultural deviance. In the end, Hirschi found that his bonding ideas were supported by the data analysis and that bonding, in his view, was a superior explanation of delinquent behavior over other leading theories.

You might think that the scientific process ends there. The steps were followed and there was support for the hypotheses. However, remember: refinement – the procedure that continues to develop a theory by examining exactly how the theory works to explain behavior – is a part of this process as well. For example, Hirschi used only males in his study. In addition, he did not find much support for his "involvement" measure. How does his bonding theory apply to females? Subsequent research would have to address this question and the scientific method would have to be applied to this variation on the theory. Can you think of other questions?

It will become clear throughout this book that most theoretical work, such as the above example of social bonding theory, is intended to expand our knowledge of social processes and establish connections between variables related to crime and antisocial behavior. This research process is called basic research. However, each chapter in the book will include a section on the policy relevance of each theory. Program evaluation and research on specific problems are forms of applied research where the main goal is to create solutions to problems that are of interest to decision-makers and policy-makers. Action research, which will be discussed further, is one way to combine basic and applied research so that practitioners and policy-makers can use scientific research based on sound theory to make decisions on effective prevention and intervention initiatives. This is often accomplished through partnerships between academics and practitioners (such as a university professor and the local police department) where a participatory and collaborative research process takes place. This process often yields useful information based on scientific research to solve local problems.

Elements of a theory

A theory has been defined by Kerlinger and Lee as: "a set of interrelated constructs (concepts), definitions, and propositions that present a systematic view of phenomena by specifying relations among variables, with the purpose of explaining and predicting phenomena."[10] Theory attempts to link and articulate the relationship between variables of interest. For example, two concepts that a theorist may wish to connect, as in the above example, are bonding with one's mother and delinquent behavior. Sometimes a theorist might propose a specific relationship in the form of a proposition (sentence) such as "Bonding to mothers will decrease delinquency." The chief aim in the social sciences is to explain a relationship between two concepts.

In order to explain relationships, a theorist should attempt to establish causation. In other words, bonding *causes* a reduction in delinquency. To establish cause, a few things must occur: (1) correlation, (2) a logical or theoretical basis for the relationship, (3) temporal order, and (4) lack of spuriousness. First, a theorist must find a correlation. A correlation is established when two concepts or variables "move together" or are associated with one another. As one goes up, the other goes up (or down) and vice versa. As bonding to mothers goes up, delinquency goes down and as bonding decreases, delinquency goes up. Or, perhaps, one's sex is related to crime such that males are more closely associated with delinquency than females. Correlation is just a statistical relationship and one must be careful to remember the popular saying "correlation does not mean causation." It is only the first step and alone is not enough for the theorist to claim an explanation.

Second, the relationship must make common sense. There is a whole website on "funny correlations" such as a strong correlation among the number of people who drowned by falling into a pool and the number of Nicholas Cage films. However, there is no common-sense explanation for this and, thus, it fails the second step in establishing cause.

Third, after finding a correlation and ensuring that it makes sense, a theorist must find out if the cause comes before the effect. This generally requires some data over time. Sometimes, cause and effect is hard to establish and, in fact, variables may have reciprocal effects. For example, a theorist would be wise to look at bonding in early childhood to predict delinquency in the teen years. This is a good test of temporal order. However, it could be the case that becoming involved in delinquency damages bonds. Your mother would probably not be happy if you got into fights and stole from people.

Therefore, delinquency in the early teen years may affect bonding in later teen years. More data, over a longer period of time, is the key to establishing the third element of a causal explanation.

A similar issue, related to but distinct from causal order, is the problem of tautology. Tautology refers to when the cause, or explanation, for crime is part of the definition of crime as well. For example, some theorists believe that psychopathy is a major cause of crime. However, some definitions of psychopathy include criminal behavior (i.e., someone is considered a psychopath because they engage in crime). In essence, criminal behavior would then be a cause of criminal behavior. This is tautological and results in circular reasoning which must be avoided in theorizing.

Finally, the theorist must account for a spurious correlation. This is perhaps the toughest to grasp and the most difficult to establish. A relationship is spurious, and therefore not causal, if there is a third concept that is related to both original variables that accounts for the "true" relationship. As we will see later in our discussion on control theories, proponents of self-control theory suggest that the relationship between bonding and delinquency is spurious because bonding actually impacts levels of self-control (the more bonded you are with parents the more self-control you develop) and it is self-control that increases or decreases delinquent behavior. It is this third variable (or concept) of self-control which is the *cause* of delinquency.

When theories and propositions continually receive support, they sometimes turn into laws. Laws are those theories that are "proven." Some laws exist in the natural sciences such as Newton's Law of Motion. However, as you might imagine, laws largely do not exist in the study of human behavior. Given human behavior's complexity and the difficulty of manipulating and conducting experiments on human beings, no theory of crime has yet been proven and turned into a law.

While the primary goal of social science theory is to look for explanations of behavior, there are two other efforts worth mentioning: (1) interpretation, and (2) critical analysis. Interpretation is the effort not so much to establish cause but to understand a concept from multiple points of view. This effort yields itself to phenomenology and other methodologies related to the subjectivist perspective discussed previously. Critical analysis is when a theorist seeks to uncover the weaknesses and shortcomings of a theory or policy in order to make improvements or suggest alternatives. It should be noted that science in itself is to be critical. Only through trying to disprove something can we move toward "proving" a theory (we can come close but never absolutely prove a theory in the traditional sense). As Karl Popper states in his classic work *The logic of scientific discovery*, "The point is that whenever we try to propose a solution to a problem, we ought to try as hard as we can to overthrow our solution, rather than defend it."[11]

Micro and macro theory

Theories can also attempt to explain phenomena at different levels. Levels can be at the individual (or person) level and/or at the group level (e.g., neighborhood, state, country). As we will see in the following chapters, some theories, such as theories of psychopathy, low self-control, and strain, attempt to explain why certain people commit antisocial acts. These are called micro-level theories. Other theories, such as subcultural or institutional anomie theories, are more interested in why we see certain groups (even countries) of people who are antisocial. These are called macro-level theories. Recently, some theorists have attempted to combine micro- and macro-level theories (as well as to include an intermediate meso-level) for a broader picture of why crime occurs.

Some of the earliest theories of antisocial and delinquent behavior were decidedly individualistic. In colonial times, people were believed to be possessed by demons which explained their poor behavior and later it was people's biology or psychology that caused them to be bad. In each case, the explanation was on the individual or micro level and elements of the larger society or social context were ignored.

In the early 1900s, a shift in thought was beginning to take place and was prominently advocated by researchers at the University of Chicago (later becoming known as the "Chicago School"). Theorists in this vein believed that the causes of criminal behavior were not from the individual alone but also from society and the social environment. Concepts such as poverty, inequality, concentrated disadvantage, social support, social disorganization, and later collective efficacy were variables used to explain why certain areas tended to be more criminogenic than others (i.e., to have higher crime rates). Macro-level theories seek to explain why groups or areas have higher crime rates than others and their explanations tend to include certain social variables.

While theories tend to emphasize one level of explanation over the other, efforts have been made to integrate the two. This is important because, as criminologists Messner and Rosenfeld state in their book *Crime and the American dream* based on their macro-level Institutional Anomie Theory, "Any macro-level explanation of crime will inevitably be predicated on underlying premises about individual behavior."[12] For example, as we will see when we discuss social disorganization theory (a macro-level theory), early theorists believed that *individuals* who were immigrants were more likely to commit crime and because immigrants from many different nations lived in the same geographical locations those *environments* were more likely to have high crime rates.

When using purely micro- or macro-level theories, it is important to avoid certain assumptions about individuals or groups whom you are *not* studying. If you are using a macro-level theory, it is unwise to make assumptions about individuals and vice versa. This is related to findings that show what is true of individuals is not always true of groups of those individuals and that characteristics of groups do not apply to everyone in those groups.

Theory and underlying assumptions of human behavior

Criminology is the study of criminal behavior. This can be separated from criminal justice theory which is concerned with the explanations of the operations of the criminal justice system. Criminology, as such, is concerned with accounting for criminal behavior. As already discussed, crime is socially constructed and includes behavior which we (as society) deem punishable. Crime, if committed by someone under the age of 18, is called delinquency. Both crime and delinquency are behaviors that are officially prohibited and punishable. Antisocial behaviors include those that are not prohibited by law but are still seen as poor or bad, including aggression (yelling or "getting in someone's face"), cheating, and manipulation. In this book, crime, delinquency, and antisocial behavior will be used interchangeably for the most part as criminology seeks to explain all of these concepts, and most theories do not seek to distinguish these behaviors.

Criminological theories often start with thoughts on the origins of human behavior and because criminology seeks to explain "bad" behavior – there are assumptions about the nature of man. In other words, is man naturally (i.e., born) bad or good? Do people have a natural tendency to be self-interested or cooperative? Or perhaps man is born a "blank slate" and all behavior is acquired later. Different theories make different assumptions about people, and this is important.

Relatedly, theorists sometimes favor explanations that are based in either nature or nurture. Theories based in the nature perspective believe that it is human nature, specifically biology, which is the driving force behind behavior. Nurture refers to environmental factors such as how we were raised and interact with others that influence behavior. While there has always been some tension between the two (sometimes called the "nature vs. nurture debate"), biosocial criminology – discussed at length in Chapter 11 – advances the idea that both are important in behavior and work together, not in opposition.

Since underlying assumptions of theories will be discussed at length in the following chapters, they will only be introduced here. Some theories, specifically control theories, assume that people are inherently self-interested and, because it is easy to get things when we cheat, manipulate, or take advantage of others, we are naturally inclined to act criminally. Thus, as the name of the theory implies, society must control us in order to reduce crime. On the other hand, strain theories argue that we are generally fairly cooperative and need a "push" into crime. Usually the push is a social strain such as poverty, academic stress, or discrimination. Other theories (such as learning theories) assume that people are born a relatively blank slate, and argue that people must learn their behaviors through interactions with others.

Society itself is also subjected to assumptions, with three major orientations: (1) consensus, (2) pluralism, and (3) conflict. Some theories assume that people are generally on the same page when defining and condemning certain behaviors. Most people, regardless of age, sex, race, and location, agree that murder, rape, and robbery are bad things to do to people. Therefore, society is defined by consensus or agreement in what is right and wrong, which remains fairly stable over time. Conversely, some theorists view society as diverse, being made up of many different points of view which are often, but not always, in disagreement about the wrongness of behavior. This is the pluralistic view. Society from a pluralistic viewpoint is continually changing and interacting. The conflict perspective is in agreement with the pluralistic perspective in that society has many groups but argues that these groups are based on different interest groups that are constantly in conflict with one another. The conflicts are over power and position in society. The powerful at the top of society get to define what is criminal at the expense of the less powerful.

Theory, science, and paradigms

As we see with the scientific method, a good researcher's work is never done. There are always more questions that exist to refine a theory and different perspectives that need testing in the first place. That is the glory of science. It is there to be used to explain our physical and social world. And because science is continually being applied to answer new questions and revise old ones, our knowledge is constantly changing. Most of the time, the change is incremental or very small over a fairly long period of time but sometimes it is profound – changing the way we view the world.

For centuries, people – including scholars – believed that the sun, moon, stars, and other planets revolved around the earth. It made sense that everyone thought the earth was the center of the universe because they believed that God made the earth first for man and then the rest of the universe. In the sixteenth century, a Polish mathematician and astronomer argued that it is not the earth but the sun which is at the center of the universe. In his book, *De revolutionibus orbium coelestium* (*On the revolution of the celestial orbs*), Nicolas Copernicus put forth a new theory of the universe which sparked the "Copernican Revolution."

Importantly, Copernicus's new model was one based on science and not religion. This did not sit well with others – especially those of faith. However, as is the process of science, others after Copernicus, including Johannes Kepler and Galileo Galilei, built upon his model and further proved his heliocentric (sun at the center) model. Just because this revolutionary idea was based on science does not mean that everyone accepted the new evidence. In fact, Galileo was forced to recant his position after the church threatened him with death. While he escaped death, his fellow astronomer and friend, Priest Giordano Bruno, was not so lucky. After refusing to disavow his beliefs, the church burned Bruno alive and threw his ashes in the Tiber River.[13]

Copernicus's model represents what Thomas Kuhn calls a scientific revolution. When traditional thoughts are challenged and then repeatedly disproven by the process of science, a new idea or set of ideas emerges. As we saw with Bruno, not everyone is quick to accept the new line of thinking, and it may still take years, or even decades, for everyone to come around to the same way of thinking. Luckily, today, people do not get burned at the stake – but people have been fired or even sued because of some of their research findings and interpretation of those findings.

Questions remain today as to whether or not criminology is its own field of study, with its own unique sets of questions and methods to answer them, or if it should exist within already established fields such as sociology or social psychology. While these complex issues will not be explored in depth in this book, there is little doubt that criminology is broadly concerned with harm, antisocial behavior, and deviance from the norms in society. Answering questions related to these areas requires knowledge from a wide array of fields (e.g., biology, psychology, sociology, public health, philosophy, and many more). As we progress through the book, it will become evident just how interdisciplinary and multidisciplinary the field of criminology is.

Summary

Before concluding this chapter, a word must be added about the idea of a proposition being a "fact" or "truth." In mathematics, truth is fairly straightforward. Two plus two equals four. It always does. We can be sure that our result is "true." In social sciences, like criminology, we can never, with 100 percent accuracy, "prove" something. Instead, we have to accumulate a significant amount of evidence in support of a theory to explain behavior. A theory won't explain all criminal behavior all the time – but it should do a pretty good job most of the time.

In his book *The greatest show on earth: The evidence for evolution,* retired Oxford University professor and nationally renowned scholar Richard Dawkins[14] makes the case that while we cannot definitely prove theories in social sciences, we can come very close, and that evolution is one of these theories. Actually, Dawkins believes that evolution is a fact despite not being something that is proven like a mathematical equation. "A scientific theorem" writes Dawkins,

> has not – cannot be – proved in the way a mathematical theorem is proved. But common sense treats it as a fact in the same sense as the "theory" that the Earth is round and not flat is a fact, and the theory that green plants obtain energy from the sun is a fact.

The interpretation here is that "fact" is rather different between mathematical proof and scientific proof. He adds, "All are scientific theorems: supported by massive quantities of evidence, accepted by all informed observers, undisputed facts in the ordinary sense of the word." In criminology, we have not yet reached a place where any one (or a combination of) them has obtained the status of "fact."[15] The theories discussed in this text have received support – some considerable support – but still fall short of "massive quantities" as Dawkins states. Perhaps someday there will be a theory that achieves the status of a fact in this sense.

Science might by now seem to be dispassionate and a mechanical way of viewing the world. I hope I make the case now, and throughout the book, that this could not be further from the truth. Science and empirical research are the foundations of a moral and productive society. Science can lead to medicine to cure disease, to tools to make our jobs easier and safe, and to programs and policies that achieve safety and justice. More broadly, it allows us to understand how things work in the world which often leads to a more empathetic society. I will conclude this chapter with a quote by writer Michael Shermer[16] from his book *The moral arc*: "One path (among many) to a more moral world is to get people to quit believing in absurdities. Science and reason are the best methods of doing that."

Notes

1 Sabra, 1989.
2 Kirk, Raven, & Schofield, 1983.
3 Kirk, 1954.
4 Tappan, 1960.
5 Monte, Zane, & Heard, 2015.
6 Caulkins, Kilmer, & Kleiman, 2016.
7 Agnew, 2011.
8 Sabra, 2007.
9 Hirschi, 1969.
10 Kerlinger & Lee, 2000: 9.
11 Popper, 1959: 16.
12 Messner & Rosenfeld, 2008: 42.
13 Singer, 1950.
14 Dawkins, 2009.
15 Dawkins, 2009: 13.
16 Shermer, 2015: 7.

Further reading

Dawkins, R. (2013). *An appetite for wonder: The making of a scientist*. New York: Random House.
Deutsch, D. (2011). *The beginning of infinity: Explanations that transform the world*. London: Penguin Books.
Hirschi, T. & Selvin, H. C. (1967). *Delinquency research: An appraisal of analytic methods*. New York: Free Press.
Nickles, T. (2012). *Scientific discovery, logic, and rationality*. New York: Springer Science & Business Media.
Shermer, M. (2015). *The moral arc: How science and reason lead humanity toward truth, justice, and freedom*. London: Macmillan.

Pre-Enlightenment theories

2

Introduction	13
Theory	14
Classical Greek and philosophical perspectives	14
Pagan perspectives	16
Christian and monotheistic perspectives	17
Naturalistic perspectives	19
The Enlightenment and the emergence of contemporary criminology	20
The case of Abigail Williams: the 11-year-old witch	20
Empirical support	22
Remaining questions	22
Policy	22
Summary	23

Introduction

Many texts on criminological theory gloss over – or fail to cover at all – theories before the Enlightenment period beginning in the eighteenth century. This is understandable since, prior to the Enlightenment, criminology was not yet a science (perhaps not yet an "-ology") and did not adhere to a system in which it could investigate its claims and reproduce its findings in a valid and reliable way. Contemporary criminology borrows heavily from ideas that emerged during the Enlightenment period, but the significance of the reorientation of thought during this period is due to the contrast that it had with prior religious doctrine. In this chapter, we will explore the oldest explanations of criminality leading up to the Enlightenment period and how they shaped the course of criminology.

Theory

It may be a stretch to call the perspectives in this chapter theories because they are not testable, for the most part, using the scientific method. While early Greek philosophers put forth ideas which are the precursors of today's theories, they were not in a position to outline the testability of their theories. The reliance on moral authority and, later, the reliance on religious morality is not something that is testable using modern scientific methods.

The demonic and theological perspectives are not empirical – you cannot see or measure the evil that was thought to lead to criminal behavior. This is a major difference between the early theories discussed in this chapter and those of the following chapters which are empirical or positivistic theories. However, even though perspectives relating criminal behavior to demons, evil, and other un-seeable factors lack scientific merit (and probably seem very silly today), they did dominate in society from the earliest times up until about the 1700s. Arguably, people still believe in the power of evil to some extent today, as casting out demons and exorcisms are still practiced in some areas around the world.

This chapter explores the perspectives of ancient Greek philosophers to those philosophers closer to the Enlightenment as well as clergy and religious figures throughout history who have put the blame of criminal behavior on otherworldly evil. Sometimes theories of crime are related to demons and the devil, while at other times crime is a reflection of the innate evil of society more broadly. Sometimes individuals are controlled by evil entities – and need to be exorcised – while others are acting freely on behalf of the evil entities such as witches who do the devil's bidding. Either way, prior to the Enlightenment, crime was defined as acts against moral or religious doctrine while criminality was due to weak morals or weak faith. While these theories have lost most of their prominence in today's thinking, we do see the re-emergence of weak morality and self-control in theories to be discussed later in the book.

Classical Greek and philosophical perspectives

Before formal mechanisms of social control and punishment were in place, any victimization experienced by a person was to be met with retaliation. If you didn't take revenge, no one else would. This was the basis of "blood feuds" where people and families had long-standing rivalries that were bloody and costly, sometimes lasting through several generations. Without any formal police or court systems, this appeared to be the only system for recourse, and today, in inner cities across the USA, a similar cycle of violence is reminiscent of this part of history.[1] This may not be surprising in that, even though there exist police and courts, the criminal justice system is viewed as illegitimate and untrustworthy; therefore, people in these neighborhoods often police themselves.

The first sets of "laws" to address crime were found in *lex talionis*. The basis of *lex talionis* is the well-known adage "eye for an eye, tooth for a tooth." These laws, found in the Bible, Koran, Torah, and several other religious texts added some control over punishment of evil-doers.[2] If a crime took place, retaliation was sanctioned by society (governments), but only if it was proportional to the crime. This type of control over sanctioning is evident in the Code of Hammurabi around 1800 BC.[3] To be sure, one can read the laws set forth in the Code of Hammurabi and notice that they are extremely harsh compared to today's standards and many crimes laid out in the laws are not crimes today. For example, if a child hit his father, his fingers would be chopped off. Overly harsh, yes, but there are at least some restrictions on the types of punishments to be handed out for the crimes of the day.

During pre-modern times, the explanations for these types of crimes were generally seen as lack of morality or evilness. Crimes such as disrespecting elders, the church, and the government were seen as the product of low morality and low self-regulation. Those weak in spirit and self-control could easily be swayed by outside influences and corrupted. Rehabilitation was not considered by *lex talionis* and punishment was to be elicited in order to promote justice and repentance.

The readings of Greek philosophers reveal another take on the origins of criminality and the responses that society should take when crime occurs. Society, according to Plato (428–348 BC), should be based on the following four qualities or "virtues": (1) wisdom; (2) courage; (3) discipline; and (4) justice. When discussing crime, the fourth virtue is the most important, but, as you will see, the third virtue of discipline (and self-discipline) has a role to play. For Plato, the moral laws of society are what should matter and not the laws of the gods. He discussed four types of offenses in his treasured book *The Republic*, including: (1) crimes against religion (e.g., disrespect of the church); (2) crimes against the state (e.g., treason); (3) crimes against persons (e.g., assault, drug use); and (4) crimes against private property (e.g., stealing). Those with few or no morals were more likely to be criminal and anything that went against the moral law of society was therefore a crime.

While the role of morality was a large part of explaining criminal behavior in ancient Greece, Plato did talk about causes of crime beyond just weak morality. In particular, he linked morality with self-discipline. Those who could not control themselves and regulate their own behavior were likely to act immorally. He states, "self-discipline is surely a kind of order, a control of certain desires and appetites."[4] He goes on to explain that when people are rational in a society there is no "civil war"; thus, the society itself is self-controlled. Plato's views appear to be a very old precursor to self-control and self-regulation theories that dominate the current theoretical landscape. In fact, this theory of behavior is often referred to as *akrasia* or a lack of self-control, and emerged from Plato's transition (his own theoretical development) from earlier intellectualist dialogs to his later psychological dialogs.[5]

Plato also believed that other factors might overpower self-discipline or make it more difficult to use. "Bad upbringing or bad company" might also influence the ability to employ self-regulation. In fact, his statement that when "the smaller forces of one's better element are overpowered by the numerical superiority of one's worse," self-discipline is more difficult to activate.[6] This is oddly prophetic of later theories, which will be covered in this book, such as strain and social learning theories which argue that definitions and strains can accumulate to increase the likelihood of crime.[7] Plato certainly appeared to recognize the role of societal factors in the ability to self-regulate.

Further, Plato stamped his thoughts in his work on early forms of criminal justice from his ideas on behavior. He was an early supporter of restorative justice as opposed to the Hammurabian retributive justice. His views that humans were naturally good, wanted to do the right thing, but sometimes did not *know* the right thing to do, led him to support a form of justice that better helped others see the good way to act as opposed to merely punishing them. Being good was the only way to happiness – so any way to promote the ability to self-regulate and act well was a worthy effort for Plato.[8]

For Plato's student Aristotle (384–322 BC), crime was the result of internal desire. Crime was committed out of free will when desire pushed someone into a criminal act. Therefore, crime was explained by a breakdown of self-regulation by desire and crimes were "chosen" out of a freely willed decision (free will plays a huge part in theories emerging out of the Enlightenment period). Often what makes a crime a crime is that it creates inequality and damages the just distribution of goods in society. Like Plato before him, Aristotle believed that criminals were severely deficient in their emotions and desires as well as unable to control themselves. Therefore, criminals should not be entirely responsible for their behavior. Rehabilitation should be tried first but, if unsuccessful, people should be abandoned, incarcerated, or put to death (a precursor to "get-tough" policies seen today).[9]

In the early centuries AD and into the 1200s, most of the authority on crime and criminality came from the clergy and the church. Guiding principles for morality and justice were not derived from politicians or society but largely from priests. To rebel against the church, as Bruno did, often ended in torture and death. The Greek philosophers who commented on criminal behavior diverted slightly from their predecessors who relied on *lex talionis* and even from those who came after and who, as discussed next, relied on the word of God to instruct their theories and responses to crime.

Two major figures of faith who commented on crime and criminality before the Enlightenment are St. Augustine of Hippo (354–430 AD) and St. Thomas Aquinas (1225–1274 AD). St. Augustine was a Bishop in Hippo (in modern-day Algeria) and the son of a Christian mother and pagan father, who believed that sin was a "falling away from God." He called this the eternal law or the law of God. Human beings, too, had their laws, or temporal law as he called it, but these laws were only just when aligned with eternal law. Every man, according to St. Augustine, carries the sin of Adam and Eve with them but all people are redeemable if they come to God. However, people can fall prey to sin by succumbing to elevated self-esteem and vanity. "Pride, he says, 'the craving for undue exaltation,' is 'the cause of all human offences."[10] This view of crime may not be surprising, as St. Augustine, before turning toward the church, was surrounded by extreme wealth. His friends were often party-goers who were fond of drink and women. An eventual disdain for this life forced him to consider a different life – one of faith.

Similar to St. Augustine of Hippo, Saint Thomas Aquinas, a Dominican Friar, believed that sin (i.e., crime) was against eternal law set forth by God. However, this law was also the law of reason. In this and in many ways, Aquinas built upon the ideas of Aristotle whose writing had recently been discovered during the thirteenth century. This "natural law" could be observed by seeing the good in the world through the eyes of faith. He saw no difference between the law of reason and the law of God. He also believed that criminal acts were violations of both the law of reason (or society) *and* the law of God. Thus, crime described those activities that violated the natural law and should be dealt with.[11]

Aquinas also believed that crime is a violation against humanity as well as against God Himself. For him, victimizing a person is evil because the victim is innocent, and it is a victimization against God directly. The perpetrator may be punished by God by being sent to Hell as well as suffer from the penalties of the land set by society. The way to avoid a life of immorality is to lead a life of virtue. The best way to do this is to become an adherent of the Christian church which instills the moral code by which we live.

Again, the role of morality and reason rings throughout theories of crime and law prior to the thirteenth century. We will see how this leads into and influences Enlightenment thinkers such as John Locke and Thomas Hobbes. Before that, we must focus more on theological perspectives that existed in society up until the Enlightenment and, to a much lesser extent, today.

Pagan perspectives

Starting several centuries before Aquinas, pagan perspectives were very common in Europe. Paganism refers to religions that are generally polytheistic (many gods), animistic (non-human gods such as plants and animals), and pantheistic (the divine universe). Paganism has a longer history than monotheistic religions (discussed in the following section), including most modern religions such as Christianity, Catholicism, Judaism, and Islam. Prior to the ninth century in Europe, individuals generally believed in many gods who all vied for their loyalty. If people enraged the gods they would pay. The gods were particularly angry when people committed crimes and expected that they be punished harshly by those in power. Those who were to commit even non-violent crime such as theft were often gutted or burned alive in sacrifice to the gods.[12]

During the pagan era, society consisted of small families, or slightly larger clans. Clans sometimes had similar traditions at times but at other times diverged quite considerably. However, most clans operated as small "cults" that consisted of ceremonies such as feasts, drinking, and sacrifices.[13] Those who committed crimes did so not only against their victim but also against the whole clan and were to be dealt with harshly. Common punishments included drowning, burning alive, beatings, and hanging. Criminals were seen as evil-doers controlled by evil itself. Because these clans were polytheistic, they did not unify evil under only the devil but viewed evil as more holistic – existing and controlling people in a grand sense.

The harsh punishments discussed earlier, such as burning someone alive, were common among Celtic clans, but, in England and Germany, there were "softer" punishments. Most popularly, criminals would have to pay money to their victim (as we see today in restitution) as well as a sum to the king or tribe leader (as we see today in fines).[14] The idea was that fines would help repair the harm that the offense caused the victim and the victim's family, clan, or tribe. This is not unlike the more recent forms of justice in today's society which are related to restorative justice – the idea that crime harms people and communities, and that the responses to crime should be to repair that damage.

Christian and monotheistic perspectives

Christian perspectives increased following the ninth century, after the pagan era, and gained prominence in the 1400s. Christian perspectives were similar to the pagan perspectives only in that criminal behavior from this perspective was thought to be the result of evil. Beyond that, the perspectives were quite different. While pagans served many gods and were afflicted by several evil forces, those who viewed crime through Christian perspectives believed that crime was due to either the Devil (or Satan) or another demon who worked at the behest of the Devil (who was the "head demon" as it were). Either way, like earlier perspectives, people who committed crimes did so because of some otherworldly force, or forces, that would have to be addressed for the behavior to stop.

There were two main avenues for evil to penetrate an individual through this perspective. First was through temptation. A weak-willed person who did not have a strong relationship with God could be easily deceived and manipulated by evil. In this way, evil could tempt people into doing its bidding which was often considered criminal behavior. The second was through possession. Evil forces were able to inhabit the body of those who had weak faith while those with strong faith were able to "fight off" evil spirits. In any case, proponents of this theory of criminal behavior blamed the individual for not being strong enough in faith to ward off evil spirits.

Imagine this. The year is 1486 in Germany and an expelled clergyman, Heinrich Kramer, publishes the book *Malleus Maleficarum*. This book, also known as *Hammer of witches*, outlines what constitutes demonic possession and witchcraft, and how to prosecute witches. Kramer's intention was, first, to convince readers that witches were real and a threat to society; and second, to instruct others on how to successfully prosecute witches. This second effort was of a personal nature, as his expulsion from the church was the result of an unsuccessful prosecution. The book, while of questionable influence, was used inside the formal courtroom and went through about 30 editions. Recently, in 2009, a translation was published by Cambridge University Press.[15]

Over the century following the publication of *Malleus Maleficarum*, the idea that witchcraft was real and a threat to society grew. In Scotland, in 1597, King James VI of Scotland (also later King James I of England) published a dissertation on demons and their infiltration of man entitled *Daemonologie.* Along with describing prior witch trials (of which King James was a part), the book promotes "witch-hunting." In fact, the book is said to have influenced infamous witch-hunter Matthew Hopkins whose efforts between 1644 and 1646 resulted in the prosecution and execution of about 300 accused witches (Figure 2.1).

Figure 2.1 Matthew Hopkins the witch-hunter

Source: Hopkins (1647).

Figure 2.2 The Love Potion

Source: De Morgan (1903).

Less than half a century after the publication of *Daemonologie*, witchcraft hysteria hit the United States (Figure 2.2). During the course of the year 1692, fourteen women and five men were executed after accusations of witchcraft in what became known as the Salem Witch Trials. Even two dogs were accused of being possessed and put to death. Many more people were accused, but not executed, during this time.[16]

Naturalistic perspectives

Naturalistic perspectives submit that the natural order of the world is to be revered and cherished. From this perspective, everything is related under one umbrella of nature (people, animals, plants, and all other life). These perspectives suggest that crime and criminal behavior are part of the laws of nature and that this behavior impacts all life on earth. Interestingly, naturalists were among the first to really incorporate science into their worldview. In some ways, naturalism led into the Enlightenment period where science was seen as the basis of all knowledge.

The Enlightenment and the emergence of contemporary criminology

The perspectives covered in this chapter largely ended with what is known as the "age of Enlightenment" or "Enlightenment" for short. As the moniker makes perfectly clear, the age of reason intended to do away with ideas and thoughts that were influenced by God and religion. For the first time, church and state were to be viewed as separate and laws were to be decided and punishment delivered by man. The Enlightenment will be described and discussed at length when rational choice is introduced later in the book but it is worth noting its importance here. Along with the Enlightenment came the views of René Descartes, who proposed a "rationalist philosophy," and John Locke, whose *Leviathan* established the major view of society as a social contract between individuals. Perhaps most important for the social sciences was Immanuel Kant (1724–1804), who espoused the positivistic view of the study of man.[17] In sum, the Enlightenment ushered in a new era of science and reason to guide the study of man and his behavior. Criminology was just a century away from its birth.

The case of Abigail Williams: the 11-year-old witch

One of the most famous cases that emerged out of the Salem Witch Trials was that of a young girl named Abigail Williams. When Abigail was about 11 years old, she started acting awkwardly according to those in her village. She would flail about with her arms and legs, contort herself into unusual positions, and scurry around hiding under tables. When asked, she reportedly told others that she was possessed and could not control her actions. Logically, then, the villagers attempted to locate the source of her possession.

It is likely that Abigail's accusations of someone possessing her are what initiated the witch-hunt that culminated in the Salem Witch Trials. The history of what became of Abigail is mixed, but there is no record of her death nor a known resting place for her body. Some material suggests that she may have died before her eighteenth birthday, but these materials do not name her specifically. Her story has been retold in works such as Arthur Miller's *The Crucible* and her name has been brought up several times such as in Jon Turteltaub's movie *The Sorcerer's Apprentice* and even the American black metal band Abigail Williams.

While demonology is not the scientific approach that would explain Abigail's behavior, it remains uncertain what would cause her well-documented strange behavior: flailing arms, arched back, and uncontrollable shaking. There are a few explanations that are more scientific. The first is that Abigail may have suffered from a variety of different seizures. Grand Mal seizures lead to unconscious convulsing and muscle stiffening, while similar symptoms are common for myoclonic seizures. Second, the behavior is congruent with those who have been diagnosed with Huntington's disease. Those who have a mutation of a specific protein (named the Huntington Protein) experience shaking – often violently – along with flailing body parts. In Salem, others were accused of being possessed for similar behaviors. Interestingly, Huntington's disease, like many disorders, is largely genetic. It may be no wonder that many in the village displayed similar behaviors with one another.[18]

In the early months of 2014, Latoya Ammons relayed a unique and strange story to Indiana Police Captain Charles Austin. She had told Captain Austin that her family had been possessed by evil demons and that her house was haunted. As a 36-year veteran of the police force, Austin was not amused. Doing his duty, he visited the house in Gary several times to follow up with the family. In the end, the Indystar news outlet quoted Austin as saying, "I am a believer."

Captain Austin was not the only "believer." Workers from the Department of Child Services, other family members, and a catholic priest joined the ranks of those who either witnessed or believed that the family was truly possessed. After moving to a new house in Gary in November 2011, the family experienced their home becoming filled with and surrounded by huge black flies (this was in November when black flies are generally dormant). Later, the family could hear footsteps coming up the basement steps and, one time, Ammons even found wet footprints after seeing a "shadowy figure." Despite many efforts to lock the doors and protect themselves, the disturbances continued.

The mysterious occurrences culminated in a particularly odd event on March 10, 2012. Latoya Ammons' mother, Rosa Campbell, was woken up by her granddaughter's screaming and ran to her room. Campbell found her 12-year-old granddaughter levitating above the bed. After praying with Rosa, the girl descended back to her bed. The Ammon family decided that they needed more help.

After consulting a priest and clairvoyants, the Ammon family built an altar in the basement and performed several ceremonies to ward off the evil spirits. This did not work. The Ammon children began to grin at their mother in sinister ways and their voices deepened. Each time, their eyes bulged with evil intent. The youngest talked to a ghost who said he had been killed and was once thrown out of the bathroom by an invisible force. The 12-year-old girl was hit on the head so hard by her bed's headboard that she needed stitches. With nowhere else to turn, the family consulted their physician. A skeptic like Captain Austin, the physician reluctantly visited the home. While there, the boys cursed the doctor and mysterious forces threw the boys against a wall. Police and ambulances drove the boys to a nearby Christian hospital.

At the hospital, the family was visited by psychiatrists and the Department of Child Services (DCS). The psychiatrists determined that the family was "sound of mind" but while there, the boys had growled at the case workers. In a further evaluation, the DCS worker stated that during an interview, the 9-year-old boy walked backwards up a wall and did a flip back to the ground. The DCS worker made a formal report – writing that the family could very likely be affected by an "evil influence."

The case progressed, leading to a home visit by Captain Austin and other police along with the DCS caseworker. The visit was filled with strange occurrences, including flickering lights, moving window blinds, and even a malfunctioning car seat in a detective's car. This was the "last straw" and the Ammons family, along with a local priest, decided to do an exorcism. The exorcism proceeded in three parts in which law enforcement was present for all but one part. After the exorcism was completed, and the family moved out of the house, there were no other complaints of odd happenings by either the Ammons family or the new residents at the house.

When thinking about demonological theories, one is tempted to only look at times before the Enlightenment. This makes sense, as this was the heyday for such explanations. We can never really know whether these stories are fabricated or involve the pranks of people trying to get attention. However, belief in the supernatural continues today and, if one looks, can still be found from time to time.[19]

Empirical support

At this point, you will probably not be surprised to hear that empirical support for demonological theories is non-existent. Demonology itself is not a scientific endeavor and cannot be subjected to empirical study. However, this does not mean that such theories do not have validity in the minds of those in society. For example, in 2001, Andrea Yates drowned her five children in a bathtub in Houston, Texas. When the police asked her who did it, she told them, "Satan."[20] Others, like those in the Ammons family discussed earlier, likely believe at least parts of their own stories, and so do their families.

On the other hand, the pre-Enlightenment philosophers created a large foundation of ideas from which new theories were developed. The influence of gods, God, or other divinities cannot be proven, but their ideas of morality, self-discipline, rationalism, and justice have made their way into contemporary thinking and criminal justice practice. These facets of their ideas *can* be tested in some specific ways which will be discussed later in the book.

Remaining questions

What remains to be seen is how much theorizing and criminal justice practice will be influenced by the concepts discussed in this chapter. Will the criminal justice system continue to operate on the idea that people are rational and self-interested? Will law continue to be founded on the social contract? Will theories continue to integrate elements of rational choice and self-regulation or, perhaps, incorporate some of the ideas on morality and even evil? Ideas have a way of coming "full circle" and may come back around in some form or another.

Policy

The philosophies of the ancient Greeks, bounded to morality and rationality as they were, were especially fond of efforts to rehabilitate people who did not have the self-discipline to control themselves. This is not unlike many programs today that aim to instill self-control among their participants. However, the ancient Greeks also thought that when rehabilitation fails, a person should be abandoned or left for dead. This, thankfully, is not the policy of the day today.

Because demonological theories are not empirical and do not have many devotees in modern society, rarely are policy efforts modeled after them. In the past, as we have seen with the Salem Witch Trials, the only forms of punishment or intervention have been extreme punishment, imprisonment, or death – sometimes a combination of all three. Witch-hunters, cunning folk, and diviners (those who acted almost like psychologists who had insight into those who could use magic) were all people whose help could be elicited during this time to track down individuals suspected of evil. Often these individuals acted as the police, tracking and investigating the use of evil magic and a "trial by ordeal" would commence. One popular ordeal was "ducking" whereby the accused would be bound and thrown into water. Witches, naturally, would resist the immersion and float. However, one would have to wait until the very end to ensure that one was not a witch. Therefore, the innocent would surely drown. Their families, perhaps, were consoled by the fact that they were not a witch.[21]

Some commentators have made the observation that the theories or perspectives discussed in this chapter serve as scapegoats for society. By ostracizing those who are "truly evil" everyone else is absolved of their own poor behavior and perhaps their responsibility for the behavior itself. This "othering" makes delinquents the bad people and others the good people, removing any guilt from those good people. Today, this is often how school shooters and terrorists are depicted. They are evil, despicable people who are really the "bad guys." They are deranged and suffer mental illness, and are solely responsible for their acts – society is not to blame.[22] Perhaps the way we look at certain people in society has changed only a little.

Summary

A lot of ground has been covered in this chapter (from hundreds of years BC up until the Enlightenment period) very quickly. This is due to the very monolithic way of viewing crime and criminality during this long period. People acted deviantly because of their lack of morals or their possession by some evil in the world. Not only were explanations closely related to religious beliefs, but so too were the punishments. Knowledge about the brain (psychology), genes (neuroscience), and most physiology (biology) was not around at this time, so the integration of knowledge was not possible. However, it should be apparent that there were great minds of the time that added a step on the huge staircase up to the integrated criminological sciences that we have today.

Notes

1 Brunson, 2007.
2 Zaibert, 2016.
3 Breasted, 2003.
4 Lee, 1987: 201.
5 Vlastos, 1991.
6 Lee, 1987: 201.
7 See Agnew, 1992; Sutherland, 1934.
8 Allen, 2009; Vlastos, 1991.
9 Ross & Brown, 2009.
10 Dyson, 2001.
11 Regan & Baumgarth, 2002.
12 Farrington, 1996.
13 Schild, 1981.
14 Hibbert, 1963.
15 Mackay, 2009.
16 Schiff, 2015.
17 Israel, 2001.
18 Woolf, 2000.
19 Story retrieved from the *Indy Star* (www.indystar.com/story/news/2014/01/25/the-disposession-of-latoya-ammons/4892553/).
20 Rafter, Posick, & Rocque, 2016.
21 Einstadter & Henry, 2006.
22 Szasz, 1970.

Further reading

Allen, D. S. (2009). *The world of Prometheus: The politics of punishing in democratic Athens*. Princeton, NJ: Princeton University Press.

Hollingworth, M. (2010). *The pilgrim city: St Augustine of Hippo and his innovation in political thought*. London: Bloomsbury Publishing.

Maggi, A. (2001). *Satan's rhetoric: A study of Renaissance demonology*. Chicago, IL: University of Chicago Press.

Normand, L. & Roberts, G. (2000). *Witchcraft in early modern Scotland: James VI's demonology and the North Berwick witches*. Exeter: University of Exeter Press.

Pfohl, S. J. (1994). *Images of deviance and social control: A sociological history*. New York: McGraw-Hill.

Schiff, S. (2015). *The witches: Salem, 1692*. London: Hachette.

Lombroso and early biological theories

3

Introduction	25
Theory	26
Origins	26
Recent developments	32
The cases of Carrie Buck and Abdelmalek Bayout: the genetic basis of crime	35
Empirical support	36
Remaining questions	37
Policy	37
Summary	38

Introduction

Criminology took a sharp turn with the beginning of the Enlightenment in the eighteenth century. Obscure religious explanations of crime and antisocial behavior were no longer trusted, since they could not be tested using scientific methods. This led to the emergence of a positivistic model that would be applied to the study of crime. Positivism is a philosophical orientation which states that all ideas and theories can be subjected to the scientific method to test their validity. Positivism slowly led to the rejection of theism as discussed in the previous chapter and toward criminology – the scientific study of crime and the criminal.[1]

Early positivistic theories attempted to study the criminal himself and explanations were placed upon a foundation of "individual differences." In other words, what makes criminals *different* than the rest of us, law-abiding and upstanding citizens? During these early years, criminology was almost synonymous with biocriminology – locating criminality within the biology of the individual.[2] The most famous and influential biocriminologist was Cesare Lombroso who has been named the "father of criminology" because of his systematic and scientific study of the criminal (and not the accuracy of his theories). However, Lombroso built upon the work of older theorists and theories as much as others then built upon his ideas. This chapter will begin with the foundations of biocriminology and discuss the recent advances in genetics and neuroscience which have eclipsed the older versions of the criminal and criminality. The large body of biosocial research and theories will be reserved for a later chapter dedicated to the science of merging environmental and biological causes of crime.

Theory

There is not one biological theory of crime, but several that arose shortly before and after the Enlightenment period. The earliest of these theories argued that a person's biological appearance – their face and physical features – reflected their true inner spirit. People deemed to be ugly or marked by large foreheads and pointed noses, large lips, and dark in color were supposed to be reflecting a criminal inner self. Later, the very popular theory of crime founded in phrenology claimed to be able to predict criminality based on bumps on the head which reflect the size of "faculties" in the brain related to behavior. The larger the section of the brain controlling particular behavior, the more it is used to carry out that behavior.

Theories of criminal behavior associated with body type and features reached their pinnacle in Cesare Lombroso's "criminal man" who he argued had several "stigmata," not unlike those promulgated by early theorists. Lombroso claimed that criminals were inherently different than non-criminals and could be identified based on their biology. His theories took a major hit in the 1900s when more sophisticated research proved him wrong but biological theories remained strong and theories relating to body type did not completely die out, emerging again in the work of Sheldon and Eleanor Glueck, among others.

Today, as mentioned earlier, biocriminology has largely been replaced by a more interdisciplinary and multidisciplinary model. Biosocial criminology incorporates knowledge from biology, sociology, psychology, public health, and many other fields. However, there are echoes of earlier biocriminology that are worth noting – particularly when considering the policies and practices that emerge from biological knowledge. This history is traced in this chapter, leaving in-depth conversation on biosocial criminology until later, and concluding with a look at how biocriminology still informs some of our laws and policies today.

Origins

In 1535, Giambattista della Porta (1535–1615) was born into a wealthy Napoleonic family outside of Naples, Italy in Vico Equense. During this time, Italy was a bastion for discovery and experiments leading to fields such as cosmology and "magic." Given his lifelong interest in his craft and his obsession with new knowledge, he would later go on to be known as the "Professor of Secrets." He was very popular with the public, and his first book, *Magiae naturalis libri IIII* published in 1558, was a hit. However, he did not score any points with the government and church who closely watched over della Porta for his entire career (this should come as little surprise given the time period in which he lived coupled with the discussions from the previous chapter).[3]

At the age of 49, della Porta published *Humana physiognomia* in 1584. Human physiognomy provided a model in which all living things could be related through their structure and resemblance. He closely studied the faces of human beings and concluded that beautiful people were also morally good and that people who resembled animals (i.e., "ugly") were more likely to be criminals and morally weak. For example, an individual with a sloped forehead and large beak-like nose would resemble a raven or crow and thus

Incuruus à fronte nafus.

Figure 3.1 Della Porta: Raven, Owl, and Man

Source: Della Porta (1586).
Credit: National Library of Medicine (NLM).

ESTHER, DAUGHTER OF "DADDY" KALLIKAK

Figure 3.2 The Kallikak family

Source: Kallikaks [digital image] (2005, July 1). Available at: https://commons.wikimedia.org/wiki/File:Kallikaks_guss-big.jpg#file; Esther [daughter of "Daddy" Kallikak] (2004, June 24). Available at: https://en.wikipedia.org/wiki/File:Kallikak_esther.jpg.

be sneaky and animalistic, and likely to go to prison (Figure 3.1). He also studied the contours of individuals' hands – a precursor to today's "palm-readers."[4]

Physiognomy was popularized by della Porta and others in the 1500s, but the idea itself is much older. In fact, ideas inherent in physiognomy may be found in the writings of Aristotle and Pythagoras in ancient Greece. It is written that Socrates himself received an evaluation from a physiognomist. A notoriously odd-looking man, his evaluation did not go well.[5]

Readers at this point may find physiognomy laughable and ridiculous, but during della Porta's time it was actually revered as a credible science. In fact, the idea that someone's outer features, such as their face, can be measured to reveal their internal character was novel and accepted with open arms. If a person's features could be reliably measured, then their future could be predicted. Criminals could be identified early in life and stopped. We know now that there is little correlation between physical features and criminal behavior (the beak-like nose is one that this author particularly takes exception to), and the idea had disastrous consequences during della Porta's time. He, and others, were much more likely to link the physical features of darker individuals to those of animals – systematically damning a whole group of individuals to criminality leading to widespread racism and discrimination. This work foretold of a dark period in criminology to come hundreds of years later in the eugenics movement.[6]

Over a hundred years after della Porta's death, but inspired by his writing, Zurich-born Johann Kaspar Lavater (1741–1801) developed physiognomics – cementing della Porta's ideas in a field of study. Lavater was a Swiss writer and protestant pastor who latched onto the idea that physical appearance could lend insight into individual character. His family consisted of physicians, and it was their hope that Lavater would follow in their footsteps.[7] While carrying with him a curiosity about medicine, he was primarily concerned with advancing his involvement with the church. It may have been this combination that led him to use della Porta's ideas and search the body as a window to the soul.

While his works were similar to those of della Porta, Lavater was more interested in correlating outer appearance, or beauty, with *specific* internal mental states, whereas della Porta related the two more generally. Lavater called this the "correspondence between the internal and external man."[8] His writings were popular in the latter half of the eighteenth century – including a pocketbook version of his writings so that people could judge the character of those they had just met – but this slowly diminished as others, who we will discuss below, entered the scene. This did not please Lavater who was known to be quite narcissistic. His behavior was considered vain and, after the French overran the Swiss in 1799, he was shot by a French soldier and later died in 1801.[9]

In the later 1700s and into the 1800s, one could find oneself in a social club receiving a reading of the bumps on one's head. Emerging from the ashes of della Porta's and Lavater's physiognomy, the new field of phrenology rose. Phrenology was the system of reading the contours ("bumps") on people's heads in order to reveal their character (and, thus, likely future). It is Franz Joseph Gall (1758–1828) who is credited with founding phrenology, but it was his student/research partner, Johann Spurzheim (1776–1832), who expanded and solidified the idea.[10] Together, they brought about a hugely popular and influential method for identifying criminals and predicting criminal behavior.

Phrenology was based on the idea that the brain was the organ of the mind which itself is the amalgamation of several other organs, or faculties, such as combativeness and destructiveness. If the organ is large (indicating that it is very active), then it will produce a bump on the skull which is large. By reading the bumps, one can tell which faculties are being used the most, indicating which behaviors are being exhibited by the individual. For instance, if I am a deceitful person, tricking people all the time, I will

---

a. The unification movement sought to conglomerate all the various territories around the Italian peninsula into the "Kingdom of Italy."

have a bump where deceitfulness lies because I am using it all the time like a muscle. This system was thought to be very scientific and a reliable way to predict someone's behavior, especially criminal behavior. Born out of the Enlightenment era, Gall and Spurzheim hoped that the science of phrenology would replace the old theological systems of thought. And, to their liking, it mostly did.

Gall was fascinated by how his schoolmates were different from himself and how even his own brothers and sisters were quite different from one another. Although he fancied himself a great thinker and philosopher, he failed to keep up with his peers in memorization. He noted that those who excelled in memory were those with large, prominent eyes. He reasoned that this must have something to do with their superior ability to memorize material. He became so obsessed with the idea that he began taking molds of people's skulls, collecting skulls, and even stopping people on the street who he thought had interesting "protuberances."[11] While Gall's view of the human being was largely deterministic (you are born one way and stay that way), Spurzheim claimed that faculties can change in response to environmental factors such as nutrition, exercise, and self-discipline. This achieved widespread support, especially among the medical community. He was flown all over the world to speak on his thoughts, including widely in the United States where his ideas had strong appeal. After an exhausting tour, Spurzheim passed away in Boston in 1832 where his remains can be found today.[12]

As mentioned in the introduction to this chapter, in the mid-1800s, a man by the name of Cesare Lombroso made his name among the scientific community. Lombroso was a physician born in Italy to Jewish parents who was profoundly interested in all aspects of human life. He studied at the University of Pavia in Italy – something he shares with Cesare Beccaria, another Italian scholar – and joined the unification movement[a] shortly after graduation. It was here that he made his study of 3,000 soldiers which became the basis of criminal anthropology presented in his 1876 book *The criminal man*. Unlike earlier theorists who were overly concentrated on the brain and facial features, Lombroso was also interested in criminal lifestyles, attitudes, and behaviors.[13]

Based on his work in *The criminal man*,[14] Lombroso posited that criminals are actually less evolutionarily advanced than "normal people." He believed that criminals were what he called ativisms, namely evolutionary throwbacks to an earlier time who were marked by stigmata such as sloped foreheads, protruding jaws, big facial features, and asymmetry in the face and body. These individuals were born that way and, therefore, born criminals. In the same year of *The criminal man's* release, Lombroso took up a position at the University of Turin in Italy where he studied prisoners. This led to elaborations on the book which went through five editions – each one adding to his view of criminality and criminals.

Charles Goring (1870–1919), a medical doctor trained at the University of London in England, set about testing Lombroso's ideas that criminals were physically different from non-criminals. He wanted to know if criminals had the stigmata that Lombroso said plagued their brains and bodies.

After a comprehensive study, in which he paired up with famous statistician Karl Pearson, and which went on to be published as *The English convict* in 1913, Goring concluded, contrary to Lombroso, that there were no significant differences in the brains and bodies of criminals and non-criminals. Given the careful methodology applied to the data collection and sophisticated statistical techniques used to analyze the data (not to mention the added validity of having one of the world's most celebrated statisticians on your team), the findings were a substantial blow to Lombroso's theory. Had Goring not conducted his study, there is no telling how long Lombroso's ideas would have dominated criminology. However, Goring concluded that there *is* substantial support for a hereditary basis of criminal behavior and for a link between brain defects and criminal behavior – spotlighting a continuing influence of biology on antisocial behavior.

Around the same time that Lombroso was working on his theory behind the criminal man, others in the United States were developing another related, but ultimately different, approach to the study of crime. If Lombroso and other theorists of the time were correct, namely that criminals were born bad, then there should be some consistency passed down through the generations in families of criminal behavior. In other words, criminality would have to be at least partially inherited. It may come as little surprise to learn (or remember) that Charles Darwin's *On the origin of species* was published in 1859 when US sociologist Richard Dugdale was 18 years old.[15] Building on Darwinian evolutionary concepts and Lombrosian theory, Dugdale conducted a study of one family, fictitiously named the Jukes, which was published in 1877. As an active and involved community member, Dugdale was involved in several local organizations in his early adult home of Ulster County in upstate New York. One of these organizations was the Prison Association of New York. After being tasked with inspecting a series of jails in the area, he noticed that many of the prisoners he encountered were related to one another. He set out to explain this occurrence using a scientific analysis.

Using a combination of official local records and personal interviews (a fantastic early example of mixed-methods research), Dugdale collected data on the related individuals in the "Jukes" family. After collecting data on 709 individuals (540 of Juke blood and 169 who married in), Dugdale found that 140 had been criminals. Many were thieves and prostitutes, and seven took their own lives. In all, Dugdale estimated that the state (through welfare and incarceration) had spent around $1.3 million on the Jukes family over the course of 75 years. Despite having found significant evidence of a hereditary component to criminality – there were many more criminals than you would expect in any "normal" family – he was very careful to suggest that this was only one study, and one that needed to be replicated. In addition, he was adamant that heredity was not the only "cause" of crime and that environmental factors were hugely important as well.[16] Through his work, perhaps Dugdale was one of the earliest biosocial criminologists. Although he had offered these cautions, others took his information and made claims that criminality was the product of "bad blood" carried through generations by inheritance and that eugenics would be a way to cleanse society of the bad people.

Richard Dugdale, frail and sickly throughout his life, suffered from congenital heart disease and passed away in his early forties. A strong advocate for science and social change, he would have likely been appalled at how his research was used by others in the eugenics movement – an effort to "cleanse" society of "bad people" through sterilizing, executing, and incarcerating people assumed to be criminal. One eugenicist followed Dugdale's work with his own examination of a "wayward" family. Henry Goddard, who led an institution for the "feebleminded," traced the family tree of a woman in his institution named Deborah "Kallikak" (a pseudonym meaning good–bad). The analysis began with Deborah's great-great-great grandfather, Martin. Martin eventually became an upstanding citizen with a large, wholesome family in New England (Figure 3.2). However, before all that, Martin had a small fling with a "feebleminded" barmaid who went on to have her own family, as did her children. While Martin's New England family continued to have several generations of intelligent, well-behaved members, the Kallikaks went on to have generations of feebleminded children with a host of problems. Goddard concluded that feeblemindedness was inherited, as evidenced by the moral and intelligent legitimate family tree compared to the "tainted" side of the tree shaped by Martin's one-night stand with the barmaid.

This line of research, while seriously flawed, does have a ring of truth to it. We will revisit hereditary and genetics-based criminological theories later in this chapter and later in the book. The theories discussed below have been supported by modern scientific analysis and divert fairly substantially from the theories presented in this section.

From della Porta and Lavater's physiognomy to Gall and Spurzheim's phrenology to Lombroso's born criminal all the way through the hereditary studies of Dugdale and

Goddard we have covered quite a lot of ground. I will finish with two theorists, with similar theories, who revisit and expand upon earlier theories centered on physical body features.

After a hiatus, the role of the body and physical features in the explanation of crime re-emerged in the mid 1990s with the work of William Sheldon, and Sheldon and Eleanor Glueck (who were husband and wife). To be clear, I will use Sheldon to refer to William Sheldon and "the Gluecks" to refer to the work of Sheldon and Eleanor Glueck. While the theories of these researchers, called constitutional theories because they rely on measurement and analysis of how the body is constituted or made up, were more sophisticated than those of older theorists (such as della Porta and Lavater) they have been largely discredited by modern researchers. Interestingly, there does seem to be a mini-resurgence in criminology examining the relationship between body type and behavior that does, in fact, lend some support to the ideas of constitutional theories.

Sheldon, a University of Chicago-trained psychologist, developed a system of examining body shapes in an effort to link body type to behavior. His choice of study was probably influenced by his mentor at the University of Chicago, the anthropologist Sante Naccarati, who was studying body shape and temperament. Sheldon went on to formalize this study, calling it somatotyping. In his 1940 book *The varieties of human physique*, Sheldon described three body types and, in the second edition in 1942,[17] their corresponding behaviors. Endomorphs were soft and round with a viscerotonia temperament (relaxed and sociable). Ectomorphs were skinny and frail with a cerebrotonia temperament (restrained and asocial). Finally, mesomorphs were muscular and athletic with a somatotonia temperament (outgoing and active). Mesomorphs were more likely to be criminal than the other groups. Sheldon did not believe that his categories were totally mutually exclusive but rather existed on a continuum such that an individual would receive a score on each type. For example, an obese man with no muscle would receive a score of 7–1-1.[18]

Sheldon concluded that criminality was genetic and that it was "bad genes" that led to certain body types and behavior. Because he believed that this genetic relationship was determinant of behavior, he supported eugenic solutions. Eugenics proposes that society should promote the reproduction of "good genes" and inhibit "bad genes" from reproducing through methods such as forced sterilization and long-term imprisonment. Along with his contemporary Ernest Hooton, who picked up where Sheldon left off, he promoted the "science" of eugenics. Hooton himself wrote and spoke widely about the benefits of the US eugenics movement until his death in 1954.[19]

Sheldon and Eleanor Glueck revitalized constitutional theory in the mid-1900s. After their very influential study described in *Unraveling juvenile delinquency* in 1950, which studied 500 delinquent boys and 500 non-delinquent boys, one of their major conclusions was that the delinquent boys tended to be "superior" in physique (and masculine), mesomorphs, and tended to mature somewhat later than the non-delinquents. Body type was not an intended focus of the book and was a result that they largely stumbled upon in the course of their research.[20]

Given what the Gluecks thought was an important conclusion to their study, another book was published in 1956 which focused entirely on the body and crime called *Physique and body type*.[21] Here, the Gluecks expanded upon their findings, suggesting that delinquent boys have body types which make offending less difficult, such as muscular physiques that enable strength and speed. On the other hand, endomorphs, who are generally lazy and aloof, are much less likely to act out their desires and drives than mesomorphs. Therefore, they are much less likely than endomorphs to be involved in delinquency. Much later, in the late 1900s, criminologists Robert Sampson and John Laub reanalyzed the Gluecks' data and, somewhat surprisingly, found that there were more mesomorphs represented in the delinquent group even after using more sophisticated modern statistical techniques. However, these results did not hold up over time as the Glueck boys grew older.[22]

Recent developments

Following what Rafter refers to as "criminology's darkest hour" and the atrocities of Nazi experiments and the abhorrent policies related to eugenics, the biological approach to explaining criminal behavior lost favor. While some psychological and biological ideas remained in the backdrop of the field of criminology, there were no longer many who championed the biological approach. However, a resurgence of the biological approach may be seen in recent years. Most of these perspectives fully acknowledge (as Lombroso did in his later years) the role of the environment in behavior. Many contemporary theorists also believe that some combination of biological and environmental factors influences behavior. In fact, the term "biosocial criminology" has gained favor because this perspective gives weight to both perspectives (the biological and the social). This is the focus of an entire chapter in this book – Chapter 11 – so the discussion in the following section will highlight the work of a handful of theorists who focus on one topic area or factor that they believe is the main causal force in leading to criminal behavior.

In 1979, C. Ray Jeffery published *Biology and crime*,[23] one of the first books to focus on biology and its relationship with crime since the classic theories fell from grace. He contends that biology can have a strong impact on delinquency – especially early learning disabilities. He also makes the case for looking at the brain and brain development in children early in their education, as this is a critical point in time to both identify disabilities and attempt to correct for them. Throughout the book, he is cautious to not suggest that biology works alone (without the environment) and argues that more research is needed in examining the biology and crime link. However, he remained a proponent of biologically informed criminology until his death. For example, he published an article in the *Journal of Criminal Justice Education* in 1993 stressing the need for more biological training in criminology given the importance of biology for behavior.[24] The response, to incorporate biology into criminological training, has been slow to come,[25] but there is reason to be optimistic that a more holistic criminological training is on the horizon with the rise in awareness of the importance of biology, and especially genetics, for behavior.

Lee Ellis, one of the remaining living criminologists who championed the resurgence of the biological approach in criminology, came out with his work on the genetic basis for criminal behavior in his 1982 article "Genetics and criminal behavior" followed up by his work on evolution and criminal behavior in "Criminal behavior and r/K selection: An extension of gene-based evolutionary theory" in 1988.[26] Ellis, throughout his career, has been concerned with integrating genetics and evolution into the study of criminal behavior. Of course, the two are intimately intertwined. Evolution is the basis for the survival of genes which persist, in large part but not entirely, due to their ability to increase the chance of sexual reproduction. The rK theory states that an "r" strategy for sexual reproduction includes the rapid production of offspring with little direct care for each child (also called a "fast" life history). The "K" strategy is the opposite – fewer children with extensive direct care for each child (also called a "slow" life history). Human beings, as a species, adhere to the K strategy[b] –– but there is variation in the human population. Ellis suggests that criminal behavior is linked to a strategy closer to the "r" side of the spectrum. The less care for children and more time spent on seeking thrills and

---

b. Compare human beings with mice. It is not uncommon for mice to have 40 offspring in one year. It would be almost impossible for mice parents to care for each one to any great extent and many will fall prey to predators. However, say even 20 survive (50%); that is still a lot of mice! Those are pretty good odds for mice – but human beings would not be okay with these odds. Now consider: spiders generally have a few hundred offspring per year

obtaining illicit income, the more violence is likely to be experienced for those individuals. We will revisit this idea to a great extent later in the book when we discuss biosocial criminology in Chapter 11.[27]

During the resurgence in the 1970s, more attention was paid to biology and individual differences in the explanation of criminal behavior. This continued into the 1980s. In the mid-1980s, the work of two theorists received arguably the most praise and most dissent in recent years in the field of criminology. Harvard University professors James Q. Wilson and Richard J. Herrnstein published *Crime and human nature* in 1985 and argued that, among other factors, crime is largely the result of low intelligence. Intelligence, also, is mainly the result of genes which are passed down by parents through heredity.[28] These hereditary personality traits are stable and very hard to change.

Crime and human nature, along with a similar book authored by Richard Herrnstein & Charles Murray almost a decade later, *The bell curve,*[29] was extremely divisive in the field of criminology. Some praised the work as a straightforward, empirically based theory of criminal behavior while others attacked the work as misguided and misrepresentative.[30] Either way, this body of work ushered in new ideas about the link between crime and biological factors such as intelligence. Today, this conversation is still contentious, with some arguing that intelligence is poorly measured while others argue that it is among the best measured constructs in psychology. Some argue that intelligence is unrelated to behavior after controlling for confounding factors, while others maintain that it is a robust predictor of behavior across individuals and groups. It appears that these debates will continue well into the future and the policy implications of intelligence research will be contested for some time to come.

In 1990, Diana H. Fishbein, C. Eugene Bennett Chair of the Prevention Research Center at Penn State University, published a paper in *Criminology* outlining what she saw as the way forward in biological criminology. In particular, she outlines four requirements for a revised biocriminological investigation of antisocial behavior, including the following:

> (1) establish the relevancy of biology to the study of crime; (2) develop the groundwork for including biological data in criminological theories; (3) design research projects using compatible measurement instruments, data sets, and statistical techniques; and (4) determine the boundaries of practical applications of biological findings.[31]

According to Fishbein, in order to accomplish these requirements, criminology must be informed about and design studies that incorporate knowledge from endocrinology (e.g., hormones), neuroscience (e.g., the brain and neurotransmitters), and genetics. While Fishbein's work, in total, advocates a biosocial investigation in crime, her early work focused on integrating a biological perspective into the study of criminality or what she calls maladaptive behaviors.

Around the same time of Fishbein's writing, University of Pennsylvania psychologist, Adrian Raine, was researching and writing about the role of the brain in criminal behavior. In his classic 1993 book, *The psychopathology of crime: Criminal behavior as a clinical disorder,* Raine covers a wide range of factors related to brain structure and function while also focusing on other biological maladies related to lead exposure, risky pregnancies, and diet/nutrition.[32] This focus picked up on what Fishbein had written about in the early 1990s, and Adrian Raine's work has gone on to immensely influence the study of crime. In 2015, Raine received the book award from the Biosocial Criminology Association for his most recent work, *The anatomy of violence,* which has brought his work on the brain basis of crime up to date.[33]

Along with the study of the brain, Raine has examined other physiological processes that can lead to criminal behavior. Of course, these processes ultimately have some effect on the brain which is the primary influence on behavior. For example, teaming up with his student at the University of Pennsylvania Jill Portnoy, Raine explores the mechanisms behind the relationship between low resting heart rate and criminal behavior (one of the most replicated findings in criminology, according to the authors). Low resting heart rate, a physiological function in the body, has been linked to criminal behavior for two major reasons: (1) it is an uncomfortable state that people tend to cope with by raising their heart rate through thrilling activities (like crime); and/or (2) it enables some people to engage in crime without becoming stimulated like most people who become anxious and scared. The authors replicate the low resting heart rate and criminal behavior link and, in addition, provide evidence that it is sensation seeking, and not necessarily "fearlessness" that is the link between low resting heart rate and criminal behavior.[34] This body of work continues to provide evidence that biological function has a part to play in criminal behavior.

Recently, the Brain Genomics Superstruct Project was launched to bring together massive amounts of data on the brain in order to understand human behavior. Drawing from a recent article by Holmes and colleagues, this states: "the Brain Genomics Superstruct Project (GSP) was initiated to yield a dataset of structural, functional, behavioral, and genetic information on a large number of clinically normal participants that could be analyzed on its own or combined with other large-scale data collection efforts."[35] This is a massive effort to make available the scans of over a thousand people to correlate brain structure and function to multiple sets of human behaviors: a truly exciting endeavor whose promise is yet to be seen.

The heritability of criminal behavior is of much current interest to criminologists. To explore whether criminal behavior, and the traits that lead to this behavior such as impulsivity, anger, and callousness, are passed down genetically from parents to offspring, researchers use a behavior genetics model where variations in a trait are explored across a population. Researchers engaging this model use twins, adoptees, and families to identify similarities and differences among children who share (and do not share) genetic and family backgrounds. For example, if identical twins are more similar than dizygotic twins on some trait, this suggests there is likely a genetic component to the trait. If adopted children are more similar to their biological parents in comparison to their adoptive parents, this, again, would suggest a genetic basis to behavior.

Behavior genetic and candidate gene studies have provided researchers with a solid foundation for exploring the role of genes and the environment in behavior. These studies generally find that for just about every phenotype there is some role for both genes and environment and often they work together to produce behavior. However, there are limitations to these studies. For example, behavioral genetic designs lend insight into the possible distribution of variance across genes and environments but tell us nothing about *which* genes matter the most and in what combination. Candidate gene studies tell us something about probable genes that influence behavior but nothing about the other tens of thousands of genes that may play a role in producing behavior.

Ultimately, what some have argued for is full genotyping of the human organism. While costly and time consuming, this allows researchers to examine the entire genome for an individual and all of their genetic variants (called alleles). While the genes making up the human organism are incredibly similar (and we are very similar to other organisms), we have different versions of the same genes. These alleles can be related to behavioral phenotypes (e.g., aggression, impulsivity, depression) and genotyping can help understand the alleles related to these behaviors and traits.

Recently, human genome mapping has increased as costs and the time it takes to genome an entire human have decreased. Studies that include the analysis of the entire genome are called genome-wide association studies (GWAS). Often, researchers will refer to these studies as GWAS or *Gee-waz*. GWAS studies have linked several genes and alleles to a variety of antisocial behavior.[36] Genes, along with the environment, impact various personal traits that, in turn, impact everything from the likelihood of owning a firearm,[37] to enlisting in the army.[38] These findings by themselves tell us little about the actual genes involved in promoting the behavior and even less about the specific mechanisms that lead to the behavior, but that is the job of GWAS studies which can further pinpoint specific genes and begin to clarify just how genes lead to certain behaviors.

Much of the research conducted today is biosocial in nature – looking at how one's biology (such as genetic makeup) and the immediate surrounding environments (such as one's neighborhood or family life) combine in different ways to influence behavior. This type of examination is often called gene by environment (GxE) interaction studies, since research often looks for how one's genes and environment interact in producing behavior. This perspective has sparked much interest among criminologists and produced a hefty amount of research from criminologists such as John P. Wright, Kevin Beaver, Brian Boutwell, J.C. Barnes, Jamie Vaske, Danielle Boisvert, Joseph Nedelec, Eric Connolly, and Joseph Schwartz (to name just a few). In fact, so much influential work has come from biosocial criminology that a separate chapter is dedicated to the work later in this book. Therefore, we will hold off on discussion until then.

The cases of Carrie Buck and Abdelmalek Bayout: the genetic basis of crime

Carrie Buck was the daughter of Emma Buck – a woman who was rumored to prostitute herself and to be an alcoholic. Carrie and Emma lived in very poor conditions, often on the streets, depending on others for help. In 1920, Emma was evaluated by psychiatrists who determined that she was "feebleminded" – a term used during this time to describe someone with low intelligence. A feebleminded person could range from an idiot at one end (someone with the mental capabilities of a toddler or younger) to an imbecile, with a moron being somewhere in-between.

Emma, being feebleminded, was sent to the Virginia State Colony to join other imbeciles kept in captivity. Upon her arrival, her genitals were promptly "cleaned" with mercury, leaving her sterile. Carrie, without her mother, was sent to live with foster-parents where she was abused and raped which resulted in pregnancy. Carrie, like her mother, was brought before the court and determined to be feebleminded – a moron: Middle Grade to be exact – and sent off to the same place (her daughter, unsurprisingly, was sent to foster care).

Carrie was observed by a doctor at the Virginia State Colony who wanted to sterilize her, like her mother, because of "bad heredity." However, this time, a legal order was needed to set the standard for all cases of the same ilk moving forward. *Buck vs. Bell* (1927) was argued before the US Supreme Court who determined that sterilization was an acceptable policy for dealing with imbeciles. Months later, surgeons cut Carrie's fallopian tubes and closed the incisions using carbolic acid. The Buck lineage could not continue.

More recently, genetics has made its way into the courtroom and has often been used as a *mitigating* factor in sentencing of those found guilty. In this way, genetic contributions to behavior have led to lighter sentences and a reduction of culpability. This is highlighted by a contemporary court case which found the offender, Abdelmalek Bayout, guilty of murder.

In 2007, in Italy, a Muslim citizen named Abdelmalek Bayout was insulted by another citizen, Walter Felipe Novoa Perez – a Columbian living in Italy at the time. Perez had insulted Bayout because he had been wearing eye makeup for religious purposes. As a result of the insult Bayout stabbed Perez, killing him. In court, Bayout's attorney argued that he had genes that predisposed him to act violently. A biological test found that Bayout had low activation of the MAOA enzyme. Because of this, argued Bayout's attorney, he could not control his behavior after being provoked by Perez. The judge agreed – subsequently knocking a year off his sentence.

Unlike Carrie Buck who was deemed a "bad seed" destined to fail, genetic predispositions to violence have been brought to the court as a mitigating factor (often unsuccessfully). However, questions abound as to how we should use genetic information in the courtroom. What genes should be considered when determining sentencing? Where is the line drawn between genetic determinism and free will? These questions are likely to become more pressing as genetic testing becomes easier and less costly and knowledge about genetic influences on behavior increases.

Empirical support

At this point it may already be clear what we can take away from biocriminology but this question deserves careful consideration. First, the biocriminology that emerged from the sixteenth through the nineteenth centuries has largely been disproven. There may be a ring of truth here and there but, overall, the theories from this time period are not useful in today's world. However, work using behavior genetics, molecular genetics, and GxE studies has advanced the understanding of the origins of criminal behavior.

In the early years of the 2000s, the work of criminologists J.C. Barnes and Brian Boutwell, along with their mentor Kevin Beaver, brought a behavior genetics design to the table in order to explain the origins of several criminological issues. In 2011, Barnes, Beaver, and Boutwell conducted a behavior genetic study on the taxonomy laid down by Terrie Moffitt (discussed at length later in this book) who proposed three major groups of (non)offenders: life-course-persistent, adolescence-limited, and abstainers. Moffitt suggested that there were significant neurological and genetic underpinnings to these groups – particularly those in the life-course-persistent group who refused to change their poor behavior over time. They found that genetics accounted for between 56 and 70 percent of the life-course-persistent groups, 35 percent for the adolescence-limited group, and 56 percent for the abstainer group.[39] Similarly, in 2012, Barnes and Boutwell examined change and stability in offending behavior. Genetics explained almost all of the stability in criminal behavior – similar to their previous study on persistent offending – while unique environmental factors explained most of the change in offending.[40] Taken together, it becomes clear that genetics has some bearing on types of offending behavior and especially offending out of the norm (persistent violent offending). These effects are only possible with some methodological design that is sensitive to genetic predisposition.

In addition, a large knowledge base has accumulated regarding the relationship between intelligence and crime. At the individual level, intelligence is shown to be one of the strongest and most persistent factors related to criminal behavior.[41] IQ levels at the county level are also found to be related to crime rates, suggesting that areas lower in IQ experience high levels of criminal behavior.[42]

In his book *Intelligence*[43] and in his personal interview, intelligence researcher Stuart Ritchie discussed the role of IQ in a host of behavioral and health outcomes. He states in our conversation,

> Another clue that our measurements of intelligence are accurate is that scores on the tests predict things in the real world that we'd expect "smarter" people to do better. For instance, intelligence test performance is very strongly related to educational attainment, and also predicts occupational success. Studies in the field of cognitive

epidemiology have found that those with higher IQs tend to live longer, potentially because of the effects of intelligence on things like socioeconomic success, but also on health and safety: smarter people tend to be able to look after themselves more effectively, being less likely to smoke, binge drink, or get into fights. So the tests are not just reliable, but they are *valid* in the real world, too.

In sum, intelligence may not be the only factor involved in delinquency, but it may be a very important one.

Remaining questions

There is little doubt that criminology has benefitted from research which considers genes, and physiological functioning, in criminal behavior. The empirical support for the role of genes and the brain in behavior is quite robust and these findings have informed theory in significant ways.[44] Candidate gene studies and GWAS studies in particular have been important in pinpointing important genes for further scientific research. There remain, to be sure, many questions for future research to tackle.

While research has identified genes associated with behavior, we still know relatively little about how these genes impact the brain which, subsequently, influences behavior. Those genes are also likely to interact with other genes (called epistasis) as well as the environment in very complex ways. Further, gene expression is influenced by several factors, including naturally occurring processes in the body related to transcription of genes. Transcription factors are mechanisms in the body that control the expression of the genes, turning them "on" or "off." The process is sometimes influenced by the environment and is specific to certain situations. This process remains ambiguous.

Policy

For better or for worse throughout history, biologically based criminology has influenced the development of public policy. In the early years, when biology was largely viewed as the end-all be-all of criminal behavior, the policy implication is quite clear – society must prevent criminals from breeding and interacting with the public. This would include sterilization (as seen in the Carrie Buck case), incarceration (so as not to interact or breed with the public), and execution. This, as Nicole Rafter states, led to "criminology's darkest hour" in the eugenics movement in the early 1900s.[45]

Luckily, today, the infusion of biology into criminology does not resemble that of the past. In fact, by exploring biology, one can identify the environments that are most important for the study of antisocial behavior and explore the effects of poverty, nutrition, abuse, and neglect on brain and body functioning, providing avenues for policy that make for a safer and more just world.[46] One recent case exemplifies this fact well. In *Roper vs. Simmons* (2005),[47] the Supreme Court ruled that individuals under the age of 18 are not as responsible as adults and should not be sentenced to death. This decision was made, in part, from a knowledge of neuroscience which suggests that brain development, especially those areas related to emotion regulation and decision-making, are not fully developed until the mid-twenties.[48]

Recently, researchers have begun to explicate exactly why certain antisocial intervention programs are effective. For example, cognitive behavioral therapy has been a mainstay in the prevention and intervention field and has now accumulated an overwhelming literature, suggesting its effectiveness in reducing criminal behavior.[49] Vaske, Gaylean, and Cullen proposed in a 2011 paper in the *Journal of Criminal Justice* that cognitive behavioral therapy is so effective because it is based in brain science and has appreciable effects on areas of the brain related to behavior, especially the prefrontal and orbitofrontal cortices.[50]

Summary

Overall, it is likely that along with the expansion in knowledge about the genetic and environmental correlates of disease and mortality, the role of genetics will continue to be explored in criminology. Society has reduced the cost and labor associated with genome studies, enabling researchers to focus more closely on how genetics influence biological function and more researchers are able to account for genetic causes of behavior than ever before. The field has learned a great deal from this work but more research is certainly needed. Fishbein's words still ring true: "Although biological techniques in the assessment of human behavior are still under the microscope and definitive answers have yet to surface, the foregoing description of biological foundations for behavior provides evidence of their applicability and value."[51]

While the lessons of della Porta's physiognomy in the 1600s, Gall and Spurzheim's phrenology in the 1700s, and Lombroso's criminal man in the 1800s still reverberate through recent biological criminology, the methods and insights from recent work are dramatically different from these earlier theories. We may not gain much from looking at the shape of someone's face or skull, but perhaps we can by looking at the structure and function of their brain or the organization of their genetic code. The future will tell us how much we can learn from and apply a biological model in the exploration of antisocial behavior.

Notes

1 See the seminal work of German philosopher Immanuel Kant, *Critique of pure reason* (1781), which introduces his thoughts on positivism.
2 Rafter, Posick, & Rocque, 2016.
3 Kodera, 2015.
4 Rafter, Posick, & Rocque, 2016.
5 Tsouna, 1998.
6 See Rafter, 2008.
7 Lavater & Holcroft, 1878.
8 From *Essays on physiognomy,* 1789 (cited in Rafter, Posick, & Rocque, 2016: 23).
9 Chisholm, 1911.
10 Tomlinson, 2005.
11 Spurzheim, 1815, esp. p. 263.
12 Walsh, 1972.
13 DeLisi, 2013.
14 Lombroso, Gibson, & Rafter, 2006.
15 Darwin, 1968 [1859].
16 Dugdale, 1877.
17 Sheldon, 1940, 1942.
18 Rafter, 2007.
19 Rafter, 2004.
20 Glueck & Glueck, 1950.
21 Glueck & Glueck, 1957.
22 Sampson & Laub, 1997b.
23 Jeffery, 1979.
24 Jeffery, 1993.
25 Wright et al., 2008.

26 Ellis, 1982, 1988.
27 To preview this discussion see Boutwell et al., 2015.
28 Wilson & Herrnstein, 1998.
29 Herrnstein & Murray, 1994.
30 See Fraser, 2008.
31 Fishbein, 1990: 28.
32 Raine, 1993.
33 Raine, 2013.
34 Portnoy et al., 2014.
35 Holmes et al., 2015.
36 See, e.g., Rautiainen et al., 2016; Salvatore et al., 2015.
37 Barnes, Boutwell, & Beaver, 2014.
38 Beaver et al., 2015.
39 Barnes, Beaver, & Boutwell, 2011.
40 Barnes & Boutwell, 2012.
41 Loeber & Welsh, 2012.
42 Beaver & Wright, 2011.
43 Ritchie, 2016.
44 See Moffitt (1993) for one such example.
45 Rafter, 2010.
46 Rocque, Welsh, & Raine, 2012; Vaughn, 2016.
47 *Roper vs. Simmons*, 543 U.S. 551, 125 S. Ct. 1183, 161 L. Ed. 2d 1 (2005).
48 Steinberg et al., 2009.
49 Hofmann et al., 2012; McCart, Priester, Davies, & Azen, 2006.
50 Vaske, Gaylean, & Cullen, 2011.
51 Fishbein, 1990: 56.

Further reading

Denno, D. W. (1990). *Biology and violence: From birth to adulthood*. New York: Cambridge University Press.
Herrnstein, R. & Wilson, J. Q. (1985). *Crime and human nature*. New York: Simon and Schuster.
Jeffery, C. R. (1979). *Biology and crime*. Beverly Hills, CA: Sage.
Pinker, S. (2003). *The blank slate: The modern denial of human nature*. London: Penguin.
Rowe, D. C. (2002). *Biology and crime*. Los Angeles, CA: Roxbury.

4 The city and social disorganization theories

Introduction	40
Theory	41
Origins	41
Recent developments	45
The case of Rochester, New York: a great city with great problems	49
Empirical support	50
Remaining questions	51
Policy	52
Summary	53

Introduction

In the late 1800s and early 1900s, the United States experienced an explosion of immigration – mainly from places in Europe like Ireland and Italy. Most immigrants settled in large cities such as New York, Chicago, and Boston, but many went to mid-sized or smaller cities as well. Fewer went to rural areas looking for work. Cities were attractive to newcomers to the USA, since most of the jobs at the time were industrial, manufacturing jobs. As immigrants settled into the city and found work, the city began to diversify, with individuals from all parts of the globe practicing their own customs and values.

This movement of people into large cities created a social phenomenon of much interest to social scientists of the late nineteenth and early twentieth century. For criminologists, a shift could be seen in the approach taken to understand crime. On the heels of the Italian School's focus on the individual and their biological or physical makeup, a new orientation focused not so much on people themselves, but on areas of violence and other delinquencies. The main question here was not "why are people criminals?" but "why are areas high in crime?" This made sense, as crime was something found to be concentrated in the new American city. Pockets of crime could be seen in particular areas of the city and not so much in others. Importantly, despite the people who lived in these areas and any shifting of demographics, these areas remained high in crime.

Theory

There may have been no better place to study crime at the turn of the twentieth century than Chicago, Illinois, and it is probably not surprising that many of the most influential criminologists who studied crime at the time were teaching at the University of Chicago. Many theorists who focused on the role of cities and neighborhoods in causing crime came out of Chicago. The theoretical frameworks from which the bulk of theories discussed in the following pages came was appropriately dubbed "The Chicago School."

The Chicago School emphasized features of the neighborhood or city as a whole in producing crime and violence. Similar to ecology in environmental sciences, there are features about an area, such as socioeconomic status, resource scarcity, residential mobility (i.e., residents moving frequently), and culture conflict (e.g., not knowing the language of your neighbor or their customs). All of these elements can culminate in what many theorists saw as social disorganization. When communities and their members are poor, have to fight for jobs and other resources, and know very little about the people who surround them, it creates a perfect recipe for crime and violence. This was something that was picked up on by the Chicago School originators in the early 1900s and continued on by their students for the better part of a century.

Origins

It should be noted that a concern with neighborhoods and high crime levels was not something that started entirely with the Chicago School, although the focus may have been solidified by it. A few others paved the way for the reframing of crime as caused by social environment, as opposed to individual biology or psychology. W.E.B. Du Bois's *The Philadelphia negro,*[1] one of the seminal pieces in all of social sciences, laid down several issues facing African Americans in the USA after slavery. While it was published at the end of the nineteenth century, his work began decades earlier. For Du Bois, high crime rates in African American communities were the result of racism, lack of resources and support provided to the African American community, and the disruption in the lives of Blacks forced to migrate out of their home country into new communities in the US. As he notes, "if men are suddenly transported from one environment to another, the result is lack of harmony with the new conditions [...] lack of harmony with the social surroundings leading to crime."[2]

Born in Massachusetts in 1868, Du Bois had a relatively advantaged upbringing when compared to most African Americans of the time. He did well at school and ended up graduating with a Ph.D. from Harvard University. He went on to teach at the University of Pennsylvania and to study Blacks in the city of Philadelphia. His position as an African American professor uniquely situated him to study this community from a scholarly standpoint.

His work in the city of Philadelphia led him to believe that it was city life – filled with striving for material wealth over community cohesion – and the influx of Blacks into areas with few opportunities to advance in society that created the perfect concoction for crime. Given this view and his distrust of material wealth, Du Bois would later lose faith in capitalism altogether and the United States in general. He moved to Ghana prior to his death in 1963.[3]

It is possible to get an entire degree in criminology without hearing a word about sociologist (or perhaps more appropriately philosopher) Georg Simmel. While not a researcher of crime per se, his ideas played a role in the development of social theories of crime in the city. Born in Berlin in 1856, Simmel was exposed to the typical European city of the 1800s. In his writings, it appeared that Simmel wasn't particularly fond of city life, proclaiming that the city is where people lose their community-oriented spirit and become individualistic. He also wrote on how the city can disorient one with bright lights and incessant noise. This type of disorientation might lead, at its worst, to a delirium that may be accompanied by criminal behavior.[4]

Simmel was also keen to theorize about the currency of the city, money which he believed led to the objectification of society and to the isolation of the individual from the larger society.[5] This is not unlike the ideas of his contemporary Émile Durkheim, who believed that modern society was moving away from a close-knit rural community toward an impersonal, individualistic society. Durkheim in France and Simmel in Germany (along with Simmel's contemporary in Germany, Ferdinand Tönnies) shared some thoughts, and their theories may be seen to travel without them across the seas to the Chicago School of Sociology and even into the thoughts of others such as Willem Bonger, discussed below, who (along with Simmel and Tönnies, in particular) lamented the impersonal, egoistic nature of modern society. It is interesting that even before the birth of the Chicago School, Simmel was intent to study and report on city life and how it might influence behavior – setting the stage, in some ways, for an entire school of sociological thought.

Following in the footsteps of Du Bois and Simmel, a newspaper man in the early 1900s was keenly interested in race relations and social issues in Chicago. This man, Robert Park, entered journalism in 1887 and continued in the profession until 1898. In those ten-plus years, Park became intimately knowledgeable about city life. Through his occupation at the time, he saw much evidence of cooperation and people working together in what ecologists call symbiosis. He also saw conflict, particularly among Whites and Blacks and within minority communities. He called this "invasion, dominance, and succession," as conflict often arose from a new group invading the community, dominating the native group, and then stabilizing as a mixed community (Park used the example of different species of trees populating an empty field to illustrate this concept).[6] Park is considered by many to be the father of "human ecology."

The human ecology model provided the Chicago School with a focus on the human being within his or her environment or context. This resonates even today as criminologists such as Gregory Zimmerman from Northeastern University, who examines the role of self-control and delinquent peer relations within specific neighborhoods,[7] and Mark Berg from Iowa University, who examines the victim–offender overlap in areas strong in the code-of-the-street ethos and those that adhere to traditional norms, continue to explore the unique ways in which neighborhoods shape behavior.[8] In most cases, context plays a role in how strongly a theory or individual variable is related to criminal behavior. This has led Harvard criminologist Robert Sampson to quip: "context is everything."

One of Park's colleagues at the University of Chicago was fellow professor Ernest Burgess. Burgess bought into Park's human ecology model but took issue with some of the ideas making up the "invasion, dominance, and succession" concept. For Burgess, this process not only expanded cities at the edges but led to a specific pattern of growth within the city as well. Burgess went on to publish these ideas with Park in the 1925 classic *The city: Suggestions for the study of human nature in the urban environment.*[9]

Burgess developed locales that he believed existed in the city which he called concentric zones. These boundaries were concentric since they were envisioned as circles around the city, and zones since they represented different environments in which to live. The innermost circle (Zone 1) was the business district. The manufacturing jobs that drove in immigrants existed in this zone. Naturally, the zone right outside Zone 1, namely Zone 2, was where the working class lived. This zone is where those looking for industrial jobs lived, including recent immigrants and blue-collar workers. Zone 2 is very important for criminal theory, as this is where the most crime was hypothesized to occur.

Zones 3 and 4 included the residential areas of the city where middle-class America lived. Overall, the residents here were better-off economically and there was less crime in these zones. Zone 4 bumped up against the suburbs in Zone 5. Zone 5 was where the richest people lived and commuted to work further into the city. These individuals were able to come and go into the city as they pleased.

Today, the zones developed by Burgess are not likely to be exactly as he hypothesized them to be, but the idea is similar (see Figure 4.1). Certain areas within the city are strongly impacted by crime and violence, and these areas are marked by considerable disadvantage and poor physical and mental health. Those who can escape these areas generally do so. Other areas are wealthy and not plagued by the same level of crime and disadvantage. As Burgess suggests, these areas tend to be on the outskirts of the city, close to suburban neighborhoods.

The study of the city, as described and analyzed by individuals such as W.E.B. Du Bois, Robert Park, and Ernest Burgess reveals a host of social factors that impact crime rates within certain areas of the city. Another phenomenon of great interest during this time was the emergence of gangs and delinquent groups. The city, it appeared, not only bred

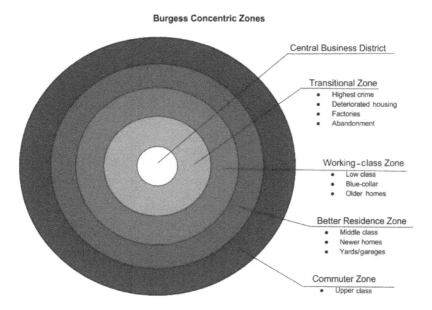

Figure 4.1 Burgess's concentric zones

Source: Adapted from Sampson & Walsh (2015).

crime, but groups of individuals committed to violent behavior that operated within the city especially in those zones identified as criminogenic by Burgess and others. This was of interest to one of Robert Park's doctoral students, Frederick Thrasher, who completed a dissertation on Chicago gangs which he later published in 1927, two years after his mentor's book, *The city*. Thrasher's *The gang: A study of 1313 gangs in Chicago*,[10] would go on to be one of the time-honored classics in the field of criminology and the first major work in gang research specifically.

In the Chicago tradition, Thrasher highlighted the structure of the city and how it influenced the emergence and development of gangs and the violence in which their members partake. To Thrasher, the gangs he studied in Chicago sprang up in the most disorganized areas where they could carry out their delinquent behavior without being interfered with – in what he called "interstitial" areas. "The characteristic habitat of Chicago's numerous gangs is that broad twilight zone of railroads and factories, of deteriorating neighborhoods and shifting populations, which borders the city's central business district on the north, on the west, and on the south," writes Thrasher in poetic style. He continues,

> the gangs dwell among the shadows of the slum. Yet, dreary and repellent as their external environment must seem to the casual observer, their life is to the initiated at once vivid and fascinating. They live in a world distinctly their own – far removed from the humdrum existence of the average citizen.[11]

Thrasher's introduction evokes the excitement of the city that Simmel touched upon. Gangs thrive on this excitement and stimulation. This would be echoed by Jack Katz in his 1988 book *Seductions of crime*.[12] This lifestyle, to those such as Thrasher and Katz, pulls people "into the shadows" so to speak and into gangs to lead an exciting and fast-paced life. Thrasher also incorporated the city structure introduced by his professor, Ernest Burgess, in explaining where gangs are dispersed among the city – outside the business district in disorganized communities.

The Chicago School culminated in the publication of *Juvenile delinquency and urban areas* in 1942 by two Chicago School criminologists Clifford Shaw and Henry McKay.[13] While often lumped together as virtually one person, Shaw and McKay were dissimilar in many ways. Clifford Shaw was born on a farm in Indiana in 1895. His father owned over 85 acres and a small general store which Shaw hung around quite frequently in his youth. In his early years, he often missed school and got involved with minor delinquencies. He eventually cleaned up and headed to the ministry before he became disenchanted with the church and joined the Navy. It was after the Navy and on the urging of others that he went to the University of Chicago to study sociology. He never finished his doctorate, but his work in the community earned him the director spot at the Institute for Juvenile Research.

Unlike Shaw, who was a master organizer and community mobilizer, McKay was the quintessential researcher – a statistician and careful analyst. Born in 1899, he was the son of a man who owned over 300 acres in South Dakota and was himself the son of a Scottish immigrant, which likely played a part in the theorizing that he did on immigration and crime. McKay only completed one year at the University of Chicago and spent much time after at the University of Indiana where he became very close to criminologist Edwin Sutherland (discussed in Chapter 6 on differential association and social learning theories) which certainly influenced his thinking about how norms are transferred intergenerationally within disorganized communities. When Shaw and McKay started the Chicago Area Project (CAP) in 1932, McKay was the analyst while Shaw "hit the streets" getting grants and other funding. Some said Shaw used his early hustling skills to maintain the work that CAP was doing in the community.[14]

Shaw and McKay's work, while central to the Chicago School's focus on communities, also incorporated some of the work of criminologist Edwin Sutherland, the theorist behind Differential Association. As mentioned in the Introduction to this book, it is difficult to neatly silo criminological theories into their own, separate categories. Many theorists combine multiple perspectives and borrow from other theorists to form their own theories. This is common and the reader should take note that the development of criminological thought is a scientific one, each subsequent theorist building on what came before them.

By far the work of most influence to Shaw and McKay was that of Robert Park and Ernest Burgess. Their foundation, on which Shaw and McKay built, went on to become the staple for social disorganization theory. In Burgess's Zone 2 where crime was most prevalent, so too were a host of other social problems. Three of these problems were: (1) poverty; (2) heterogeneity; and (3) transiency. First, those who lived in the transition zone were fairly low on the economic ladder. They did not have a lot of resources to buy homes, go to the best schools, or move out of the inner city easily. Second, the individuals living in this zone were very diverse (or heterogeneous), often consisting of multiple ethnicities with different customs and languages, making it hard to associate with one another. Third, due to several factors, such as not having money for rent, residents in these areas moved around the zone frequently, making them a transient population incapable of forming strong bonds with neighbors who only lived in the same area for a short period of time.

When residents cannot form bonds and do not have an investment in their community, it is not hard to see why crime might increase. Shaw and McKay confirmed the idea that crime is, in fact, higher in the transition zone (Zone 2). Not only that, but over time, the area remains high in crime regardless of who lives there. This indicated that there may be something about place, as opposed to people, that causes crime.

In *Juvenile delinquency in urban areas,* Shaw and McKay differentiate between high-income economic areas (like the suburbs) where residents share common goals and attitudes and low-income areas where there is conflict among residents in terms of goals, values, and attitudes. Resources are abundant in affluent areas, allowing them to incorporate mechanisms of social control such as neighborhood organizations, churches, and service centers that keep people busy and out of trouble. In low-income areas, resources are stretched, prohibiting mechanisms of social control that keep people out of trouble. In these communities, residents, especially youth, are free to associate with other delinquents, join gangs, and engage in illegal activities. Delinquent attitudes develop among these groups and are transmitted through generations. Shaw and McKay suggest that affluent areas are organized while low-income areas are disorganized.

The theory of social disorganization, as developed by Shaw and McKay, incorporates elements of control theory (a macro-level version of control) as well as differential association. Further, it is easy to see where social disorganization incorporates insights that were provided by Frederick Thrasher in *The gang.* Much later, Elijah Anderson's *Code of the street* appears to borrow from Shaw and McKay's ideas about the development of values and attitudes toward violence common in disorganized communities.[15] As Anderson echoes almost 60 years later, boys in the city are often involved with delinquent groups and, even if they are not, they are aware of the attitudes and values that permeate life in the city.

Recent developments

The city appears to have gripped scholars in the late 1800s and early 1900s and, for the most part, has not let go. While specific theories and orientations have waxed and waned, a fascination with inner-city crime is a mainstay in the field of criminology.

Along with this fascination, there has been significant development in the theories since the days of Park, Burgess, Shaw, and McKay. It is likely that one piece in particular profoundly changed how social disorganization and theories of the city were viewed and accepted in the (relatively) recent past.

In 1978, Ruth Rosner Kornhauser published her major work in *Social sources of delinquency* – an expansion of her dissertation completed at the University of Chicago in 1975 and edited from her hospital bed following a stroke. This, for many, is viewed as *the* most important piece of scholarly work of the past 50 years. Unfortunately, Kornhauser suffered chronically from the effects of the stroke, passing away at a young age and leaving the field with this one genius work – which many refer to as just "Sources."

In *Sources*, Kornhauser admits to one major personal flaw; her past life as a strain theorist (anomie and strain theories are discussed in Chapter 5, but feel free to glance at them before reading this section). As an adherent to the tradition of anomie and strain theory, she believed that crime was the result of a society that had unattainable goals and values which strained its citizens and could not regulate their behavior. After considering the literature, and the results of empirical studies, Kornhauser was struck with what she saw. The evidence clearly supported social disorganization/control and not strain/anomie. Theoretically, Kornhauser began to believe that social disorganization was the culprit behind deviant behavior. Therefore, she endeavored in *Sources* to make the case for social control/disorganization theories – and to obliterate other theories in her wake.

There are several points that Kornhauser makes in *Sources* (and all readers are encouraged to take a close look at the original book – however difficult it may be to get through during the first read), but a few deserve careful discussion. First is the idea of attenuated culture. While many theorists in the traditional Chicago School viewed disorganized communities as having a separate value system, Kornhauser believed that this is not the case. This view was even more exemplified in the anomie literature that came after the Chicago School which argued that it was the clear rejection of conventional norms that led to criminal behavior. To Kornhauser, everyone shared the same system of values, but it was how strongly people were able to hold onto these values that mattered. If they were weakly applied by individuals, the likelihood of crime increased.

Kornhauser also reformulated social disorganization, particularly the approach adopted by Shaw and McKay, into a more modern social control theory. If the majority of people ascribe to similar goals and values, and when these values systems weaken there is crime, then the link must be in the way that society is able to control crime when there is discord among its members. By borrowing from Travis Hirschi and earlier control theorists (discussed in later chapters), she set the stage for both macro- and micro-examination of crime through the lens of social control.

A very practical contribution to disorganization theories was proffered by a dynamic scholarly duo, Patricia and Paul Brantingham. The Brantinghams did not deny the influence of neighborhoods in the production of crime and, in fact, have been staunch proponents of exploring how the environment exacerbates or alleviates crime. However, they were also keenly aware that people *interact* with their surroundings and are not just passive passersby. Through a thorough exploration of how people navigate and interact with their environments, one may be able to design the environment to reduce criminal behavior.

In their 1981 *Environmental criminology*,[16] the Brantinghams argue that the distribution of offenders (i.e., people) and targets (i.e., places for crime) combine to produce a criminal event. Building on work by Oscar Newman and his views discussed in *Defensible space*,[17] they suggest that the environment be designed and surveilled to reduce crime. For instance, one can move places of work away from the inner city where crime is rampant to the outskirts of the city or to suburban areas less susceptible to crime. Increasing the surveillance of the neighborhood by businesses and employees can reduce crimes such as theft and burglary. Overall, they take the sole focus on the offender and put it on the intersection of people in places. This was a quite novel approach at the time and is making a comeback as of late in contemporary "criminology of place."[18]

The vast amount of literature that accumulated on social disorganization and the importance of place throughout the twentieth century led criminologist Rodney Stark to organize a theory of deviant places in the later 1980s. In "Deviant places: A theory of the ecology of crime," published in the journal *Criminology* in 1987, Stark argued that because certain places experience considerable stability in high crime rates regardless of who lives there, theories which contend that "certain people" are the cause of crime need to be replaced by a theory of "certain places."[19] Many have taken this to heart and have combined both levels of theory.[20]

Other researchers, too, took seriously the idea that theory should address places of crime and expand the theoretical propositions of place-based criminology. Criminologists Robert Bursik Jr. and Harold Grasmick, in 1993, published *Neighborhoods and crime* in which they argued that social disorganization theories would benefit from a more holistic perspective of community.[21] In particular, they envisioned neighborhoods as controlled by three mechanisms of social control: (1) private (e.g., family, friends); (2) parochial (e.g., acquaintances); and (3) public (e.g., schools, churches, youth centers). These levels of social control may weaken when there is a state of flux within the city – for example, when immigrants settle in large numbers within a community. This flux leads to disorganization, in Shaw and McKay's sense of the term, reducing social control and increasing crime.

After Shaw and McKay's work in the early 1940s, social disorganization theories enjoyed several years in the theoretical limelight but turned relatively stale in the 1950s through the 1970s. In the 1980s, criminologist Robert J. Sampson revitalized the social disorganization perspective by moving beyond the components discussed by Shaw and McKay. Sampson, very differently from Shaw and McKay, grew up in the industrial city of Utica in upstate New York in the 1970s amid a terrible economy. Crime was fairly routine and his own family home was burglarized when he was just a child. He went to the State University of New York at Buffalo for his undergraduate degree and was a fairly average student. Following graduation he returned to Utica to sell shoes. When that proved to be strenuous and hardly lucrative, he decided to apply to graduate school. He was lucky to slip into the Master's degree program at the State University of New York at Albany on probationary status without any funding.[22]

At Albany, Sampson buckled down and became very interested in the relationship between culture and social structure. His mentor, criminologist Robert Bursik, urged him to further connect *why* social disorganization creates an environment conducive to crime – something which early social disorganization theories had yet to explain. This, and other ideas, ruminated in Sampson's head, particularly in his farmhouse where he roomed with friend and colleague Casey Groves.[23] This was the beginning of the idea of collective efficacy – a modern update to the Chicago School's social disorganization theory (which Sampson and Groves formally tested together in 1989, leading them to further develop the collective efficacy approach[24]).

For Sampson, the most important component of keeping the neighborhood safe is the ability of residents to come together to address crime. For example, when children are found to be scuffling in the street, a neighbor (perhaps someone unrelated to them) will come to break up the fight and show that it is unacceptable to be fighting in the community. The same would go for anyone doing/selling drugs, painting graffiti, or flashing gang signs. If no one in the community addresses the criminal element there is no reason for it to stop, leading to more crime. This essential ability of residents in the community to identify crime and then respond to it, mostly informally, is called collective efficacy. In neighborhoods where there is high collective efficacy, residents are able to effectively intervene when crime is seen and therefore enjoy lower crime rates than those where crime is allowed to be overlooked.[25]

There are several elements of collective efficacy that impact area-level crime rates. First, adults in the community must monitor the play of children on the streets. Residents must know if children are engaging in poor behavior such as drug dealing, skipping school, and fighting. Second, residents must be willing to intervene when they witness poor behavior. Generally, people are more willing to intervene when they have strong ties to their neighbors. Finally, visible signs of disorder must be addressed such as dilapidated buildings and graffiti which signal to others that individuals do not care about their neighborhood. When people feel comfortable intervening in these issues, do not fear their neighbors, and have a good sense of shared values among residents, then crime rates will be low (Figure 4.2).

Sampson also teamed up with urban scholar William Julius Wilson to provide an explanation for violence in the city – especially violence committed by African Americans. Unlike Shaw and McKay who believed that values differed between the upper and lower classes (where African Americans disproportionately live up to today), they argue that violence is *not* valued but represents a logical *choice* to those in the lower class. Racial segregation and persistent racial inequality provides a context (i.e., inner-city neighborhoods) that are so far removed from middle-/upper-class contexts that ways of thinking about and solving problems are fundamentally different.

Sampson and Wilson introduce the term *cognitive landscapes*, which represents the appropriate standards and expectations of behavior in a specific area. In isolated inner-city communities, which lack resources and mechanisms of social control, violence is a logical choice to respond to problems related to joblessness, housing discrimination, and disrespect (this is the cognitive or *thinking* part of the equation). The isolated landscape, or community, prevents those individuals who live in these neighborhoods from interacting with those who have more tools to deal with societal problems. Unfortunately, this isolation and ingrained way of doing things makes intervening in the cycle of violence marked in these communities very challenging and difficult.

Georgia State University criminologist Barbara Warner contends that the bulk of the focus of social disorganization theories and research has been on structural disorganization and has overlooked cultural disorganization. Cultural disorganization deals with the role of values in different parts of society. Shaw and McKay mention differences in values, and Sampson and Wilson discuss cognitive landscapes as producers of behavior, but exactly how cultural values in the inner city are different from middle-/upper-class values did not receive much attention until the 1990s. Warner's work has expanded upon social disorganization theories by paying particular attention to how mainstream cultural values are weakened, or attenuated, in the inner city. Unlike others, such as Shaw and McKay, as well as some anomie theorists, Warner follows the lead of Ruth

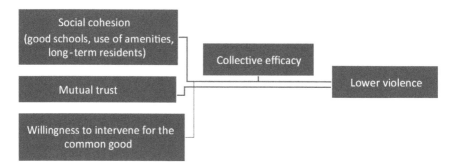

Figure 4.2 Collective efficacy theory

Source: Higgins & Hunt (2016).

Kornhauser, who argues that values and beliefs are shared among almost everyone in society. No one *really* values violence, manipulation, and deception. Even those in communities that are plagued by high violent crime value safety, trust, and cooperation. It is just that in these communities traditional values are weakened by structural forces such as poverty, disadvantage, and inequality.

In 2003, Warner expanded upon Kornhauser's ideas, spring-boarding off of her statement that cultural values are "not rejected […] just disused."[26] In other words, values do not vary greatly across communities, but how well people adhere to these values *does* vary. When people do not adhere well to conventional values of trust, conformity, and respect, society cannot do much to provide effective social control – resulting in crime. Warner expands on this in our discussion. "Kornhauser's argument about variance in the strength of the culture rather than variation in the content of the culture, made Shaw and McKay's theoretical arguments much more clearly about social control," she states. "That is, when the culture was weak, informal social control was less likely to occur, and therefore delinquency had lower costs and could more easily arise. A deviant subculture was not necessary to provide motivation for delinquency."[27]

The case of Rochester, New York: a great city with great problems

Social disorganization theories consider, remember, places and not necessarily people. The theoretical approach seeks to explain why crime *rates* are higher in some places over others. These questions are seen almost every day in the news media and particularly during presidential campaigns. The attention is almost always on the high crime within inner-city communities marked by poor schools, disorganized neighborhoods, and broken families. I worked for several years in one mid-sized city, Rochester, NY, that exemplified many of the characteristics in social disorganization theory (Figure 4.3).

Figure 4.3 Rochester, New York

Photo credit: Photograph taken by Kyle McHargue.

First, and most importantly, Rochester, NY is a beautiful, and safe, city overall. The majority of people who live there are friendly, responsible, and non-violent. This is true of every city, but, like every city, there are pockets of crime – areas throughout the city where violence is more ordinary than in other parts of the city. I became intimately familiar with these parts of the city when working on various crime prevention projects, including Project Safe Neighborhoods with my mentor, criminologist John Klofas, at the Rochester Institute of Technology. In the 1930s through the 1940s, when my grand-father was attending Rochester schools, the city was booming. It had a population of over 320,000 people and ranked in the high 20s for the most populated in the country. Kodak, the film and camera company which started in Rochester in the 1880s, was in full swing. In the 1980s and 1990s, when my father worked for Kodak, there were just over 240,000 people living in Rochester – a sharp decline of almost 100,000 people over a few decades – but the economy was doing well and the city was generally in good shape. However, in the 1990s until the 2000s, the collapse of Kodak and other local busi-nesses such as Xerox, meant massive job layoffs – my father included. Today, the popula-tion of Rochester is under 210,000 ranking it 105th in the United States for population – a reduction of over 4 percent across the past decade and almost 37 percent of the size it was at its peak.[28] It ranks much higher, generally first in the state, and among the top 10 of mid-sized cities in the USA for violent crime.

Violent crime is high as an average in Rochester, NY. Again, the violence is concen-trated. In the city, some have taken to calling a crescent-shaped area of the city from the southeast to the northwest the "fatal crescent." It is in this crescent that most violent crime occurs. On average over the past decade, the homicide rate for Rochester has been about 19 per 100,000 people or about 41 homicides a year. This rate tracks along with Richmond, VA and Pittsburg, PA, and is well above cities like New York and Chicago.[29]

In the crescent of Rochester, not only are crime levels elevated, but so is almost every indicator of social disorganization one can think of. For example, by request of then District Attorney Michael Green, the Center for Public Safety Initiatives at Rochester Institute of Technology, where I was employed as a graduate research assistant through-out my Master's program in the mid-2000s, mapped household poverty, child poverty, single-parent-headed households, early pregnancy, and several health indicators, and found, unsurprisingly, that these factors mapped almost identically on top of violent crime. I remember vividly giving this presentation, flipping map by map, wondering what little, if anything, had changed from one to the next. This would also not come as a surprise to other scholars of communities who examine not only crime but the many layers of disadvantage in the most at-risk neighborhoods.[30] In fact, a recent publication by criminologists John Hipp and Charis Kubrin found that changes in inequality and racial–ethnic heterogeneity coincided with change in crime not only for the specific neighborhood under examination but also for a zone of two-and-a-half miles around the neighborhood. This highlights the widespread effects of neighborhood (or "egohood" as the authors call it) change on local crime rates.[31]

Empirical support

While many of the early social disorganization theories have been dealt a hit by empiri-cal research, the central idea that neighborhood plays a role in crime causation remains strong. Today, the theory is being tested and expanded. In 2003, criminologists Charis Kubrin and Ronald Weitzer reviewed some of the equivocal empirical support for social disorganization theory, particularly the idea that social ties decrease crime,[32] and high-lighted four areas that still need fleshing out. First, there needs to be a greater use of dynamic models that can account for change in community structure and subsequent changes in crime. Second, research must investigate the reciprocal nature of social disorganization and crime. For instance, it must be known not just how social disorganization leads to crime but how crime may also lead toward (more) disorganization. Third, neighborhood contextual effects on individual behavior must be investigated. In other words, how do factors of a neighborhood, such as disorganization, violence, and cohesion, impact individual-level factors like self-control, stress, and behavior? Fourth, the spatial dynamics and "spillover" effects of crime must be more closely examined. What is going on in the neighborhoods close to the most disorganized and crime-ridden neighborhoods?

Some evidence has begun to examine Kubrin and Weitzer's four areas of concern. In his book *Great American city*,[33] Robert Sampson discusses many of these issues, including how, at least in Chicago and in a handful of other cities, neighborhoods are extremely stable in terms of their level of disorganization and crime. Those that do change often see a change in *both* crime and disorganization. A spate of recent contextual research indicates that aspects of the neighborhood have a significant impact upon individual-level characteristics, including moderating the effects of self-control[34] and delinquent peer associations[35] on crime. The empirical research on spillover and spatial effects has increased substantially over recent years, along with the methods to investigate these issues, including the study mentioned earlier with Kubrin and Hipp in 2017. The jury is still out on how disorganization and crime in one neighborhood affect adjacent neighborhoods and how crime-prevention effects in one neighborhood disperse either crime or the benefits of prevention, an area of study that is ripe for further investigation.

Another area of social disorganization theories that is understudied but receiving increased attention is the role, or rather the intersection, of race, gender, and inequality. Sociologist Andrea Leverentz of the University of Massachusetts at Boston and co-author Monica Williams, a criminologist at Weber State University, tackled some of these issues in their recent article which appeared in the journal *Criminology*. They demonstrate how public and parochial forms of social control (borrowing from Bursik and Grasmick, among others) work together to prevent crime (as opposed to separately) for different places and among different people. From our discussion, Leverentz states,

> public and parochial networks work together, or not, in different types of places and among different groups of people. These processes are also historically contingent, both in terms of social contextual factors that may shape resident involvement and in terms of specific histories of places that may shape perceptions of what seems possible or necessary. So, for example, some people and some places have much higher levels of legal cynicism, and much more suspicion about formal systems of control. Some places, because of legal cynicism *or* because of geographic isolation, may have a strong sense of self-reliance; that they must take care of their own problems because no one else will. All of these factors come together to shape how community crime control plays out in different places. In this sense, we're pulling together related concepts to extend these earlier ideas.[36]

Clearly, research needs to tease these interactions apart and consider more nuanced views of the role of neighborhood in crime causation.

Remaining questions

Various aspects of social disorganization theory have received support and, if anything, the early work of the Chicago School theorists laid the foundation for contemporary work on the criminology of place and social processes in intercity communities. However, the world is continually changing and, much like the early 1900s, the role of immigration and social change is being re-examined. In the USA, executive actions by President Donald J. Trump have banned immigration from specific countries and restricted foreign travel, and deportations of immigrants have increased exponentially – actions based, at least partially, on the notion that immigrants are the cause of violent criminal behavior. This flies in the face of much empirical research,[37] but questions remain as to whether or not specific individuals, who emigrate from particular areas or who are part of specific factions in society, are more likely to engage in crime or terrorist acts than others. So far, evidence does not support this claim, although more research is needed.

Theories that have been developed to explain crime in the city have recently been applied to crime in the suburbs and rural areas. For example, D. Wayne Osgood and Jeff M. Chambers applied social disorganization theory to rural areas and found that, in support of the theory, residential instability, family disruption, and ethnic heterogeneity were all related to high crime rates.[38] This finding was replicated later using several non-metropolitan counties throughout the United States.[39] A handful of other studies suggest that the mechanisms behind social disorganization theory are not all equally related to crime in rural areas which questions the utility of using social disorganization as a main theoretical construct to explain crime in rural areas.[40] More research is needed here to reach firm conclusions.

Policy

Social disorganization theory, then and now, has clear implications for society and communities. If disorganization is the cause of crime, organizing society and communities may be able to stem violent in the most violent places. The first and most obvious program based on social disorganization theory was the Chicago Area Project (CAP). The CAP was the brainchild of Clifford Shaw, and took up a considerable amount of his time and effort in the 1930s and 1940s. It was the program that he hustled for over many years in Chicago. Shaw's goal was to establish organization in a few of the most crime-ridden neighborhoods in 1930s Chicago. His initial efforts were to gather and mobilize parents and families in the most disorganized neighborhoods. By organizing families, he was able to establish the Russell Square Community Committee that would provide opportunities for youth to be lured out of the seduction of gang activity and into prosocial programs.

Shaw not only mobilized parents but also sought to incorporate the ideas and efforts of delinquent youth. He even brought together delinquents and parolees returning to the community for their insights into how to stop violence. He was among the first to actively recruit and hire ex-felons for crime prevention programs. Today, the CAP remains active in Chicago, providing education, job training, and recreation programs to youth in the city.[41]

In the late 1960s and early 1970s,[42] Oscar Newman presented a straightforward strategy to decrease crime in urban areas which he called "defensible space." Defensible space made suggestions on how space should be designed and utilized in urban neighborhoods, particularly housing projects. He suggested designing paths to limit open movement around housing projects, grouping housing units together to increase visibility of the street and backyards, and increasing surveillance of communities. These strategies would allow for quick detection of criminal activity and prevent the easy commission of crime in the first place.

In his frustration, Newman vented in his publication with the Housing and Urban Development organization in 1996, *Creating defensible space*, about the misunderstandings around his theory. "Defensible space," Newman began, "is not about fencing. It is about the reassignments of physical areas and areas of responsibility – the demarcation of new spheres of influence."[43] In other words, his frustration stemmed from policy that claimed to be in the vein of defensible space but was just based on a watered-down version of the perspective. Instead, defensible space is intended to take a broad approach to environmental design and architecture that decreases opportunities for crime while increasing social surveillance. A popular approach in the 1980s and 1990s, there may be a resurgence of the perspective as micro-level research on crime (focusing on small street segments)[44] and methods like risk terrain modeling,[45] which seek to identify physical features of the environment that attract crime, continue to increase.

Not long after Newman's work on defensible space, Paul J. Brantingham and Patricia L. Brantingham expanded upon this line of thinking to more closely align criminal actors and environmental space. In 1981, they published their seminal piece *Environmental criminology*.[46] Their contribution in this work was expanding on how individuals (i.e., criminals) interact with their environmental surroundings in the commission of crime. They also stressed the importance of how police interact with the community and the role of fear of crime in neighborhood efficacy. They saw that fear of crime could severely, and negatively, impact area crime levels.

Continuing on from their work in 1981, the Brantinghams expanded their insight on environmental criminology to include other concepts and tools. They formalized a "criminality of place" in 1995[47] and provided insight into community-based analysis of crime using an environmental framework in 2004.[48] Together, they provided avenues to conceptualize how local environment can contribute to criminal behavior and how contemporary tools of analysis can improve crime analysis and prevention. Their work on environmental criminology and criminology of place continues today.

In 1982, James Q. Wilson and George L. Kelling introduced a theory of crime that expanded upon the traditional social disorganization approach.[49] They argued that crime and disorder in the form of graffiti, boarded-up houses, and, of course, broken windows signaled to people that no one cares about the community. If no one cares about the community, then why would crime stop at graffiti and not escalate to drug selling, gang wars, and homicide? The broken windows theory gained much acceptance in the years following its initial release and has even been referred to as "the bible of policing."[50]

Policing for the next two decades following the release of *Broken windows* heeded the advice of Wilson and Kelling. Despite the original policy intentions of the pair, policing strategies from zero-tolerance, to stop and frisk, to community policing have been credited to addressing signs of disorder to prevent larger crime. Others, such as Bernard E. Harcourt[51] and Ralph B. Taylor,[52] question the efficacy of broken windows policing and suggest that the policy that came out of the perspective has increased crime and disorder and led to diminishing trust in the police.

Summary

Social disorganization and theories of the city emerged in the late 1800s amid migration in several areas around the globe. These theoretical approaches reached their apex in the work of Shaw and McKay before slightly declining in dominance as social learning theories, discussed in Chapter 6, gained traction. However, the efforts of Sampson and his contemporaries have reinvigorated and more carefully specified the theoretical approach, making for an exciting new view of crime and deviance in the city. It should also be noted that the seeming dominance of social disorganization theories has received some backlash as of late. Some social control theorists, such as Northeastern criminologist Simon Singer, argue for more consideration of suburban areas, and a whole rural criminology movement, spearheaded by scholars such as Joseph Donnermeyer and Walter DeKeseredy, suggests that rural areas need more attention and consideration. These and other perspectives will be discussed at length in the following chapters.

Notes

1 Du Bois, 1899.
2 Du Bois, 1899: 235.
3 Ritzer & Goodman, 2004.
4 Simmel, 1903.
5 Simmel, 1907.
6 Park, 1936.
7 Zimmerman, 2010; Zimmerman, & Messner, 2011.
8 Berg et al., 2012.
9 Park & Burgess, 1925.
10 Thrasher, 1927.
11 Thrasher, 1927: 3.
12 Katz, 1988.
13 Shaw & McKay, 1942.
14 Hayward, Maruna, & Mooney, 2010.
15 Anderson, 2000.
16 Brantingham & Brantingham, 1981.
17 Newman, 1972.
18 See Hipp & Kubrin, 2017; Weisburd, Groff, & Yang, 2012.
19 Stark, 1987.
20 See, in particular, Miethe & Meier, 1994.
21 Bursik & Grasmick, 1993.
22 Sampson, 2011.
23 See Sampson, 2011; Hayward, Maruna, & Mooney, 2010.
24 Sampson & Groves, 1989.
25 Sampson, Raudenbush, & Earls, 1997.
26 Warner, 2003.
27 Warner, Personal Interview, October 12, 2016.
28 Population data taken from: www.biggestuscities.com/city/rochester-new-york.
29 Paliwal, Cabrera, Dougherty, & Klofas, 2016.
30 For example, Sampson, 2012; Sharkey, 2013.
31 Hipp & Kubrin, 2017.
32 See Bellair (1997) for evidence in favor of social ties, Kubrin & Weitzer (2003) and Bursik (1988) for evidence that questions this relationship.
33 Sampson, 2012.
34 Zimmerman, 2010.
35 Zimmerman & Messner, 2011.
36 Leverentz, Personal Interview January 21, 2017.
37 Martinez, Stowell, & Lee, 2010; Stowell, Messner, McGeever, & Raffalovich, 2009.
38 Osgood & Chambers, 2000.
39 Bouffard & Muftic, 2006.
40 See Kaylen & Pridemore, 2011, 2013.
41 For more information on CAP's history and current efforts: www.chicagoareaproject.org/.
42 Newman, 1972.
43 Newman, 1996: 3.
44 Weisburd, Groff, & Yang, 2012.
45 Caplan & Kennedy, 2011.
46 Brantingham & Brantingham, 1981.
47 Brantingham & Brantingham, 1995.
48 Brantingham & Brantingham, 2004.
49 Wilson & Kelling, 1982.
50 Cullen, 1997.
51 Harcourt, 2009.
52 Taylor, 2001.

Further reading

Desmond, M. (2016). *Evicted: Poverty and profit in the American city.* New York: Broadway Books.

Harding, D. J. (2010). *Living the drama: Community, conflict, and culture among inner-city boys.* Chicago, IL: University of Chicago Press.

Sampson, R. J. (2012). *Great American city: Chicago and the enduring neighborhood effect.* Chicago, IL: University of Chicago Press.

Sharkey, P. (2013). *Stuck in place: Urban neighborhoods and the end of progress toward racial equality.* Chicago, IL: University of Chicago Press.

Wilson, W. J. (2012). *The truly disadvantaged: The inner city, the underclass, and public policy.* Chicago, IL: University of Chicago Press.

5 Anomie and strain theories

Introduction	56
Theory	57
Origins	57
Recent developments	60
The case of Tanya Mitchell: the stressed killer	63
Empirical support	63
Remaining questions	64
Policy	64
Summary	65

Introduction

Early theories of social disorganization focused heavily on the city landscape and features of city life that lead to crime. As we have seen, immigration increased in the US during this time and many people came to the US to achieve the American Dream. While conditions deteriorated overseas, manufacturing jobs were burgeoning in America. Along with this came an expectation that anyone could "make it" and that all you had to do was work hard and do good, and the Dream was yours. The story of Andrew Carnegie, a poor immigrant who moved to the United States from Scotland in the mid-1800s, rang in the heads of new immigrants. If Carnegie could come from poor roots, pull himself up by his bootstraps, lead the American steel industry, and become a millionaire – then why couldn't everyone else?

Although prospects for a good life were increasing in the US, opportunities to succeed and the ability to achieve the American Dream were not equal for everyone. It seemed as though Carnegie was the exception that proved the rule. Mobility out of a hard life of poverty was rare. In fact, in cities across America, immigrants were making only a fraction of what they needed to feed their families (in Chicago that was, on average, 38 percent of what was needed to feed a family of four; in Buffalo, NY, outside where I grew up, it was about 50 percent of what was needed). Immigrants and natives alike all wanted to achieve success, make money, and support their families. Some were able to do so while others could not. Further, some individuals did not accept the traditional American goals and either replaced them or were left in a state of disorientation – in other words, they didn't know what to think.

Social theorists during the early and mid-1900s began to wonder how the goals of US citizens impacted crime rates. As expectations for the good life rise, what happens to those who cannot achieve such lofty goals? Two main approaches emerged along this line of inquiry. First, theorists wondered, at the societal (or macro) level, how US expectations led citizens to become violent – and, in particular, more violent than their European counterparts. Second, what are those individual-level factors that put stress and strain on people (e.g., the stress to make money and support a family) and influence criminal behavior?

Theory

Following mass migration into major cities in the US and in other countries across the globe, we had a different-looking society from centuries past. With the convergence of cultures and conflicting values, a new perspective on society was beginning to be molded. What was the true goal of this new society? What should people strive for in life? The answers were sometimes unclear and some goals were so out of reach that scholars began to argue that the society was largely normless, leading to a state of disorientation and despair called anomie.

Other theorists discussed in this chapter have made a handful of further observations. First, what happens when individuals in society strive to achieve monetary success but fail to get there? Second, what happens when people reject the norms of society or are not even sure what the goals of society are, and so make up their own? Third, what are all the stresses and strains that people experience and how are they related to crime? Examining these types of questions is the job of anomie and strain theorists.

Origins

The Western world was grappling with an overwhelming movement from rural to urban areas in the late 1800s and early 1900s, and these patterns were evident in Europe as well as the US. In particular, France saw movements from agricultural areas to larger cities such as Paris. One philosopher, considered to be one of the founding sociologists of the time, Émile Durkheim, took note of these events. A conservative by today's standards, he was interested in acquiring the academic fortitude to provide the moral guidance he thought society sorely needed at the time. He was profoundly impacted by the anti-Semitism that existed in France and particularly the court martialing of Jewish Army captain Alfred Dreyfus (Durkheim was raised Jewish by a long line of rabbis). He attributed the anti-Semitism to the moral depravity of society.[1] Coupled with what he saw as the transition of society from agrarian to urban life, Durkheim provided a functional sociology to the study of crime and society.

Durkheim suggested that emigration from rural areas, where people trusted and valued one another, to urban cities, where the small town life gave way to normlessness, created a society characterized by anomie. Anomie, according to Durkheim, was the lack of a consistent set of values and goals ascribed to by citizens of a society, leading to that society's inability to regulate itself. For the individual, Durkheim states that anomie "spring[s] from society's insufficient presence in individuals [...] thus leaving them without a check-rein."[2] In other words, when the values and regulations of society fail to instill themselves within the individual, there will be no brake on behavior. Strong bonds do exist in modern society, what he called organic solidarity, but absent this solidarity crime is likely to emerge.

For Durkheim, anomie was a major factor influencing high crime rates. Where values and goals are in flux or unknown, members of a society turn to crime to achieve their own ends. Durkheim also argued that the cause of crime could be found totally outside the individual – in society. What he called "social facts," such as anomie, were solely responsible for behavior – not biology or psychology.[3] Because of his views about society and the influence of social facts on behavior, Durkheim is often credited with being the "father" of sociology. Importantly, he argued that sociology must be guided by empirical science.[4]

Some readers, who may be familiar with criminological theory, may wonder whether Durkheim's anomie theory – this normless society that cannot regulate the behavior of its members – is a theory that belongs to, or started, the strain tradition (as covered in this chapter) or whether it belongs to the line of thought common to social control theories (covered in Chapter 8). This is a good question and many would debate exactly where the theory belongs. The reasoning for including Durkheim's theory in this chapter is due to the historical relevance of anomie in establishing a long line of macro-level anomie and micro-level strain theories (along with variations of strain theory at the macro level) as well as his influence on and mentorship of others who continued in the anomie/strain tradition in later years. One of these individuals is the famed sociologist Robert Merton.

Merton, who was deeply influenced by Durkheim, borrowed the concept of anomie to explain the American milieu in the early 1900s. Born as Meyer Schkolnick to Eastern European Jewish immigrants in 1910, Merton grew up in a poor neighborhood in South Philadelphia. To make some money, he conducted magic shows and used the stage name Robert K. Merlin. The Merlin part seemed to stick and he changed it to Merton shortly after. From then on, he was almost exclusively known as Merton (his parents welcomed this "Americanization").[5]

In Philadelphia, Merton saw first hand that many people in America were able to go to good schools, achieve academic success, and go on to secure steady employment. These individuals were able to achieve the American Dream – complete with a job, car, family, and other material goods. Some people, however, were not able to achieve this monetary success that brought with it all the luxuries of the American Dream. Due to the overwhelming focus of American culture on monetary success, those individuals unable to achieve the Dream were put under enormous strain. In order to cope with this strain, individuals could adopt one of five modes of adaptation which formed the basis of Merton's theory.[6]

First, the most common strategy was conformity. These people used legitimate means to achieve monetary success (or not) such as going to college, obtaining a job, and working hard. Others decided to give up on the American Dream, and "go through the motions" while putting very little effort into achieving monetary success. These are the people that, day-in and day-out, go to the same job, clock in and out, and go home at the end of the day (kind of like zombies). Merton called this ritualism. Important for the purposes of crime and delinquency, other people, unlike the ritualists, want to achieve monetary success and will adopt other means besides legitimate ones to get what they want. Merton called this innovation. These people, instead of going to a job, find alternative means to get money such as drug dealing, robbery, stealing, and human trafficking. This group is by far the most delinquent.

Conformity, ritualism, and innovation all contain some aspiration of cultural goals of monetary success and some form of the means to get there. Merton also recognized two groups of people who reject both America's dream of monetary success and the legitimate ways to get there. The first is retreatism. Here, people decide to "drop out" of society. This could mean literally dropping out of school or the workforce, or living on the margins of society. These people are often homeless, drug users/abusers, and alcoholics. They neither care for success nor try to achieve it through any specific means. Finally, some groups are characterized by rebellion. These people reject both monetary success and the legitimate ways to get there and instead *substitute* alternative goals and means. These individuals often support alternative political systems and value systems such as anarchy, socialism, and communism. Later, we will discuss the maximizer, which was added by criminologists Daniel Murphy and Matthew Robinson and which captures people who make use of more than one, adaptation.[7]

In the mid-1950s, as poverty and economic disadvantage began to attract political attention, despite overall prosperity in the US, sociologist Albert K. Cohen put forth a subcultural theory of deviance which was based on anomie theory.[8] In fact, Cohen was one of Robert Merton's students and borrowed many ideas from his mentor. Subcultural theories argue that delinquents, and especially delinquent gang members, adhere to alternative value systems. While most of us value conformity, cohesion, and trust, delinquents value things like respect, toughness, and violence.[9] Cohen believed that young, lower-class youth experienced status frustration when they were not able to achieve middle- or upper-class status in society. This frustration from blocked opportunities encouraged these youth to develop their own set of values (aside from monetary success) such as violence and respect. These value systems were created in an effort to turn middle-class values "on their head." Many youth rejected education and legitimate work, dropped out of school, and began engaging in delinquent activity to make their way and to attain respect. For Cohen, these youth actively engaged in behaviors that were totally against the mainstream and truly bred of a counterculture in the US. Later, many social learning theorists (discussed in Chapter 6) and social control theorists (discussed in Chapter 8) would rally against the subculture idea.

Shortly after Cohen's writing in 1955, two sociologists added a key part to his theory and to subcultural theories based on anomie. Richard Cloward and Lloyd Ohlin developed what they called opportunity structure theory whereby they pay close attention not only to blocked *legitimate* opportunities but to blocked *illegitimate* opportunities.[10] Not everyone who cannot achieve middle-class success can all of a sudden use illegitimate means to attain success. Someone who is frail or weak will not likely be able to rob others and those who have no connection with drug dealers cannot automatically become drug dealers themselves. Therefore, there are many subcultures that develop when people cannot achieve middle-class success.

Cloward and Ohlin describe three types of subcultures that emerge from the existing opportunity structure. The first is the criminal delinquent subculture. These subcultures are what we generally think of when we hear about street gangs. Individuals who make up this subculture are generally involved in robberies and thefts as a means of monetary gain. In order to get into the criminal delinquent subculture, a person must have someone to vouch for them or they must prove themselves to the group. The second subculture is conflict gangs. Conflict gangs are smaller groups of delinquents who engage in a variety of crimes and usually emerge in impoverished areas. These are the loosely knit gangs that are common today. Third are the retreatist gang members. Like Merton, Cloward and Ohlin described these individuals as people who escape their daily strains by using drugs and alcohol and retreating from society. While they may engage in some crime it is generally non-violent.

Recent developments

Robert Merton described the strain or stress that came with trying to acquire monetary success which was the basis for why people adapted and engaged in delinquent behaviors. Criminologist Robert Agnew in the early 1980s began to theorize about additional strains that might cause someone to engage in crime. Specifically, he used a social psychological approach that was rather different from the macro-level, sociological perspective espoused by earlier anomie theorists. Over the next 30-plus years, Agnew has formulated and revised a general strain theory (GST) of crime.[11] GST incorporates more strains than classical anomie theory and explains which types of strains are more likely to be associated with crime and why.

Strains, as described by Agnew, can be real (or direct), vicarious, or anticipated. Losing your job is a real direct strain, but anticipating losing your job is also stressful. A close friend who loses a job may affect you emotionally as well (you would experience this strain vicariously through your friend). The major sources of strain that Agnew has outlined (which may all be experienced directly or vicariously, or be anticipated) are failure to achieve positively valued goals (this is classic anomie theory's contribution but includes goals other than monetary success), the removal of positively valued stimuli (such as the removal of a parent from the home due to divorce), and the introduction of negative/noxious stimuli (such as abuse and neglect). These strains increase the likelihood that one will cope, or attempt to overcome the stress from these factors, using illegitimate means such as delinquency.[12]

Over time, critics argued that almost anything can be a strain, making Agnew's theory superfluous (and certainly not parsimonious). This "kitchen-sink" critique pushed Agnew to refine his theory, explicating the types of strains that are most likely to lead to delinquency and how they do so. First, Agnew suggests that certain strains can be more criminogenic than others. Strains that are: (1) perceived to be unjust (e.g., discrimination); (2) perceived to be high in magnitude (e.g., victimization); (3) associated with low self-control; and (4) perceived to create an incentive for criminal coping are more likely to lead to criminal coping than other types of minor strains.[13]

However, not everyone commits crime even though they are exposed to a strain or even many strains – some perhaps very severe. Agnew also states that there are character traits of individuals that protect against delinquent behavior. When individuals are: (1) even-tempered; (2) highly intelligent; (3) creative and thoughtful; and (4) self-confident, they are less likely to cope using delinquent means and more likely to cope using pro-social means such as sports, listening to music, or seeking help. Strain theory also suggests that coping may be partially dependent on gender. Males have been found to cope through externalizing (fighting and aggression) while females tend to internalize (self-harm and drug abuse).[14]

Recently, through several publications including two pieces in the journal *Criminology*, Agnew has used strain as a foundation to think about broader theories of violence. While traditional anomie/strain theories argue that a person has to be "pushed" into crime, Agnew's thoughts on social concern acknowledge that although people are often naturally inclined toward self-interest they are also socially concerned.[15] In our personal interview, Agnew states:

> Individuals high in social concern care about the welfare of others, in large part because of their empathy with and sympathy for them; they desire close ties to others; they follow certain moral intuitions, such as the inclination to avoid harming innocent others; and they are inclined to conform to the behavior and views of

others. These inclinations are in part "natural," meaning they have a strong biologi-cal basis and are widely shared.[16]

In essence, our nature is neither completely self-interested nor completely socially concerned but a mix of both, and that may be a good start for theorizing about criminal behavior.

In a second article, Agnew uses strain theory's argument about conditions, or fac-tors, that increase the likelihood of deviant coping in response to strain as a foundation to explain delinquency. In this piece, Agnew focuses on susceptibility and resilience. The factors that make a person more vulnerable to coping with strain in a deviant way increase susceptibility and those that insulate and make a person persevere are consid-ered to increase resilience. By considering these two factors together, the likelihood of criminal behavior may be estimated to some degree.[17] In addressing crime the solution is easy: increase resilience and decrease susceptibility.

After the boom of social disorganization theories in the early 1900s, the theo-retical landscape gave way to anomie and strain theories. While anomie/strain theo-ries began to wane in importance themselves in the 1960s and 1970s, there was a comeback of sorts in the 1980s and 1990s. It was noted earlier that Émile Durkheim had initiated a long line of scholarship on the role of the social environment con-cerning individual behavior. Criminologist Francis Cullen benefitted indirectly from Durkheim through guidance from his mentor Lloyd Ohlin – himself a student of Robert Merton.

Cullen has incorporated elements of anomie and strain theory throughout his career. In his 1994 address to the Academy of Criminal Justice Sciences, he outlined a the-ory of social support that built on traditional anomie theories in the vein of Durkheim and Merton.[18] In his address, Cullen expands the concept of social support by Lin who defines it as "the perceived or actual instrumental support and/or expressive provisions supplied by the community, social networks, and confiding partners."[19] With this in mind, the theory incorporates ten major propositions.

On the macro level (and meso level), Cullen argues that (1) crime rates will be higher in societies that lack social support such as welfare to the poor. He also mentions that (2) neighborhoods and communities that lack social support, like close relations between friends, neighbors, and community organizations, will have higher crime rates. Based on these propositions, Cullen argues that the US experiences high violent crime rates because it is a less supportive society.

On the individual, or micro level, Cullen proposes that social support can act as an insulator from crime. Of particular importance is the family, and (3) the more support a family gives to an individual the less likely crime is to occur. In addition, the more support society gives to families the lower the crime rate will be. He also argues that this will be the case for peers and social networks in that (4) the more social support given to individuals through peer relationships the less likely crime is to occur.

Specific to strain theory, Cullen suggests that (5) social support steers people away from strains and (6) it provides avenues for offenders to avoid a life of crime throughout their lives. Even (7), anticipation of not receiving support (true or not), will increase crime as a person is likely to believe that they don't have the support of others and must figure it out for themselves. Interestingly, Cullen also argues that (8) giving social support can decrease involvement in crime by transforming individual identities and improving a positive view of the self. Finally, (9) when social support for conformity exceeds social support for crime and (10) when social support leads to effective social control, crime will be unlikely. Together, Cullen provides an integrative and largely strain-based theory of criminal behavior.

Think back to classic anomie theory as envisioned by Robert Merton. The Ameri-can Dream was the achievement of monetary success. However, many people cannot achieve this dream and go on to incorporate illegitimate means to do so. Those who have the illegal means available to them, as Cloward and Ohlin point out, may choose these means to achieve their monetary success. In the 1990s, two criminologists, Steven Messner and Richard Rosenfeld, latched on to this idea and put anomie theory into an international context.[20] Their major research question was "Does the American Dream promote high crime rates in the US when compared to other countries?" Importantly, Messner and Rosenfeld noted how the US is so focused on the economy (i.e., money) that other institutions such as the family, school, and politics are largely ignored. They call this institutional anomie – leading to Institutional Anomie Theory.

It is this imbalance of institutions that Messner and Rosenfeld view as problematic. Families are sacrificed in order to maintain the 9 to 5 workday, schools begin and end at times that accommodate work schedules (even though this may not be best for learning), and politics rarely focus on families and neighborhood but more on the economy ("It's the economy, stupid!"). This institutional imbalance is the cause of high crime rates in the US according to Institutional Anomie Theory (IAT) and the solution is decommodification. Decommodification entails reducing the influence of the economy and focusing on a more holistic society that values all institutions as important. In effect, this would re-establish institutional balance.

Comparative criminologist Nikos Passas has, in the past 20 years, proposed a slightly revised strain theory which is heavily reliant on insight from IAT that has an international twist. Passas suggests that globalization and neoliberalism play a large part in creating anomie of various strengths across the globe. "Globalism," he states, "refers to the degree of interconnectedness and the increase or decrease of linkages. By contrast," he continues, "neoliberalism refers to an economic and political school of thought on the relations between the state on the one hand, and citizens and the world of trade and commerce on the other."[21] Passas believes that when neoliberalism reigns, and there is asymmetry across international communities, global anomie is the result or "dysnomie" as he calls it.

> Dysnomie literally means "difficulty to govern" and is obtained when the following three conditions are present: a lack of a global norm-making mechanism, inconsistent enforcement of existing international rules, and the existence of a regulatory patchwork of diverse and conflicting legal traditions and practices.[22]

When these institutional controls are weakened, criminals are emboldened and can better get away with their crimes. In this way, Passas's view is very Durkheimian in nature as it focuses on societal regulation of behavior.

Another recent extension of strain theory includes the work of criminologists Matthew Robinson and Daniel Murphy. They believe that there is another category which Merton left out of his original typology; this is what they call "The Maximizer."[23] As Robinson explained to me in our personal interview, they stumbled upon this idea quite fortuitously one day. He states,

> It was a discussion in the hallway of our old building where Dan Murphy was talking about a fictional construction contractor making a legitimate living by building bridges (conformity) who cut corners by knowingly using substandard concrete to save money (innovation). The question was, is it possible to conform and innovate at the same time?

The answer to this was yes. He continues, "the maximizer is one who engages in conformity and innovation at the same time. He or she (usually he) is one who aims to maximize wealth by any means necessary, legal and/or illegal."[24] So, from this discussion and subsequent theorizing, "The Maximizer" was born and incorporated into the theory of anomie (Table 5.1).

Table 5.1 Merton strategies + The Maximizer

Modes of adaptation	Culture goals	Institutional means	Criminal behavior
Conformity	Accept	Accept	Reject
Innovation	Accept	Reject	Accept
Ritualism	Reject	Accept	Reject
Retreatism	Reject	Reject	Accept
Rebellion	Reject/replace	Reject/replace	Accept
Maximization	Accept	Accept	Accept

Source: Adapted from Murphy & Robinson (2008).

The case of Tanya Mitchell: the stressed killer

Tanya Mitchell was married to her husband for over 20 years. Over those years he would beat her repeatedly and emotionally abuse her. One day he told Tanya that he was going to kill her. At that moment she thought there might be only one choice left – to kill him first. So she did. In 2002, Tanya was convicted of second-degree murder and subsequently incarcerated.

After securing an attorney and as photographs of Tanya's cuts and bruises from years of abuse surfaced, the courts re-examined her case several years later. With no prior criminal history and evidence that she was an upstanding citizen, she was released from prison in 2013. She states that even after her husband's death she felt controlled by him and has only recently escaped her abusive past.[25]

Tanya's story is not unique. It is a story that is similar to that of millions of other women. One can make sense of her crime through the lens of strain theory. Tanya's years of abuse were a strain that was severe in magnitude and frequency, occurring over the span of 20 years. The abuse was likely to be seen as unjust and unfair given that the strain was coming from an intimate partner whom one is supposed to love and trust. Despite Tanya's clean record and history of conformity, the abuse was enough to push her into crime.

As Agnew and others have found, experiencing neglect and victimization is one of the strongest predictors of future delinquency (see more on this in Chapter 14).[26] This empirical finding may allow for not only a better theoretical model for criminality but also a key entry point for prevention policy which will be discussed shortly.

Empirical support

Tests of strain theory, broadly, have provided support for the perspective. Various types of strains have been shown to lead to delinquent behavior across many different datasets.[27] One of the most potent strains, which has received considerable empirical support, is the role of direct and indirect exposure to violence and later delinquent and antisocial behavior.[28] Exposure to these "noxious stimuli" has supported the role of strain in delinquent behavior across many studies with diverse samples and in a variety of locations.

One of the main propositions of strain theory, namely that strain leads to negative emotionality, which (in turn) leads to delinquent coping mechanisms, has received a fair amount of support throughout the past several decades. Strain theory's major prediction is that strain leads to anger, and anger is responsible for violent behavior. The work of criminologist Paul Mazerolle (among others) has provided support for this notion across several studies.[29] However, anger is not the only emotion that strain theory implicates in leading to bad behavior. Depression and anxiety can also lead to maladaptive coping. For example, strain has been found to lead to depression (which in turn leads to delinquency and self-directed harm).[30] The strain → negative emotionality → delinquency path appears to receive quite a lot of support.

According to strain theory, not everyone is strained all the time. We go through periods across our life-course of high, low, and moderate strains. The theory predicts that in periods of high strain, delinquent and criminal behavior is more prevalent. This is exactly what Lee Ann Slocum and colleagues found using a sample of incarcerated women. When individuals were going through periods of high strain, they were more likely to engage in violent and property crime as well as drug use.[31] Accumulation of strains over time has also been shown to increase the likelihood (growth) of delinquency in adolescence.[32] These studies suggest that strain theory may have potential in explaining crime across the life-course and have a place at the table in developmental explanations of delinquent and antisocial behavior.

Remaining questions

Despite a fairly supportive empirical basis for the role of strain in delinquent behavior, particularly through anger and other negative emotions, other aspects of the theory have received scant support or attention. The major area of contention in the current literature is the moderating factors that condition strain. Generally, this is tested by interacting strain and other personal or environmental factors (e.g., self-control). These conditioning factors are generally not supported in the literature.[33] While this may reflect a flaw in the theory, Agnew argues that it may be the way in which strain and conditioning variables are measured (and the data themselves) that may not be able to capture real conditioning effects.[34]

Relatedly, how strains are experienced and coped with may vary by race, gender/sex, and socioeconomic status. Studies have found substantial differences in how males and females respond to strain – generally indicating that females cope inwardly (self-harm or depression) while males focus strain outward through violence.[35] Strains related to discrimination may also be felt differently according to race and the coping of these strains may be variable across groups in society.[36] The role of socioeconomic status in strain theory remains in flux and how resource-disadvantaged individuals and communities respond to strain remains an area to be explored.[37]

While strain theory has achieved some success in explaining behavior over the life-course, more work needs to be done in this area. Agnew has recently come up with a "life-domains" theory of crime and delinquency (heavily embedded in strain theory) which has yet to receive much empirical attention (or undergo full tests of the theory). A few tests of the life-domains perspective have found some weak support but many of the theory's predictions have varying strength in their ability to explain behavior across time.[38]

Policy

Strain and anomie theories have been a mainstay in criminology across the past two decades and into the twenty-first century. Not only have they provided a foundation for empirical work – and found a fair amount of support – but they have also informed policy and practice. Policy-makers began to take the theory's predictions seriously in the mid-1900s, and policies and programs today can still be seen to utilize the information garnered from the theory.

The weight of poverty sat heavy on the shoulders of Americans in the 1950s and 1960s, particularly as the effects of urban poverty were front and center in the civil rights movement. In 1964, Lyndon B. Johnson, President of the United States, declared his "War on Poverty." This approach merged a political orientation (mostly held by democrats) and practical action by those who wanted to improve society by eliminating poverty. At the time, social scientists, such as Merton, Cloward, and Ohlin, made the case that poverty was a major cause of crime. Some believe these policies were misguided, as poverty is only a correlate and not a cause of crime and that these policies were largely unsuccessful in reducing crime.[39]

In the early 1960s, building on the national attention and policy work around issues of poverty, the program Mobilization for Youth (MFY) sought to begin an anti-poverty initiative focused on social justice for youth in the lower Manhattan area of New York City. MFY started by providing education services for youth in poverty-stricken neighborhoods and quickly expanded to providing job training for older youth. While focusing on the needs of youth, the program realized the necessity of engaging parents and families and extended services, such as counseling and mental health services, to youth and their families.[40]

Other federal programs that offered social support to low-income individuals and families were also based, at least partially, on strain theory's predictions that social strain can lead to adverse outcomes. The Comprehensive Employment and Training Act of 1973, signed by President Richard Nixon, sought to employ individuals with low incomes as well as students with summer jobs. This was followed by other efforts such as the Job Training Partnership Act of 1982.[41]

Today, several programs exist at the federal and state levels to provide services and economic assistance to those in the lower socioeconomic strata. Such programs include mentoring (e.g., Big Brothers, Big Sisters), foster care (e.g., Court-appointed Special Advocates), and various education programs. One of the most successful programs for youth appears to be the Head Start program. The Early Head Start program began in 1995 and has been evaluated by several researchers since its initiation. For instance, a 2013 evaluation found that Early Head Start improved cognition, language, attention, behavioral problems, and the health of individual participants up to age 5, and maternal outcomes, including parenting, mental health, and employment.[42]

Robert Agnew has put forth his own prevention and intervention plan which is based on strain and anomie theories. He outlines three approaches that would eliminate strains, help individuals avoid strains, and intercede where people do experience strains to make them less severe. First, he suggests employing "strain responders." These individuals would identify and intervene in youth who show early signs of stress or who are referred by other people or agencies. Second, social support centers should be established as one-stop shops to provide resources and education to youth and families who experience high levels of strain in their lives. Finally, and more challenging, Agnew suggests altering the larger social environment to focus less on material success and more on helping each other and cooperating on societal goals.[43]

Agnew's final goal for policy is not unlike suggestions from others such as Steven Messner and Richard Rosenfeld. Informed by their Institutional Anomie Theory, they argue that larger social structures must be addressed to significantly influence crime. In particular, teachers, parents, and other community leaders must help change the current interpretation of the American Dream (which is focused on monetary success) to also incorporate other successes. In addition, those who commit crime should not be seen as abnormal or demonized for their behavior but instead should be seen as products of their environment in need of social support.[44]

Summary

Anomie and strain theories have a rich history that is steeped in a sociological understanding of crime and criminality. However, recent research also contributes an understanding of the biological impacts of stress and strain on the human body and decision-making processes. While the evidence supporting strain theory is mixed – particularly on what specific strains lead to crime, how different people cope with strain, and the additive and interactive effects of strain and other factors – a new understanding of strain theory through a multidisciplinary lens may increase its empirical strength.

Regardless of the particular strengths and weaknesses of the theory, it may have informed public policy more than any other criminological theory. From early "War on Poverty" efforts to federally funded education and work programs, the idea that social support can decrease crime and increase socio-behavioral health has remained to this day. It may be a good bet that strain theory will continue to develop and be tested by researchers for years to come.

Notes

1 Ritzer & Goodman, 2004.
2 Durkheim, 1951 [1897]: 258.
3 Durkheim, 1951 [1897].
4 See also Durkheim, 1982 [1895].
5 Hayward, Maruna, & Mooney, 2010.
6 Merton, 1938.
7 Murphy & Robinson, 2008.
8 Cohen, 1955.
9 See also Miller, 1958.
10 Cloward & Ohlin, 1960.
11 Agnew, 1985, 1992.
12 Agnew, 1985, 1992.
13 Agnew, 2001.
14 See Posick, Farrell, & Swatt, 2013.
15 Agnew, 2014.
16 Personal Interview with Robert Agnew, December 30, 2016.
17 Agnew, 2016.
18 Cullen, 1994.
19 Lin, 1986: 18.
20 Messner & Rosenfeld, 2012.
21 Passas, 2000: 21.
22 Passas, 2000: 37.
23 Murphy & Robinson, 2008.
24 Robinson, Personal Interview, July 13, 2016.
25 See http://progressive.org/dispatches/abuse-victims-fight-fair-sentencing/.
26 Agnew, 2002; Posick, 2013.
27 Agnew et al., 2002; Broidy, 2001.
28 Agnew, 2002; Eitle & Turner, 2002; Zimmerman & Posick, 2016.
29 Mazerolle & Piquero, 1997; Mazerolle et al., 2000; See also Maschi, Bradley, & Morgen, 2008.
30 Manasse & Ganem, 2009; Posick, Farrell, & Swatt, 2013; Sigfusdottir, Farkas, & Silver, 2004.
31 Slocum, Simpson, & Smith, 2005.
32 Hoffmann & Cerbone, 1999.
33 See, e.g., Button, 2016; Moon & Morash, 2017; Ousey, Wilcox, & Schreck, 2015.
34 Mazerolle & Maahs, 2000; McClelland & Judd, 1993.
35 Posick, Farrell, & Swatt, 2013; Piquero & Sealock, 2004.
36 Piquero & Sealock, 2010; Simons et al., 2003.
37 Aseltine, Gore, & Gordon, 2000.
38 De Coster & Kort-Butler, 2006; Ngo et al., 2011.
39 See Jencks, 1992.
40 See more information on the organization's official website (www.mfy.org/about/about-mfy/).

41 Mangum, 1983.
42 Love et al., 2013.
43 Agnew, 2010.
44 Messner & Rosenfeld, 2012.

Further reading

Agnew, R. (2006). *Pressured into crime. An overview of general strain theory.* Los Angeles, CA: Roxbury.

Cloward, R. A. & Ohlin, L. E. (1960). *Delinquency and opportunity: A theory of delinquent gangs.* New York: The Free Press.

Cohen, A. K. (1955). *Delinquent boys: The culture of the gang.* New York: The Free Press.

Durkheim, E. (1951). *Suicide: A study in sociology.* Glencoe, IL: The Free Press.

Messner, S. F. & Rosenfeld, R. (2012). *Crime and the American dream.* Boston, MA: Cengage Learning.

Passas, N. & Agnew, R. (Eds.). (1997). *The future of anomie theory.* Boston, MA: Northeastern University Press.

6 Differential association and social learning theories

Introduction   68
Theory   69
Origins   69
Recent developments   70
The case of the Boston Marathon bombing: learning crime and terrorism   73
Empirical support   74
Remaining questions   75
Policy   75
Summary   76

Introduction

After Cesare Lombroso established the field of criminal anthropology in the 1800s and methodically studied the brains and bodies of criminals, his pioneering approach to the study of criminals established a positivistic criminological science that continues almost two centuries later. Although Lombroso, and other researchers in the biological tradition, along with the emergence of the Chicago School theorists, made their mark on the field, harsh critiques were leveled against criminology in the early 1900s. The most devastating critique of the field of criminology was proffered by Jerome Michael and Mortimer Adler. In 1933, Michael and Adler published a now famous report (often referred to as the Michael–Adler Report) where they discussed what they saw as the three major flaws of criminology. These were: (1) criminological research has been futile; (2) the reason for the futility of research in criminology is the incompetence of criminologists in science; and (3) the current methods of criminological research should be abandoned and scientists should be imported into criminology from other fields.[1] Following their report, there was certainly a need for someone to step forward in defense of the blossoming endeavor that was criminology.

Shortly after the release of the Michael–Adler[2] report, Edwin Sutherland – the theorist behind differential association theory as discussed in this chapter – fired back at Michael and Adler, arguing that criminology was a new field experiencing all the growing pains typical of any emerging field of study. As his own contribution, Sutherland offered a sociological perspective on criminology that became the guiding paradigm in criminology for much of the twentieth century. Today, sociological explanations of crime and criminality remain prevalent, but efforts to integrate biological, psychological, and sociological theories have become increasingly popular, particularly in addressing the nature vs. nurture debate[3] which will be the focus of later chapters.

Theory

As a sociologically trained criminologist from the Chicago School, Edwin Sutherland chose to focus on the social aspects of criminal behavior as opposed to the biological origins that emanated from the Italian School. However, instead of focusing as much on place as did his predecessors, Sutherland believed that crime is the result of learning from people to whom one is close. Crime, therefore, is taught from one person to the next. It is not so much the place that promotes delinquency as the people who reside in those places and how they reinforce each other's behavior. He called this idea "differential association." Because people associate with different peers and have different friends, they learn different things from one another (this is the "differential" part of differential association). If those with whom someone associates commit crime, the person is likely to learn that behavior and continue to do it. If close associates do not commit crime and instead conform to appropriate behavior, the person is likely to be non-criminal or learn to quickly reshape their poor behavior.

Differential association theory survived relatively untouched for several decades until the work of Ronald Akers in the 1960s. Akers agreed with much of Sutherland's theory but saw a hole in his work. While Sutherland adequately described the association between people in society, he failed to elaborate upon exactly *how* they learn from one another and what maintains this behavior over time. Akers, drawing upon psychological theories of the time, brought in "differential reinforcement" to coincide with Sutherland's differential association. In other words, it is not just *who* you associate with, but how those individuals *motivate* your behavior.

The idea that humans learn from one another and support or admonish the behaviors of others is the central pillar of social learning theories. Social learning theory remains a dominant force in criminology and continues to develop, making it a robust approach to the explanation of criminal behavior. This chapter will begin with the theories of Gabriele Tarde and Edwin Sutherland before moving into the contemporary theories of Akers and his contemporaries in the mid- to late twentieth century who have furthered the study of social interaction and the effects of associating with delinquent peers.

Origins

In the late 1800s and early 1900s, a French psychologist by the name of Gabriel Tarde was making waves in the social sciences. In fact, he made it a point to take on one of sociology's greats – Émile Durkheim. Tarde believed that Durkheim's sociology, based in macro-level "social facts," overlooked the importance of the individual. He disagreed with both Durkheim's theory and his methods of sociological investigation.[4]

For Tarde, what was most important in human behavior was the role of imitation. He presented his most influential thoughts in his 1890 book *The Laws of Imitation*.[5] For him, if we want to know how people learn to behave, we have to first look at who they imitate. Most people imitate the people who they are close to and spend the most time around. Sons will imitate their fathers and daughters their mothers. However, children may also imitate others in their communities and schools if they look up to them and wish to be like them. In this way, it is at the individual level that people learn from others and there exists a social contagion of behavior. If people around you act a certain way, so will you. About 30 years after Tarde's death in 1904, one of the giants in criminological theory, Edwin Sutherland, would use his ideas in one of the most influential theories in criminology: differential association.[a] In particular, Sutherland would list imitation as one of the many social ways in which a person can learn behavior from others. This would set the stage for contemporary social learning theories in criminology.

As mentioned previously, Edwin Sutherland was responsible for putting criminology back on the map in the 1930s by providing a criminological theory for the ages.[6] Sutherland believed that criminal behavior was learned just like anything else is learned and that you learn from others with whom you are close. From these two main principles, Sutherland developed his Differential Association Theory (DAT) along with nine principles that make up the theory.

First, Sutherland believed that (1) criminal behavior is *learned* and is most likely to influence behavior when it (2) is learned in *interaction* with people with whom one communicates. He also states that criminal behavior is most likely to make an impact upon an individual when it is learned from (3) *intimate* personal groups such as family and friends. The groups (4) teach others not only *how* to commit crime but also the *motives* and *rationalizations* for committing crime. These (5) motives and rationalizations are derived from *definitions* that are favorable or unfavorable toward the law. Definitions are another way of saying *attitudes* toward the law leading to motivation for obeying or disobeying the law.

Sutherland also outlines how definitions and associations contribute to the acquisition and continuation of criminal behavior. He argues that (6) a person becomes delinquent when the definitions for breaking the law exceed the definitions for conforming to the law. There is some cost–benefit analysis which is conducted by the individual and is based on what people teach each other regarding the law. Importantly, Sutherland says that (7) people who associate with one another do so in varying frequency, duration, priority, and intensity. Those with whom we spend a lot of time and whom we respect, trust, and admire will be those from whom we wish to learn and model our behavior. The methods and definitions that are learned from these individuals are (8) learned like anything else, such as arithmetic and fixing a broken light bulb. Finally, Sutherland believes that (9) criminal behavior is an expression of general needs and values but is not explained by those needs and values. In other words, people engage in crime to meet some need (say to obtain money) but money does not explain why someone becomes a criminal because most people look to acquire some wealth and do so using non-criminal means.

Recent developments

Sutherland's DAT theory was very popular from the 1930s into the 1960s (and his principles remain important for criminological theory today). Beginning in the 1960s,

---

a. Tarde not only influenced Sutherland and social learning theories but he also had a major influence on early Chicago School thinkers such as W. I. Thomas, Florian Znaniecki, and Robert Park.

sociologist Ronald Akers began to think about what was missing from Sutherland's Differential Association Theory. Akers wanted to better define what motivates people, beyond mere definitions, to engage in crime and then continue to act delinquently. He believed he had found what he was looking for in the foundations of operant psychology.

Ronald Akers was born in 1939 in New Albany, Indiana to blue-collar parents. He learned the value of hard work, discipline, and religion from his parents. Both of his parents were factory workers who did not make it far in school – his father made it to sixth grade and his mother to eighth. Akers himself received good grades but was often truant, and was considered to have something of a conduct problem. He did overcome this issue and went on to graduate with a doctorate under the tutelage of critical criminologist Richard Quinney (a prominent scholar discussed in Chapter 7), and made his way on to the Faculty at the University of Washington. It was here where he met his collaborator Robert Burgess (not to be confused with Ernest Burgess from the Chicago School) who brought a psychological behaviorism perspective to the department. Also working with his colleagues Walter Chambliss and, later in 1969, Travis Hirschi, he incorporated several perspectives into a revised social learning theory.

In 1957, just before Akers began to theorize about extensions to DAT (Figure 6.1), American behavioral psychologist B. F. Skinner released his book *Verbal behavior* where he discussed how communication can influence behavior and the process by which this happens. He believed that people were motivated, or not motivated, by others to maintain a certain behavior.[7] Skinner went on to discuss complex human behaviors which Akers adopted for explaining criminal behavior. In particular, Akers added differential reinforcement to DAT to form a more comprehensive social learning theory (SLT) of criminal behavior or what was originally called differential association-reinforcement theory.[8]

SLT, therefore, consisted of four main principles. The first two – (1) differential association, and (2) definitions – were borrowed almost directly from Sutherland. People learn definitions favorable or unfavorable to criminal behavior from those with whom they associate (the association part) and people associate with different peers (the differential

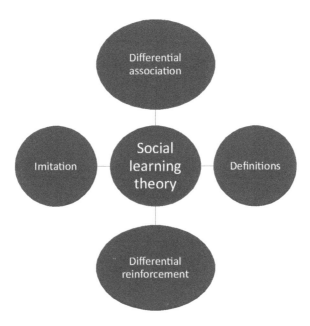

Figure 6.1 Akers' extensions

Source: Akers (2002).

part). Akers added (3) differential reinforcement to get at why someone might continue or desist from criminal activity. If criminal behavior is positively reinforced (e.g., to gain status/respect, acquire goods/money) and if one is able to avoid punishment for one's bad acts (e.g., family doesn't find out, law enforcement doesn't find out) then behavior is likely to continue. If criminal behavior is negatively reinforced through punishment or disapproval, then this behavior is likely to stop.

Akers added one more concept to SLT. People also learn through (4) imitations. This is a little nod to Tarde who also believed that imitation is an important part of behavior. People imitate those whom they respect and look up to whether they be family, peers, or celebrities. Akers notes that imitation is a minor factor in the continuation of criminal behavior but it is a strong predictor of initial engagement in criminal behavior. The differences between Sutherland and Akers are shown in Table 6.2.

Around the same time that Akers and Burgess were writing and formulating their perspectives, Albert Bandura was also arguing that behavior is learned through imitating close relatives and friends and that there is a response from society when behavior is imitated that is either positively or negatively reinforcing.[9] For example, if a child imitates a good behavior, like helping a friend, they will be positively reinforced by parents and friends. If the imitation is of a bad behavior, such as shoving another child, this behavior will be negatively reinforced through disapproval and/or punishment. Bandura also argued that a person learns when others are rewarded or punished. In that sense, someone can learn from someone else what is socially acceptable and unacceptable and thus partake in or avoid these behaviors such as when an older sibling is punished for behaving poorly (e.g., underage drinking).

Bandura added a very important aspect to social learning theories that had not received much previous attention. He believed that there were certain mediating processes between input from the environment (behavior to be modeled) and the output (behaving like the model). He mentions four major mediators that received attention in his 1986 work *Social foundations of thought and action: A social cognitive theory*. For a

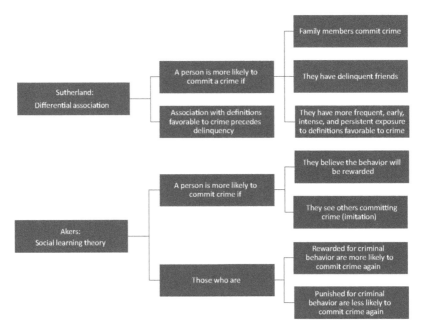

Figure 6.2 Akers' social learning theory

Source: Akers (2002).

behavior to be effectively learned and replicated, one must: (1) pay careful attention to that behavior; (2) retain and remember the behavior; (3) be able to physically and mentally reproduce that behavior; and (4) be motivated to perform and continue the behavior. Important in his thinking was that many times throughout the day we are exposed to behavior that we can, if we choose to, imitate. But this is not always wise or possible.[10] For example, I may want to be just like Albert Einstein and pay attention to his theories and be motivated to act like him, but it will be hard for me to retain his behaviors and reproduce them because I am not a genius. Likewise, I may want to imitate the behavior of the best baseball player to play the game (of course, Derek Jeter) but not be physically able to do so because of physical limitations. Together, these theorists consolidated a psychosocial theory of criminal behavior that has continued to influence the field of criminology and to set a firm foundation for contemporary theories.

Today, those who follow in the footsteps of social learning theorists have capitalized upon one of the strongest correlates of criminal behavior: association with delinquent peers. In fact, using delinquent peer association is one of the major ways in which researchers account for the differential association and social learning perspectives. Given the long line of research which shows that people imitate and learn from close relatives and peers, and often adopt their behaviors, social learning rests heavily on the role peers play in promoting and sustaining delinquent behavior.

Perhaps the best evidence for the peer effect and the role of social learning in crime comes from the seminal book *Companions in crime* by University of Texas, Austin criminologist Mark Warr.[11] "Criminal conduct is predominantly social behavior," states Warr in his introduction. "Most offenders are imbedded in a network of friends who also break the law, and the single strongest predictor of criminal behavior known to criminologists is the number of delinquent friends an individual has. Furthermore," states Warr, "most delinquent conduct occurs in groups; the group nature of delinquent behavior is one of its most consistently documented features."[12] Warr's claims are not unfounded but are backed by evidence throughout the book. Echoing his evidence, a 2010 meta-analysis supported the strength of social learning and peer association in the link to delinquency,[13] and many others have contributed to the knowledge base of delinquent peers and delinquent behavior.

It may also be the case that it is not just how many delinquent peers one has, but characteristics of peer networks themselves that can influence delinquent behavior. Criminologist Dana Haynie, using peer network data from the National Longitudinal Study of Adolescent to Adult Health (Add Health), found that when individuals have close-knit delinquent peer groups and when they are more central in those peer groups, they are more likely to be delinquent than when they are part of loose-knit groups and/or peripheral members of those groups.[14] In a separate study with the same dataset, she found that while most peer networks contain both delinquent and non-delinquent peers, individuals with more delinquent friends than non-delinquent friends tend to be more delinquent themselves.[15] This also holds for gang members. The more an individual is embedded within their gang structure, the longer they stay involved with the delinquent gang.[16] Social network and embeddedness theories[17] are recent extensions and elaborations on social learning theories and point toward fruitful avenues for future research, especially as rich network data, and the techniques to analyze such data, become increasingly available to researchers.

The case of the Boston Marathon bombing: learning crime and terrorism

On April 15, 2013, I can remember vividly sitting in my apartment office in Medford, Massachusetts working on a paper and chatting online with my friend and fellow Northeasterner, Michael Rocque. We had both just finished our dissertations and were getting ready to make our transitions out into the world. I had a position starting in the fall at Georgia Southern University and he was the incoming director of research at the Maine Department of Corrections. It was a happy time.

In the early afternoon, Mike writes, "turn on the news." Someone had set off multiple bombs at the Boston Marathon – about five miles from my apartment. We both had many friends at the event – some even running. I had no idea of the extent of the atrocity at the time, but later found out with the rest of the nation that three people ended up dead and over 250 injured – having been scarred, burned, and lost limbs. The manhunt was on for the perpetrator(s).

The following day I was heading down to Georgia to house-hunt with my wife which meant making our way to Logan Airport and heading out of Boston. The images of armed officers lining Airport Way stick in our minds to this day. They were not armed with handguns, but with the biggest machine-guns we had ever seen. We were able to leave Boston and saw in the meantime that the culprits of the bombing were caught. One had been shot and killed, and the other was taken into custody. The perpetrators, two brothers, Dzhokhar Tsarnaev and Tamerlan Tsarnaev, had set off two pressure cooker bombs at the marathon and walked away to let the carnage ensue (the bombs were able to be detonated remotely).

Tamerlan, the eldest brother, died in a firefight with law enforcement during the manhunt (as did a Massachusetts Institute of Technology officer), while the younger brother, Dzhokhar, was captured shortly thereafter – himself being shot multiple times, but not fatally. During interrogations, Dzhokhar told police that his brother had been the mastermind behind the bombing because he had been upset about US intervention in Iraq and Afghanistan. He was furious over what he saw as an assault on Islam and wanted to harm the US. The Boston Marathon was just the unfortunate place where the brothers could do the most harm to civilians. Dzhokhar said that his older brother had "recruited" him only recently to aid in his efforts.

While an outcast himself, Dzhokhar seemed to look up to and follow his older brother. Like many of us with an older sibling or cousin, we tend to want to imitate them and learn from them, as they appear cooler and wiser than we are. The relationship between the Tsarnaev brothers and their behaviors are in line with the predictions of social learning theory. Dzhokhar wanted to imitate his brother, at least to some extent, and learned from him the reasons why he should commit the atrocity he came to commit. It is likely that he also learned the "means" with which to commit the crime from his older brother. Interestingly, an interview with University of Pennsylvania psychologist Adrian Raine points to another possibility (or an additional possibility). Dzhokhar detonated the bomb and witnessed the carnage, yet walked away "cool as a cucumber." This is indicative of deficits in the prefrontal cortex and a marker for low physiological arousal which may have plagued the young offender.[18]

Empirical support

Social learning and differential association theories have received much empirical support. In particular, associating with delinquent peers and ascribing to a value system that promotes criminal behavior (i.e., definitions favorable to crime) are among the strongest correlates of crime.[19] Research spanning from the 1970s through the early 2000s finds that associating with delinquent peers increases one's own delinquent activity.[20] Furthermore, spending unstructured socializing time with peers (delinquent or not) has been shown to increase delinquency.[21]

Social learning has also found success when put to a "head-to-head" test with other criminological theories. Essentially, social learning variables remain significant, even after controlling for a host of other variables, and tend to have the greatest effects on delinquency.[22] Furthermore, social learning theory has received recent support in explaining some contemporary issues. For example, social learning has been shown to account for the occurrence of terrorism[23] and the use of novel drugs.[24] As discussed later in Chapter 12, social learning theory has also had success in explaining crime and delinquency across international contexts.

Remaining questions

One of the major problems that has continued to plague social learning theories, and theories suggesting that delinquent peers are among the most powerful factors in crime causation, is that of *projection*. Those who have made this complaint against social learning theories argue that in self-report studies – by far the most common method for testing social learning theory – individual respondents have the tendency to "project" or attribute their own behaviors on to their peers. For example, if respondents are themselves substance users who often get drunk and use drugs, they are more likely to say that all their friends do this too when they might not. Empirical research has supported this critique. Bowling Green University criminologist John Boman and colleagues studied the issue of projection using self-report data and found it to be a significant problem. Respondents were likely to project their own behavior on to their friends and to overestimate their friends' delinquency – particularly low-level delinquencies that are more frequent than violent crime.[25]

I followed up with Boman to discuss some of the other areas of social learning research that are likely to be popular in upcoming years. "Some of the current projects researchers are actively investigating [are] how social learning may work differently for people who are dating, behavioral similarity (called 'homophily') in offending, offending with other people, the role of friendship quality, and studies of friendship pairs and social networks," he points out. "Since it is well-known that friends do influence crime, the main issues of these active research agendas focus on determining the specific mechanisms through which friends influence crime." I believe Boman is correct – these do seem to be among the most relevant and pressing concerns in this area of research and I would not be surprised if he is right in that these areas will see increased attention in the future.

One of the most long-standing debates in recent criminology relates to the "birds of a feather flock together" concept. For criminology, an open question is whether or not individuals learn how to behave from one another or whether people behave in a certain way and *then* flock together with others who exhibit the same behaviors (the latter is a frequent claim of control theorists). Reciprocal relationships between delinquent behavior and delinquent peer association were tested by Ross Matsueda and Kathleen Anderson in 1998. They found that, indeed, there is a reciprocal relationship between the two variables but that the effect of delinquency on later association with delinquent peers was stronger than the reverse.[26] While an important study, it leaves room for future research.

Finally, there are large questions as to whether or not people ever internalize a counterculture value system at all. The definitions that Sutherland discusses and the subcultures described by Cohen, and Cloward and Ohlin, may, in the end, not even exist. Perhaps, as Kornhauser suggested, there is no separate culture or value system but just attenuated culture. Some social learning theorists have themselves rallied against the notion of subcultures and separated themselves from subcultural theories. Regardless, questions about how people learn values are reinforced for having or not having those values, and the methodological questions that arise when testing social learning theory remain largely open for future research.

Policy

Social learning theory has a fairly long history of influencing social policy and prevention programming. In the 1950s, shortly after Sutherland solidified his theory of differential association, the Highland's Project initiated Guided Group Interaction (GGI). This initiative was predicated on the idea that people learn from one another, particularly in groups. The effort hoped to capitalize on the social processes behind learning pro-social behaviors. Following GGI, juvenile probation in the 1960s and 1970s began to provide alternative care for young adults who would reside in a semi-residential support center to learn pro-social skills from staff and peers. In the 1980s, the Teaching Family Model provided in-home married couples with the skills to effectively become surrogate parents for at-risk youth.

Many of the programs started in the latter part of the twentieth century have been disbanded or significantly revised. However, there are contemporary initiatives that rely on social learning models. The Oregon Social Learning Center (OSLC) is at the forefront of providing programs based on a social learning theory framework. Its founder, Dr. Gerald Patterson, wanted to structure social policies and interventions around a scientifically valid theoretical framework. For him, this theoretical framework was social learning theory. Although Patterson passed away in 2016, the OSLC carries on his legacy by providing services to children and adolescents using a framework based on social science research.

The OSLC developed three major programs that utilized the insights provided by social learning theory. First, the Adolescent Transition Program teaches youth and their parents effective discipline and social skills to improve the chances of finishing school and attaining a job. Second, the Multidimensional Treatment Foster Care Program provides in-depth training to parents who wish to foster children until they are placed in homes. Finally, a program offered by the OSLS which focuses on children in first and fifth grade is the Linking the Interests of Families and Teachers initiative. This program seeks to understand the daily interactions of children and their peers to establish pro-social relationships early on in life.

Importantly, new statistical methods are enabling researchers to quantitatively examine the links among people in society. Social network analysis focuses not only on people but the *ties among people* in explaining behavior. Individuals are not seen as independent sculptors of their behavior but part of larger networks that have symbiotic and bi-directional effects on one another. This increases the usefulness of research for policymakers.

Summary

Edwin Sutherland's differential association theory marked a watershed moment in criminology by providing the field with a theoretical foundation in the 1930s. So influential were Sutherland's ideas that the whole field of criminology took a sociological turn that remains strong today. This is in part due to the efforts of Ronald Akers who expanded upon Sutherland's theory in the 1960s, along with others who incorporated operant conditioning into social learning models to produce a more well-rounded theory. Social learning theory at the micro and macro levels as well as expansion of the theory to include social and biological factors by criminologists and Akers himself have become prominent in theorizing about crime today.

Notes

1 Laub, 2006: 237.
2 Michael & Adler, 1933.
3 DeLisi et al., 2010.
4 Vargas et al., 2008.
5 Tarde, 1980 [1903].

6 Sutherland, 1934.
7 Skinner, 1957.
8 Akers, 1968.
9 Bandura, 1977.
10 Bandura, 1986.
11 Warr, 2002.
12 Warr, 2002: 3.
13 Pratt et al., 2010.
14 Haynie, 2001.
15 Haynie, 2002.
16 Pyrooz, Sweeten, & Piquero, 2013.
17 See, e.g., Hagan, 1993.
18 Raine Interview (www.youtube.com/watch?v=J-D2iWjUWiM).
19 Pratt et al., 2010; Warr, 2002.
20 Chappell & Piquero, 2004; Krohn, 1974; Warr, 1996.
21 Osgood & Anderson, 2004.
22 Matsueda & Heimer, 1987; Posick, 2013.
23 Akers & Silverman, 2004.
24 Miller, Boman, & Stogner, 2013.
25 Boman et al., 2012.
26 Matsueda & Anderson, 1998.

Further reading

Akers, R. L. (1985). *Deviant behavior: A social learning approach*. Boston, MA: Wadsworth Publishing.
Akers, R. L. (2011). *Social learning and social structure: A general theory of crime and deviance*. New Brunswick, NJ: Transaction Publishers.
Warr, M. (2002). *Companions in crime: The social aspects of criminal conduct*. Cambridge, MA: Cambridge University Press.

7 Labeling and critical criminology

Introduction	78
Theory	79
Origins	80
Marxism	80
Labeling	82
Recent developments	84
Peacemaking	84
Left realism	84
Feminist criminology	85
Green criminology	87
Queer criminology	88
The case of Brock Allen Turner: sexual assault and violence against women at Stanford	88
Empirical support	89
Remaining questions	90
Policy	90
Summary	91

Introduction

The past few chapters discussed the progression from the Italian School in the late 1800s to the Chicago School in the early 1900s through learning theories and strain theories. It is important to be cognizant of a parallel set of theories that originated in the early 1900s which continue to reverberate through and inform many theories today. Critical criminology (which will be discussed along with labeling theory in this chapter) views society in conflict as opposed to in consensus. In fact, a segment of critical criminology has been named "conflict criminology." While there are different sects of critical criminology, and we will discuss a handful of the most prominent ones in this chapter, they have a few main themes that permeate them all to some degree. That is: (1) individuals and groups in society are in conflict; (2) crime is defined and punished mainly by the elite in society; (3) issues pertaining to the underclass such as environmental rights, LGBTQ rights, gaps in wages, and corporate corruption are ignored by the elite. The elite, because they define and punish crime, have the power to label individuals as criminals and treat them as "bad" people.

Critical criminology seeks to understand crime as defined by the elite and to examine the criminal justice policies and practices in responding to crime. Critical criminology also puts a spotlight on underserved and understudied populations such as the lower class, racial/ethnic minorities, women, and the environment. Again, while not new, these issues often fall through the criminological cracks and are not afforded much attention in major theories of crime. Critical criminology offers a somewhat different approach to criminology than more traditional theories, and often intends to motivate others toward achieving social justice.

Theory

Labeling theory has its roots in the early 1900s when criminologists began to become more concerned with delinquent behavior – and how to respond to it . Some of these criminologists believed that children were being unfairly labeled as being delinquent (or "bad") when their behavior was really just "kids being kids." Once stamped with the label of a delinquent, over time, the individual would come to accept that label and act accordingly. If everyone calls you a bad person, even if you don't initially believe it, after so many people tell you the same thing over a period of time, you come to accept it.

Labeling theory argues that deviance is normal – people, especially young children, are going to get into trouble. This does not mean that they are bad or that their behavior is out of the ordinary (thus, such behavior is not actually deviant). On the contrary, it is very normal and we should expect it. After children grow up and mature, they will stop their wayward behavior. The worst thing society can do, say labeling theorists, is to overreact to the delinquency of adolescents. Once the label of delinquent, criminal, "bad," has been applied to a person, they will then come to accept their label and continue their poor behavior. It is the label that leads to the escalation of delinquency and not usually the people themselves. The way to stop poor behavior is to either ignore it (as some labeling theorists suggest) or intervene appropriately without stigmatizing the person (as proponents of restorative justice suggest).

Labeling theory and labeling theorists are generally quite critical of the criminal justice system and suggest that its intervention in the lives of citizens does more harm than good. By having police officers, prosecutors, judges, and corrections officers label people as criminal, convicts, and all sorts of other names, they are creating more violence than they are stopping. Therefore, labeling theory is placed within the larger framework of critical criminology.

There are several critical theories that will be discussed in this chapter, many of which have a foundation in Marxist thought. In the 1800s and early 1900s manufacturing was taking off worldwide and industry itself was booming. While this expansion of manufacturing and industry did provide jobs and opportunities for many people, the process of production was controlled by the rich and powerful – or the "elite." While workers produced the products to be sold to consumers, they had no say in the process; nor were they offered rights to their products. Marx referred to this as alienation from labor. This alienation of the underclass and control by the elite resonated with critical criminologists. These criminologists suggested that the elite control normal citizens through laws and punishment that serve their own purposes and not the lives of the poor and working class. Given this subjugation of a whole class of people and laws enacted against them, critical criminologists are unsurprised that crime is concentrated in poor communities that are defined as criminal and policed in a way that maintains the current class structure.

Along with critical theories that place the blame for crime on the elite by focusing on the economic relationship between the upper and lower classes, another set of theories focuses on the power differential between males and females. Feminist theories focus on the devaluing of females in society and the relegation of women to a lower position in society so that men can rule at the helm. Feminist criminology examines the discrimination and neglect of women in a patriarchal (i.e., male-dominated) society and places the blame for crime on male dominance which labels female behavior as criminal (e.g., prostitution) and forces women into deviance by discriminating against them.

Feminist criminology is not only interested in explaining the delinquent behavior of females but also in placing women's issues at the forefront of the field of criminology. These theorists argue that we should pay more attention to issues such as date rape, intimate partner violence, human trafficking, and the like because these crimes disproportionately harm females. Feminist theorists (who, by the way, are both women and men) seek to explain why females commit crime, why certain behaviors that are mostly committed by females are deemed to be criminal, and what kinds of crime affect women in society.

Along with labeling, Marxist, and feminist theories of criminal behavior, other theories and approaches have been proffered in recent years which have a critical bent. This includes green criminology which is concerned with the degradation of the environment and queer criminology which examines the behavior and victimization of often neglected groups of individuals, including lesbian, gay, bisexual, and transgender (LGBT) individuals. Intersectional research and theories consider how multiple lines of disadvantage come together and intersect to influence violence (e.g., focusing on the plight of black females, poor black males, poor immigrants). While diverse, the theories in this chapter add to the vibrancy of the criminological landscape and offer many avenues for future research to test and refine modern criminological ideas.

Origins

While there are several theories that may be called "critical" and while these theories are far from all the same, there are recurring elements that appear across most critical theories. Most significantly, critical theories of crime focus on power differentials between the upper and lower classes as well as power differentials among the government and citizens. Often, these theories argue that those in the upper strata, as well as the government itself, define and use laws to maintain their power. Laws are used to keep the lower strata where they are, and the people that inhabit those strata from moving upward, by criminalizing behaviors of those who might threaten the position of the elite (or government actors). On the other hand, individuals in the lower strata commit crime because they are discriminated against or in an effort to improve their social position. Critical criminologists believe that the best way to eliminate, or at least reduce, crime is to reorganize society by moving toward a more equitable (often communist or socialist) society. The major critical theories are discussed in this chapter along with theories about the societal reaction to criminal behavior – namely labeling theory.

Marxism

Hopefully it will come as no surprise that the man behind Marxist criminology was none other than Karl Marx himself. It bears taking note that Marx's ideas were influenced by the German philosopher G. W. F. Hegel (1770–1831). Hegel taught at the University of Berlin and his philosophical orientation influenced much German thought at the time – including that of the young Karl Marx. However, while Marx borrowed from Hegelian philosophy, he diverged in significant ways. Marx, as opposed to Hegel, believed that wealth, material, and the state were *real* and not abstractions as Hegel proposed. Marx was also upset that Hegel was merely interested in philosophizing about the world and not changing it (who are often called "armchair" academics today). Marx believed that scholars should have an active hand in creating social change – something he called *praxis*.[1]

After receiving his doctorate in philosophy in 1841, Marx was already seen as somewhat of a pariah. He was too radical for most employers and had difficulties finding employment. He ended up finding a job in journalism and so his writings took flight.[2] The running theme throughout Marx's work was the conflict between the upper and lower classes.[a] Most important to Marx was that the lower class (the proletariat) sold their hard work and labor (and the products of this labor) to the upper class (the bourgeoisie) for wages. Once the bourgeoisie had the labor, and all materials/products resulting from that labor, they controlled the entire production process from start to finish. This alienation, to Marx, was a significant cause of crime. Marx, and his co-author Friedrich Engels, believed that criminals inhabited the lowest rung of society, the lumpenproletariat. The lumpenproletariat were a separate, third class of society who victimized others because of their objectification by the capitalist system. Since all of society's most important problems, including criminal behavior, were the result of capitalism, the only way to stop crime and victimization was to transform to a socialist society.

Marx was very concerned with several sociological and political issues, and crime, while a part of his philosophy, was not the major focus of his writing. In 1905, one of the first Marxist criminologists, Willem Bonger, published *Criminality and Economic Conditions*.[3] Like Marx, Bonger believed that the alienation and exploitation of the proletariat by the bourgeoisie was the foundation of criminal behavior. He also believed that capitalist societies, overall, created an atmosphere in which people cared much for material things and little for one another. Thus, capitalist societies bred egoism at the expense of altruism. Where people cared more for material things rather than other human beings, crime was likely.

At around the same time as others in Chicago were writing and theorizing about urban crime problems, a Swedish-born criminologist at the University of Pennsylvania was pondering the implications of societal conflict and the role that this conflict had on criminal behavior. Born in Sweden in 1896, Thorsten Sellin moved to Canada to live with his father in 1907 and went on from there to earn degrees in Illinois and Pennsylvania before his appointment at the University of Pennsylvania. He was quite a worldly scholar, spending time in France, Italy, Sweden, Canada, and the United States. He could also speak fluent Swedish, English, French, and German. Besides being well traveled and educated, many reported that he was one of the kindest people they had met.[4]

For Sellin, society was made up of different classes of individuals (a classical critical perspective) and these classes had different cultures with different definitions of norms – what is appropriate in civil society. These differences in values and behaviors led to class conflict. In addition, for Sellin, the law represented the majority and the powerful in society – not the poor or underprivileged. He rejected the idea of state-defined criminal behavior for this reason (it only reflected behaviors thought to be bad by the upper class). Regardless of how the state defined crime, because the upper and lower class would always butt heads on the values of their cultures, this conflict is a fact of society.

In 1938, Sellin published his most influential article, "Culture conflict and crime." In this piece, he solidified his view that different classes were characterized by different

---

a. A set of critical criminological theories are called "conflict" theories and seek to place crime in the context of struggles between different groups in society.

cultures and that the "cause" of crime is just that these cultures do not agree on acceptable behavior (although Sellin did concede that some behavior, like murder, is universally condemned). He considered this clash of the two cultures as "primary conflict." He also stated that even a unified culture, sooner or later, would evolve into multiple cultures, each with its own set of norms. There would also be conflict among these "splinter groups" that would be less severe than the fundamental conflict experienced by the two major societal groups (upper and lower class). This he called secondary conflict.[5]

Sellin's work (which continued up until his death at the age of 97) influenced many other prominent theorists both within cultural conflict criminology and outside of it. In his original *Theoretical criminology* in 1958, George Vold used Sellin's ideas about culture conflict but tempered the view that there were clear and separate cultures in society. He suggested that society is one culture, but that groups form to serve their own needs. These groups vie for political power and the most effective group ends up wielding the power of the state.[6] Ten years later, in *Criminality and legal order*, Austin Turk borrowed from these ideas but focused more on the state and criminal law. For him, culture conflict is needed, even beneficial, for continually examining whether the status quo is justified. If it is not, then there will be societal conflict as groups not in power rebel against the enforcement of the law as developed by those in power.[7] Finally, it should be noted that Sellin mentored Marvin Wolfgang, who went on to found the *Delinquency in a birth cohort* study, arguably one of the most influential studies in all of criminology.[8]

Labeling

Pause for a moment and think about your teenage self – the 13-, 14-, 15-year-old you. What did you do with your spare time? Did you ever get into trouble? I bet the vast majority of you (and I would wager that's almost 100 percent of you) engaged in some deviant behavior such as skipping class, talking back to your parents, or sneaking a sip of your parents' whisky. For others of you, particularly if you are male, you may have done something a little more deviant such as stolen from someone or someplace, got into a serious fight, sold drugs, vandalized someone's property, or perhaps even burglarized a home. These acts are fairly common, particularly for young males, and those acts could have sent you to jail or even to prison. I am guessing that most who are reading this made it out relatively unscathed. Perhaps some of you reading this were not so lucky and ended up involved with the juvenile or criminal justice system. There are serious implications with being exposed to the criminal justice system (CJS) and labeling theorists view this official contact with the system as harmful but avoidable.

From as far back as the early 1900s, academics have argued that the delinquent label sets a person up for failure. In 1938, Frank Tannenbaum placed the blame on society for delinquent behavior as well as the creation of gangs. He argued that normal juvenile activity, which is sometimes deviant, such as getting into schoolyard scuffles, may be demonized by adults in the neighborhood. This leads young individuals to start to see themselves as deviants and to meet up with other youth – so demonized – to form gangs. In this way, the mere fact that others label young people as deviant creates the actual deviant. He believed that if this behavior was just recognized as normal and largely ignored, nothing more would come of it except for a limited few.[9]

Radical policy implications were espoused by some in the 1950s and 1960s (to be discussed in more detail later). Edwin Schur had perhaps the most drastic view which he expressed in his book *Radical non-intervention*. As the title implies, he suggested that society, literally, should not respond to crime. Since the criminal justice system could do no good, and only serves to make people *more* criminal, not less, we should all ignore juvenile deviance.[10] As might be expected, this idea did not marshal much support. However, others built on this idea to offer similar suggestions with slightly different twists.

In 1951, Edwin Lemert wrote a comprehensive text entitled *Social pathology* in which he laid the groundwork for the role of social interaction in the emergence of certain behaviors. It was in this text where he first used the terms that would come to be associated with his name: primary and secondary deviance.[11] Lemert expanded on these terms along with his theory behind deviant behavior in his 1972 book *Human deviance, social problems, and social control*. It was in this text that Lemert solidified the relationship between the deviant actor and the criminal justice system.[12]

For Lemert, the origin of criminal behavior is "polygenic" or emerging from a variety of sources. To him this is fairly uninteresting and normal. Most people commit some deviant behavior and he called this initial form of poor behavior primary deviance. Primary deviance is not, technically, the first and *only* act someone might commit, but it is the first significant act for which someone is caught. If those who catch the individual stigmatize them by labeling them as "bad," or "delinquent," or "mean" and further isolate and control the individual, it is likely that, at some point, the individual will accept those terms and fulfill them by continuing their delinquent behavior. Since this occurs after the initial poor behavior, Lemert called this secondary deviance. He was much more concerned with this type of behavior (or reaction to behavior) and believed that society should try to avoid labeling in this way as it leads to much larger problems than minor primary deviance.[13]

Ways in which we *should* address deviance were confronted by other theorists during this time. In a key publication in *The American Journal of Sociology* in 1958, sociologist Harold Garfinkel described what he called "degradation ceremonies."[14] Degradation ceremonies can be very harmful when they are intended to humiliate and lower the status of the person being punished. Punishments that intend to produce guilt and shame further degrade personal identity and status within the community. Punishment through incarceration is an example of this type of degradation, as it intends to produce guilt and shame as well as change the identity of a person to that of a criminal.

Degradation ceremonies can be positive. When moral indignation is the goal, denouncing the morality of an act but not necessarily the person, group solidarity can be preserved and even enhanced. When degradations are public, collaborative, and preserve the dignity of people and society, they have the potential to produce positive outcomes for everyone. In essence, when the goal is group governance and not individual humiliation, the denouncing of an act will be successful.

Akin to Lemert, sociologist Erving Goffman, in the 1960s was very concerned with a specific type of labeling – that of stigma (or stigmatization). Such stigma could come from the types of interventions, or ceremonies, that Garfinkel talked about. To Goffman, it is people and society as a whole that labels others and stigmatizes them with a specific identity, whether or not that identity is a "true" identity. It doesn't matter that a person is naturally good, generally behaves well, and is a productive member of society if they have stigma about them put there by society.

In the first pages of his book *Stigma*, Goffman discusses the effects of stigma.

> While the stranger is present before us, evidence can arise of his possessing an attribute that makes him different from others in the category of persons available for him to be, and of a less desirable kind – in the extreme, a person who is quite thoroughly bad, or dangerous, or weak. [...] He is thus reduced in our minds from a whole and usual person to a tainted, discounted one.[15]

This is often how we view those convicted of a crime or who have mental illness. They no longer retain their "normal" selves but are effectively stigmatized and reduced only to their one act or set of behaviors that set them apart from others for the worst.

Recent developments

Following earlier labeling theorists, criminologist John Braithwaite agrees that labeling individuals in stigmatizing ways leads them to commit more crime and not less. He also argues that we can see how this leads to higher crime rates in entire societies where there is a lack of community and people are dealt with in a harsh and impersonal way which stigmatizes their behavior. However, he disagrees with a radical non-intervention strategy. In fact, he believes much the opposite. We must intervene. The important part is *how* we intervene. The CJS is very important in crime intervention as it is a last stop, last resort, to dealing with the issues of crime and delinquency. Programs such as restorative justice are successful alternatives to law enforcement tactics, and are aimed at dealing with juveniles and preventing system involvement that could damage the development of adolescents who could be helped in more productive ways.[16]

In a similar vein to Braithwaite, Robert Sampson and John Laub have written about the impact of labeling on the desistance process. Echoing others, they suggest that labeling theory offers a truly developmental theoretical approach to the study of delinquency in that it is concerned with what happens to people from when they are labeled and over their life-course. "Labeling may thus lead to an alteration of one's identity, exclusion from 'normal routines' or conventional opportunities, and increased contact with and support from deviant subgroups," they state. "All three, in turn, may lead to further deviance."[17] Labeling in a developmental sense (to be discussed in Chapter 10) explains what they call cumulative disadvantage. One example is that the criminal label leads to failure to get a job which leads to poverty which then leads to resorting to crime to obtain money to live. Similar to others, Sampson and Laub suggest providing opportunities to serve as turning points in a person's life and limiting the chance that someone's path to success is "knifed off" by a deviant label.

Peacemaking

Born out of critical criminology, and conflict/Marxist criminology in particular, is a focus on addressing crime through peaceful rather than punitive or coercive means. The criminologist who has proffered the greatest number of ideas behind peacemaking criminology is Richard Quinney.[18] For Quinney, crime represents suffering. To alleviate crime, one must alleviate suffering. Therefore, our response to crime and violence cannot perpetuate this suffering, as may be seen with campaigns such as the War on Drugs and harsh crime control policies that invoke mandatory minimums and the death penalty. These forms of punishment serve only to increase crime and violence. The criminal justice system should instead be committed to reducing violence by promoting peacemaking. This idea is very much in line with other theorists already covered, such as Garfinkel and Braithwaite. In fact, most theorists from the critical tradition believe that restorative justice may be the best philosophy to be applied to reduce crime because it increases community cohesiveness and does not use the divisive nature of the criminal justice system.

Left realism

The late criminologist Jock Young combined critical criminology with a refocus on street crime. As opposed to some radical criminology and the anarchist perspectives that permeated conflict theory in the 1970s and 1980s, Young proposed a critical perspective which he called "left realism." This perspective sheds a new light on the offender not as a radical revolutionary but as a person who can do real harm to others and to society. While maintaining that street offenders are often influenced by the larger social structure and subjugated by the powerful in society, left realism takes seriously the circumstances of both the offender and the victim.[19]

Contemporary Marxist criminologists follow in the footsteps of their predecessors and believe that capitalism and the market society lead to a criminalistic society but divert from the classic theorists in several ways. First, while classical Marxists believed that criminals were generally not responsible for their offending ways given that they were the oppressed class, contemporary Marxists believe that crime does cause real harm which should be addressed. Second, while capitalism may be the major cause of criminality, it is not the *only* cause of crime. Contemporary Marxist criminologists are often referred to as left realists. Left realists also believe that pragmatic solutions to the crime problem must be sought over the utopian dream of a socialist society.[20]

Criminologist Elliott Currie exemplifies this position. Currie believes that the market society, indeed, generates crime. Societies with a "harsh capitalism" where the free market economy dominates and social welfare is low have higher crime rates than societies with a "compassionate capitalism" which provide safety nets in the form of social welfare and health care for its citizens.[21] The United States, according to Currie, as well as others,[22] exemplifies a harsh capitalism with its obsession with the free market and individualism. Other countries, such as Scandinavian countries like Sweden and Norway, capture compassionate capitalism – establishing social welfare programs that allow for generous work leave and anti-poverty programs.

Feminist criminology

To shift gears slightly, one thing may have become obvious over the past six chapters. Most theories of crime are developed by men, who study male offenders and fail to take into account sex differences in offending behavior (of course there are exceptions even as far back as Lombroso and Ferrero's *The female offender*[23]). This changed, in some ways, with the growing concern over women's issues during the Women's Movement of the 1970s.[24] Shortly after the peak of the civil rights movement of the 1960s, society became more cognizant of other important issues such as those that concern women and children (it may not be surprising that these two issues went hand-in-hand). With the attention turned toward women's issues, feminist criminology made its entrance into the field. Feminist criminology is concerned with rectifying the neglect of women and crime by focusing on four major questions: (1) Are the explanations of crime the same for males and females?; (2) Why do men commit more crime than women?; (3) What explains the seeming "closing of the gap" between males and females?; and (4) How does the field of criminology become more inclusive of women's issues as well as promoting the efforts of female criminologists?

In 1975, two landmark works were released by two feminist criminologists. The first major work, *Sisters in crime: The rise of the new female criminal* by Freda Adler argues that the Women's Movement led to greater equality among men and women essentially "masculinizing" society. Women entered the workforce, became economic contributors to their family, and took on leadership roles just like men. Because of this equalization, women also entered criminality much like their male counterparts.[25]

Interestingly, Adler was not immune to the sexism of her time. Born in Philadelphia in 1934, she came of age as the United States was going through the Great Depression. Her mother wanted to become a doctor but found that this path was very much blocked for her as a woman in the early 1900s. For Adler, this signaled that she must overachieve in school. She was a bright student in high school and went on to attend the University of Pennsylvania in 1952. When she joined the Faculty at Temple University in 1971, she did not escape subtle (and not so subtle) sexism. She recalls that she often received correspondence addressed to "Fred A. Adler." Despite her experiences and line of work, she never considered herself a feminist criminologist.[26]

Later in the same year that Adler released *Sisters in crime*, Rita Simon published her book *Women and crime*, where she argued something different from Adler. Whereas Adler proposed that women were "masculinized" and increased their involvement in all types of crime, Simon believed that women were merely "emancipated" and increased their exposure to opportunities for crime. In other words, nothing about females changed internally; they only increased their external exposure to opportunities for *specific types* of crime that would be provided by entrance into the workforce.[27] Subsequent research has been brought to bear on these theories which will be discussed toward the end of this chapter.

Later criminologists who studied females and crime, as well as the gender/sex gap in crime, moved on from the liberation hypotheses proposed by Adler and Simon in the 1970s shortly after the Women's Movement. In the 1980s, Meda Chesney-Lind pointed out another likely cause of female criminality: patriarchy. A patriarchal society is dominated by males who overwhelmingly view women as inferior and as objects. This leads to the victimization of females at the hands of males, including both physical and sexual abuse. This control and abuse of women by men often leads females to run away from home, skip school, become homeless, and engage in criminality such as drug use, theft, and prostitution. Chesney-Lind argues that particular attention should be paid to the "pathways" into crime that are unique to females.[28]

A very different view of female criminality (or lack of criminal activity) was proffered by evolutionary psychologist Anne Campbell. In her "staying alive hypothesis," Campbell argues that females try very hard to avoid any violence because they are more invested in caring for children. The cost of their life would likely mean the cost of their children's (and future children's) lives. Campbell does not deny that women do engage in crime but most of this crime is in line with this reasoning – women commit crimes which help their survival or the survival of their children such as theft of food/clothes or killing in self-defense. Rarely are they involved in dangerous criminal activities such as aggravated assault, robbery, or murder.[29]

Criminologist James Messerschmidt approaches the study of gender and crime rather differently from each of these female scholars. Opposed to seeing liberation or patriarchy as the end-all-be-all of criminal behavior, he suggests that criminality, especially for men, exists on a spectrum of masculinity. Masculinity is the concept of what it means to be a man; this differs from person to person and is particularly influenced by race and gender. Social forces (e.g., poverty, history, disenfranchisement) characterize the concept of maleness and structure male social action.

For Messerschmidt, crime is in part a resource for "doing gender." For middle- and upper-class males, who generally have resources at their disposal, their way of showing their masculinity or "doing gender" is to make money, be successful, and have access to women. If the way toward these goals is blocked, they may resort to sexual harassment of women or white-collar crime. For lower-class males, particularly black males, "doing gender" is different. If the avenues for success are blocked, their masculinity is proved through violence. For all races and classes, Messerschmidt believes that proving masculinity reinforces the dominance of males over females and is a cause for social concern.[30]

With renewed attention to women's issues, feminist scholars, and others, are now increasing their attention to how sex and gender intersect with other demographic factors of disadvantage such as race, ethnicity, and age. This approach, called intersectionality, which is not entirely new, started in 1989 when Crenshaw used the term to explain women of color in politics. Since that time, others have used intersectionality to measure the interaction of gender, race, ethnicity, and immigration status on several outcomes such as victimization,[31] pre-trial release,[32] and domestic violence.[33]

Intersectionality research falls squarely within the critical tradition. Researchers have "recognized that certain groups of individuals cross lines, or categories, of oppression," write Blackwell and Cruze, "experiencing oppression based on more than one social category, or socially benefitting because of statuses attained across more than one category."[34] The doubly disadvantaged or advantaged likely experience different pathways into and out of delinquency based on the intersections of their demographic backgrounds. This is very much related to what is known as "pathways" research. Pathways research has illuminated the paths by which women and men of various backgrounds find themselves moving into trouble and getting out of trouble as well as what trouble they happen to get into in the first place.

Green criminology

Before finishing the discussion on critical criminology, two recent efforts should be discussed: Green criminology and Queer criminology. In the 1980s, general business practices in the United States began using and/or depleting natural resources at a rate not seen in prior decades. Environmental harm caused by human pollution, destruction of ecosystems, and animal poaching/trafficking makes the world a more dangerous place and costs society more than street crime. Yet, criminology is relatively silent on these harms. Green criminologists, however, are not. The rise of green criminology, beginning in the 1990s through the work of Michael J. Lynch and others, has gained some traction over recent years as concerns about global climate change and the destruction of natural ecosystems and decreasing biodiversity are rising.[35]

Green crime is quite a broad term including crimes as diverse as poaching, animal trafficking, and polluting the environment. However, there are links between many of the crimes that are of interest to green criminologists. In our conversation, criminologist Michael Lynch, from the University of South Florida, states:

> Generally green criminology is the study of: (A) how humans harm ecosystems; (B) how those harms affect other life forms (ecosystems and nonhuman species); (C) the content of environmental law and how law responds to environmental crimes (the content of environmental law and whether it controls and punishes environmental crime); and (D) the distribution of pollution which can include studying how pollution affects human behavior (e.g., whether exposure to lead pollution generates crime).

This definition provides for a consolidation of aims of green criminologists who are all, in some way or another, concerned about how we as a human species cause harm to the environment and what the effects of that harm include.

Green criminology, with its focus on non-traditional harm, fits well within critical criminology's concern with harm that falls outside of what the state formally defines as crime. Green criminology also implicates the rich and powerful as the primary offenders of environmental destruction and other environmental crimes. Corporations and the state are often found to be the worst offenders in environmental harm but often evade prosecution or any responsibility, as laws are difficult to enforce and offenders are hard to identify.[36]

"Green" problems are international in scope. In today's interconnected world, climate change and other green harms are global – affecting all of humanity. This has led to international efforts to ameliorate environmental problems such as the United Nations' International Panel on Climate Change and the Kyoto Protocol. The Kyoto Protocol, an international agreement to reduce greenhouse gas emissions, has been signed by 191 nations[b] – the United States is not one of them.[37] Despite these concerns, green criminology has yet to make a significant impact upon criminology *writ large* even as it slowly grows within the field.

Queer criminology

Probably most recently, Queer criminology has made its emergence into the field of criminology. Queer criminology (or the "queering of criminology") considers victims of a broad variety who are vulnerable or ignored such as the LGBTQ community, women, and minorities. The subfield is concerned with the criminal behavior of these groups as well as their victimization.[38]

Queer criminology is also concerned about the intersection of multiple lines of disadvantage – as discussed earlier. While concerned with LGBTQ individuals, queer criminologists also look at how gender identity and sexual identity intersect with race, ethnicity, class, and so on.[39] Therefore, like many other theoretical approaches discussed in this chapter, Queer criminology challenges traditional approaches to the explanation of crime and considers an alternative approach concentrated on those who are located on the fringes of the social structure.

The case of Brock Allen Turner: sexual assault and violence against women at Stanford

On January 17, 2015, a young woman attended a fraternity party with her younger sister at Stanford University in California. The atmosphere at the fraternity party was that of most college parties – dancing, mingling, and drinking. After "drinking too much too fast,"[40] the woman found herself in a terrible situation – waking up as she was being wheeled around in the hospital. She did not know at that time what had happened to her.

In court, evidence came out of what did happen to the woman that night after she lost consciousness. A young Stanford swimmer, Brock Allen Turner, sexually assaulted the young woman next to a garbage dumpster on the street. An examination of the victim's body and the results of the rape kit revealed that Turner had sexually assaulted the woman by penetrating her with his fingers. Nurses who were part of the Sexual Assault Response Team (SART) examination noted penetrating trauma including bruising and bleeding. Pine needles were found in the woman's hair and vagina.

The court proceedings illuminated several issues of both the court process and social justice. Impact statements were read by several members of both the defense and prosecution. The woman's impact statement was seven pages long, making a splash on the internet and social media as people lauded her courage and willingness to share her story with the world. She vividly described the aftermath of the incident and the effect it had on her life.

Impact statements were also read by both of Turner's parents. These were largely met with outrage. Snippets of the parents' statements circulated around social media, including the father's statement that "His life will never be the one that he dreamed about and worked so hard to achieve. That is a steep price to pay for 20 minutes of action out of his

---

b. As this book was being completed, US President Donald J. Trump joined the US to Syria and Nicaragua as the only three nations to not sign the Paris Climate Agreement to cut greenhouse gas emissions in an effort to halt global climate change.

20 plus years of life." His mother's statement included lines such as "My once vibrant and happy boy is distraught, deeply depressed, terribly wounded, and filled with despair. His smile is gone forever – that beautiful grin is no more. [...] We are devastated beyond belief. My beautiful, happy family will never know happiness again." Neither parent's statement had anything to say about the young woman who was victimized.

The court found Turner guilty. The maximum that he could receive for his crimes was 14 years in prison. Many around the nation believed that Turner would be sentenced harshly given the seriousness of the crime. He received six months in jail and probation. In the time that it took to finish this book, he has already been set free and returned to his home. The sentence struck a chord in the general public, with many even calling for the removal of the judge because of the lenient sentence. For many women especially, this was another blind eye to the issues of female victimization.

Feminist criminology is acutely interested in the issues surrounding female victimization and the criminal justice responses to female victims. In this case, two outcomes rose to the surface. The first is the amount of victim blaming, particularly by the parents of the accused. Alcohol and promiscuity were identified as the culprits of the crime and the female victim was seen as at least partially responsible for her victimization, as she got drunk and could not control her actions. Feminist criminologists have long pointed out that, in a male-dominated society, the popular view is that "boys will be boys" and that young girls must protect themselves. Often boys and men are not taught to control their behavior but to see themselves as superior to girls and women.

The second issue that rises to the fore in this case is the lenient sentence that the guilty man received. The man's life was seen to be too precious and promising to be "wasted" by a long and harmful prison sentence. His potential and position in society (as a straight, upper-class, white male) was seen to be privileged and a harsh sentence would damage what the man could become. In the process of protecting the man from harm, the criminal justice system failed to address the needs of the female victim. While the majority of the public were outraged by the sentence, the criminal justice system did very little to respond to the victim's needs.

Empirical support

Since this chapter has presented various perspectives, the empirical support is mixed depending on which perspective is under investigation. However, there has been some consistency in the support for various theories in this chapter. For example, research is conclusive now that human-facilitated climate change is occurring and impacting entire communities, leading to conflict.[41] In addition, exposure to environmental harms, such as lead and pesticides, has a negative impact upon health and behavior.[42] Exposure to environmental harm is shown to not be random across the population but to disproportionately impact the poor and minorities.[43] Therefore, many radical and critical criminologists are keenly interested in this exposure and the resultant impacts upon human health and behavior.

In terms of labeling theory, while specific tests of some of the theory are hard to operationalize, researchers have sought to test whether or not official sanctioning (i.e., labeling) leads to a net positive or negative effect on individuals. A *Campbell Systematic Review* of 29 randomized controlled trials (one of the most rigorous kinds of empirical tests) indicated that the juvenile justice system produced undesirable effects on individuals and did not work to reduce crime.[44] This research raises doubts on the ability of the juvenile justice system to produce positive effects for individuals and society.[45]

Feminist criminology has provided empirical support and justification for examining the unique experiences of girls and women and their encounters with crime. While many factors work similarly for increasing delinquency for both males and females, other factors work differently according to the gender of the individual.[46] This is particularly the case for externalizing and internalizing behaviors where males are more likely to externalize (e.g., fight) and girls internalize (e.g., self-harm).[47] In addition, an entire volume by biosocial criminologists Anthony Walsh and Jamie Vaske shows how evolutionary and biological factors account for the differences between male and female criminality.[48] Without gender-sensitive models, accounting for personal identification of sex and biological sex, these effects would not be uncovered, suggesting the continued use of gendered models.

Competing perspectives from feminist criminology have also received attention from empirical research. For example, in 1989, criminologist and pioneering researcher on women and crime Darrell Steffensmeier and colleagues evaluated four hypotheses from feminist theory that seek to explain women's increase in violence over recent years: (1) gender equality; (2) female economic marginality; (3) opportunities for female-based consumer crimes; and (4) formalization of social control. They found that gender equality and female economic marginality were both poor predictors of crime while opportunities for female-based consumer crimes and formalization of social control were good predictors of crime.[49] This lends support to some feminist perspectives, but not all.

Remaining questions

As society becomes more diverse and cognizant of the issues that plague individuals from multiple walks of life, critical criminology may morph into separate subfields that investigate the offending and victimization patterns of vulnerable and neglected groups. Criminology has only begun to consider the role of sexual and gender identity in crime and victimization and intersectionality research is relatively nascent. Therefore, the empirical base evaluating these theories is small or even non-existent. As people and cultures change, criminology faces the challenge of keeping up with the explanation of crime and empirically evaluating theories as they emerge into the theoretical landscape.

Policy

In the 1970s, as mentioned earlier in this chapter, Edwin Schur released his book *Radical non-intervention*. His aim in the book was to promote a specific view of crime and a straightforward response to crime. His solution: do nothing. To Schur, formal sanctions in the form of arrest, prosecution, and incarceration did nothing but make a person worse and exacerbate the crime problem. Therefore, the only way to decrease crime was for the formal justice system to "lay off" and let informal mechanisms take their course such as parental support, community cohesiveness, and school investment.[50] Needless to say, this idea did not catch on. Not many were able to endorse such a dramatic change to the system. In fact, as we will see, the United States became more punitive than ever following these ideas and formal intervention, especially incarceration, skyrocketed in the 1970s.

Marxist criminologists often agree with radical non-intervention and strict Marxists go further with societal change by suggesting that there be a total transformation of society from a capitalist system to a total socialist system. A similar idea is brought forward by anarchist criminologists who view all power structures as flawed and leading to an unequal society. To anarchists, the criminal justice system is the epitome of power and authority in society, and should be dismantled in favor of an egalitarian approach to justice where all members of society can partake in the justice process. Many anarchist criminologists are in favor of a decentralized process such as restorative justice (discussed momentarily).[51]

A more recent approach to reducing the labeling effect of formal sanctions and, for many, a more reasonable approach compared to radical non-intervention and total socialism is diversion programming. Diversion comes in many forms but always includes an alternative, less severe sanction for an individual receiving punishment. Today there are a host of diversionary programs and courts that seek to rehabilitate and not stigmatize those individuals who have offended.

Diversion programs are generally used for youth and mainly for those accused or found guilty of minor or non-violent crimes. Popular diversion efforts include prosecution in alternative courts, such as youth court, over traditional courts, restorative justice, and family treatment programs. The evidence as to the effectiveness of diversionary programs to reduce recidivism and produce net positive effects is mixed. For instance, a recent meta-analysis indicated that only family treatment programs and researcher-led restorative justice programs produced a sizable reduction in recidivism.[52] A meta-analysis on restorative justice programs a few years later indicated similar results, indicating that in over 21 studies, restorative justice had a net reducing effect on recidivism.[53]

In his influential piece *The way of peace: On crime, suffering, and service*, Richard Quinney begins by stating: "No amount of thinking and no amount of public policy have brought us any closer to understanding and solving the problem of crime." He continues, "The more we have reacted to crime, the farther we have removed ourselves from any understanding and any reduction of the problem."[54] His statement has elements of both labeling theory and peacemaking criminology. For Quinney, one must transform oneself first, and then commit to service through peacemaking. One strategy to alleviate suffering and establish peace in society is restorative justice and other peacekeeping practices.

Central to restorative justice is what John Braithwaite calls disintegrative shaming and reintegrative shaming.[55] The current criminal justice process seeks to blame the offender and find them guilty in a court of law. Essentially, a fine, community corrections, or incarceration follow this guilt-seeking process. These practices "disintegrate" bonds with society and a person's self-identity – likely leading to more crime. Restorative justice and peacekeeping intends to shame the *act* that a person committed but not the person who committed the act. Instead, the process is centered on restoring bonds between victims and offenders as well as their communities and welcoming the offender back into the community. This process, namely reintegrative shaming, restores harmony and peace – reducing crime and violence.

Recently in the United States and in much of Europe, many criminologists have argued for the decriminalization of certain acts such as drug use and prostitution (along with other "victimless" crimes). Decriminalization is different from legalization (which is also being discussed for many acts defined as criminal) in that it does not necessarily propose that certain acts go unpunished but that punishment should not result in sentences reserved for criminal acts such as imprisonment or long-term probation. Most research on drug legalization and decriminalization shows that there is relatively little to no impact upon property and violent crime rates.[56] Results from Australia indicate that decriminalizing sex work does not increase the prevalence of paying for sex.[57] The research on these issues, taken together, appears to suggest that legalization and decriminalization of drugs and victimless crimes have little or no impact upon crime rates but do have the potential to reduce incarceration rates.[58]

Summary

This chapter has covered a lot of diverse, but related, ground. Although there are several modern versions of both labeling and critical approaches to explaining crime and criminal justice behavior, the roots of these perspectives originated quite a long time ago.

While it is often difficult to measure and test parts of these theories (and some critical criminologists directly reject such empirical research), there is evidence to support aspects of labeling theory and conflict theory. Further, parts of these theories are integrating with other perspectives, such as desistance and strain perspectives, to expand prediction.

While diverse, there are a few themes that connect these theories. Critical theories (including labeling) focus on power struggles in society, question the utility of the criminal justice system in responding to and preventing crime, and seek to promote social justice and change. Today, critical theories inform criminal justice practice. Restorative justice, specialty courts, and prevention programs tailored to women and minorities all utilize elements of critical theories. While the future of critical theories is blurred, with a changing society the continued use of theoretical perspectives is likely to continue in criminology and may even expand.

Notes

 1 Ritzer & Goodman, 2004.
 2 Frailing & Harper, 2016.
 3 Bonger, 1969 [1905].
 4 Melossi, 2010.
 5 Sellin, 1938.
 6 Vold, 1958.
 7 Turk, 1969.
 8 Wolfgang, Figlio, & Sellin, 1972.
 9 Tannenbaum, 1938.
10 Schur, 1973.
11 Lemert, 1951.
12 Lemert, 1972.
13 Lemert, 1972.
14 Garfinkel, 1956.
15 Goffman, 1963: 2–3.
16 Braithwaite, 1989.
17 Sampson & Laub, 1997a: 139.
18 Quinney, 1993.
19 Young, 1979; 1987.
20 Einstadter & Henry, 2006.
21 Currie, 1997.
22 See Messner & Rosenfeld, 2008; many have made the astute observation that Institutional Anomie Theory is founded on the same principles as Marxist thought.
23 Lombroso & Ferrero, 1895.
24 For a good example of the women's movement and how it affected crime legislation see Best, 1997.
25 Adler, 1975.
26 Hartmann & Sundt, 2011.
27 Simon, 1975.
28 Chesney-Lind, 1989, 2006; see also Daly & Chesney-Lind, 1988.
29 Campbell, 1999; see also Campbell (2013) for a great review of female psychology generally.
30 Messerschmidt, 1993.
31 Katz, 2000.
32 Demuth & Steffensmeier, 2004.
33 Erez, Adelman, & Gregory, 2009.
34 Blackwell & Cruze, forthcoming.
35 Lynch & Stretesky, 2001.
36 Crank & Jacoby, 2015.
37 Lynch & Stretesky, 2016
38 Ball, 2014.

39 See Woods, 2014.
40 See www.buzzfeed.com/katiejmbaker/heres-the-powerful-letter-the-stanford-victim-read-to-her-ra?utm_term=.gqR0wqAyj#.gdJngqwGQ.
41 See Myers et al., 2015.
42 Boutwell, Beaver, & Barnes, 2014; Lynch & Stretesky, 2001.
43 Stretesky, 2003.
44 Petrosino, Turpin-Petrosino, & Guckenburg, 2010.
45 See also Paternoster & Iovanni, 1989.
46 See Heimer & De Coster, 1999.
47 Posick, Farrell, & Swatt, 2013.
48 Walsh & Vaske, 2015.
49 Steffensmeier, Allan, & Streifel, 1989.
50 Schur, 1973.
51 Pepinsky, 1978; Wieck, 1978.
52 Schwalbe et al., 2012.
53 Wong et al., 2016.
54 Quinney, 1991: 3.
55 Braithwaite, 1993.
56 Maier, Mannes, & Koppenhofer, 2017.
57 Rissel et al., 2017.
58 See Husak (2002) for a discussion on multiple issues of legalization and decriminalization.

Further reading

Beirne, P. & South, N. (2013). *Issues in green criminology*. New York: Routledge.
Loader, I. & Sparks, R. (2013). *Public criminology?* New York: Routledge.
Melossi, D. (2008). *Controlling crime, controlling society: Thinking about crime in Europe and America*. Cambridge: Polity Press.
Reiman, J. & Leighton, P. (2015). *The rich get richer and the poor get prison: Ideology, class, and criminal justice*. New York: Routledge.
Tannenbaum, F. (1938). *Crime and the community*. Boston, MA: Ginn.

8 Social and self-control theories

Introduction	94
Theory	94
Origins	95
Recent developments	97
The case of Randy Kraft: the successful serial killer	101
Empirical support	102
Remaining questions	102
Policy	103
Summary	104

Introduction

Theories of criminal behavior usually pose the question, "Why do people commit crime?" This makes sense. If we want to understand why people commit crime, we ask the question as to why they might become involved in such behaviors. Do they hang out with bad people? Are they stressed out or strained by society? Or maybe they have biological deficits that push them into crime. Social control, and by extension, self-control theories, ask a different question, "Why *don't* people commit crime?" In other words, instead of being pushed into crime or learning crime, control theories argue that people are already predisposed to commit crime. Why *wouldn't* we do it? Control theories seek to answer this question.

Theory

Classical control theories argue that people must either be controlled by society to not commit crime or learn internal (or self-) control to be able to regulate themselves throughout their daily lives. It is no wonder that these theories are called "control" theories. Indeed, they see people in need of control so that they will not follow through with their natural inclinations to act in self-interest in ways that often contravene social norms.

Another departure which control theories had to make from mainstream criminology was that if one is to determine how someone is controlled, some sort of self-report survey must be used. Simply, someone must be asked what types of factors they believe control their behavior. Police data do not lend themselves nicely to answering this question. Along with the rise of social control theories came the rise of self-report surveys. These theories, and to some extent these methods, are the focus of this chapter.

Origins

One of the early pioneers of control theory was Albert Reiss Jr., a sociologist from the University of Chicago. Reiss was among the first theorists to suggest that regulation of behavior comes from internal and external controls. External controls are social controls that come from society and its institutions.[1] He states, "From the perspective of the person, institutional control lies in the acceptance of or submission to the authority of the institution and the reinforcement of existing personal controls by institutional controls."[2] Thus, a control is placed on an individual's behavior when an institution in society (say, church) provides a norm (say, generosity) that is internalized by the individual.

Similarly, personal controls "are an index of the person's definition of how he will act in certain situations."[3] Essentially, for Reiss, personal controls are ideals that individuals have regarding appropriate social behavior that are non-delinquent. He also believes that individual controls are rational ways of thinking and acquiring the needs for a productive life. When the individual (or ego) is weakened, delinquency is likely. This way of thinking about individual and societal controls paved the way for theorizing about the many ways in which an individual's behavior can be controlled – especially the work of contemporaries such as Walter Reckless.

It is likely not a surprise that social control perspectives came from University of Chicago students. In 1925, Walter Cade Reckless, a student of Robert Park and Ernest Burgess at the University of Chicago, as well as an accomplished violinist, completed his dissertation on vice in Chicago where he investigated drugs, gambling, and prostitution on the streets. After graduating from Chicago, he began his professorial career at Vanderbilt University but moved to Ohio State University shortly thereafter. There, he met his collaborator Simon Dinitz, and together they began to theorize and write about juvenile delinquency in urban neighborhoods. Dinitz was 27 years Reckless's junior but they formed a strong professional and personal bond that would span several years and several academic articles.[4]

Reckless's early work and his later collaborations with Dinitz led him to hypothesize about the forces that contribute to delinquent behavior. He believed there were many forces that were either internal or external to the individual which led to delinquency. This departed from the social disorganization perspective of other University of Chicago theorists in that Reckless and Dinitz were concerned not only with neighborhood-level factors but also with individual-level factors that contribute to crime. Internal factors were found within the individual, including their morality and religious beliefs. External factors included parents, teachers, and peers. In Reckless's view, these forces contained behavior – preventing delinquency. Therefore, his theory would be called containment theory and was one of the first fully fledged control theories that explained factors which contained or prevented a person from engaging in poor behavior.

Reckless also wrote on the idea of the self-concept as an internal containment or insulator against crime.[5] Along with his collaborators Simon Dinitz and Ellen Murray,

Reckless began with the question, "What insulates an early teen-age boy against delinquency?"[6] By asking 30 teachers in the most delinquent areas of Columbus, Ohio which kids they thought were unlikely to come into contract with the police or the juvenile justice system, the researchers identified 192 males of whom 125 ended up as part of their sample of insulated boys. They concluded of the boys that

> the vast majority defined themselves as being stricter about right and wrong than most people, indicated that they attempted to keep out of trouble at all costs and further indicated that they tried to conform to the expectations of their parents, teachers and others.[7]

Overall, this research highlights the importance of self-concept, or identity, which is an important insulator against delinquent behavior and sets the stage for later work on identity that continues to show similar results through its ability to control individual behavior.[8]

Around the time when the control perspective was picking up in the 1950s, another issue arose. What is the best measurement of delinquency and what sampling strategy would be best to use in tests of theory? For the most part, the sociological perspectives that had dominated the 1900s had used information from official sources of data or from clinical samples, such as prisoners and psychiatric patients. One criminologist had a different idea. To offer the best test of theory, one should use a sample of those who are most likely to engage in minor delinquency and perhaps some more major forms more infrequently. For F. Ivan Nye, this would be school students.[9] While not the first to use school samples in theory research, he did write extensively on using school-based samples and used these samples to test the propositions of theories – including control theories.

Based on his research, Nye also extended control theory in a few different ways. Similar to Reiss and Reckless, Nye viewed the family as a strong social control along with individual controls. From this jumping-off point, Nye suggested that a social control like the family can result in individual, indirect, and direct control on behavior. For example, parents can directly control behavior by spending time with their children, monitoring their behavior, and supervising their play. It can also be the case that absent direct control, the individual's behavior will still be controlled when away from parents because children fear or anticipate disapproval from their parents if they engage in bad behavior. Ultimately, these can both influence and/or lead to individual control or conscience.[10] It will become clear how much this line of thinking influenced not only current control theories but also self-control theories to be discussed shortly.

Along with concepts of internal/external, individual/social, and direct/indirect controls, it is prudent to discuss one additional component that rounded out thinking about controls during this time period. Rutgers University criminologist Jackson Toby introduced the concept of "stakes in conformity" in his 1957 paper appearing in the *Journal of Criminal Law and Criminology*. For Toby, juveniles who are not committed to being productive members of society and who do not form strong relationships with their families and society would have little to lose by becoming involved with delinquent groups and gangs. Every juvenile can be tempted into a delinquent gang but most have relationships and a commitment to society that they do not want to damage or lose. He calls these bonds "stakes in conformity" and these stakes are what control individual behavior keeping juveniles on the straight and narrow.

In 1957, a seminal article was published in *American Sociological Review* by Gresham Sykes and David Matza which presented a theory of criminal behavior that was similar to social learning but with a control theory twist. Sykes and Matza agreed with Sutherland that delinquent behavior is learned. One does learn criminal behavior from others and, when definitions favorable to law violation outweigh those for conformity, crime and delinquency is the result. However, the key mechanism, or linkage, between definitions and crime is neutralization.[11] They also agree with control theorists in that when individuals are bonded to society and do not want to jeopardize those connections, they can get around this guilt by qualifying their behavior.

For Sykes and Matza, the reason people commit crime is that they are able to use definitions to justify their behavior. While most juveniles know that crime is bad, and that one should not engage in violent acts, they can be "freed up" to do so by justifying (or neutralizing) their behavior. Thus, neutralization theory as proposed by Sykes and Matza is a control theory, suggesting that most people are restrained from committing crime but can be freed to do so with proper self-justification.

Sykes and Matza discuss five major justifications or neutralizations people use before committing crime: (1) denial of responsibility; (2) denial of injury; (3) denial of victim; (4) condemnation of the condemners; and (5) appeal to higher loyalties. First, if a person can deny that they are responsible for the crime then they have nothing to worry about (e.g., "I accidentally hit the kid with my baseball bat"). Second, one can deny that there was any injury from the act and therefore no one is hurt (e.g., "I use cocaine, but I don't hurt anyone and it is my own business"). Third, someone can deny that there was any real or true victim or that the victim deserved it (e.g., "Sure, I stole $100 dollars from the man's wallet, but he is rich and won't even miss it"). Fourth, by condemning the condemners one is able to justify a delinquent act by focusing not on one's own behavior but on the behavior of those who disapprove of the delinquent act (e.g., "Yes, I voted twice, but the whole system is rigged and politicians are all corrupt"). Finally, by appealing to higher loyalties, one can justify one's behavior as necessary or in self-defense (e.g., "Yes, I beat the kid up, but he bullied my friends and I always stick up for my friends").

Recent developments

While social control theories enjoyed attention prior to the 1970s, especially in the 1950s when control theories were being developed and messaged by sociologists and criminologists, it was Travis Hirschi who was responsible for promoting the perspective in criminology. Travis Hirschi was born in 1935 in Rockville, Utah. His parents were educated only through the eighth grade, but they made an impression on him which was apparent in his professional work. After joining and finishing a stint with the Army, he enrolled at the University of California at Berkeley. After finishing his doctoral degree, he spent time at the University of Washington, University of California at Davis, the State University of New York at Albany, and the University of Arizona. He is among the most prolific and influential criminologists of his time. He passed away in 2016 while this book was being written.

In 1969, Hirschi published his penultimate work in *Causes of delinquency*. This book was a reformulation of his dissertation where he proposed that the causes of delinquency involved a lack of the bonds that tie people to society. According to Hirschi, an individual bonds with society (and the people in it) in four major ways: (1) attachment to significant others; (2) commitment to conventional behavior; (3) involvement in conventional activities; and (4) belief in society's normative system. A person can be bonded in one or more ways and all four in conjunction make up a person's overall social bond.

The elements of Hirschi's bond require a little more elaboration to fully understand his contribution to criminology. Attachment refers to the relationship an individual has with significant others – most importantly parents. Hirschi states that someone's attachments to significant others, including parents, peers, and teachers, prevent him or her from engaging in delinquent acts because the person fears that engaging in delinquency would damage those bonds.

Commitment, the second main component of social bonding, is the extent to which a person believes in the law and in pro-social behavior. This is akin to Sutherland's "definitions," but Hirschi reframes this as "stakes in conformity" which borrows from Toby's conceptualization of social control. To the extent that an individual engages in and is rewarded for pro-social behavior, that person becomes committed in socially acceptable ways of life. Again, a person would not want to damage a good job, marriage, or report card by engaging in poor behavior.

Involvement in conventional activities refers to an individual's investment of time and energy in pro-social activities such as school work, sports, and extra-curricular activities. The more a person is committed to engaging in pro-social activities, the less time and effort will be spent on antisocial activities. Involvement is often described with the adage "idle hands are the Devil's workshop."

The final element of Hirschi's social bonding theory is belief in a society's normative system. This refers to an individual's acceptance of a general value system within a society. He contends that individuals are less likely to engage in delinquent acts when they have respect for people within society and adhere to the rule of law. Even if a person lacks the other three elements of the social bond, it may be belief in the law and the moral obligation to obey rules that restricts someone from engaging in crime. In sum, the social bond is what controls someone's behavior, and thus forms the basis of social control theory in criminology.

Throughout the 1970s and 1980s, social control theories received much support from theorists and through empirical research. Along with social learning and strain theories, social control rounded out the "big three" theories of criminal behavior. Hirschi not only wrote and expanded on social control theories but he engaged in a wide range of research. Much of this was with his collaborator Michael Gottfredson who was his undergraduate student at the University of California at Berkeley.

Aside from theorizing on the role of age and crime, criminal careers, and measuring crime, Gottfredson and Hirschi adopted a theoretical approach that would come to dominate criminology from 1990 up until today.[12] In their 1990 book *A general theory of crime*, Gottfredson and Hirschi put forth the idea that low self-control was the major contributor to delinquent behavior. They defined crime as "acts of force or fraud undertaken in pursuit of self-interest"[13] and said that people make rational decisions about whether or not to engage in crime in order to maximize benefits and pleasure as well as to minimize cost and pain (this is the classical deterrence argument for criminal behavior – or any behavior for that matter). It is important to note that their definition includes crime but also a wide range of antisocial behaviors that they call "analogous acts." Again, this does not require any specific explanation as to motivation. Criminal behavior is only the means through which to achieve pleasure or avoid pain.[14]

The central thesis in *A general theory of crime* is that individuals with low self-control will engage in criminal and deviant behavior because they are only concerned with short-term pleasure at the expense of long-term pain (i.e., consequences). Delinquent acts are immediately gratifying, simple to commit, and generally exciting. They are often the quickest way for someone to get what they want (why work hard for a new cell phone, just steal one!). They also argue that individuals with low self-control are impulsive, prefer simple tasks rather than complicated ones, pursue risk-seeking activities, prefer physical tasks rather than mental tasks, easily lose their temper, and are self-centered.[15] Alternatively, people who develop high self-control are likely to consider the long-term consequences of their behavior and resist the temptation to engage in antisocial behavior.

This leaves one unanswered question: How do people develop self-control? According to Gottfredson and Hirschi, effective parental socialization during early childhood is the most important factor in the development of self-control. They state that parents must engage in three major activities to instill self-control in their children: (1) monitor their children's behavior; (2) recognize their children's bad behavior when it occurs; and (3) effectively and consistently punish their children's deviant behavior. According to Gottfredson and Hirschi, this will instill self-control and lead children to consider the long-term consequences of their behavior and delay gratification until a later time. If parents fail to instill self-control, generally by the age of around 8, the child will never develop adequate impulse control at any other time during their life. In this way, self-control is a time-stable trait according to Gottfredson and Hirschi.

Five years after Gottfredson and Hirschi's *A general theory of crime*, criminologist Charles Tittle presented his control theory which he called control-balance theory. Not surprisingly, control-balance theory is firmly placed on the foundational idea of control which Tittle describes as: (1) the degree to which others and a person's surroundings can limit the options for their behavior; and (2) the extent to which an individual can escape from the controls placed upon them and exercise their own control over others. Important to the theory is the concept of the control ratio (the calculation of control imposed upon a person relative to the control that they have over others). Crime is likely when there is a control imbalance.[16]

A control imbalance can be in either direction. First, a person can have a control deficit which occurs when the control that an individual can exercise is exceeded by the amount of control they are under. Second, a person can have a control surplus which occurs when that person has a lot of control over others but is himself (or herself) under very little control. Tittle believed that control deficits would be related to street crime (to gain back some control) while control surpluses would be related to white-collar crime (as control over others is conducive to this type of behavior). For Tittle, control balance is needed for crime to be effectively controlled.

Others besides Hirschi and Gottfredson have worked on developing social control theories and testing their propositions. Criminologist Barbara Costello (who has written extensively on the theoretical conception of social control and social bonding and how to measure these constructs) teamed up with Paul Vowell to develop and test a – then – new measure of social control. In response to a previous study by Ross Matsueda,[17] a proponent of differential association theory, Costello and Vowell suggest that the most appropriate way to conceptualize certain attitudes toward the law and antisocial behavior is not by using "definitions" as Sutherland and Matsueda do, but through the "belief" mechanism proposed in social bonding theory. Costello and Vowell support their theory by using statistical analysis showing that certain questions about attitudes toward law-breaking and conformity load together (i.e., correlate) on a "second-order latent construct" (a fancy way of saying that these items correlate with one another to form an overall measure of belief) and that this belief measure is highly correlated with other social bond measures as opposed to social learning/differential association measures.[18]

For generations, criminology has focused on criminality in large cities. Social disorganization theories and even those of strain and social learning assume that crime and criminals are in urban areas, in close proximity to one another. Missing from this line of scholarship is a concern for crime in suburban and rural areas. Fortunately, recent research from Simon Singer, a criminologist from Northeastern University, has shed light on crime in the suburbs.[19] He uses a social-control theoretical approach to explain why, even in relatively safe places, people engage in deviant behavior.

For Singer, crime in the suburbs must be interpreted through the lens of modernity. "Criminological and sociological theories have always had a modernity component to them," Singer states in our personal interview. He continues,

> But they tend to put all the cards on the family, or in the aggregate the community. A theory of relational modernity says modern-day life is more complicated than that. And to reduce complexity you need to understand what children and adolescents

are up against in terms of modern-day expectations. Those expectations might be narrowly defined in terms of grasping societal demands for complexity, autonomy, and rationality – as they are encountered in one social setting after another.[20]

At the heart of Singer's theory is that context matters. Social control and social bonding matter but why those bonds matter, and with whom those bonds are made, is a matter of time and place. Singer calls these attachments relational because of the different relations that we all have with people or institutions in society. When prompted, Singer states, "This is where I go beyond Hirschi's social control theory, and explicitly state that affluent communities are better prepared to provide these relational attachments, particularly in positional form." Along with the new focus on rural criminology, Singer and others are pushing toward a suburban criminology as well.

One approach to combine the insights from several control perspectives comes from Swedish criminologist Per-Olof Wikström. His theory of criminal behavior combines insight from individual (e.g., levels of self-control) as well as contextual (e.g., morality of the immediate environment) factors. Appropriately, Wikström calls his perspective Situational Action Theory (SAT). SAT first and foremost views crime as the violation of a moral rule. A theory of action is important for Wikström in that it allows the researcher to understand the causal mechanisms of the environment that brings the individual to action.[21]

SAT begins on the premise that beliefs and morals vary across individuals. Some people are selfish and impulsive while others are sympathetic and rational. These individuals will have different likelihoods of engaging in crime. However, the setting those individuals are in is also important. A person, even one with low self-control, may choose not to engage in crime in a setting of high morality such as a church or elementary school. Settings can also have strong deterrent qualities. If a person is consistently in a context that has strong deterrents (say, video cameras or armed security guards), these environments will prohibit criminal activity and make crime an unlikely course of action. The immediate environment can promote crime as an alternative action when it is of low morality or low in deterrents (such as unlit parks, street corners, and seedy nightclubs). In essence, SAT argues that crime is a *choice* and that choice is guided by individual characteristics and the environments to which people are exposed. A theory must account for both to have a true conceptualization of the causal mechanisms in the choice to engage in criminal activity.

At this point, readers may be confused or wondering whether there is a relationship between social bonds and self-control. According to Travis Hirschi, the answer is yes. He was critical early on of self-control, or internal controls, and favored social control. This was clearly evident in his 1969 study. So what happened?

In 2004, Hirschi offered his perspective on the relationship between self- and social control in the *Handbook of self-regulation*. In this publication, he makes clear that he views social bonds, particularly those to parents, as *leading* to the development of self-control. Having self-control *is* the bond to society and represents the bond one carries throughout one's daily activities.[22] This echoes much of the work in *General theory of crime* but is framed using his social bonding approach.

More recently, another Travis has chimed in on the subject of self-control. Criminologist Travis Pratt has attempted to integrate self-control theory into a life-course framework. This may seem impossible in light of the original theory, but Pratt makes a convincing argument. The two *can* be integrated when self-control is viewed as dynamic and changing over time and self-control is examined as a cause of selection into significant life events. He clarifies his position by introducing ten propositions for the new self-control model: (1) self-control predicts problem behavior across the life-course; (2) self-control varies across individuals over time; (3) self-control increases after the peak crime years; (4) self-control predicts selection into negative life events; (5) self-control impacts coping strategies following negative life events; (6) self-control links neuropsychological deficits with early-onset offending; (7) self-control influences sensitivity to the maturity gap; (8) self-control influences sensitivity to informal and formal social control across the life-course; (9) self-control predicts selection into social ties and turning points across time; and (10) self-control influences the quality of social ties across the life-course.[23]

There is some work to be done on this model if it is to be evaluated. Pratt clues me in on how this may be possible.

> In terms of thinking about self-control, the first thing we need to do is just get comfortable with the reality that self-control is dynamic and fluid within individuals. Among social and behavioral scientists who study self-control, only criminologists whose reading on self-control has been confined to Gottfredson and Hirschi still cling to the idea of stability.

I tend to agree with his sentiment here. He continues,

> Pretty much everybody else is cool with the idea that self-control is malleable over the life course. And in terms of future studies, in addition to longitudinal work that extends into later stages of the life course, I think that experimental work on self-control and self-control depletion is likely to prove most useful in the next decade or so.[24]

His last point is a good one; as other researchers have implied,[25] self-control may be like a muscle, usable for a little while but tiring out after being used. Thus, self-control may even fluctuate in the short term. This is surely relevant to antisocial behavior, but, as of yet, it is understudied.

The case of Randy Kraft: the successful serial killer

Randy Kraft had a normal childhood. He grew up in a quiet town in Southern California. His childhood home overlooked strawberry fields in a rural area outside of Orange County. Both of his parents were hardworking individuals who both made time to spend bowling with him as well as his three older sisters. All in all, Randy grew up as a normal child in a normal family.[26]

Randy was also very smart. He was placed in accelerated classes in high school and went on to obtain a degree in economics at a prestigious liberal arts college. With an IQ of 129, he fit in very well at his job after college as a computer consultant. He was meticulous, forward thinking, and gregarious. Randy certainly had self-control.

Randy also had a strong penchant to kill. Between September 1971 and May 1983 he murdered 64 people (at least); mostly by strangulation, but sometimes by shooting them. Like in his other life as a computer consultant, he was meticulous and careful. He would spend time with his victims, often over a drink, and then drug them before torturing them, raping them, and ultimately killing them. He would then dump his victims out of his car on the freeway, leading to Randy becoming known as "The Freeway Killer." He kept a detailed "ledger" of his victims which provided police with a clear starting point for investigating, prosecuting, and locking him up in San Quentin prison while awaiting execution.

Randy made, unfortunately, a very effective serial killer; but he is the exception that proves the rule. Most murderers are impulsive, lacking much self-control. This is one reason that murderers usually only kill once. They are often sloppy, do not carefully plan their attacks, and do not anticipate the responses to their actions. Randy did. He carefully planned every murder. Research by Adrian Raine and his colleagues shows that "successful" psychopaths have heightened executive control when compared to "unsuccessful" psychopaths. In fact, successful psychopaths tend to have greater executive functioning than do members of the general public.[27]

The case of Randy Kraft is very unusual. This chapter documented the prominent role of low self-control in antisocial behavior and the protective functions of high self-control and executive functioning against several negative life outcomes. However, self-control, as Randy shows, can make someone an effective and "successful" criminal or psychopath. This points to the interesting and counter-intuitive nature of self-control and behavior. It also highlights another important issue. If Randy had high self-control, what other factors were responsible for his awful behavior? It is likely that a multitude of biological, psychological, and sociological variables came together to influence Randy's behavior and it is the job of developmental and biosocial criminology to explore these possibilities (these will be discussed in Chapters 10 and 11, respectively).

Empirical support

Social bonding/social control and self-control theories have received a considerable amount of empirical support across the past half-century or more. An early review of Hirschi's social bonding theory was conducted by Kimberly Kempf in 1993. Her review may be summed up by a quote she uses from Albert Cohen stating that social control theory is "fertile but not yet fecund."[28] She saw promise in the basic tenets of the theory but wondered about its ability to generalize across social categories, including biological sex. Others have answered that call, at least in part, and conducted studies since Kempf's original work. Based on the results of a meta-analysis of 74 published and unpublished manuscripts of over 55,000 individuals, Hoeve and his colleagues found that poor attachment to parents was significantly linked to delinquency in male and female adolescents. The size of the effect of parenting on delinquency was moderate across the studies under examination.[29]

In 2000, a meta-analysis was released evaluating the efficacy of self-control theory in explaining criminal behavior. This analysis revealed that self-control is a strong predictor of crime and delinquency regardless of the specific operationalization/measurement of the concept. Further, self-control is robust across various types of samples and over time. However, self-control does not mediate or account for all crime, as other types of theories, such as social learning theory, also receive support.

Other pieces of evidence lend some support to various aspects of self-control theory. For example, evidence supports the idea that self-control is not dependent on age,[30] accounts for crime for both boys and girls,[31] and explains antisocial behavior across race and ethnicity.[32] However, there is now little support for the idea that self-control does not change over a person's life-course.[33] Moreover, self-control does not appear to emerge only from parental socialization but from a host of other biological[34] and social sources.[35]

Hirschi's revised concept and scale of self-control has also been evaluated. One study, conducted by Michael Rocque, Gregory Zimmerman, and myself examined the psychometric properties of Hirschi's new measure (basically investigating how good a measure the new conceptualization is) as well as how well it explains crime compared to past measures. We found that his new conceptualization was theoretically and psychometrically sound, but it did not outperform the most common measure of the construct of self-control (the Grasmick et al. (1993) scale).[36] Overall, self-control can be measured in multiple ways and is a robust predictor of crime. Theoretical research in this area still needs to work out the best conceptualization and measure of self-control.

Remaining questions

Despite a lot of work being done exploring the measurement, properties, and theoretical value of social and self-control, there is much still to learn. I have thought about these issues again with Michael Rocque along with criminologist Alex Piquero in a recent book chapter for the volume that first published Travis Hirschi's reconceptualization of self-control in 2004: *The handbook of self-regulation.*[37] First, there is still no consensus on how to best measure social bonds (as evidenced by Matsueda and Costello's work mentioned earlier) as well as self-control. Some studies have used attitudinal measures[38] while others have used behavior-based measures.[39] Still, Hirschi himself has argued for a new measure of self-control that appears to be "bond-based" as opposed to purely self-control.[40]

Social control theories assume that the motivations for crime are everywhere and that everyone is predisposed to act antisocially if it is in their best interest. Therefore, they have not had much to say on how *opportunity* for crime plays a part in the explanation of the type and extent of criminal behavior – yet this would appear to be an important component of the theory. Some studies, like the previously mentioned article by Grasmick and colleagues, as well as the one by Tittle, Ward, and Grasmick, include measures of opportunity to commit crime, but there is still very little known as to how it impacts the commission of criminal behavior.[41]

Finally, social control theories (and particularly self-control) are known to be highly correlated with delinquent and criminal behavior, but it is still out for questioning whether or not the theory is completely general – accounting for all crime at all times – and whether self-control is the most important factor in explaining criminal behavior, or whether it is just one theory among many that influences certain behavior. Some of the previous literature in this chapter has tried to address these issues, but the evidence remains mixed. Theory testing does not seem to be on the downswing and perhaps many of these issues will have answers (or at least consensus) in the next couple of decades.

Policy

Policies are rarely explicit about which theoretical framework they use to base their efforts (and usually don't use any!) and control theory tends not to be an orientation that influences policy directly; rather, a few programs incorporate the lessons from control theories. In the past several decades, some communities have attempted to establish a Police Athletic League (PAL). One site in Baltimore has led the way. They state:

> A cornerstone of PAL programs is the active participation of Baltimore City Police officers who serve as role models, mentors, and caring adults for young people. With a combined focus on character development, academic enrichment, arts and cultural activities, and athletics, Baltimore PAL is distinct from many other youth programs.[42]

It is evident that this program borrows from social control theory by establishing bonds between youth, police, and the community, and engaging at-risk youth in productive activities.

One of the most popular programs in America is the Drug Abuse Resistance Education program (DARE). DARE of America states,

> D.A.R.E. is a comprehensive K-12 education program taught in thousands of schools in America and 52 other countries. D.A.R.E. curricula address drugs, violence, bullying, internet safety, and other high risk circumstances that today are too often a part of students' lives.[43]

While not explicit in the mission statement or literature, DARE is predicated on the bonds that students form with law enforcement, their peers, and teachers to steer clear of drugs and violent behavior. Unfortunately, the effects of the DARE program show very little impact upon actual drug use and attitudes toward drugs and alcohol.[44]

Similarly, the Gang Resistance Education and Training (GREAT) program seeks to establish societal bonds in order to provide children with resources and knowledge to avoid gangs and delinquent groups. As with DARE, a uniformed police officer delivers the program to students during school hours. Unlike DARE, the GREAT program established more empirical support.[45] However, the effects of the program are fairly small and the cost–benefit of the program is still in question.

As much as bonding and self-control perspectives can inform what *to do*, they also inform as to what *not to do*. In particular, harsh penalties such as mandatory minimum sentences do little to address the true causes of crime which are lack of parental bonding and the under-development of self-control. In addition, along with selective incapacitation (identifying chronic offenders for long prison terms), these policies ignore the observation that almost everyone ages out of crime. As Gottfredson and Hirschi note, by the time the criminal justice system finds and prosecutes chronic offenders, they are already decreasing their involvement in crime and will shortly desist from crime altogether. Therefore, policies, and research, that attempt to identify career criminals and trajectories are unproductive and a waste of money.[46]

Summary

Following the introduction of differential association and social learning perspectives in criminology, social control theories slipped in to dominate the landscape of behavioral theory. While social learning theories assumed that people were mostly born as "blank slates" which society could shape into the people they wanted to become, social-control theories flipped this around. They assumed that people are born with innate tendencies such as the drive to pursue pleasure and avoid pain. Thus, in order to mold behavior, natural impulses must be controlled to promote positive, pro-social behaviors.

Theoretical and empirical work on social control perspectives blossomed in the 1950s as academics such as Reiss, Reckless, Nye, and Toby fleshed out and tested the idea that people with bonds and stakes in conformity are more likely to refrain from crime than those who do not feel connected to society. Those individuals who develop strong internal and external controls were shown to be insulated from crime while those with low self-regulation and poor self-identity were shown to engage in antisocial behavior.

Subsequently, in the late 1960s and early 1970s, the work of Travis Hirschi brought the control perspective to criminology. He was responsible for formalizing the control approach by focusing on bonding to parents and society. Following this earlier work, he paired up with Michael Gottfredson to establish the self-control perspective which is currently one of the most popular and empirically supported theories of crime and antisocial behavior. Today, control theories continue to be refined as theorists debate the best ways to conceptualize and measure social and self-control. Control theories are also being integrated with other types of theories, including those from biosocial criminology, deterrence theory, and rational choice theories.

Notes

1 Reiss, 1951.
2 Reiss, 1951: 201.
3 Reiss, 1951: 203.
4 Huff & Scarpitti, 2011.
5 Reckless, Dinitz, & Murray, 1956.
6 Reckless, Dinitz, & Murray, 1956: 744.
7 Reckless, Dinitz, & Murray, 1956: 745.
8 See Rocque, Posick, & Paternoster, 2016.

9 Nye & Short, 1957.
10 Nye, 1958.
11 Sykes & Matza, 1957.
12 See Hirschi, 2011.
13 Gottfredson & Hirschi, 1990: 15.
14 Hirschi firmly believed that social-control theories were compatible with rational choice theories. See Hirschi, 1986.
15 Gottfredson & Hirschi, 1990: 90.
16 Tittle, 1995.
17 Matsueda, 1982.
18 Costello & Vowell, 1999.
19 Singer, 2014.
20 Personal interview with Simon Singer, January 29, 2016.
21 Wikström, 2006.
22 Hirschi, 2004.
23 Pratt, 2016.
24 Personal interview with Travis Pratt, February 28, 2016.
25 Muraven & Baumeister, 2000.
26 The story of Randy Kraft comes from Adrian Raine's *Anatomy of violence* – see esp. pp. 61–64.
27 Ishikawa et al., 2001.
28 Kempf, 1993: 144.
29 Hoeve et al., 2012.
30 Tittle, Ward, & Grasmick, 2003.
31 LaGrange & Silverman, 1999.
32 Vazsonyi & Crosswhite, 2004.
33 Burt, Simons, & Simons, 2006; Hay & Forrest, 2006.
34 Beaver et al., 2008, 2009b.
35 Botchkovar et al., 2015.
36 Rocque, Posick, & Zimmerman, 2013; Grasmick et al., 1993.
37 Rocque, Posick, & Piquero, 2016.
38 Grasmick et al., 1993.
39 Tittle, Ward, & Grasmick, 2003.
40 Hirschi, 2004.
41 Grasmick et al., 1993; Simpson & Geis, 2008; Tittle, Ward, & Grasmick, 2003.
42 Subhas & Chandra, 2004: i.
43 Obtained from www.dare.com/.
44 Ennett et al., 1994; Rosenbaum et al., 1994.
45 Esbensen & Osgood, 1999; Esbensen et al., 2001.
46 Gottfredson & Hirschi, 1986.

Further reading

Black, D. (1984). *Toward a general theory of social control: Fundamentals*. Cambridge, MA: Academic Press.
Hay, C. & Meldrum, R. (2015). *Self-control and crime over the life course*. Thousand Oaks, CA: Sage.
Hirschi, T. (2011). *The craft of criminology: Selected papers*. New Brunswick, NJ: Transaction Publishers.
Matza, D. (1967). *Delinquency and drift*. New Brunswick, NJ: Transaction Publishers.
Tittle, C. R. (1995). *Control balance: Toward a general theory of deviance*. Boulder, CO: Westview Press.

9 Deterrence and rational choice theories

Introduction	106
Theory	107
Origins	107
Recent developments	110
The case of John Snow's old maps and new models of policing	114
Empirical support	115
Remaining questions	117
Policy	117
Summary	118

Introduction

Take a minute to recall all the way back to Chapter 2 and early theories of criminal behavior which invoked the power of evil forces to control one's actions. These theories dominated the explanation of crime up until the Enlightenment in the mid-1700s. While many Enlightenment ideas and thinkers challenged the theologically oriented theories, one man's work (which was likely the work of many men) changed the way in which society viewed criminal behavior. This man, Cesare Beccaria, is usually given the honor of being the "Father of Criminology." His famous *An essay on crimes and punishments* changed not only the way we view criminal behavior, but the way we respond to it as well.

Drawing upon several theorists before him along with contemporary thinkers of the time, Beccaria brought forth "classical theory" which argued, much like Francis

Hutcheson and Montesquieu before him and along with his contemporary Jeremy Bentham, that individuals are rational beings who are first and foremost concerned with their own well-being.[1] Human beings try to "maximize their pleasure and minimize their pain" as Bentham argued. Given that crime is an easy way to get what you want, it is often the preferred strategy to reach goals. That is, however, unless society increases the pains and reduces the rewards associated with criminal behaviors. This is the idea behind deterrence theory. People will be deterred from their natural impulses to commit crime if society steps in and makes the acts risky and simply not "worth it."

Rational choice and deterrent strategies dominated the theorizing about behavior until the Italian School when they lost a bit of favor. However, there has been a resurgence of classical ideas and of deterrence theory. Theorists such as Mark Stafford and Mark Warr have revised classical theory to incorporate the influence of punishment as well as avoiding punishment, while others, more recently, such as Raymond Paternoster and Shawn Bushway, rest their work on desistance upon a foundation of human rationality. This chapter discusses the development of rational choice and deterrence theoies from their inception during the Enlightenment through the present day.

Theory

Classical theory argues that the causes of behavior are natural – not supernatural. They arise for very practical reasons. Due to people being self-interested, they will often do things that harm others because this gets them what they want. However, no one wants to be the brunt of an attack or theft. Therefore, being rational creatures, people have given up some of their freedom to be protected by the state. Thomas Hobbes called this informal agreement the "social contract." If one breaks the contract, one must be punished.[2] In this way, classical theory is also an explanation of the criminal justice system. If people are rational, which classical theory says they are, then people can be deterred from harming one another using the strategies implicit in deterrence theory (newer theories in this vein are often called neoclassical theory, as they rely on this classical notion of human behavior). To be a deterrent, the criminal justice system must be sure to catch offenders, swiftly punish people who harm others, and ensure that the punishment is severe enough to outweigh the benefits of crime. This is the crux of Beccaria's "certain, swift, and severe" mantra.[3]

Origins

The history of the Enlightenment period (and the years just prior and after) is very rich, as are the ideas and thoughts that emerged from this time. It was not only a time of great intellectual development but a period of great social change across the globe. Although the crux of action occurred in Europe, there were widespread effects of Enlightenment ideas all across the world, and particularly in the United States.

Pertinent to criminology, an Irish Reverend, Francis Hutcheson (1694–1746), wrote widely immediately prior to the emergence of the Enlightenment period.[4] He was influenced by John Locke and, in turn, inspired the writings of other popular philosophers, including Adam Smith (his student) and David Hume. Hutcheson believed that man (i.e., human beings) has many senses, including a sense of beauty, a public sense, a sense of honor, and so on. Among these is a moral sense. The moral sense opposes innate self-interest (this is akin to social-control theories and why many see these two theories as very compatible). If developed, the moral sense can out-battle the self-interest of an individual. Importantly, this meant a few things to Hutcheson. First, one may be deterred from committing crime by building or appealing to the moral sense. Second, harsh punishment is unlikely to deter crime because it does not appeal to the moral sense. Third, punishment should be carefully calibrated such that it is not overly abusive but appeals to the morals of the individual and can outweigh self-interest. In many ways these ideas set the stage for other Enlightenment thinkers to expand upon the nature of man and the ways to control poor behavior.

Meanwhile, in France, Charles-Louis de Secondat, Baron de La Brède et de Montesquieu (1689–1755), was a contemporary of Hutcheson with similar ideas. It is probably not surprising that this philosopher simply went by the name of Montesquieu. In any case, Montesquieu grew up in a noble family in Bordeaux, France and attended the University at Bordeaux. After receiving a degree from the university – a law degree – he served as a local magistrate (i.e., judge). As a magistrate, he saw many things he considered wrong with the criminal justice system; he felt obligated to share these with others and he sought to implement strategies to improve the system.

Like his predecessors and contemporaries, Montesquieu had many reservations about harsh punishment. He was a critic of harsh punishment and an advocate of fair punishment which he equated with "advanced" societies (only animals and uncivilized beings would torture and kill). Specifically during this period, he was appalled by the prosecution of witches and those who were accused of witchcraft (see Chapter 2). Montesquieu believed that there was not enough evidence to charge people with witchcraft and that, if convicted, the punishment should flow from the crime – which, in many cases, was no crime at all.[5] In this way, Montesquieu argued that any punishment should be equivalent to the crime. Taken together, Montesquieu brought two major ideologies to law and punishment: rationality and proportionality. These two concepts would follow through the years of the Enlightenment and continue to direct criminal justice efforts today.

The work of Hutcheson and Montesquieu led into the ideas of the individual who is often dubbed the founder of criminal justice/criminology: Cesare Beccaria. Beccaria was born in Lombardy, Italy in 1738 and died in 1794. He attended the University of Pavia as well as the Jesuit School of Parma, both located in Italy. During this time he particularly noted the involvement of the church in policy-making and was dismayed at the intrusion of the church into the political process. He ardently believed that the two should be kept separate (as did the Founding Fathers of the US constitution and many others who borrowed from Beccaria's ideas). Interestingly, he fell in love and married a "lower-class girl" which was frowned upon by his family and community. This stoked the fire within Beccaria, leading him to challenge the aristocracy and form ideals contrary to their expectations. Perhaps without this history, not only would criminology and criminal justice look very different today, but so would the rest of civilization.[6]

Much of Beccaria's involvement in scholarly pursuits was through the Academy of Fists, an organization that fought against the church and bureaucracy which he joined with his fellow Italian colleague Pietro Verri (who would eventually call Beccaria lazy). During his time with the Academy, Beccaria wrote a scathing review of the current justice system and what he saw as a corrupt and ineffective justice process. In *On crimes and punishment*, published in 1764, he offered a sweeping reconsideration of the role of law and punishment in society.[7] Here, he consolidated the thoughts of others such as Helvetius's rational society, Hobbes's social contract, and Hume's association of ideas to construct what he saw as the appropriate response to crime. The social milieu was already primed by Hutcheson and Montesquieu and his ideas took off.

The crux of Beccaria's philosophy of law and punishment was that it should be "certain, swift, and severe." To him, if punishments were to be effective they had to be certain. If the chance of getting caught and punished for committing a crime was low, then it really did not matter if the law proscribed a harsh sentence. Second, we are rational beings and learn from getting punished for behaving poorly. If the law was too slow, and did not swiftly punish someone for committing a crime, they would not connect the punishment to the crime; therefore, they would not learn to stop such behavior in the future. Finally, also because we are rational beings, the punishment for a crime had to be sufficiently severe to outweigh the benefits of committing a crime. If the punishment was weak (what people often call a "slap on the wrist") there would be no reason to stop doing the crime if its benefits outweighed the punishment. However, he was a staunch critic of overly harsh punishment (as were his predecessors), including the death penalty. For Beccaria, overly harsh punishment would cripple society and lead to societal backlash. Thus, sentences must be proportional (fit) to the crime.

A somewhat parallel story may be found in one of Beccaria's contemporaries: Jeremy Bentham (1748–1832). Bentham was influenced by many of the same philosophers as Beccaria, especially Helvetius who discussed the rational society and Adam Smith who formulated the basis for rational choice and also theorized about the behavior of rational beings (Figure 9.1). Bentham himself used some of Beccaria's ideas in his own "hedonistic calculus" which he outlined in *The principles of morals and legislation* published in 1789.[8] For Bentham, people weighed the costs and benefits of engaging in particular behavior. After calculating each, the person would act in a way that maximized pleasure and minimized pain (often known as the pleasure–pain principle). He also noted that everyone does this calculus – even madmen. For him, even the seemingly irrational criminal or psychopath was a calculating creature.

Interestingly, like Beccaria, Bentham fell in love with a woman from the lower class. He, too, was shunned. In his case, at his father's request, he left the relationship and never entered into another one for the rest of his life. He was an unusual man who didn't like to engage in any irrational behavior (such as drinking or lying in bed without sleeping). Upon his death, at his request, he was mummified and placed in the University College of London. He wanted his friends to meet with his body periodically to "discuss utilitarianism."

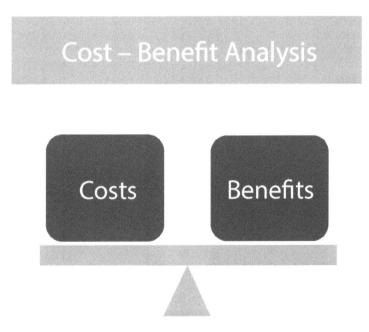

Figure 9.1 Rational choice framework

Source: Clarke & Cornish (1985).

Recent developments

While elements of rational choice, utilitarianism, and hedonistic calculus appeared in theories throughout the following centuries, some theories stressed these factors more clearly than others and there has even been a resurgence of rational choice theories in the past several decades. Along the way, in 1968, economist Gary Becker wrote a piece on the economic aspects of illegal behavior, hoping to spark a new flame for rational choice theories. He stated,

> Beccaria and Bentham, explicitly applied an economic calculus. Unfortunately, such an approach has lost favor during the last hundred years, and my efforts can be viewed as a resurrection, modernization, and thereby I hope improvement, of these much earlier pioneering studies.[9]

Becker believed that crime, like any behavior, is an economic decision that takes into account the probability of apprehension and the probability of conviction. Further, the criminal justice response is also based on economic principles which take into account available resources and their allocation, as well as the calibration of punishment to get the most "bang for the buck." Becker quantified the economic calculus through an equation that weighed costs and benefits, and others have added to his equation, so that the probability of committing a crime given specific costs and benefits could be calculated.

This type of calculation has been challenged by many scholars. Two in particular are Willem de Haan and Jaco Vos from the Netherlands. Using personal accounts from street robbers, de Haan and Vos challenge the notion that criminals are rational. In fact, they point to several aspects that seem to contradict the rational choice perspective. They found that street robbers were impulsive (not thinking about their crime at all) and driven by emotional factors that really did not allow for the cold calculations that are implicit in the rational choice model. These scholars argue for a more effective approach to explaining crime that accounts for the emotional forced behind criminal behavior.[10]

Rational choice is a theory in its own right, but it also informs other theories. Many theories implicitly incorporate ideas of a rational criminal into their framework for explaining criminal behavior. Two of these theories are lifestyles theory and routine activity theory. Both suggest that offenders are rational and are motivated to commit a crime whenever the benefits outweigh the costs. Lifestyle theory tends to look at the behavior of those who become the victims of a criminal incident, while routine activity theory examines the criminal event and how individual and situational factors merge to make crime more likely.

In their 1978 book *Victims of personal crime: An empirical foundation for a theory of personal victimization,* Hindelang, Gottfredson, and Garafalo discuss a theory of victimization that is rooted in rational choice and deterrence which they refer to as lifestyle–exposure theory. They believe that the motivations for crime are natural and that anyone, when presented with ample opportunity, will commit crime and it is the lifestyles that people lead that bring them into contact with risky people and situations that increase their exposure to victimization.[11]

The authors evaluated their theory using the National Crime Survey (NCS) which provided data from 1972 and 1974. This is one of the first major theories developed from self-reported crime and victimization data. They found that victimization varies across people and demographic groups, and that the reason for this is that lifestyles also vary across people and groups. Lifestyles, they state, are "routine daily activities both vocational and leisure activities."[12] Certain lifestyles insulate one from exposure to violence, such as going to school, going to work, and spending time with family, while others, such as going to clubs and hanging around with delinquent peers, will increase exposure to victimization.

Building on lifestyles theory, and using very similar terms, routine activity theory was developed by Cohen and Felson in 1979 to explain the circumstances of criminal victimization following World War II. Specifically, they wanted to explain the increase in the crime rate between 1947 and 1974 in the United States. They define routine activity as "any recurrent and prevalent activities which provide for basic population and individual needs, whatever their biological or cultural origin."[13] Following World War II, they noted some major changes to routine activity, such as more women entering the workforce, leaving homes unoccupied, and more women coming into contact with other people. These changes, they argued, influenced crime rates. In addition, they wanted to respond to economic theories which assumed that when the economy is great, crime goes down. Yet, in the 1960s, the economy was booming and so was crime. Routine activity theory was their solution to that paradox.

Central to their thesis is the convergence of three factors necessary for the commission of crime, including: (1) a motivated offender; (2) a suitable target; and (3) the absence of capable guardianship. A motivated offender refers to any individual who wants to commit a crime. This is left relatively unexplored by routine activity theorists, since they contend that motivated offenders exist everywhere and criminal motivation is constant (again this is the rational criminal actor approach). Instead, the theory focuses on opportunity to commit crime.

Opportunity for crime includes the second element of routine activity theory: that of a suitable target (Figure 9.2). A suitable target may be either an item or an individual viewed as attractive to motivated offenders. Researchers have examined what they call

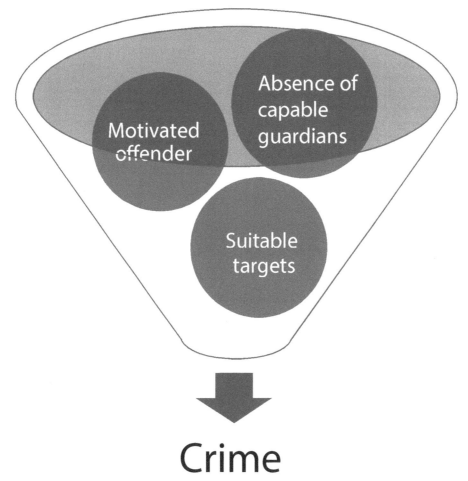

Figure 9.2 Routine activity theory (RAT) framework

Source: Cohen & Felson (1979).

target suitability, especially in terms of items and not people, by evaluating the target's Value, Inertia, Visibility, and Accessibility, known as VIVA. Others have recently added more elements, such as Concealable, Removable, Valuable, Enjoyable, and Disposable or CRAVED.[14] Essentially, the smaller, more valuable, and more accessible a target is, the more likely it will be stolen or victimized.

The final element of Cohen and Felson's routine activity theory is capable guardianship. Guardianship refers to the informal and formal controls that are present at a specific spot to monitor people and property. Formal guardians include specific people like police and security guards and protective systems like cameras and alarms. Informal guardianship is more common than formal guardianship and includes neighborhood citizens who look out for one another during the course of their daily lives. By increasing guardianship, one can lower the chances of being victimized.

Routine Activity Theory (RAT) which focuses on large-scale, macro-level factors, and lifestyles theory which focuses on individual factors and behaviors, offer two related but distinct theories couched in the rational choice/deterrence literature. Later, in 1981, Cohen teamed up with James Kluegel and Kenneth Land to develop an integrated theory that combined insight from both Lifestyle and Routine Activities Theory (LRAT). They rely on four concepts, including: (1) exposure to crime; (2) proximity to crime; (3) target attractiveness; and (4) guardianship. Together, these factors help explain an individual's propensity for and exposure to victimization.[15]

First, according to Cohen, Kluegel, and Land, exposure is "physical visibility and accessibility of persons or objects to potential offenders at any given time or place."[16] Borrowing from lifestyles theory, LRAT argues that individuals put themselves into harm's way by getting into risky situations, which leads to the potential to be victimized. Proximity, they state, is where people live most of their lives and how close they are to large numbers of people who are potential offenders.

Target attractiveness, the third component in Cohen, Kluegel, and Land's theory, is defined as the desirability of a person or object for the potential offender. For example, a homeless person is not an attractive target for robbery given that they likely do not have many material possessions to steal. A wealthy businessman stumbling out of a bar drunk at 2 a.m. would be a much more attractive target. Likewise, a first-generation iPod is a much less attractive target than a brand-new smartphone that is half the size but has 100 times the capabilities. Finally, the fourth element, guardianship, is borrowed from the original routine activity framework. They do, however, pay more attention to homogamy. Homogamy suggests that people with similar personalities and interests will likely associate with one another. If an individual shares common factors with offenders, it is more likely that they will associate with offenders. Thus, homogamy increases exposure to potential offenders which, in turn, increases the risk of being victimized.

Classical rational choice theory, as envisioned by Jeremy Bentham and others, was quite simple: people seek to maximize their pleasure and minimize their pain. If crime gets people what they want, and it doesn't cost them very much (or at least not as much as they gain), then it makes perfect sense that people would commit crime in that situation. This "hedonistic calculus" – what Bentham saw as a calculation conducted by individuals when deciding what course of action to take – relied on a simple view of cost–benefit. Today, theorists have been expanding this view and incorporating a wide range of costs and benefits as well as different "calculations" behind the decision to offend or not to offend.

Most deterrence theories up until the 1980s focused on general and specific deterrence. In other words, how do laws and punishments deter crime by making it uncomfortable for the person being punished (specific deterrence) and by signaling to others what can happen if you commit crime (general deterrence)? With all the attention on experiencing punishment, there was little attention on *avoiding* punishment.

This changed in the 1990s with the work of Mark Stafford and Mark Warr. First, Stafford and Warr believed that the distinction between specific and general deterrence was not theoretically useful, as the same people experience both. However, more useful is the distinction between experiencing punishment and avoiding punishment. Like specific and general deterrence, there could be specific and general experience with punishment avoidance which would figure into the calculus of committing crime. For example, if someone gets caught one out of every 100 times they commit a crime, their direct experience with avoiding punishment will likely influence them in continuing to commit crime. As well, if a person sees that others keep avoiding punishment and hardly ever get caught, they may be more likely to engage in crime themselves. This reconceptualization of deterrence strengthened the theoretical approach in the early 1990s and set the stage for later deterrence theorizing.[17]

Along similar lines to Stafford and Warr, criminologist Bruce Jacobs saw a major gap in deterrence research and sought to fill it with an additional component of the theory. For Jacobs, deterrence theory is overly focused on specific and general deterrence on a large, macro scale which ignores the more micro-level feature of deterrability. For example, in order to come up with effective strategies for punishment, one must know how would-be offenders perform their "calculus" of costs and benefits as well as how deterrable someone is.[18] Offenders high in psychopathy are very hard to deter because they do not learn from their punishment. Similarly, older offenders who are hardened and recalcitrant are not likely to be easily deterred whereas younger, more malleable youth are more likely to be influenced by punishment. Jacobs suggests that more research needs to be done in this area for deterrence research to be truly effective in reducing crime.

Most recently, Albany criminologist Justin Pickett, along with colleagues Sean Roche and Greg Pogarsky, presented an emotion-based theory of deterrence. This is a start to addressing some of the concerns of both de Haan and Vos, and Jacobs, who all agree that there is some emotive aspect to criminal behavior. Beginning with the premise that early deterrence theorists assumed that there was an emotional reaction (fear) to the prospect of being punished, these criminologists sought to expand upon the emotional factors implicated in deterrence research. Since fear is important for deterrence theory – a person is unlikely to think twice about committing a crime if they just don't care or don't fear getting into trouble – whether and in what ways people fear the consequences of violating the law is important. In addition, people are not uniformly fearful of formal sanctions[19] and, in fact, individuals with a low resting heart rate[20] are more likely to become involved in crime, possibly because of their low level of fear (since they do not become aroused by the prospect of getting caught) of the consequences of their actions.

Pickett and colleagues examine five major components that take deterrence theory to a new level. First, fear is different from cognitive appraisal of the chance of getting caught (e.g., "I might get caught, but who cares"). Second, perceptions of getting caught should predict levels of fear. Third, perceptions of the risk of sanctions should mediate situational signals and fear of apprehension. Fourth, fear of apprehension should have a larger effect on criminal decision-making than perceived sanction risk. And fifth, perceived sanction risk should have an indirect effect on criminal decision-making through fear of apprehension.

The results of their own study of the theory provided strong evidence that perceived risk and fear of apprehension are distinct concepts, and both are important for understanding criminal decision-making. Perceived apprehension risk was positively related to fear of apprehension, and background factors do impact fear but through generalized perceived risk. Further, fear mediates the effects of perceived apprehension risk on criminal decision-making and is the strongest predictor of situational intentions to offend. Overall, fear appears to be an integral component of deterrence theory, one that has largely been neglected, but which deserves continued examination.

The case of John Snow's old maps and new models of policing

In the mid-1800s, a deadly illness hit Britain. Citizens were falling ill around the city with little explanation as to what was plaguing the city's inhabitants. The illness, later to be called cholera, was infecting citizens at an alarming rate and the medical experts of the time blamed "miasma." A miasma, namely noxious air containing contagions, carried the illness to inhabitants of the city. Miasmas were blamed for many other diseases, including the "black death." One medical expert, Dr. John Snow, had a different opinion. Instead of the miasma, Dr. Snow believed that cholera was spread through drinking water. To prove his theory, he mapped out the city of London and the locations of drinking-water pumps (remember: this is the 1800s). Around the pumps he mapped cases of cholera. He found that cases of cholera clustered around the pumps and became more infrequent the further away from the pump one was. Dr. Snow had mapped "hotspots" of cholera. Not only did he advance the study of cholera, which was, in fact, spread through drinking water, his work also ushered in the field of epidemiology.[21]

In recent decades, criminological researchers have realized that crime acts similarly to contagious diseases in many ways. Spots in neighborhoods can be identified where crime is prevalent. Crime in these "hotspots" spreads like the cholera in 1800s London – hot in the center and slowly decreasing in intensity from the center. Instead of cholera, violence often starts with a street gang or delinquent group, and crime is high around the neighborhoods where the group associates and areas near the hotspot experience elevated crime levels. As one moves further away, crime is seen to decrease precipitously.

Researchers and policy groups that approach crime in this manner look to identify the source of violence, halt the spread of violence, and "treat" those who are impacted by violence. Physician and epidemiologist Gary Slutkin founded Cure Violence – a model for crime that views violence as a public health issue and argues that crime should be approached as such. In the Cure Violence model, whole communities are engaged to change how violence is perceived and responded to. Insiders, often street outreach workers who themselves have a past history of violence and/or incarceration, are enlisted to intervene in beefs and conflicts that arise on the streets.[22]

The model promulgated by John Snow and relied upon by contemporary scholars such as Slutkin is intended to offer an approach to reduce crime as well as to increase the reliance and trust in law enforcement. Recent incidents in the United States have led to a crisis of trust in law enforcement – particularly line officers. The distrust in law enforcement has existed in minority communities for decades, if not centuries. The shooting death of Michael Brown, in Ferguson, Missouri, marked a boiling point for police–community relations. On August 9, 2014, Brown, an 18-year-old black man, was shot and killed by Officer Darren Wilson – a 28-year-old white man. While the details are disputed, Brown was unarmed at the time he was shot and, some witnesses say, he had his hands up. Regardless of the details, the community rallied together to protest the poor treatment of the black community by police officers. The Black Lives Matter national movement (perhaps international at this point) was borne out of the Ferguson events and has gained momentum after similar cases involving a black citizen being killed by police officers have plagued the nation.

Coinciding with these tragic events has been an uptick in violent crime in select major cities across the nation – some of which have not seen an increase in several years. Some have argued that the increase in crime is due to the "Ferguson Effect." Perhaps the strongest proponent of the Ferguson Effect, Heather MacDonald, the Thomas W. Smith Fellow at the Manhattan Institute, argues that because the community distrusts the police and is violent toward them, law enforcement has essentially "backed off" enforcing the law in certain neighborhoods, leading to an increase in violent crime. MacDonald published these views in her book, *The war on cops.*

Others, such as criminologists Richard Rosenfeld, Justin Nix, Bradley Campbell, David Pyrooz, and Scott Wolfe, believe that there are alternative answers to the rise in crime in certain areas. First off, not all cities experienced an increase in crime from 2014 to the present day, limiting a general Ferguson Effect that impacts all cities equally. Second, the reasons that crime rates rise and fall are notoriously hard to figure out. Entire volumes and journal issues have been dedicated to this issue, with little agreement. The changes in crime rates are probably the best examples of theoretical debates and disagreement on the theoretical mechanisms behind violent behavior. Generally speaking, for the Ferguson Effect, Heather MacDonald and conservatives stand on one side which believes that the actual violent behavior of these communities is driving crime rates up and that the police are rightfully holding back on enforcement due to a "war on cops." On the other side, many criminologists believe that some version of the Ferguson Effect is likely to be one of many contributors to the rise and fall of crime rates but that the theoretical mechanisms behind the fluctuations are much more nuanced. As an alternative, it may be the loss of legitimacy of law enforcement itself that is the driver of crime increases and the lack of trust of citizens in the police is resulting in less reliance on formal law enforcement in solving crime problems. This echoes the concepts found in theories such as Gary LaFree's Legitimacy Theory[23] and Lawrence Sherman's Defiance Theory.[24] These cases are meant to be a segue into the recent research using deterrence research.

Empirical support

As mentioned previously, routine activities (and modern rational choice theories) were staging a comeback of sorts around the same time that self-report surveys were also gaining traction (as were the control theories mentioned in Chapter 8). This convergence led to the symbiotic relationship between theory and empirical testing. These theories continued to be refined and subjected to more and more testing. First, much of current research shows that the risk of being victimized is increased when individuals live and stay closer to potential offenders.[25] This includes living in disorganized areas with little informal social control. On the flipside, ownership of expensive goods and possession of cash can increase the risk of encountering victimization.[26] This is compounded by the fact that risky neighborhoods face a plethora of challenges, including infant mortality and sexually transmitted diseases, indicating the need for holistic crime prevention programs that can meet the multiple needs of individuals living in these areas.[27]

RAT suggests that individuals who expose themselves to risky environments and people will be more likely to be the victims of violence and/or theft. If you leave your home, go to a party, or just hang out with friends, RAT argues that you have already increased your risk of victimization (however slight it may be). Before you question this, there is good evidence that engaging in normative behaviors such as going out on the weekend, and spending time with family and friends around the holiday, increases the risk of victimization.[28] The cost–benefit is likely in your favor to go ahead and engage in normal social behavior, as routine activities like those just mentioned only marginally increase the risk of criminal behavior (and it is not worth shutting yourself in to never see the light of day only to reduce being victimized when the likelihood of something major going wrong is relatively slight). However, those who engage in risky behaviors, particularly when hanging around those who are involved in delinquent activity or engaging in the behavior themselves, can exponentially increase the chances of being victimized.[29] So go ahead and attend the party, but think twice about becoming involved with people and activities that are particularly risky!

Moving beyond the insights provided by social disorganization, recent efforts to contextualize crime have moved toward examining specific places and the reasons why certain places are more criminogenic than others. Specificity has increased to the point where certain addresses, neighborhood segments, and streets are being identified as being criminogenic. Crime is concentrated within what researchers call "hotspots" and identification of these high crime areas is essential in providing focused prevention/intervention services to affected communities and their members. For example, as few as 3 percent of addresses in Minneapolis, Minnesota produced over 50 percent of calls to the police in a study in the early 2000s.[30] A study in Seattle, Washington similarly found that just 5 percent of street segments produced 50 percent of all crime incidents during a 14 year period.[31] Focusing on these hotspots can have appreciable effects on reducing crime, as evidenced by a recent Campbell Corporation systematic review which revealed that 20 out of 25 hotspot initiatives uncovered significant drops in crime and disorder.[32]

It should be noted that advances in technology have enabled advanced research on crimes within local contexts. Programs like Geographical Information Systems (GIS) and software packages such as those for risk terrain modeling and social network analysis have allowed researchers to fine tune their investigations on neighborhoods and crime. Along with the technological advances, there have also been methodological advances. GIS technology has led researchers to engage in rigorous spatial analysis including risk terrain modeling which combines spatial analysis with multivariate regression analysis.[33] Here, the researcher can examine a host of variables within specific areas such as household income, exposure to lead, and others to identify what factors are related to crime rates with the areas.

The insight provided by RAT which states that people who spend more time in risky environments will be more likely to be victimized holds across several social environments. People who spend more time in the online environment are more likely to be at risk of a computer infection[34] as well as being cyber-stalked than those who limit their time online.[35] Studies have also revealed that spending more time instant messaging is linked to an increase in being the victim of cyberbullying and that capable guardianship in the form of filtering software may prevent some of this type of bullying – but far from all.[36] More time spent on the internet and emailing increases the risk of phishing attacks[37] and being hacked.[38] Time spent in the virtual sphere has only recently been studied empirically, but, given the societal importance of computers and online activity, it is not a far stretch to believe this line of research will continue, especially in criminology.

The level of support for deterrence theory is more mixed. A large-scale meta-analysis found that measurable effects in studies which incorporated variables related to deterrence theory were "modest to negligible" and "much weaker than those found in meta-analyses of the relationship between criminal/deviant behavior and peer effects and self-control."[39] The most supported facet of deterrence theory appears to be the certainty of punishment and much less the severity or swiftness/celerity.

Focused deterrence appears to hold much more promise for reducing crime. To reiterate, focused deterrence concentrates law enforcement on specific populations such as gang members, frequent violent offenders, and drug market offenders. These strategies are found to achieve medium-sized reductions in crime in studies that use rigorous designs including randomized studies.[40] Focusing interventions on specific types of crime also appears to be fairly productive in reducing the targeted offense. For example, law enforcement efforts to deter speeding by increasing the penalties associated with driving above the speed limit have found moderate success.[41]

Overall, the evidence suggests that the most effective parts of deterrence theory are targeted interventions and those that increase the certainty of being caught. There is modest or no support for the severity of punishment which calls into question the efficacy of crime prevention strategies that ignore the certainty of detection in favor of harsh punishments. Increasing reliance on research to guide policy may lead to changes in how society responds to crime which can already be seen with programs such as Swift-Certain-Fair which has received bipartisan political support.[42]

Remaining questions

Researchers are still teasing out the relative contributions of certainty, severity, and celerity (swiftness) to criminal behavior. A premier study on this issue was conducted by criminologists Daniel Nagin and Greg Pogarsky which revealed several important conclusions about deterrent policies. First, certainty and severity predicted offending but celerity did not. Second, extralegal consequences of behavior appear to be about as influential as the legal consequences of behavior. Third, the influence of the severity of sanctions is related to that person's "present orientation," and finally, the certainty of punishment is much more influential than the severity of punishment.[43]

Similarly, and in line with the work of Bruce Jacobs discussed earlier, deterrence may rely on the deterrability of the individual being targeted. We still know little about which types of individuals are more deterrable than others, aside from those who show strong psychopathic traits.[44] It will likely have to be the case, especially if punishment remains the focus of the criminal justice system, that those who are most persuaded by punishment will have to be identified, while those who are recalcitrant may need alternative treatment or just incapacitation.

There is still much to learn about how exactly traits and environmental exposure shape later behavior. This is often called the state dependency vs. population heterogeneity debate. What matters most for individuals? Is it their traits and characteristics (such as their IQ, level of self-control, or level of psychopathy) that contributed to their selecting a certain environment to commit crime and harm others (this would be the population heterogeneity argument which suggests that people's personalities shape their routine activities and their experiences)? Or is it that specific things happen to an individual (say, they are victimized) and those precise experiences shape their later behaviors (i.e., they go on to commit crime)? Evidence remains mixed, but routine activities and the population heterogeneity perspective do appear to play at least some part.[45]

Policy

One of the strengths of the routine activity and deterrence approaches is that they have straightforward policy implications. Not surprisingly, the work around focused deterrence has led to a change in the way in which many departments carry out their law enforcement activities focusing on specific groups as opposed to broad, jurisdiction-wide deterrence strategies.[46] Routine activity theory suggests that policy actors should focus less on the criminal and more on the situation that gives rise to the crime. Therefore, it is the immediate environment that is often manipulated to control crime. The next time you go to a club late at night, see if they give you plastic cups instead of a glass or a beer bottle. This is to reduce injury when the glass is used as a weapon. Or, the next time you go to a sporting event, notice if they stop selling alcohol at some point (usually the seventh inning of baseball games and the second half of football games). This is to reduce drunkenness and driving while intoxicated. Finally, at each of these events, notice "security" – whether they be bouncers, guards, or police. This is an effort to increase supervision at these events. All of these crime prevention techniques are modeled after the insight provided by routine activity theory.

It may not even be debatable at this point that deterrence theory established the role of the criminal justice system in the United States and many other countries across the globe. It has continued to direct most criminal justice policy and practice.[47] While the work of Beccaria, Bentham, and later Enlightenment thinkers drove the penal ideology that punishment should be swift, certain, and proportional to the crime, a strict deterrent and rational approach to dealing with criminals increased in the 1970s following the expansion of civil rights in the 1960s. Some believe that this was a response to increasing crime, but others suggest that the increase was an intentional effort to control specific parts of the population, particularly racial minorities, who were at the time gaining political and civil rights.[48]

In their 1992 publication, Malcolm Feeley and Jonathan Simon describe what they see as "The New Penology." The new penology, they state, "considers the criminal justice *system,* and it pursues systemic rationality and efficiency. It seeks to sort and classify, to separate the less from the more dangerous, and to deploy control strategies rationally."[49] According to the new penology, if offenders are rational then they can be deterred by a rational system – and the most rational and deterrent mechanism of punishment is incarceration. It may be little surprise then that incarceration skyrocketed in the early 1970s, and continued to rise until about 2015.[50]

Recently, during the "Reagan years" in the United States and shortly after in other nations, such as the Netherlands, "tough on crime" legislation led to the enactment of several deterrent policies including mandatory minimums, three-strikes laws, and truth-in-sentencing. Many of these policies had the intention to deter criminals by offsetting the offender "calculus" by increasing costs of crime, making it not worthwhile to engage in bad behavior. However, rather than reduce crime, many of these policies increased the number of those who got caught up in the system and institutionalized them for long periods of time with little rehabilitation. When they returned to society, recidivism was likely. In addition, these policies have resulted in drastically disproportionate effects on minorities (particularly African Americans).[51] This questions the utility and fairness of policies based almost exclusively on a deterrent philosophy.

A deterrent philosophy has infiltrated not only the criminal justice system but also schools. Many scholars have noticed that schools are acting as a gateway into the penal system. Youth at school who "acted up" and were mostly dealt with informally are now being arrested by law enforcement officers in school or being suspended or expelled. These exclusionary policies are found, again, to be biased toward minorities and lead to a host of long-term maladies. This so-called school-to-prison pipeline has been dubbed the "new disciplinology" by some academics.[52]

Summary

The history and development of rational choice and deterrence theory is rich and fascinating. Beginning (mostly) with the Enlightenment period and penetrating modern-day theories, the idea that people choose to engage in behaviors that maximize pleasure and minimize pain is a mainstay in criminological thought. In fact, almost the entirety of the US criminal justice system is based on the principles of rational choice and deterrence, and many countries around the globe have followed suit.

The legacy of theories based in rational choice is complicated. In some ways, rational choice theories (and policies) are a double-edged sword. One edge is the very straightforward theory and policy implications of the theory. If one is to increase the costs of crime and decrease the rewards, crime should go down (and is often shown to do just that). However, the other edge reflects the nefarious side of the theory that has increased harsh punishments, quadrupled the prison population, and has caused severe damage to segments of the population: all this with relatively little impact upon crime rates. Rational choice and deterrence theories may have promise, but this promise appears to lie in specific parts of the theories and when the insights are applied to policy with a specific eye on the potential enormous costs to society.

Fortunately, academics and policy-makers appear to be working together to ensure that empirically based research is guiding public policy. It seems very unlikely that deterrence theory will ever be totally done away with and it probably never should be, given the decades long support that most of the theoretical propositions have received. With increasing interest in the treatment of marginalized groups, the hope is that the theories discussed in this chapter can increasingly become more effective and more just may be realized.

Notes

1 See DiCristina, 2012.
2 Hobbes, 2006 [1651].
3 Beccaria, 2009 [1764].
4 This discussion is largely based on *A system of moral philosophy* by Hutcheson (1755).
5 Montesquieu, 1748.
6 Yar, 2010.
7 Beccaria, 2009 [1764].
8 Bentham, 1988 [1789].
9 Becker, 1968: 45.
10 De Haan & Vos, 2003.
11 Hindelang, Gottfredson, & Garofalo, 1978.
12 Hindelang, Gottfredson, & Garofalo, 1978: 241.
13 Cohen & Felson, 1979: 593.
14 Clarke, 1999.
15 Cohen, Kluegel, & Land, 1981.
16 Cohen, Kluegel, & Land, 1981: 507.
17 Stafford & Warr, 1993.
18 Jacobs, 2010.
19 Raine, 2013.
20 Portnoy & Farrington, 2015.
21 See also Fine et al., 2013.
22 Slutkin, 2013.
23 See LaFree, 1998.
24 See Sherman, 1993.
25 McNeeley, 2015.
26 Sampson & Wooldredge, 1987.
27 Ousey, 2017.
28 McCarthy et al., 2014.
29 Henson et al., 2010; Posick, 2013.
30 Sherman, Gartin, & Buerger, 1989.
31 Weisburd et al., 2004.
32 Braga, Papachristos, & Hureau, 2014.
33 Caplan & Kennedy, 2011.
34 Bossler & Holt, 2009.
35 Welsh & Lavoie, 2012.
36 Navarro & Jasinski, 2012.
37 Hutchings & Hayes, 2008.
38 Xu, Hu, & Zhang, 2013.
39 Pratt et al., 2008: 383.
40 Braga & Weisburd, 2012.
41 Watson et al., 2015.
42 See Kleiman, Kilmer, & Fisher, 2014.
43 Nagin & Pogarsky, 2001.
44 See DeLisi, 2016.

45 Wittebrood & Nieuwbeerta, 2000.
46 Weisburd, Groff, & Yang, 2012.
47 DeKeseredy & Schwartz, 2017.
48 Alexander, 2012.
49 Feeley & Simon, 1992: 452 [emphasis in original].
50 Clear & Frost, 2015.
51 Tonry, 1995.
52 Rocque & Snellings, 2017.

Further reading

Clear, T. R. & Frost, N. A. (2015). *The punishment imperative: The rise and failure of mass incarceration in America*. New York: New York University Press.

Felson, M. & Boba, R. L. (2010). *Crime and everyday life*. Thousand Oaks, CA: Sage.

Jones, D. A. (1986). *History of criminology: A philosophical perspective* (Vol. 82). New York: Greenwood Press.

Tonry, M. (1995). *Malign neglect: Race, crime, and punishment in America*. New York: Oxford University Press.

Welsh, B. C. & Farrington, D. P. (2009). *Making public places safer: Surveillance and crime prevention*. New York: Oxford University Press.

Developmental criminology

10

Introduction	121
Theory	122
Origins	122
Recent developments	123
The case of Stanley "Tookie" Williams, III: from gang leader to children's book author	129
Empirical support	130
Remaining questions	131
Policy	131
Summary	133

Introduction

Many of the theories that have been discussed thus far in this book have dealt with factors, or a set of factors, that increase or decrease involvement in delinquency. Sometimes these factors are additive, accumulating within the individual, or interactive, relying on the effects of other factors. The bulk of these theories explain why a person at any given time may engage in or refrain from delinquent behavior. What has not been discussed in any great detail up until this point is how these factors change, or remain the same, across someone's lifespan. The contexts that people find themselves in change over time and so do individuals themselves – at least to some extent. Developmental theories seek to investigate involvement in delinquency across someone's life or "life-course."

Importantly, these theories suggest that while some things change and some things stay the same over a person's life, the relative importance of certain social and biological factors waxes and wanes across the life-course. According to this notion, it is important to uncover the individual and societal factors that matter in causing behavior and establish the developmental stage during which they are most important. In addition, it is imperative that crime prevention and intervention capitalize on the dynamic nature of the causes of criminal behavior in order to decrease antisocial behavior.

Theory

While there isn't one specific developmental theory of crime, there are several components that appear over and over again in these types of theories. First, developmental theories start with the premise that early childhood is an important (probably *the* most important) time for influencing later behavioral and health outcomes. The biological factors a person is born with – their genes, physiology, and neurology – coupled with their environmental exposure – to toxins, adverse life events, and parents – all have an impact upon how the child develops into early adolescence. Thus to understand behavior, one must understand the confluence of these risk factors and how they play a part throughout the early life-course.

Developmental theories are also concerned with ways in which the human organism changes over time. Most developmental theorists do not argue with the findings from psychologists that many personality traits are relatively stable across the life-course. However, they tend to believe that people do change, and that biological and environmental influences on people change as a person progresses through life. For example, good evidence now suggests that self-control, heritability, and the importance of family and peers for the behavior of individuals change over time.[1]

Third, developmental theories often incorporate knowledge from various sources, including sociology, biology, psychology, and criminology. Because developmental theories consider the growth (and degeneration) of the human organism, theorists using this framework often consider how the brain develops (neuroscience), the contribution of genetic predisposition to behavior (behavior and molecular genetics), and the relative importance of social factors such as family bonding, association with delinquent peers, and neighborhood and school climate (sociology). Often, developmental theories are grouped in with "integrated theories" because of this very reason – they integrate knowledge from multiple perspectives and on several levels (e.g., individual, family, community). In this chapter, I will discuss what I believe are developmental and life-course theories of antisocial behavior and how they can inform public policy.

Origins

True developmental and life-course research is relatively new. So, again, I will take some liberty in the definition of "origins." There are, no doubt, a few examples of pioneering developmental criminologists who are worthy of note. Harvard sociologists Sheldon and Eleanor Glueck conducted several studies beginning in the 1920s that all followed individuals over time. Sheldon received his doctorate in 1924 from Harvard and Eleanor followed with her doctoral degree in education. While Sheldon went on to be a Harvard professor, Eleanor was a research assistant from 1930 until 1953. She was promoted to associate in 1964 despite the incredibly similar body of work to her husband, Sheldon. Harvard was the last Ivy League school to admit women and Eleanor experienced discrimination throughout her entire career. Both of the Gluecks, who grew up during World War II, experienced discrimination based on their Jewish heritage. Despite these obstacles, they contributed perhaps the most rich data sources to test developmental criminology and desistance from crime of any scholar of the time – and maybe since.

The Gluecks' first study was completed in 1930 and published as *500 criminal careers*. This study sampled men released from the Massachusetts Reformatory. They ended up re-interviewing the men twice, five years apart, after the baseline interview.[2] In the second study, the Gluecks interviewed 1,000 boys who came into contact with the Boston Juvenile Court when they were around 13 years of age on average. They followed up with these individuals after ten years.[3] In a third study, the Gluecks focused on females by interviewing 500 women and publishing the results in *Five hundred delinquent women* in 1934.[4] This focus on females is another reminder of how prescient of the concerns of criminological research the Gluecks were, and how they were careful to establish a broad research base for the study of human behavior.

The Gluecks were able to examine many features of crime and criminal behavior that were elusive to earlier criminologists. In particular, by following up with participants at several points after the baseline interviews, they could pay attention to how behavior changes (or stays the same) over time. Their studies merged on a couple of very important findings. First, for almost everyone, offending decreased over time. Even serious frequent offenders appeared to stop offending as they grew older. Second, even for those who did continue to offend, their behavior became less serious over time. The Gluecks did not specifically use the term desistance – although that is how criminologists would refer to these phenomena today – but they did call this process maturation. They did not go on to define maturation with any clarity but left this up to future researchers.[5]

Not very long after the Glueck studies, in the 1950s, criminologist Marvin Wolfgang initiated a longitudinal study that would further define developmental criminology. He, along with his colleagues, followed all boys born in 1945 in Philadelphia from age 10 to age 18. Similar to the Gluecks, he found that offending peaks in adolescence and then slowly decreases over time. In addition, he uncovered another very important criminological "fact." A small proportion of the sample – about 6 percent – contributed to almost 60 percent of all criminal activity.[6] A subsample of the original Philadelphia cohort was followed until age 30. Again, echoing the Gluecks, Wolfgang's research team found that the most serious crimes were committed in the teen years and declined over time. The prevalence of offending also decreased over the young adult years. However, some chronic offenders in adolescence did continue to offend into adulthood, suggesting that there is both continuity and change over a person's life-course.[7]

While life-course research was gaining traction from the 1930s into the 1980s, theorizing about continuity in and desistance from crime was lagging behind. The Gluecks' maturation concept remained ambiguous and empirical research from others did not carefully tie in the theoretical links to the findings of age and crime. One exception to this was the work of control theorist David Matza (the same Matza who worked with Gresham Sykes on developing techniques of neutralization). In 1964, with the release of *Delinquency and drift*, Matza described the offender throughout the life-course as an actor who chooses to either continue offending or "drift out" of delinquency. For him, individuals are not compelled to commit crime nor are they committed to any specific delinquent subculture. At the same time, those who continue to commit crime are not altogether different from law-abiding individuals. One take away from Matza appears to be that drifting in and out of delinquency is normative, and that most people, regardless of delinquency status, are relatively the same.[8] Still, as one can see, there was a lot more explaining to do.

Recent developments

One of the first criminological theories that was inherently developmental in nature was brought forth by psychologist Terrie Moffitt. Moffitt, not surprisingly, is a developmental psychologist interested in several negative health outcomes – crime and delinquency being just two. In fact, the field of criminology may not have had the insight from Moffitt at all if it had not been for an unfortunate parachuting accident that left Moffitt with a broken leg. Unable to do much except sit behind a desk, she switched to a theoretical dissertation, leading her on the path toward theorizing about the neuropsychological underpinnings of antisocial behavior.[9]

Moffitt proposed that there are two major types of offenders with two very different developmental trajectories.[10] The first trajectory includes the most typical types of offenders. In fact, it is the trajectory that most of us, including those of you reading this book, follow. They are the adolescence-limited (AL) offenders who have average childhoods, dabble in some minor delinquency during their adolescent years, and largely stop by late adolescence or early adulthood. A large portion of the population belongs to this trajectory.

The second developmental trajectory is less common, belonging to under 10 percent of the population (and closer to about 6 percent). This trajectory exemplifies the life-course-persistent (LCP) offenders of Moffitt's theory (Figure 10.1). These individuals start their offending early, often before their teen years, engage in violent crimes, and continue well into adulthood. These offenders typically have neuropsychological deficits that stem from factors such as maternal drinking and drug use, poor nutrition, and abuse/neglect. The results of these deficits are a reduction in verbal and executive functioning, leading to learning difficulties, reduced problem-solving abilities, impulsiveness, and irritability.

Moffitt also discusses how these early deficits, and subsequent behaviors, are related to a continuing trajectory toward delinquency. Children with the deficits discussed earlier are hard to get along with and irritate people around them. In several ways, interactions exist between the person (child) and their environment. Children with neurocognitive deficits often evoke negative reactions (evocative interaction) from frustrated parents and face ostracization from peers who would rather not be around them. These children often "overreact" (reactive interaction) to environmental strains such that children without neurological deficits are able to interpret and respond to their environments using non-violent problem-solving, while those with disabilities are unable to solve problems and become angry or frustrated. These children also actively search out environments that are consistent with their personalities and behaviors – what Moffitt calls "proactive interaction." By selecting and evoking reactions from the environment, there is hardly a setting where these children find themselves that is not conducive to violence. Thus, the life-course-persistent developmental trajectory is set early and persists throughout life.

Around the same time that Moffitt was proposing and developing her developmental theory of LCP and AL offenders, criminologists Robert Sampson and John Laub were simultaneously developing their life-course theory of delinquent behavior. In what is now one of the most celebrated and recounted stories in contemporary criminology, John Laub had fortuitously stumbled upon the Gluecks' data while in a basement at Harvard University. Along with colleague Robert Sampson, the two painstakingly re-created the data and subjected the information to the most recent statistical and theoretical analyses of the day.

Sampson and Laub, in their seminal book published in 1993, *Crime in the making: Pathways and turning points through life*, suggest that several factors set an individual up for failure or success.[11] Early conduct problems and poor temperament set the stage for offending, but strong, positive family, school, and peer bonding can inhibit poor behavior across the life-course. So important was bonding for Sampson and Laub that they specifically discuss the idea of social capital. Social capital describes the resources one can accumulate as one encounters and bonds with others (or with institutions) in society. Where some people accumulate social capital, others accumulate disadvantage (poverty, discrimination, a criminal record, etc.) which ultimately leads to a life of crime.

Even for those who have accumulated disadvantage and few bonds to pro-social people and institutions, Sampson and Laub found some hope for change. Specific turning points in one's life were able to put people back on the right track and lead to desistance

Figure 10.1 Moffitt: Life-course-persistent vs. adolescent-limited offenders

Source: Moffitt (1993), 674.

from crime. In a follow-up of the original Glueck boys, Laub and Sampson found that marriage to a supportive spouse, a good job, and military service were turning points that came about, often by chance, and which enabled the boys to stop offending. Laub and Sampson published these follow-up interviews with the Glueck "boys" (who were 70 years of age or older at the time of the interviews) in their second book on their life-course theory, *Shared beginnings, divergent lives*. As the title implies, many people are born into similar circumstances, but their pathways and developmental trajectories can differ through the life-course.[12] In all, their work (which is now a quite substantial body of literature) has provided the field with a foundation for future research on developmental and life-course theories of delinquent and criminal behavior.

Not everyone "agrees" with the specifics of Sampson and Laub's theory – called the age-graded theory of informal social control. One group of theorists, led by criminologist Peggy Giordano, suggests that Sampson and Laub's theory overplays the role of chance in finding and taking advantage of turning points which they call "desistance by default" as opposed to focusing on the opportunities and agency behind desistance from crime. For Giordano and her colleagues, desistance is a process that does not happen by chance but is intentional. First, there have to be opportunities to change – what they call "hooks for change." Second, it is up to the individual to take hold of those hooks. The bonds and ties to society may be there, but it is then up to the individual to establish and maintain those bonds. Finally, the desistance process must contain cognitive transformation. Even if the opportunities exist and individuals seize those opportunities, if their actions are not backed up by a change in how they perceive themselves, then any change is unlikely to stick.[13]

A similar line of thinking to that of Giordano and colleagues has emerged out of identity theories of antisocial behavior. Former professor of criminology at the University of Maryland at College Park, Raymond Paternoster and his co-author, University of New York at Albany criminologist Shawn Bushway, have put forth an identity theory of desistance similar to, but different in key ways from, the previously mentioned theories of desistance. According to Paternoster and Bushway, people have a major role to play in their own life trajectory – choosing to engage in crime or stop their criminal ways by intention. Recall that Sampson and Laub believe that desistance, or stopping offending, occurs primarily "by default" with little or no effort on the part of the individual.

In this way, Paternoster and Bushway are more in line with the theory put forth by Giordano and colleagues who say that "hooks for change" must be grasped by those who want to change. For those who do not intend to change their deviant ways, the hook remains without any effort to seize it and make life better. Therefore, Paternoster and Bushway believe that human agency, or intention, plays a crucial role in the decision to stop offending. In their view, the costs of criminality weigh heavily on offenders and accumulate into a "crystallization of discontent" at which point individuals feel pushed to choose whether or not they want to make a drastic change in their life to escape the costs of poor behavior.

Robert Agnew, who was discussed earlier in this book, has also created a general theory of crime and delinquency which includes life domains that impact a person's chances of engaging in crime. Much of his theory borrows from the life-course research of others and integrates insight from control, learning, and strain theories. The domains that Agnew created impact one another and are more or less influential on the individual depending on the life-course stage (e.g., childhood, adolescence, adulthood). Agnew is careful to account for how the domains interact with one another and the life-stage that most influences a particular domain in its role in crime for a truly developmental theory of crime.

Agnew considers five major life domains: (1) the self; (2) the family; (3) the school; (4) peers; and (5) work (Figure 10.2). Within each of these domains, Agnew identifies factors that either increase motivations for crime (in the strain tradition) or constrain people's actions toward crime (in the control tradition). While there are numerous factors at each stage that influence crime, Agnew mentions a few that are of particular importance. For the self-domain, Agnew mentions low self-control and high irritability as the most important factors. Poor supervision and low parental bonding along with child abuse are the most relevant factors in the family domain, while poor teacher bonding and low grades are the most powerful predictors of delinquency in the school domain. Spending time with delinquent peers, especially unstructured and unsupervised time, is the greatest predictor of delinquency in the peer domain. Finally, unemployment or employment in a poor working environment are the most predictive of delinquency in the work domain.[14]

Importantly, Agnew acknowledges that some of the domains are more important at different stages of the life-course. For children, the family is the most important domain, as children rely on their family for support and direction. For adolescents, especially teens, the peer domain is the most important as individuals move on from their family and try to establish their own identity among their peers. For adults, the school domain is probably not at all important, but the work domain is. In addition, Agnew points out that problems in one domain likely affect others. For example, someone with low self-control (individual domain) will likely have problems in school (school domain) because they have trouble concentrating and elicit negative views from their teachers and peers (peer domain). This, in turn, will affect their chances of gaining a good job with a positive atmosphere (work domain). This dynamic and reciprocal life-course model is a strength of Agnew's theory. However, with all the variables and their interconnections, the theory is certainly not among the most parsimonious.

Figure 10.2 Agnew's life domains

Source: Agnew (2005).

A developmental approach which has itself gone through quite a developmental process was formulated through the 1990s and established in the 2000s. The integrated cognitive antisocial potential (or ICAP) theory developed by the prolific criminologist David Farrington began by addressing a series of questions that a developmental theory should be able to answer (Figure 10.3). Among these, Farrington wanted to explain why people start offending, maintain their offending, desist from offending, and why it is that most crime is diverse (people tend not to specialize in one type of crime but engage in various antisocial behaviors), peaking in the adolescent years.[15]

The basis of the theory is that individuals engage in delinquent behavior when antisocial potential is high. When an individual has few resources and low achievement they are more likely to choose antisocial ways to meet their needs (this is not unlike the strain theorists in the 1950s) – increasing antisocial potential. When individuals have antisocial models such as criminal parents and peers, their antisocial potential increases further. Farrington also distinguishes between long-term and short-term antisocial potential. Short-term potential includes intoxication, boredom, and frustration that results from immediate and current factors, while long-term potential includes persistent factors such as personality traits like impulsiveness and life event strains that have lasting impacts (e.g., child abuse). When these factors coalesce, antisocial potential peaks (often in the teen years) and tends to improve into adulthood, partially explaining the age–crime curve.

In the middle decades of the 1900s, Sheldon and Eleanor Glueck proposed the idea that maturation is a major cause of desistance from crime. Their development of this theory never came to fruition, but they did challenge future researchers to continue to explore and test theories of maturation. For decades, no one did. Recently, Bates College criminologist Michael Rocque has unearthed the lost concept of maturation.

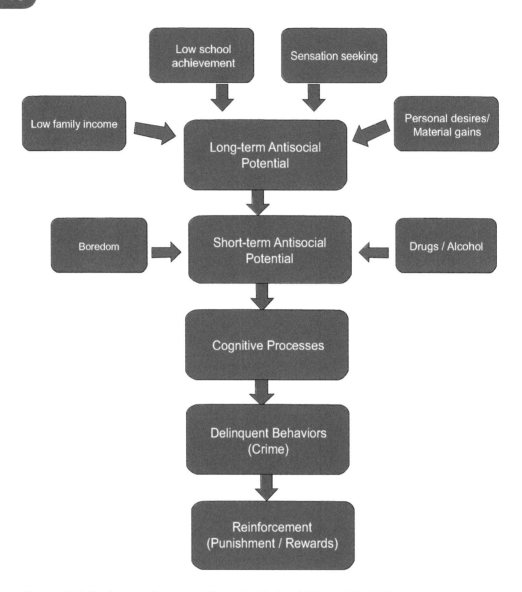

Figure 10.3 Farrington's Integrated Cognitive Antisocial Potential (ICAP) theory

Source: Adapted from The Integrated Cognitive Antisocial Potential (ICAP) theory [digital image] (2016). Available at: www.open.edu/openlearn/people-politics-law/discovering-disorder-young-people-and-delinquency/content-section-2.4.

In a theoretical paper published in 2015, Rocque proposed a theory of desistance through maturation. He defined maturation as a concept constructed from several developmental domains, including: (1) social role maturation; (2) civic maturation; (3) psychosocial maturation; (4) identity/cognitive transformation; and (5) cognitive/neurological maturation (Figure 10.4).[16] The construction of domains was an effort to address the Gluecks' call for scholars to define maturation by "dissecting [it] into its components." Rocque argued that positive changes in these domains would correspond with a reduction in criminal behavior. In a subsequent paper, Rocque and his colleagues

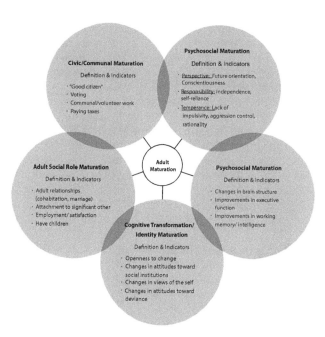

Figure 10.4 Domains of maturation

Source: Used with permission from the author.

found that improvements in the identity domain did reduce crime and facilitate desistance. Individuals who increased positive perceptions of themselves, such as seeing themselves as good, trustworthy individuals, were more likely to stop acting poorly. The main question now is how can we instill or increase people's positive views of themselves in the most effective way.[17]

The case of Stanley "Tookie" Williams, III: from gang leader to children's book author

The early life-course work of Sampson and Laub and the more recent work of Paternoster and Bushway and Rocque suggests that there are points in someone's life where there is a significant transition away from criminal behavior and toward conformity.[18] Sometimes this "just happens" and at other times there is a conscious decision to change, usually following a change in how one see's oneself – a change in identity.

This type of change is exemplified in a man named Stanley Williams III – otherwise known as Tookie.[19] Tookie grew up in South Central Los Angeles in the 1960s. The son of a single mother in her early twenties, Tookie spent his days on the streets, often being made to fight by adults in the community. In his early teens he was already getting into fights, stealing cars, and getting locked up in juvenile halls. Before his eighteenth birthday he met up with Raymond Washington, another individual in South Central who was involved with gangs and fighting. Both Tookie and Washington were sick of the neighborhood gangs taking advantage of everyone in the community and decided to create their own gang for protection. Originally known as the "Cribs" the gang quickly turned into the "Crips" which would become one of the nation's biggest and well-known gangs.

In 1979, Tookie was found guilty of four murders and sentenced to death.[20] While on the inside, Tookie's violent behavior did not stop. He was disciplined several times for assaults on other inmates and guards. However, in the 1990s, Tookie's life took a dramatic turn. He grew tired of the violence and destruction that had dominated his life. He no longer wanted to hurt people but, instead, to help people. In fact, Tookie began writing children's books about how to avoid crime and violence, particularly gangs and gang violence. He also authored memoirs about his life in the gang. His thoughts on violence prevention and peace reverberated throughout all his publications.

Activists around the country lauded Tookie's "redemption" and praised him for his efforts to instill peace within troubled communities. He was even nominated for the Nobel Peace Prize – an unlikely award for a gang member and convicted murderer. Despite these accolades and efforts to clear his name, Tookie was sentenced to death. On December 13, 2005 at the age of 51, Stanley Tookie Williams was executed in San Quentin Prison in California. These last words were played at his funeral:

> The war within me is over. I battled my demons and I was triumphant.
> Teach them how to avoid our destructive footsteps. Teach them to strive for higher education. Teach them to promote peace and teach them to focus on rebuilding the neighborhoods that you, others, and I helped to destroy.

Empirical support

Life-course and developmental theories are among the most difficult to test given that longitudinal data are needed from several individuals over a relatively long period of time. The best data would also include social, psychological, and biological factors at multiple life-stages. This is no small task and many theories are tested piecemeal using the available data. Despite these limitations, there is some impressive support for developmental theories of behavior.

The notion that people "age out" of crime is well documented and one of the brute facts of crime. Both quantitative and qualitative studies indicate that as people increase in age, crime becomes more and more "not worth it" and the criminal calculus (discussed in Chapter 9) changes such that crime is less rewarding and more costly. This leads to a decrease in offending over time.[21]

One factor implicated in this change in calculus is often a change in identity over time. In one of the premier studies on this issue, criminologist Shadd Maruna studied 30 offenders and concluded that changes in how people view their "core self" influenced offending. The more positively they viewed themselves, the less they took part in crime.[22] In a quantitative analysis of the effect of identity concept on crime in which I took part, we found that changes in the way a person views themselves (e.g., as a good person, as a delinquent person) are associated with the way they subsequently behave.[23]

Specific turning points in people's lives have also been studied to determine how well they do, in fact, reduce criminal activity among offenders. One turning point that is shown to fairly consistently predict desistance from crime is marriage. As people become committed to one another through the institution of marriage, crime (which perhaps jeopardize this relationship) is less likely to occur.[24] Similarly, employment has also been found to influence desistance from crime. Much as marriage works as a turning point, so too does having a steady, good job.[25]

Moffitt's early contention that different groups of offenders can be identified has, for the most part, been supported. While Moffitt proposed two large groups, other studies have found multiple groups that consist not only of LCP and AL offenders but also groups like extremely high persisters (who show almost no decrease in bad behavior), low desisters (who decrease offending but very slowly), and even "increasers" (who elevate their offending over the life-course).[26]

Remaining questions

There is currently little debate that different pathways exist throughout life for different individuals. However, the exact number of different pathways and how those avenues differ by sex (males vs. females), race (especially Whites vs. minorities), and sexual identification (cisgender vs. gender minorities) is still unknown. There has been significant debate considering more traditional categories used in criminology. A comprehensive review of criminal trajectories revealed that studies have found anywhere from two all the way up to seven trajectories. Most studies found three or four trajectories.[27] Others, such as Norwegian scholar Torbjørn Skardhamar, question the utility of trajectory analyses and theories about specific pathways altogether. Specifically, it appears to be inaccurate to envision trajectories as discrete categories instead of existing on a spectrum. He concludes his critique on Moffitt's AL and LCP theory, stating,

> [I]t is nevertheless more reasonable to suggest that the differences between the law-abiding and the highest-rate offenders are on a sliding scale. Although the extremes may appear to be black and white, there are considerable shades of grey in between.[28]

Although developmental criminology argues for a longitudinal study of crime that starts as early as possible and goes on for as long as possible (the ideal would be from conception to death including family history), the exact causal path from risk factors to crime is still not entirely clear. For example, scholars are still trying to figure out *what* matters about marriage that leads to desistance and even what comes first – desistance or marriage.[29] In addition, some factors that lead to desistance for certain people have no effect on others. Employment, for one, has been found to impact those in their late twenties but to have little impact upon younger adults.[30] Others argue that the family bonds that are so touted by desistance researchers matter very little and it is really the heritability of violence that matters.[31] We are a long way from settling these issues.

Policy

Policies and programs based on a developmental perspective are, of course, concerned with sustained and frequent follow-ups over a relatively long period of time. Many programs are intended to start early in a person's life, even *before* they are born, in an effort to nip bad behavior in the bud. There is good evidence mounting that this approach can be profitable in decreasing violence, improving lives, and reducing costs to society.

Desistance researchers Beth Weaver and Fergus McNeill recommend eight strategies for translating desistance research into policy. First, they recommend that policy-makers be patient. Often, we as a society want quick fixes and unfortunately desistance research shows that many of us engage in crime and most desist. To truly find out what works and to effectively help some disengage in crime will take time. Second, they suggest, like others including critical criminologists, using formal social control as little as possible and relying on informal mechanisms of control. Third, and relatedly, incarceration should be an absolute last resort given the lack of evidence regarding its ability to change behavior and reduce violence. Fourth, and related to recommendation two, relationships with others in society who are pro-social should be a focus of prevention and intervention.

Fifth, policy-makers should understand that the desistance process is different for everyone and that, sixth, the environments that impact those individuals should be a focus of all prevention/intervention efforts. Seventh, hope and positivity should be introduced into the lives of those seeking to desist, and, eighth, the ways that individuals can "make good" should be promoted by policies and programs.[32]

One program that adheres to the principles of developmental crime prevention is the Nurse Practitioner Home Visitation Program (Nurse Family Partnerships) started in Elmira, New York under the auspice of David Olds. True to early prevention, the strategy employed by the program was to begin with expectant mothers and provide them with resources on pre-natal care. Several randomized clinical trials were conducted to evaluate this program. In total, they found that the program was successful in improving the lives of children by reducing injuries and ingestions that might be due to child abuse or neglect. Children also had better emotional and language development than comparison children. The lives of mothers were improved as well. Mothers who were enrolled in the program had fewer subsequent pregnancies, greater workforce participation, and reduced dependence on public assistance and food stamps when compared to their counterparts who were not enrolled in the program.[33]

Parental programs are important, and profitable for those who have parents (or ones that care). Former Harvard professor Richard Cabot developed a mentoring program, called the Cambridge-Somerville Youth Program, almost a century ago, which would match an individual with a personal mentor. This mentorship, Cabot believed, could help correct youth by putting them on the right life track even if they had a poor family history. Mentors would tutor their mentees, assist them in seeking out medical and psychiatric treatment, and spend time with them in pro-social activities such as swimming and athletics. An evaluation in the 1930s, which placed a set of individuals in the mentoring group and a set in a non-mentoring group, was undertaken to assess Cabot's approach. Surprisingly, those in the mentoring group had *worse* outcomes. The Cambridge-Somerville Youth Program is an early example which shows that even thoughtful programs must be evaluated to see if they indeed achieve the outcomes they hope to achieve.

Broadly speaking, advocates of a developmental approach to crime prevention are against overly harsh, long punishment. Developmental criminology takes the perspective that the formative years of one's life are during childhood and early adolescence. Any disruptions during those periods can have very drastic negative impacts on a person's entire life. Therefore, advocates argue against criminal justice intervention in favor of diversionary or restorative approaches to addressing crime.

In addition, and this may be the only time you hear this, developmental criminologists often agree with Travis Hirschi and Michael Gottfredson on the uselessness of specific deterrence that identifies and harshly punishes frequent offenders. Developmental criminologists are very aware of the age–crime curve and affirm Hirschi and Gottfredson's position – by the time you identify frequent offenders they are already aging out. Long sentences in general will not be effective because they will just keep older, non-violent offenders in prison for a long period of time when they are not a threat to society.[34]

While on the topic of sentencing, some proponents of developmental criminology support re-entry initiatives that help restore the rights of ex-felons who have "paid their dues." In particular, University of Minnesota sociologist Christopher Uggen has staunchly advocated re-establishing voting rights for ex-felons as a way for them to reintegrate back into society and to have a stake in that society. Currently, there are at least five million ex-felons who have served their time, but who are not eligible to vote. These individuals are disproportionately poor and people of color. Not only are they locked out of the democratic process, they are prohibited from taking ahold of an important hook for change: voting. This may severely hinder the desistance process, as many have observed.[35]

Summary

Taking together the work of Sampson and Laub, Giordano and colleagues, and Rocque, it appears that a developmental consideration of crime commission and desistance is a very important and profitable view of criminality. Not only do people become involved in crime for some very specific reasons but so too do they stop committing crimes. Perhaps this does not only occur by chance but also from a concerted effort to do so on the part of the individual.

There is still much we need to learn about the development of crime and how and why people desist. What *are* the hooks for change? Which characteristics of individuals promote taking hold of those hooks? Surely the work of Agnew, Rocque, and Farrington can clarify some of this but, much like the Gluecks, there is a need for other researchers to come on board using insights from multiple fields to fill in the gaps. This area will undoubtedly be an integral part of criminology in the upcoming years and decades.

Notes

1 See Bergen, Gardner, & Kendler, 2007; Hay & Forrest, 2006; Steinberg, 2014.
2 Glueck & Glueck, 1930.
3 Glueck & Glueck, 1934a.
4 Glueck & Glueck, 1934b.
5 Rocque, 2015; See Rocque (2017) for a comprehensive discussion on longitudinal and developmental research.
6 Wolfgang, Figlio, & Sellin, 1972.
7 Wolfgang, Thornberry, & Figlio, 1987.
8 Matza, 1964.
9 Piquero, 2011.
10 Moffitt, 1993.
11 Sampson & Laub, 1993.
12 Laub & Sampson, 2003.
13 Giordano, Cernkovich, & Rudolph, 2002.
14 Agnew, 2005.
15 Farrington, 2003.
16 Rocque, 2015.
17 Rocque, Posick, & Paternoster, 2016; Rocque, Posick, & White, 2015.
18 Paternoster & Bushway, 2009; Rocque, 2015; Sampson & Laub, 1993.
19 See www.biography.com/people/stanley-tookie-williams-476676 for the story of Tookie Williams.
20 People vs. Williams (Cal Sup Ct April 11, 1988).
21 Paternoster, 1989; Cusson & Pinsonneault, 1986.
22 Maruna, 2001.
23 Rocque, Posick, & Paternoster, 2016.
24 Bersani, Laub, & Nieuwbeerta, 2009.
25 Uggen, 1999.
26 Tremblay, 2010.
27 Jennings & Reingle, 2012.
28 Skardhamar, 2009: 875.
29 Skardhamar et al., 2015.
30 Uggen, 2000.
31 Harris, 2009.
32 Weaver & McNeill, 2011.
33 Olds, 2006.
34 Gottfredson & Hirschi, 1986.
35 Maruna, 2001; Rocque, 2015; Uggen, Manza, & Thompson, 2006.

Further reading

Agnew, R. (2005). *Why do criminals offend? A general theory of crime and delinquency*. Los Angeles, CA: Roxbury.

Laub, J. H. & Sampson, R. J. (2003). *Shared beginnings, divergent lives*. Cambridge, MA: Harvard University Press.

Maruna, S. (2001). *Making good: How ex-convicts reform and rebuild their lives*. Washington, DC: American Psychological Association.

Rocque, M. (2017). *Desistance from crime: New advances in theory and research*. New York: Springer.

Sampson, R. J. & Laub, J. H. (1993). *Crime in the making: Pathways and turning points through life*. Cambridge, MA: Harvard University Press.

Thornberry, T. P. & Krohn, M. D. (2006). *Taking stock of delinquency: An overview of findings from contemporary longitudinal studies*. New York: Springer Science & Business Media.

Biosocial criminology

11

Introduction	135
Theory	136
Origins	136
Recent developments	137
Crash and crime: the case of stress and genetic susceptibility	143
Empirical support	143
Remaining questions	144
Policy	145
Summary	146

Introduction

The field of criminology has gone through several swings from one theoretical orientation to another. As illustrated through the first ten chapters in this book, the field has gone from a mostly biological orientation, to a psychological one, to a mostly sociological orientation. Currently, theoretical efforts have returned – partially – to their biological roots, but this time with new insight into the interplay between the environment and biology. The old nature versus nuture debate promulgated by Francis Galton in the 1800s has, for the most part, vanished. In its place a biosocial criminology has emerged. Advances in neuro-imaging, DNA analysis, and epigenetic research reveal that biology and sociology are intimately linked, having additive and interactive impacts upon behavior.

This is a truly exciting and important time for criminology. Not only is technology on the rise to be able to investigate environmental, psychological, and biological processes related to behavior, but those technologies are becoming more accessible and less expensive. We can now peer into people's brains to see how the brain is structured and how it functions. We can access hormone levels, pathogens, and whole genomes with a swab of the cheek or a few strands of hair. We can even start to analyze the microbes in our gut that contribute to emotion regulation and behavior.

Biosocial criminology, broadly speaking, is interested in how all these facets of the individual come into play in predicting antisocial behavior. While the perspective views both biology and the environment as important, scholars acknowledge that some behaviors are more genetic and some more environmental depending on what type of behavior is being examined. It also acknowledges that no behavior is entirely determined by either genes or the environment. The key is to examine the complex ways in which both biology and sociology are intertwined and help inform crime prevention.

Theory

Currently, there is no one biosocial theory of crime. Instead, biosocial criminology is beginning to uncover the various ways in which genes, physiology, and environment combine to produce behavior. This is no easy task. Even though science and technology has advanced to the place where it can begin to uncover the connections between body and environment, it is far from a place where it can identify all the genes responsible for behavior, how those genes interact with one another and the environment, and how those genes are activated or deactivated by environmental factors.

Despite difficulties in biosocial research, many recent findings have reaffirmed the importance of this approach. First, the role of the prefrontal cortex in antisocial behavior has been supported across a wide variety of studies.[1] Second, physiological factors such as heart rate and skin conductance have proven to be important in the etiology of antisocial behavior.[2] Third, gene by environment interactions (using mostly candidate genes that are theoretically linked to antisocial behavior) predict certain behaviors that are important to criminologists.[3] New genome-wide studies show that there are likely several genes that contribute small effects and add up to influence behavior.

Origins

Unlike many of the previous chapters, the "origins" of biosocial theories are, for the most part, non-existent. It is true that many early biocriminologists, such as Cesare Lombroso and Richard Dugdale, began to hone in on the role of genes/heredity and the environment in concert with one another, but these ideas were not formalized until much later. Therefore, the "origins" in this chapter are much more recent than the previous chapters and break the "rule" of defining classical theory discussed earlier.

In 1975, biologist Edward O. Wilson published a seminal book in the field of social biology entitled, aptly, *Sociobiology*. Throughout the more than 600 pages of this text, Wilson discusses the importance of examining behavior using a framework which places the human organism within his or her social context. Certainly, Wilson was not the first to suggest such a framework. However, he may be among the first to do so with such comprehensive clarity. Wilson notes and discusses the importance of evolution and biology in human development and behavior while acknowledging that the human organism is social, interacting with the environment and with other people. For the time, Wilson's views were very different from other biological and sociological theorists – especially since the nature versus nurture debate was in full swing and few fully incorporated an integrated approach to explaining behavior.[4]

Still, Wilson did not focus heavily on the role of sociobiology in criminal and antisocial behavior. This was not his sole or main focus. Shortly after Wilson's *Sociobiology*,

C. Ray Jeffery used a social-biological approach to explain crime in his 1979 book *Biology and crime*. Jeffery was very clear that biology was not the sole cause of crime and, to him, probably not even the most important cause of crime. He did believe that biology was likely related to violent individual behavior. He focused mostly on neurological (e.g., brain lesions) and physiological (e.g., hormonal control) factors that may lead to violent behavior. Importantly, and somewhat prophetically, he noted that the social environment can impact the "internal biochemical environment."[5] Up until then, most criminologists ignored the role of biology in behavior, let alone attempting to integrate it into the sociological theories of the time. And he may have even foreseen the importance of gene–environment interactions and the importance of environmentally influenced gene activation and deactivation.

Recent developments

The biosocial perspective remained a fairly fringe affair throughout the 1980s and 1990s despite the work of some luminaries in the field such as Minot State University criminologist Lee Ellis, Boise State University criminologist Anthony Walsh, and the late University of Arizona psychologist David C. Rowe. In the 2000s, criminologist John Paul Wright began teaching biosocial criminology at the University of Cincinnati. One of his students at the time was Kevin Beaver who graduated and went on to teach biosocial criminology at Florida State University. This lineage has produced a cadre of biosocial criminologists who have gone on to establish their own line of research (and students) in their own right.

Evolution

If violence and antisocial behavior is the result of biology or genes in any sense, then there must be some evolutionary advantage or some other evolutionary mechanism at play. The idea that crime and violence might be explained through an evolutionary framework is not new, as we have seen. However, criminologist Brian Boutwell of Saint Louis University and his colleagues[6] have recently offered a new, unified theory of crime using an evolutionary framework. Their theory combines insight from J. P. Rushton's *rK* theory and Terri Moffitt's life-course-persistent offending theory – with a twist.[7] What they have come up with is a testable theory of violence that has found some recent (albeit piecemeal) empirical support.

According to *rK* theory, individuals who live in resource-disadvantaged areas ascribe to a "fast" life history which is described as early maturation, high reproduction, and low investment in offspring. This is toward the *r* side of the spectrum. On the other hand, those who live in advantaged areas are more likely to fall toward the *K* side of the spectrum. The *K* life history is "slow" and marked by average or late maturation, few offspring, and intense resource investment in those offspring. It is important to note that human beings, as a species, fall toward *K* on average. However, there is variation within the human species.

The *rK* theory, note Boutwell and colleagues, maps well on the developmental theory proposed by psychologist Terrie Moffitt, as discussed earlier in the book. The more individuals move toward the *r* or fast life history, the more likely they are to engage in crime. This makes sense because those who are less invested in offspring are not going to be inhibited from committing crime as much as someone who has resources, time, and effort invested in children. Communities that ascribe to the fast life histories are more likely to see a presence of life-course-persistent offenders.

Importantly, the unified evolutionary theory of criminal offending notes that life-course-persistent offending, while appearing fairly maladaptive (who wants to hang out with or marry a life-course-persistent offender?) can survive – by not being selected out of the population – because of negative frequency dependent selection. Low rates of poor behavior may be able to be maintained in the population when the frequency is low. Because high-frequency offending (the life-course-persistent offending) is present in around 6 percent of the population it largely flies "under the radar." Active and frequent delinquents spend time together and mate with one another through assortative mating (reproducing with those who are the most similar to you), allowing these traits to be passed on. If persistent offending were to increase in the population, it might become problematic and selection would begin to naturally lower that frequency.

Psychopathy

Evolutionary theories are useful in identifying how certain behaviors survive across large spans of time. So what about those high-frequency offenders? What is it about those 6 percent of offenders who start early and stop late? Is there something to be said for them or to identify who these individuals are early on? Some potentially profitable research can be taken from work on psychopathic individuals.

Today, criminologists who use a psychological approach often look at the concept of psychopathy. It is important to keep in mind that psychopaths, or those who score high in psychopathy, aren't all serial killers and many aren't delinquent at all. Like any trait, psychopathy exists on a continuum. It is true that most individuals who score high on psychopathy have low self-control, are self-centered, manipulative, and have a grandiose opinion of themselves. Given that those characteristics of psychopathy are also those that are found to be related to criminality, criminologists have turned their attention toward the concept to explain antisocial behavior.

A recent article and book by criminologist Matt DeLisi of Iowa State University proposes that psychopathy can be used as a unifying theory of criminal behavior.[8] Psychopathy, according to DeLisi, can help explain everything from the petty thief who shoplifts to the mass murderer who unemotionally kills his victims. Just as there is wide variation among the seriousness of these types of crime, so too is there variation in the trait of psychopathy. Therefore, low levels of psychopathy can be useful to explain minor incidents of crime while high levels of psychopathy can explain violent, frequent, and persistent offending.

DeLisi expands on psychopathy as the unified theory of crime in his full-length book. "[P]sychopathy" claims DeLisi, "is the purist, most parsimonious, and frankly, best, explanation for antisocial behavior."[9] Psychopathy, according to DeLisi, is a biosocial construct. First, there is considerable evidence that psychopathy is heritable, as there is a strong correlation between parents and children and among twins compared to siblings. Second, psychopaths differ when compared to non-psychopaths concerning brain structure and function such as reduced volume in the amygdala and less gray matter found among psychopaths. In addition, psychopaths often have over-activation in sensation centers in the brain, including the right insula. Third, environmental factors such as abuse, neglect, poor parental attachment, and delinquency within the family have all been linked to psychopathy. Biological and environmental factors are important to the development and maintenance of psychopathic personality and likely influence one another along the life-course.

The psychopathy framework has found some favor within criminology. In particular, psychological criminologists, such as Adrian Raine and Andrea Glenn, have written extensively on the topic of psychopathy and have confirmed the brain-based differences that many others have discussed theoretically. They too see the promise of psychopathy to explain a wide range of antisocial behaviors. Psychopathy, and other biological factors, may be best situated in the environments within which they arise. This leads to the integration of genes and the environment to explain criminal behavior.

Gene and environment interactions

Criminology has progressed in two major ways when examining gene and environment interplay. The first is to identify what are called candidate genes for the very basic reason that they are "good candidates" for being related to behavior.[a] You probably wouldn't get very far by spending a lot of time examining the role of the BRCA1 gene in antisocial behavior – it has been linked to breast cancer risk but has little or nothing to do with behavior. Not a good candidate. However, the MAOA enzyme gene breaks down (as enzymes do) serotonin which is a neurotransmitter in the brain. A good candidate. Indeed, the gene has been linked, along with the environment, to aggression and depression. For shorthand, these studies are often called cGxE (see-gee-by-eee studies) – the c standing for candidate, G for gene, and E for environment.

These cGxE studies have shown some promise in criminology and inform many theoretical positions. The first position (consisting of two perspectives) is that when people with genetic susceptibilities *also* spend time in stressful environments they will be *more* likely to behave poorly than those who have at least one buffer against criminal behavior (either genes or a good environment). This is referred to as the diathesis–stress model. This is also called the amplification hypothesis. The effect of one amplifies the effect of the other. Similarly, those who have a genetic vulnerability are often the most impacted by their environment because their environmental stressors cannot be offset by insulating genetic factors. Often referred to as the differential-susceptibility hypothesis, this model also suggests that environmental prevention programs might work best with this population, since they are easily impacted by their environment.[10]

The second position argues that when people are doubly vulnerable because of their genes and environment, they have so many risk factors that the effect of any one will be small and the interaction between genes and the environment will actually be negative (the effect of one is *smaller* in the presence of the other). Playing off of this perspective, if one had genetic susceptibilities, they would be more likely to "shine through" and be influential in *good* environments. Relatedly, other scholars have suggested that when individuals are exposed to so many stressors from the environment they become immune or desensitized (often referred to as saturation, crowding-out, and/or desensitization effects). Therefore, no gene by environment interaction is found (or it is but in the negative direction).

Epigenetics

The burgeoning field of epigenetics offers another novel and empirically sound pathway into the future of gene and environment interplay. To be sure, the field is very new, and there are many complex issues to untangle before epigenetics becomes a theoretical mainstay in criminology.[11] However, there is now much evidence that epigenetic processes are important in studying the etiology of antisocial behaviors.

Epigenetics, very simplistically, is the alteration of gene expression without altering the underlying sequence of DNA.[12] Many regular genetic processes occur naturally within the body which regulate gene expression. Most of these mechanisms are called transcription

---

a. It should be noted and reiterated here that the genome is incredibly consistent across people (over 99 percent identical). Differences occur when the same gene contains a small difference called an allele or polymorphism. For our purposes here (and in most cases otherwise), genetic differences just mean differences in the alleles between people.

factors that either enhance or block the reading of DNA (which then inhibits the production of proteins). Another set of mechanisms are epigenetic. The two major processes that are epigenetic in nature are histone acetylation and DNA methylation. Within the field of criminology, DNA methylation has received the most attention. DNA methylation occurs when a specific enzyme (DNA methyltransferase) attaches a methyl group to a cytosine base (one of the four bases that complete the double-helix of DNA) inhibiting transcription. Both internal and external factors can influence epigenetic processes.[13]

While epigenetics is new, theories have begun to use insight from the field to develop theories of behavior. For example, Boise State University criminologist Anthony Walsh has worked with several co-authors on epigenetics and how the field can inform criminological theory.[14] While still developing as a scientific field in its own right, epigenetics asks questions about how the environment and genetics intertwine to produce antisocial behavior. Two major questions that epigenetics tries to tackle are: (1) does the environment impact the activation and deactivation of genes (i.e., turn genes on and off); and (2) are changes to the activation of genes heritable across multiple generations?

To begin with the first question, the answer is a fairly clear yes. Exposure to certain environments impacts the activation of certain genes which control behavior. This is part of regular genetic processes such as the activation or deactivation of genetic transcription that produces or inhibits the production of substances such as glucose. However, there are certain exposures, such as exposure to chronic stress, which have more stable and long-term effects on physiological functioning; for instance, long-term exposure to environmental stress and victimization which can alter endocrine production.

The second question is more complex – whether or not these epigenetic changes can be "transferred" from one generation to the next. Can what happened to your mother or father, or even your grandmother or grandfather, impact your well-being? The answer […] maybe. There are now some very interesting studies that have linked chronic stress– for example, for those who were exposed to the atrocities of the Holocaust or impacted by widespread famine– to outcomes in the children and even grandchildren of those who experienced the original stressful event. This epigenetic transmission is under scrutiny in humans but has been shown in animal studies quite regularly. It appears that chronic and severe acute stress can have an impact upon people and across generations which deserves a closer look.

Allostatic load

Both cGxE and epigenetic studies suggest that there is something about how genes (particularly those that are influential in brain activity) interact with the environment in promoting certain behaviors. One of the most influential concepts which explains the pathway from environmental stress, to biological functioning, to criminal behavior, is allostatic load. To understand allostatic load (basically the amount of stress on the brain) one must understand the role of the hypothalamic–pituitary–adrenal axis (HPA axis for short). The HPA axis is located in the brain and is the "command station" for the release of important neuro-hormones, including adrenaline, cortisol, and norepinephrine, which, together, regulate the fight-or-flight-or-freeze response. When a person comes into contact with a stressful situation, the HPA axis kicks in – releasing neuro-hormones – to address the threat or potential threat.[15]

For many people, the HPA axis does what it needs to do – it responds to threat and then returns the body back to an equilibrium called homeostasis or "allostasis." All human beings are exposed to some level of stress and their HPA axis is able to regulate their body relatively well. However, for a group of individuals who are chronically and frequently exposed to serious stressors, the HPA axis becomes overwhelmed, unable to return the organism to allostasis. Two outcomes are possible which may be criminogenic.

Hypercortisolism may occur, resulting in an excess of circulating corticosteroids leading to heightened anxiety or hypocortisolism, resulting in a reduction in cortisol leading to fearlessness.[16] Exposure to chronic stress, which is more common in disorganized communities, can lead to different responses to that stress, explaining some of the reasons why crime and violence is more common in some areas and among some individuals.[17]

Environmental exposure

Not only are individuals exposed to chronic stress in many of the poorest and most disadvantaged communities, they are also exposed to a host of environmental toxins that negatively impact the brain and biological functioning. Lead, an environmental toxin, is one of the most studied substances that has been associated with antisocial behavior and deficits in acquired traits that lead to violent externalizing behavior for both children and adults. Indeed, studies link lead exposure to violent behavior in children and adults.[18] Crime is not the only effect of lead exposure. A host of other negative consequences such as early pregnancy,[19] reduced language acquisition, intelligence, memory, and mood stability,[20] increased likelihood of ADHD,[21] and decreased IQ are all associated with increased levels of lead exposure.[22] Importantly, the effect of lead is community-wide, negatively affecting entire neighborhoods at the aggregate level, including neighborhood-level crime rates.[23]

Along with lead, other environmental toxins have been linked with socio-behavioral outcomes such as attention deficit and hyperactivity disorder, autism spectrum disorders, and delayed motor activity. This has been labeled the "chemical brain drain."[24] These neurotoxins include, but are not limited to, methylmercury, polychlorinated biphenyls, arsenic, and toluene which are associated with cognitive delays and endocrine disruption that persists from childhood to adulthood.[25] Many of these substances are found in fertilizers and are the product of certain practices such as burning rubber tires. Individuals are not equally exposed to neurotoxins, with those in impoverished areas and in substandard housing bearing the brunt of these negative effects and enduring the consequences such as elevated levels of neighborhood crime.[26]

Researchers are beginning to make headway into understanding exposure to neurotoxins. There is now quite a lot of research on industrial toxins in urban areas, but very little is known about exposure to neurotoxins in rural areas and their subsequent health outcomes. This is particularly problematic given that pesticide poisoning is especially acute in children and adolescents living in agricultural communities, such as farms, in rural areas.[27] Questions about injustice ("environmental injustice") abound, as those in the lower economic strata are unduly exposed to and suffer the consequences of exposure to harmful pesticides.

Nutrition

Research across disciplines highlights the importance of early development in various health-related life outcomes. Proper neurological health is paramount to a healthy childhood and this includes engaging in pro-social behavior. Neurological health and development is partly genetic but environmental factors also affect the structure and function of the brain. One of the most important environmental influences on brain health is nutrition.[28] In fact, poor nutrition during the preschool period is linked to antisocial behavior in childhood.[29] Again, poor nutrition is likely to hit those in poor and impoverished areas to a greater extent than their more affluent counterparts. Often, those who live in the inner city are too far away from a walkable grocery store and instead rely on "junk" food from corner stores and fast-food restaurants. This has led some to refer to these areas as "food deserts."

Nutrition is also informative in other areas of importance. Bullying in school is now one of the biggest social problems, and children who have been bullied experience several negative developmental outcomes that persist for long periods of time. Despite concern, questions remain as to the origins of bullying behavior and, because low levels of bullying are quite normative among children, the larger problem is persistent bullying behavior. Recent research reveals that persistent bullies are often malnourished and the effect of poor nutrition is especially influential for bullies who are not particularly delinquent in other areas.[30] Fortunately, this line of research has relatively clear implications. To improve safety and well-being, communities should ensure that all children receive adequate nutrition, including access to healthy foods and supplements.

Physical abuse

In one of the first studies to empirically test a truly biosocial perspective, Avshalom Caspi and colleagues (including his wife, renowned psychologist/criminologist Terrie Moffitt whose work was discussed in Chapter 10) investigated the role of maltreatment in childhood in later antisocial behavior. They found that prior abuse and neglect is a risk factor for later antisocial behavior. However, not all previously abused children went on to become antisocial in later life. Why? They found that those children with a specific allele that leads to high expression of the MAOA gene were less likely to be delinquent – in other words, they were insulated from the effects of maltreatment.[31] A second study in 2003 found that individuals who experienced stress and had a short allele polymorphism in the serotonin transporter promoter region of the 5-HTT gene were more likely to suffer and be diagnosed with depression.[32] Since then, several studies have investigated the interaction between gene alleles and environments lending at least fairly consistent support for the integration of social and biological mechanisms in the explanation of behavior, and antisocial behavior in particular.

The gut

Think about when you go into a stressful situation. For instance, you have to give a talk in front of an audience who will all have their eyes on you. Does your stomach start gurgling? Do you have a bit of a stomach ache? You may be having that response just thinking about it! Now think about when you made a quick decision about something important that you did not have time to look into. Did you make a *gut* decision? Well, maybe the relationship to these situations and the response you had are connected. Recent research on the gut–brain axis indicates that this is no coincidence.

The human body not only has human cells but also about 10–100 *trillion* microbial cells.[33] In other words, you have trillions of little single-celled friends living on and in you at all times – and friends they are. Contrary to popular belief, these bacteria are almost always beneficial, not harmful. As new research confirms, these bacteria may also help you regulate emotions and promote health and good behavior.[34]

The human microbiome (which is most plentiful and diverse in the gut) has been shown to be linked to antisocial behavior. In one study, the guts of toddlers who had poor temperaments were studied and it was found that they had less microbial diversity than their well-mannered counterparts.[35] One reason for this may be that microbes are essential for appropriate neuronal growth and activity.[36] In fact, often called the gut–brain axis, the microbiome has a part to play in maintaining allostasis in the HPA.

When the gut microbiome is interrupted (by stress or antibiotics) dysbiosis may result, influencing mental and physical health.[37]

The microbiome is still little understood by biologists and especially by social scientists. The role of the microbiome in behavior – and in antisocial behavior – is still nascent. However, given the strong relationship of gut diversity to a host of outcomes including health and behavior, it may be just years down the road before the microbiome begins seriously informing crime prevention and intervention.

Crash and crime: the case of stress and genetic susceptibility

There are many examples of how particular individuals, within specific environments, behave when exposed to environmental stressors. One in particular illustrates the biosocial perspective very well, including the concept of differential susceptibility. In the mid-2000s, the United States experienced an economic downturn that led to what became known as the Great Recession.[38] While the recession started earlier, the housing crisis that peaked in 2008 was one of the major events that occurred during this time which substantially impacted people around the country.

One of the effects of economic downturns is the added stress put on families. It was not surprising that families reported more strain during this period than they did prior to the downturn. Along with this strain comes the impact upon behaviors. It is widely known that people who are stressed are more likely to "take out their frustration" on other people – sometimes their children. Unfortunately, that is what research has found in this particular situation. Parents were more likely to engage in "harsh parenting" practices during this time, and this harsh parenting often increased, bordering on child abuse.

There is an interesting twist. Prior research also found that genetic predisposition can also lead a parent to harshly discipline their child. The dopamine gene DRD2 can increase harsh parenting practices when a specific allele in the gene is present. So, there is also a genetic component to harsh parenting on top of other types of environmental exposure.

Researchers, as you may have already surmised, wondered how those parents with the DRD2 allele responded to the economic downturn and subsequently treated their children. They found that, surely, the economic downturn increased harsh parenting across the board (among all parents) but that this increase in harsh parenting was not equal for all parents. Those parents who had the risky DRD2 allele were *much more* likely to discipline their children harshly compared to those parents without the particular variant.

This is not the only case study that provides some useful information for parents and the larger social structure. Other studies have found that certain genes modify the effect of the environment.[39] While the interplay between genes and the environment can be complex, it does highlight two potential avenues for preventing and intervening in crime.

Empirical support

It is difficult to cleanly assess the empirical status of biosocial criminology as the approach is relatively new and encompasses so many different types of studies. Overall, biosocial criminology has quite unequivocally provided evidence that personality traits (e.g., psychopathy, antisocial personality disorder) as well as behaviors (e.g., aggression, manipulation) that are often correlated with criminal behavior are the result of *both* the environment and genetics. The recipe is not always equal parts environment and genetics (say, 50 percent each) but varies depending on the trait or behavior.[40] This is an oversimplification, but an overwhelming literature shows that in one way or another, genes and environments interact with one another and with themselves to influence (not determine) behavior.

Often, there may be a combination or interaction between the environment and gene(s) that lead to behavior. Overall, there is substantial evidence for biosocial criminology in that the bio and the social matter when examining crime, but much less support exists concerning the specifics. As discussed earlier, the most replicated interaction between genes and the environment has been the MAOA gene and adverse environments. A 2014 meta-analysis indicated that the low-activity MAOA genotype was associated with antisocial behavior when coupled with childhood adversity for males but a less consistent interaction existed for females.[41]

Like MAOA, another candidate gene that has often been linked to antisocial behavior in conjunction with the environment is the 5HTTLPR gene.[42] This gene is associated with serotonin transportation in the brain and, since serotonin has an effect on depression, anxiety, and emotion regulation, it was an early candidate gene for antisocial behavior. Specific variation in this gene has been strongly linked to antisocial behavior. The 5HTTLPR variation has a complex association with behavior, as it is often found to interact with sex, race, and environment in various ways.[43]

One specific DRD2 gene variant has found similar success in predicting antisocial behavior. The DRD2 gene encodes for a dopamine receptor and certain alleles interfere with the regulation of dopamine which is an activating neuro-hormone. So, again, this is a good candidate for antisocial behavior. Studies have shown that the A-1 allele of the DRD2 gene interacts with religiosity[44] and having a father engaged in criminal behavior to produce antisocial behavior.[45] Taken together, certain polymorphisms of serotonin and dopamine-related genes seem to interact with environmental factors in producing behavior.

While new, epigenetic processes are being identified as important in the production of aggression and antisocial behavior. Not surprisingly, given the evidence for the importance of cortisol in behavior, psychologist Mark Dadds and colleagues found that increases in methylation of sites related to the production of cortisol led to increases in child-aggressive behaviors.[46] Similar findings of methylation and antisocial behavior have been uncovered when examining methylation of MAOA sites.[47] To overlook the potential of epigenetics in explaining delinquency and crime appears to be to the detriment of criminological theory.

Remaining questions

There is little doubt that researchers have learned a lot about how genes and the environment impact behavior and how they come together in producing almost every possible phenotype imaginable. Despite this increase in knowledge, the exact way that genes and the environment have direct and indirect effects on behavior, and exactly how they combine with each other, is still up for debate.

The first major issue concerns the way in which genes and the environment combine to influence behavior. On the one hand, it may be that they do not interact very much with one another but "add up" to whatever behavior is under investigation. This is called additivity. On the other hand, it may be that having a certain genetic variation or being in one particular environment over another amplifies the effect of the other variable. This is called interaction. Although much early work in biosocial criminology revealed the promise of gene and environment interactions, there is some question as to the extent to which interactions account for antisocial behavior above additivity.[48]

Not only are there likely both additive and interactive effects of genes and the environment but also additive and interactive effects among genes themselves. For example, one gene variant may be required to see the behavioral impacts of another gene. This is where things get really messy. For any behavioral outcomes, there are generally small effects of many genes on this behavior. Rarely is it the case that one gene (i.e., gene variant) is the sole cause of a specific behavior or trait (one gene, one disorder). It is usually the case that many genes come together in various ways to contribute to a specific behavior. Identifying these genes, and which environments influence the activation of these genes, is still in the beginning stages. The new field of social genomics intends to tackle some of these issues.[49]

Like many new technologies and fields of study, epigenetics has received a vast amount of popular attention. Epigenetics has the potential to clarify a lot about what society is concerned about. How do the environments in which people live impact their biology? Can the environment activate or turn on certain genes? These are the questions that epigenetics may be able to help answer. However, epigenetics is not yet well understood, leading to some heated debates in criminology.[50]

Finally, and discussed to a greater extent in the following section, the specific interventions and policies that may be developed using information from biosocial criminology are still being considered. There is even more concern over the ethical or unintended consequences of seeking to change behavior using information from both the environment and biology. One example concerns the new technology CRISPR-Cas9 which can, literally, cut out sections of DNA that may cause problems. It can also "fix" and add new genes to a person's genome, offering the potential to address a host of genetic problems related to disease and disorders. However, there is reason for caution. First, there may be ethical reasons to consider before using this technology. Should we "fix" genomes related to disorders like deafness or autism? What if we really want a child with blond hair and blue eyes? Can we make that happen? Second, there is also reason to consider unintended genetic consequences. Some research has shown that using CRISPR to edit certain genes has the potential to mutate other genes and non-sequencing sections of DNA.[51] Remember: genes often rely on one another and the environment for proper functioning. The consequences of this are unknown at this time but give researchers considerable pause for thought.

Policy

Stemming from a class that both of us took in 2008 with the late biosocial criminologist Nicole Rafter, Michael Rocque and I discussed the role of biosocial criminology in public policy. Rocque went on to team up with crime prevention luminary Brandon Welsh and biosocial criminology path-breaker Adrian Raine to come up with several examples of successful prevention and intervention strategies that are informed by biosocial criminology.[52] First, parenting programs can prevent long-term antisocial behavior by simply informing expectant mothers about the dangers of ingesting chemicals that have harmful impacts upon neurocognitive development, such as tobacco and narcotics.[53] Early school-based programs that focus on cognitive development are also shown to reduce delinquent and criminal behavior using randomized controlled studies. The Perry Preschool Project and the Carolina Abercedarian Project both show consistent, long-term benefits for those who participate. Even programs in nursery schools that focus on cognitive stimulation, physical activity, and mental health are shown to have long-term positive impacts for participants.[54] Programs that focus in addition on nutrition increase their benefits[55] and certain supplements, such as fish oil, have now been demonstrated to be effective in enhancing neurocognitive development.[56] The mantra holds true: prevention cannot start too early and programs that address neurocognitive development appear to be among the most effective in supporting healthy mental and behavioral health.

In 2016, an entire section of the journal *Criminology and Public Policy* tackled the question of how biosocial criminology can advance effective policy and programming. The main article, by Jamie Gajos, Abigail Fagan, and Kevin Beaver, argued that one of the reasons that prevention and intervention programs are only marginally successful (at best) is that most of them fail to account for any role of biology in behavior.[57] One study they pinpoint as a success story is a biosocially informed intervention developed by University of Georgia researchers. The Strong African American Families program (SAAF), a seven-session parent and child training program, teaches participants how to engage in pro-social behavior and respond positively to adversity. A genetically informed evaluation of the program found that those individuals with the short allele of the 5HTTLPR gene were more likely to engage in antisocial behavior, but the parenting program mediated this effect, confirming its positive effects on behavior.[58]

One of the more intriguing statements in the issue was made by criminologist Michael Vaughn. He states, *"Most, if not all, prevention is essentially biosocial."*[59] This caught my eye, so I contacted him to see what he meant. "[N]o preventive intervention that I am aware of," he tells me,

> is biologically free. More specifically, typical psychosocial or policy interventions attempt to change behavior but these changes necessarily involve the brain. In other words, we are obviously biological organisms and any intervention or change in behavior necessarily engages us at a biological level.[60]

For Vaughn, and the bulk of other biosocial theorists, no behavior lies outside the brain and the brain is implicated in almost every strategy that attempts to change behavior.

To date, biosocial criminology has made only limited inroads into these areas, but the tide appears to be turning. As genome-wide studies are becoming less expensive and the tools to examine genes and their interactions with other genes and the environment become more sophisticated, the possibilities for biosocial criminology in affecting public policy increase. However, along with this expansion come some very serious and important ethical questions that need to be addressed, as mentioned above.

One recent example of a biosocially informed program comes from the Economic Mobility Pathways, or EMPath, program out of Boston, Massachusetts. The idea behind EMPath is that children in poverty are desperately stuck in a cycle where environmental stressors impact the brain, leading to bad decision-making. Bad decision-making further leads to life complications and added stressors that further impair biological functioning (and so on). Any behavioral intervention program from this viewpoint must break the cycle.

One facet of the EMPath program is "The Child Bridge to a Brighter Future," a piece that targets children to assist them in improving health and well-being, social-emotional development, self-regulation, achieving independence, and attaining educational goals. A recent evaluation of the program found that about 86 percent of children increased executive functioning and about 86 percent of families reported a reduction of "chaos" in the home with improved order and alignment.[61]

Summary

Biosocial criminology appears to hold much promise for future research and policy. The approach capitalizes not only on the knowledge of sociology and other social sciences but also on the quickly advancing fields of biology, chemistry, genetics, and other "hard" sciences. Further, the approach considers the interplay between sociological/environmental and biological/genetic factors. The evidence accumulated thus far indicates that the approach could be fruitful in gaining a more accurate picture of human behavior as well as increasing the amount of variation among behavior that can be explained. To date, most of the efforts of biosocial criminology are empirical and not as yet heavy on theory. A stronger focus on theory may help push the field toward better explanations of human behavior.

Along with promise there also appears to be as much, if not more, caution. If changing environments and genetics can influence behavior, how is this best done? If some people learn better in one environment over another, do we give them special privileges over others? If it is possible to edit the genome using technologies such as CRISPR, do we go ahead and "replace" segments of DNA? In addition, if we can influence behaviors (as well as diseases) before they have the chance to manifest, say editing the genome in utero or even before by influencing the combination of genes from fathers and mothers, do we do it? What kind of society would this lead to? Time will tell, but that time is here.

Notes

1 See Glenn & Raine, 2014.
2 Portnoy & Farrington, 2015.
3 Wells et al., 2017.
4 Wilson, 1975.
5 Jeffery, 1979.
6 Boutwell et al., 2015.
7 Moffitt, 1993; Rushton & Bogaert, 1988.
8 DeLisi, 2009; DeLisi, 2016.
9 DeLisi, 2016: 9.
10 Gajos, Fagan, & Beaver, 2016.
11 See Moffitt & Beckley, 2015.
12 Weinhold, 2006.
13 Carey, 2012.
14 Walsh, 2009; Walsh, Johnson, & Bolen, 2012; Walsh & Yun, 2014.
15 Tsigos & Chrousos, 2002.
16 See Rocque, Posick, & Felix, 2015; Walsh & Yun, 2014.
17 Rocque & Posick, 2017; Rocque, Posick, & Felix, 2015.
18 Boutwell, Beaver, & Barnes, 2014; Reyes, 2015.
19 Reyes, 2015.
20 Boutwell, Beaver, & Barnes, 2014; Mason, Harp, & Han, 2014.
21 Goodlad, Marcus, & Fulton, 2013.
22 Needleman & Gatsonis, 1990; Schwartz, 1994.
23 Boutwell et al., 2016.
24 Grandjean & Landrigan, 2014.
25 Genius, 2008.
26 Mohhai et al., 2009.
27 Karr & Rauh, 2014.
28 Molteni et al., 2002.
29 Jackson, 2016; See also Jackson & Vaughn, 2016.
30 Jackson, Vaughn, & Salas-Wright, 2017.
31 Caspi et al., 2002.
32 Caspi et al., 2003.
33 Ursell et al., 2012.
34 See Gato et al., forthcoming.
35 Christian et al., 2015.
36 Cryan & Dinan, 2015.
37 Lee & La Serre, 2015.
38 A good discussion of this case is presented in Conley & Fletcher's (2017) *The genome factor*.
39 DeLisi et al., 2009b; Glenn et al., 2017.
40 See, e.g., Polderman et al., 2015.
41 Byrd & Manuck, 2014; see also Wells et al., 2017.
42 Ficks & Waldman, 2014.

43 Douglas et al., 2011.
44 Beaver et al., 2009a.
45 DeLisi et al., 2009b.
46 Dadds et al., 2015.
47 Checknita et al., 2015.
48 Chabris et al., 2015.
49 See Conley & Fletcher, 2017.
50 See Burt & Simons, 2014; Moffitt & Beckley, 2015.
51 Schafer, Wu, & Colgan, 2017.
52 Rocque, Welsh, & Raine, 2012; see also Vaske, 2017.
53 See Beaver et al., 2010.
54 Raine et al., 2003.
55 See Farrington & Welsh, 2008.
56 Hibbeln et al., 2007.
57 Gajos, Fagan, & Beaver, 2016.
58 Brody et al., 2006.
59 Vaughn, 2016: 704 (emphasis in the original).
60 Personal interview with Michael Vaughn, January 19, 2017.
61 For more program information see www.theatlantic.com/education/archive/2017/04/can-brain-science-pull-families-out-of-poverty/523479/?utm_source=fbia.

Further reading

Beaver, K. M., Barnes, J. C., & Boutwell, B. B. (2014). *The nurture versus biosocial debate in criminology: On the origins of criminal behavior and criminality.* Thousand Oaks, CA: Sage.

Conley, D. & Fletcher, J. (2017). *The genome factor: What the social genomics revolution reveals about ourselves, our history, and the future.* Princeton, NJ: Princeton University Press.

Rafter, N., Posick, C., & Rocque, M. (2016). *The criminal brain: Understanding biological theories of crime.* New York: New York University Press.

Raine, A. (2013). *The anatomy of violence: The biological roots of crime.* New York: Random House.

Walsh, A. & Vaske, J. C. (2015). *Feminist criminology through a biosocial lens.* Durham, NC: Carolina Academic Press.

Criminology in international perspective

Introduction	149
Theory	150
Origins	154
Recent developments	155
The case of the Super Bowl and sex trafficking	159
Remaining questions	159
Policy	160
Summary	161

Introduction

Critics of current mainstream criminology have lamented that mainstream criminology is American criminology. Theories, as well as their theorists, have originated in the United States with little regard for how these theories apply across the globe. Recent efforts have been made to rectify this limitation by investigating crime rates across countries, applying theories to cross-cultural tests, and developing theories with cultural factors in mind (efforts in criminal justice research have examined policing, incarceration, sentencing, and the administration of justice across the country context).

There are several benefits to studying a phenomenon comparatively. Three of these benefits are outlined by Clayton Hartjen, and include: (1) providing a global portrait of misbehavior and how societies respond to misbehavior; (2) advancing criminal knowledge by increasing the database and testing theories; and (3) casting light on international problems and providing knowledge on how to address those problems.[1] In his 1987 presidential address to the American Sociological Association, Melvin Kohn stated that comparative research is a useful tool in developing and testing sociological theories which needs to be utilized to a greater extent in the social sciences.[2] David Nelken, a comparative criminal justice researcher, further suggests that comparative criminology is useful in testing and validating explanatory theories of crime by testing the generality of explanatory mechanisms and their relationship to social context (e.g., social control).[3] Comparative criminology draws conclusions by paying careful attention to the similarities and differences between cultural contexts. This is not entirely new, as others such as Beccaria, Bentham, Voltaire, Helvetius, and Quetelet have all used a comparative method of one form or another in their pioneering research.[4] Much of what we currently know about offending and victimization, however, is confined to one country, and although research has been conducted in countries other than the US and with ethnicities other than Caucasian, few studies have attempted to use multiple social contexts within the same study.

This chapter introduces cross-cultural criminological efforts to develop and test theories in various international contexts. Attention will be paid to the generalizability of theories across context and how theories are beginning to incorporate insight from culture and context into their explanations of criminal and antisocial behavior. The benefits and challenges of international criminology will conclude the chapter, giving a roadmap for more inclusive future work in international criminology. In these ways, it departs slightly from the structure of previous chapters.

Theory

Comparative criminologist James Sheptycki defines the project of comparative criminology as "[the] attempt to comprehend similarities and differences in patterns of crime in different cultures and contexts."[5] In Sheptycki's view, comparative criminology would benefit from quantitative and qualitative approaches to the study of crime in particular by placing the results of quantitative analyses within their social, cultural, and historical contexts. This type of empirical endeavor – placing quantitative analysis within its cultural context – requires that the line between relativism and positivistic empiricism be crossed, at least in their purist forms. Pure relativism (or total relativism) states that all knowledge is based on the views of particular cultures, societies, or groups of like-minded individuals. Therefore, knowledge is completely variable. Empirical positivism attempts to uncover the truth, which is viewed as the one and only "true" truth. Here, knowledge is general and applicable everywhere at all times.

One of the major advantages of the comparative method is that knowledge of the context will help with interpretation of the data.[6] David Nelken sheds light on the controversy between those who believe that culture explains behavior and those who believe that it is the behavior of citizens that explains the culture.[7] Another caution to comparative researchers is presented and discussed by Max Travers. He argues that comparative research needs to strike a balance between the positivistic and the interpretist models of investigation. The positivist model seeks to obtain scientific facts from society which explain behavior. The advantage of this approach is that it relies on empirical facts as opposed to common-sense or gut feeling. The interpretist approach critiques this method, claiming that the model of natural science is inappropriate for studying human behavior because it neglects the individual who has free will and conscience.[8]

The first step to investigate criminal behavior and explanations of that behavior across different populations is to conceptualize the meaning of culture. There is no one way to do this and there are several ways in which scholars have conceptualized and measured culture in the past. For example, Esping-Andersen, in *The three worlds of welfare capitalism*, developed three major welfare regimes, or Keynesian welfare states, using a broad conceptualization of how macro-level economic conditions influence the configuration of state welfare. He gives a basic definition of welfare state as, "[the] state responsibility for securing some basic modicum of welfare for its citizens."[9] The welfare state does more than demarcate social policies such as handing out food to the poor or housing the homeless that existed long before the nineteenth century. Rather, "it is a unique historical construction, an explicit redefinition of what the state is all about."[10] Essentially, it is the involvement of the state in providing benefits to its citizens such as health care, financial resources, and personal freedom. The state influences the extent to which citizens rely on mechanisms of social support.

Three major mechanisms exist in every society which assist individuals in meeting the basic needs of liberty, equality, and solidarity: (1) the market; (2) the state; and (3) the family/civil society. The market is the mechanism by which people provide labor and human resources in exchange for income and other benefits. The state receives fiscal and civil contributions from its citizens in exchange for basic social and political rights. The family and civil society is characterized by mutual obligation and voluntary acts of symbiotic exchange among family members and citizens. While most societies try collectively to meet the rights of liberty, equality, and solidarity using each of these mechanisms of support, over-reliance on any one mechanism leads to an imbalance of rights. For example, a strong valuation of liberty includes freedom of the market. Unrestricted market regulation and a hands-off approach from the state promotes liberty but also leads to inequality, as not everyone is able to contribute to the market. As researchers illustrate, there is no perfect society and societies vary in their values. This, in turn, reflects their welfare regimes.[11]

Esping-Andersen identified three major welfare regimes in his analysis: (1) the social democratic regime; (2) the liberal regime; and (3) the conservative regime. The social democratic regime is marked by universalism and de-commodification with a strong reliance on state welfare. The state minimizes any inequality in the labor market by providing universal health care and benefits for the family (e.g., parental leave and worker benefits). Critiques of this regime suggest that reliance on the state reduces individual liberty in the marketplace.[12] Countries originally included in Esping-Andersen's social democratic regime are the Scandinavian countries along with the Netherlands. He does not include Iceland in his analysis.[13]

The second regime identified by Esping-Andersen is the liberal regime. These countries are characterized by "moderate universalism."[14] Benefits are aimed at those who are not able to contribute to the marketplace, but these benefits are often modest, unlike those in the social democratic cluster. First and foremost, the state encourages participation in the market economy and avoids benefits that may interfere with market functioning. Benefits are limited and recipients of these expenditures are often socially stigmatized (e.g., referred to as lazy). Freedom is the most important ideal in the liberal regime often at the expense of social equality.[15] Esping-Andersen identified Australia, Canada, Japan, Switzerland, and the US as belonging to the liberal cluster. He mentions that Ireland may also fit into this cluster, but he is not clear as to whether or not it belongs in any of his three classifications.

The last regime identified by Esping-Andersen is the conservative cluster, also referred to as "corporatist" countries. In the corporatist countries, there is a synergetic relationship between social institutions and the government. In other words, the government supports social institutions such as the family, church, and school to meet the needs of citizens instead of providing direct governmental benefits.[16] This regime also stresses the importance of work. The state will give benefits during and after contributions to the workforce. However, not contributing to the workforce often means exclusion from social benefits. Those who are unable to work often rely exclusively on the family to meet their needs. This produces a society that is heavily reliant on the male breadwinner for national solidarity. In turn, there is less equality and a rigid class-based social system.[17] Esping-Andersen places Austria, Belgium, France, Germany, and Italy into this cluster.

While Esping-Andersen developed these three major welfare regimes, others have added regimes for countries excluded from his analysis, and some slight modifications have been made by others which have also received empirical support. For example, Bonoli added a Latin regime made up of a cluster of Southern European countries. This regime is very similar to the conservative regime but stresses the importance of family to an even greater extent. There are modest social expenditures, but the state largely promotes reliance on family to meet individual needs.[18]

Culture defined

Culture represents the value system of a society marked by customs and traditions adhered to by a majority of citizens. A parsimonious operationalization of societal culture is given by House and colleagues as countries sharing a common experienced language, ideological belief system (religious and political), ethnic heritage, and history.[19] Culture is said to account for at least 25 to 50 percent of a person's basic value system.[20] Those values impact our thoughts, decisions, and behaviors. Importantly, whether definitions of culture are based on welfare states,[21] organizational leadership,[22] physical climate,[23] self-expression,[24] religion and language,[25] penal policy,[26] or capitalistic characteristics,[27] there is considerable consistency among studies in assigning countries to clusters representing a common societal culture. Of course, there are also disagreements among researchers regarding the assignments of countries to cultural clusters, but there appears to be general agreement.

Further, many argue that globalization has decreased the disparity between countries, making distinctions more difficult to make. But, as others argue, globalization has also illuminated deeply ingrained cultural differences between countries, such as differences in decision-making processes between American and German countries.[28] Despite these criticisms, it does appear that separate cultures can be identified and that, overall, there is general consensus.

To be sure, culture describes an *average* set of values and norms. Just because a person was born in a specific country does not mean that they think like everyone else in that country. Individuals are just that – individuals. However, within a country, citizens are exposed to similar macro-level structures that have an impact upon their daily lives and that direct many of their thoughts and beliefs.

Anglo-Saxon culture

Anglo-Saxon culture has mainly been characterized by individualism and competition. For example, the GLOBE study conducted by House and colleagues describes Anglo-Saxon culture as high in performance orientation and low in in-group collectivism.[29] In other words, these societies urge members of society to continually strive to improve performance (e.g., grades in school) while maintaining a strong focus on work-related success, but do not necessarily value cohesiveness in work organizations or in their families. The culture of the United States, one country included in this cluster, has been likened to American football. Gannon and Pillai state that "if you don't understand

U.S. football, you will have difficulty understanding U.S. culture."[30] Football exemplifies US culture because it values competitiveness, individual specialization, and a survival-of-the-fittest attitude. Importantly, Gannon and Pillai don't ignore cooperation in US culture (or in the Anglo-Saxon ethos, including football) – there are several examples in Anglo-Saxon culture of success through group collectivism; however, the backbone of this cooperation is to improve the self and to achieve individual goals. Cooperation exists to the extent that it furthers the individual.

Northern European culture

Northern Europe, or Scandinavia, is perhaps best known for its vast mountains and serene landscapes. Northern European culture is somewhat a reflection of this landscape. Northern (Nordic) Europe is characterized by high future orientation, gender egalitarianism, institutional collectivism, and uncertainty avoidance and low assertiveness, in-group collectivism, and power distance.[31] While Nordic people value equality and cohesiveness among their social institutions they are still a solitary people, choosing to be individualistic and self-controlled. For example, Swedes tend to value alone time and spend long vacations of up to several weeks alone for self-reflection. Denmark adheres to "interdependent individualism" where government social support is generous in order to promote individual expression. Northern European countries, in general, enjoy social support from the government in terms of childcare benefits, vacation time, and health care for the sick and elderly.[32]

Western European nations

Western Europe is often compared with other "Western" societies such as those in the Anglo-Saxon cluster, especially the US. Some suggest that Western Europe is becoming increasingly "Americanized." Anglo-Saxon countries have high scores on performance orientation and assertiveness and low scores on humane orientation and both in-group and institutional collectivism.[33] One major difference is that the Western Europe cluster scores high on future orientation. Also similar to Anglo-Saxon countries is that these nations value individualism and the free market. However, there is a stark contract between the welfare systems of Anglo-Saxon and Western European nations. Although Western European nations value a free market, they also see the value in social welfare such as benefits for the sick, elderly, and families. Therefore, social benefits such as these are much more generous in Western Europe than in Anglo-Saxon countries.[34]

Mediterranean nations

The Mediterranean cluster is known for the high value which society places on the family. For example, Gannon and Pillai describe the family in Italy as close and personal – "the greatest resource and protection from all troubles."[35] They describe the family in Spain as a "large and affectionate clan."[36] The GLOBE study reveals scores on cultural variables in this group of countries to be fairly moderate but does find that they tend to score low on humane orientation and institutional collectivism.[37] This finding suggests that while individuals in this culture tend to value close ties within the family they are wary of outsiders, especially the government and other societal institutions. Often this is related to the idea that problems should be handled within the family and not by outsiders.[38]

Latin American nations

The Latin American cluster is perhaps best characterized by "machismo." Machismo is the value that Latin American nations place on the male breadwinner who is portrayed as strong, authoritative, and someone who demands respect. Neapolitan states that "aggressive masculinity" pervades Latin American culture.[39] The GLOBE study supports this, showing that Latin American countries tend to score high on in-group collectivism and low on performance orientation, future orientation, and uncertainty avoidance.[40] Like the Mediterranean Europe (Latin Europe) cluster, Latin America values collectivism within the family and places less value on school/work performance.

Post-socialist nations

The Eastern European or post-socialist cluster contains many countries with complex histories. In their discussion of Eastern European culture, Gannon and Pillai group these countries together in a section called "torn national cultures." In other words, these countries have had to deal with a tumultuous history marked by many social and economic shifts. For example, within the past 100 years, Russia has experienced three major changes starting in 1917 when ruling by czars changed to communism. In 1992, Russia saw the fall of communism and a move toward capitalism. Currently, there is much uncertainty surrounding Russia's economic and political future, as capitalism appears to be at least partially threatened by current ideology.[41] Despite some imbalance, the post-socialist cluster shows some consistency in its cultural values and practices. The GLOBE study finds that Eastern European nations score high on in-group collectivism, assertiveness, and gender egalitarianism, and low on performance orientation, future orientation, and uncertainty avoidance.[42]

   To date, there is no one "international theory" of crime and criminal behavior. Instead, theorists have revised older theories, or developed fresh new theories, to account for differences across international contexts. For example, the work of criminologist Alexander Vazsonyi has tested the generalizability (how well a theory can explain crime across all contexts such as in different countries). Others have considered how concepts such as the dimensions of criminal careers and the victim–offender overlap fare in areas besides the United States.[43] In general, these efforts have mostly found generalizability with a hint of differences across international contexts. This reveals a rich and exciting area for criminology to take in as it moves forward.

Origins

International or comparative criminology as a specific focus is relatively new. However, comparative work in the social sciences has been conducted for centuries. The benefits of a comparative perspective have been long known to researchers. Perhaps sociology's most influential academic, Émile Durkheim, conducted one of the most well-known and earliest comparative research studies in his work *Suicide*. Durkheim endeavored to show that rates of suicide were related to the macro-level social environments specific to the countries in his study. His claim was that suicide could be understood through a sociological as opposed to a psychological (i.e., individual) perspective. To accomplish this goal, Durkheim used data from several European countries to study social contributors – "social facts" as they were to be known – to suicide. His contention was that only through a comparative lens can social facts – such as suicide – be fully understood because they are influenced by society.[44] He encouraged researchers to think independently and not to rely on common knowledge but to develop scientific facts.[45] Other social facts – such as offending and victimization – should be examined comparatively across several disparate contexts if we are to fully understand these phenomena.

Recent developments

Routine and lifestyle theories

Routine activity and other opportunity theories have been tested cross-nationally. Bjarnason and colleagues tested lifestyle theory using a sample from Iceland.[46] Their results echoed those found in the US.[47] In their study, violent lifestyles were found to be the best predictors of violent victimization. Including lifestyles into statistical models also closed the victimization gap between males and females, suggesting that lifestyle theory is capable of explaining the greater amount of victimization experienced by males.

Another study, conducted by Bennett, used a sample of 52 countries over a period of 25 years and found strong support for routine activity theory in the explanation of victimization. More support for the theory was found for property crimes than for violent crimes. Interestingly, different social structures (e.g., industrialization) moderated the effects of routine activity on property victimization, suggesting the importance of cross-national samples in theory testing.[48]

Despite research which suggests that routine activity theory is more suitable to explain property crime, support for the theory has been garnered for explaining violent crime as well. Using a sample from Canada, Kennedy and Forde found that routine activity theory did explain violent crime.[49] Their results indicated that the activities of individuals, particularly young males, are important in predicting violence. Those who spent more time walking around and visiting bars were more likely to be victimized due to their exposure to potentially violent situations.

Learning theories

Learning theories have also been subjected to cross-national tests. The main question which international research seeks to answer about social learning theory is whether or not peers are as influential in criminal behavior or exposure to victimization in one culture as they are in another. The extant literature reveals that peers influence delinquency regardless of social context. For example, Hartjen and Priyadarsini applied social learning and social control models to explain delinquency in a sample of French youth.[50] Measures of social learning were more reliable than social control measures, suggesting that operationalization of the theory is consistent in other social contexts and social learning variables were significantly related to delinquency, indicating validity in other social contexts.

Research on social learning theory in Japan supports the conclusion that delinquent peers influence antisocial behavior. Japan fosters a family-oriented culture which stresses the importance of family bonding. Research finds that a weakening of this bond is associated with delinquency. For example, Fenwick concludes that the breakdown of the family bond in Japanese youth increases the likelihood that these youth associate with delinquent peers. This, in turn, increases delinquency among those individuals.[51] Kobayashi and colleagues similarly find that individuals associating with friends outside of school increases their likelihood of offending.[52] Using samples of youth from India and the United States, Hartjen and Kethineni conclude that associating with delinquent peers is related to offending, regardless of the country being examined.[53]

Cross-national differences in social learning have also been uncovered. Research finds that socialization differs across countries which, subsequently, influences youth behavior. Arnett and Jensen use data from Denmark and the United States to compare socialization and risky behavior among a sample of youth.[54] This work reveals that American youth have fewer household rules and adults, beyond their immediate family, who assist in their socialization. Danish youth live in areas greater in community stabilization which is related to the development of positive individual characteristics such as self-control. American youth are more likely to be involved in minor criminal behavior such as shoplifting and vandalism than Danish youth. The authors suggest that the differences in risky behaviors of the two samples of youth are related to the individual's socialization. The comparative evidence on social learning theory provides partial support for its generalizability but also raises some questions about differential socialization among countries that may explain disparities in delinquency levels between cultures.

Strain and anomie theories

Strain and anomie theories have been tested in several different cultural contexts, producing conflicting results. The reasons for testing anomie theories (such as Institutional Anomie Theory) cross-nationally are fairly obvious. Mainly, this research tests the proposition that macro-level institutions and culture, such as capitalism, have an influence on criminal behavior. At the micro level, General Strain Theory posits that objective and subjective strains drive a person to commit crime. This may be contingent upon social context and what drives someone to act criminally in one cultural setting may not do so in another.

Institutional Anomie Theory (IAT) provides criminology with a relatively new theory within the anomie tradition that is particularly amenable to testing using international data. The main argument of IAT is that in countries where economic institutions dominate and overshadow other social institutions such as the family and school, there will be more crime (i.e., higher crime rates). Messner and Rosenfeld tested IAT using homicide rates from 45 countries and a variable that represented de-commodification (access to welfare benefits, income replacement value, and expansiveness of health coverage).[55] The results of their analysis showed that de-commodification was negatively related to homicide rates providing at least partial support for IAT. Other researchers who have tested IAT have come up with other results and at least one study claims that IAT is only applicable to advanced Western nations.[56] In either case, international studies have shed light on the importance of macro-level economies on crime.

General strain theory, a micro-level variant of anomie theory, has also been tested using data from countries other than the US. Baron used data from Vancouver, Canada to test whether or not strain is linked directly and indirectly to criminal behavior.[57] Results from the study indicated that strain has direct effects on criminal behavior as well as indirect effects through social learning (deviant peers) and social control (self-efficacy). Bao and colleagues used a non-Western sample of youth from the People's Republic of China to explore the mediation of anger in the link from strain to crime.[58] Similar to results in the US,[59] anger was shown to significantly mediate the relationship between strain and crime. The results of this study, and others from the US, provide evidence that strain is linked to delinquency and that strain often produces anger which mediates strain's relationship with crime.

Not all comparative studies support GST. Botchkovar and colleagues used data from Russia, Greece, and the Ukraine to test the relationship between subjective and objective strains and crime.[60] Support for strain was only found in the Ukraine with little to no support in Russia or Greece. This study challenged the major propositions of general strain theory by suggesting that the impact of strain upon crime may be contingent upon contextual factors. Additional cross-national comparisons are necessary to confirm or disprove the positive relationship between strain and criminal behavior.

Control theories

Social and self-control theories are among the most tested theories in the US and abroad.[61] Recently, cross-national data have been brought to bear on control theories. This research has tested major claims of these theories as well as the generality of their claims. This literature is generally supportive of social and self-control theories, but comparative research has challenged some of the claims made by the theories. Using a sample consisting of participants of four different ethnic backgrounds in the Netherlands, Junger and Marshall found that each of Hirschi's four components of social control theory predicted delinquency and provided theoretical explanations for delinquent acts.[62] In all four samples of youth, social control theory was substantially and significantly correlated with delinquent behavior and very few differences were found across ethnic backgrounds. However, the components taken together did not explain all the variations in delinquency and independent effects were found for components of learning theory as well (i.e., association with delinquent peers).

Collective efficacy's ability to explain neighborhood variation in crime was tested using similar sampling procedures in the US and Stockholm, Sweden. Results from this analysis showed that collective efficacy was able to explain varying crime levels in both countries, despite considerable cultural and environmental differences.[63] Mazerolle and colleagues compared results from their study in Brisbane, Australia to those from the US and Stockholm studies.[64] They, too, found strong support for collective efficacy's ability to explain neighborhood variation in crime, suggesting that collective efficacy may have far-reaching explanatory power.

One of the main arguments of control theories is that low self-control is a general cause of crime found in all places at all times. Traditional self-control theorists generally do not believe that macro-level structures directly impact criminal behavior and instead believe self-control should mediate any relationship between structure and criminal behavior. Comparative research has put this claim to test. Rebellon et al. (2008) used multi-level modeling to tease apart the contributions of social structure and self-control in explaining criminal behavior in 32 countries.[65] They found that self-control is internally consistent and reliable across countries and is positively related to criminal behavior. However, it did not fully mediate macro-level effects such as aggregate levels of parental neglect. Therefore, while self-control remained a general cause of crime it was not shown to be the *only* cause.

Self-control theory also states that the mediating link between low self-control and crime is the inability to anticipate long-term outcomes. In other words, the concept of low self-control implies that people who lack self-control will act impulsively to address immediate concerns, paying scant attention to the future costs of their actions.[66] Tittle and Botchkovar tested this conceptualization using data from Russia.[67] They found support for the generality claims of self-control theory (i.e., self-control was negatively related to criminal behavior) but results did not support the claim that it is the inability to account for long-term consequences of behavior that links the concept of self-control with criminal behavior. This indicates that while the overarching conceptualization of self-control theory may not be culturally bound, perhaps certain components of the theory operate differently depending on social context. Similarly, Vazsonyi and colleagues found that different components of self-control explained different amounts of variation in offending using a sample consisting of participants from four different countries.[68] Continued research using samples from several other countries is needed to understand the nuances and generality of self-control claims.

Results from the International Self-Report Delinquency studies

Two books have been published presenting results from the ISRD-II. First, in *Juvenile delinquency in Europe and beyond: Results from the second International Self-Report Delinquency study*, several chapters present findings from different countries which support the generality of theories to explain behavior cross-nationally. Social disorganization, self-control, risky lifestyles, and delinquent peer association are related to delinquency, regardless of the country under investigation. In addition, analysis of the ISRD-II data showed that immigrants were more likely to be offenders in most countries (but certainly not in all countries or among all immigrant groups).[69]

The second publication, *The many faces of youth crime*, expands on the findings in the previously mentioned book with specific attention to the ability of theories to explain offending and victimization across national contexts.[70] Similar to results in the first ISRD study, family bonding and parental control remain robust predictors of delinquent activity. Another control theory, self-control, was measured by items included in the ISRD-II study. Analysis showed that self-control predicts delinquency across national contexts and is also found to be related to weak bonds to the family. An interaction effect was present with opportunities to engage in crime but only in half of the country clusters, indicating a need to test particular parts of theories cross-nationally. Attachment to school and school disorganization were found to predict delinquency among boys and girls which held for both violent and property crime, even after controlling for the effects of other individual-level characteristics and structural (e.g., employment rate) characteristics. Another social control theory, social disorganization, was measured by several items included in the study and was found to positively predict delinquency, increasing the odds of offending by approximately 32 percent.

Results related to lifestyles and associating with peers are in line with the findings of the first study. Overall, youth spend a great deal of time associating with their peers. However, there are differences between clusters. For example, it is more common for youth to spend several nights a week out with friends in the Anglo-Saxon and Northern Europe clusters than in the Mediterranean cluster, where it is more common for youth to spend time with family. Consistent across clusters is the finding that boys spend more time with peers than girls and that spending time with peers is related to an increase in the odds of offending (about a 20 to 50 percent increase in odds depending on context). Similarly, spending more time with family is associated with a decrease in the odds of offending.

In sum, as stated in the final chapter of *The many faces of youth crime*, previous analyses of the ISRD-II dataset provide support for elements of self-control theory, social bonding theory, social disorganization theory, as well as routine activities theory. These results apply to the entire sample – suggesting that these theories have general applicability– as well as for the individual clusters, albeit with some variability and exceptions – suggesting the need to be sensitive to local specifications.

There are some major take-away points from international criminological research. First, evidence suggests that theories of offending and victimization have achieved some success in understanding violence and theft across several social contexts. In other words, many criminological theories are general in their overall ability to explain crime and criminality. The major theories of victimization, lifestyle, and routine activity theory are often shown to increase victimization in similar ways regardless of the national context.[71] In addition, social control, social learning, and strain theories all provide adequate frameworks for explaining crime across national contexts.[72]

Second, despite the finding that theories do a relatively good job in explaining violence cross-nationally, research finds subtle differences among social contexts. While the major tenets of theories find support regardless of the sample under consideration, often supporting claims of generality, there are subtle differences found in the operationalization of these theories that are idiosyncratic to the particular social context. For example, Vazsonyi and colleagues[73] found that separate components of self-control theory explain crime differently depending on national context, and Botchkovar and colleagues[74] found that GST only explained delinquency as expected in one country in their study but not in the others. To date, little is known about these idiosyncrasies. Generality claims of many criminological theories tend to hold cross-nationally, but variation does exist in the operationalization of several components of these theories. It appears appropriate – and essential – to bring together these literatures to construct a framework for beginning to answer the remaining questions surrounding major criminological theories.

The case of the Super Bowl and sex trafficking

Anticipation was high. Two of the best quarterbacks, Tom Brady and Eli Manning, were meeting again in the 2012 season Super Bowl in Indianapolis, Indiana. The Patriots and Tom Brady had some bad blood for Manning's Giants as they had pulled off an epic upset five years earlier in the 2007 season Super Bowl. As families and friends from all over the United States (and abroad) gathered around the TV to watch the rematch, the teams took the field in what would be another Giants win over the powerhouse Patriots.[75]

As the football game was in full force, another incident was taking place (and had been taking place for several days). Thousands of young females were trafficked to Indianapolis for sex work. The Super Bowl is noted to be the largest sex trafficking event in the United States due to the increased demand of the individuals attending the football game. Forbes reported that the 2010 Miami Super Bowl was thought to have brought in over 10,000 prostitutes to the city.[76] The National Center for Missing & Exploited Children estimates that in the US alone, one in six missing children is likely a victim of sex trafficking.[77]

Human trafficking is a serious international problem that leaves no country unscathed. The United Nations Office of Drugs and Crime reports that in 2006, 71 countries identified almost 15,000 trafficking victims (and a total of 111 provided some data on human trafficking). This number is only a small fraction of the total picture. Almost 80 percent of all trafficking is related to sexual exploitation.[78] Unfortunately, considering the demand for sex, labor, and other forced services, trafficking will likely continue. Fortunately, it appears that attention to this topic is growing, as is scholarly research in the area.

Remaining questions

International research is making a resurgence and shedding light on important issues of generalizability and cultural contingencies in explanations of crime across the world. There are fascinating questions that have yet to be answered, or even addressed, by research. There are still many questions about how cultural factors may attenuate or enhance crime and criminal behavior. This chapter has explored many of the differences between collections of countries and their average or general culture. Exactly how these differences may or may not influence crime is not yet well understood, even though some headway is being made.

As crime becomes more global and crime types like terrorism, cybercrime, human trafficking, and white-collar crime cross national boundaries, collaboration on policy and research will increase where necessary. An additional area that appears to be ripe for international research is delinquent youth gangs. Little is known about the specifics of gangs across countries and cultural contexts. I reached out to the best person I know to better understand this issue, criminologist and gang expert David Pyrooz at the University of Colorado Boulder: "it is anticipated that gang research will continue to be internationalized," he begins. "There are too many groups that assume gang-like features across the world for this to go ignored. The Eurogang program of research provided an essential platform for the type of comparative research."[79] This will require extensive planning and collaboration.

The best avenues for cooperation are only beginning to be navigated. Different laws, cultural practices, law enforcement capabilities, and social environments make collaboration on crime and justice issues very difficult. Research across nations is also challenging given that definitions of crime vary, access to human subjects is easier or harder depending on rights given to research participants, and cultural factors such as social desirability differ across certain nations.[80] Despite these barriers, official and self-report data on crime and justice will grow into the future and broader pictures of theory and policy are likely to emerge from these efforts.

Policy

Although comparative criminal justice and criminology is relatively new from an academic standpoint, the need for international cooperation in order to address crime and violence has been recognized for over a century. One of the most coordinated efforts to investigate crime that crosses national boarders is the International Police or INTERPOL. Initiated as the International Criminal Police Commission (ICPC) in 1923, INTERPOL now has the cooperation of 190 countries (North Korea is one of the few states that is not a member of INTERPOL) and has over 750 employees.[81]

INTERPOL is careful not to overstep its boundaries (literally and figuratively). The purpose of the organization is not to become involved in other countries' political processes nor to intercede in domestic affairs. INTERPOL's constitution lists two main purposes: (1) to ensure and promote the widest possible mutual assistance among all criminal police authorities within the limits of the laws existing in the different countries and in the spirit of the Universal Declaration of Human Rights; and (2) to establish and develop all institutions likely to contribute effectively to the prevention and suppression of ordinary law crimes.[82] INTERPOL has most often become involved in cases such as drug/weapon/human trafficking, terrorism, genocide, child pornography, and money laundering. These crimes are generally seen as serious crimes for all member nations and their scope often crosses international boundaries, making an international law enforcement organization a necessity to effectively catch and prosecute criminals.

You may be asking yourself: What happens if someone (or an organization) is accused of breaking international law? INTERPOL is one of the largest and most organized law enforcement agencies that investigate crime and its counterpart in the legal realm is the International Criminal Court (ICC). Individuals who are accused of violating international laws related to genocide, war crimes, terrorism, and other crimes against humanity may be brought before the ICC in The Hague, Netherlands. While the idea of the ICC has been around at least since the close of World War I, the ICC was not officially formed until almost a century later, in 2002. At present, 124 countries are ICC members of which the United States and Russia are among a few that initially signed for membership but later withdrew from the agreement.[83]

Several efforts have also been put together to govern the way in which people are treated across the globe. Even when nations go to war, there are established guidelines on how to treat prisoners of war, the injured, medical providers, and civilians. Known as the "Geneva Conventions," rules were established following the Civil War on how to treat those involved with and exposed to war. The four conventions were revised in 1949 following World War II. Table 12.1 shows the progression of the conventions and their major contributions to how individuals are treated in war. Overall, the goal is to maintain standards of human dignity and treatment even in times of war when violence is justified.[84]

Important for criminology and criminal justice, there are also international guidelines for conducting research on human beings. Following the atrocities in Germany during World War II, trials were conducted in Nuremburg, Germany to examine the "racial hygiene" agenda that was carried out by Nazi doctors and researchers.[85] For example, prisoners of war were exposed to freezing conditions to study hypothermia, prisoners were injected with immunizations to test their effectiveness on diseases and illnesses against their will and were even exposed to poisonous gasses so that subsequent administration of "antidotes" could be tested, and several medical experiments (most famously conducted by Dr. Josef Mengela – a.k.a. Dr. Death) were carried out on prisoners, including operations on live individuals, and sterilization.

To address this horrific history and to prevent coercion during research studies in the future, the Nuremberg Codes were developed to protect human subjects. Today, all research studies must be reviewed and approved by a board of experts who can judge the costs and benefits of the research and ensure that any negative outcomes will be balanced out by the positive outcomes (these are often called Institutional Review Boards (IRBs)).[86] The codes developed through this effort are listed in Table 12.2.

Summary

There is little controversy in the idea that the world is "getting smaller." Organizations are increasing their business across the globe, people move frequently between countries, and issues that affect one nation often affect many others. These connections have made the world an exciting place. However, along with the good, crime has also become more international.

To meet this relatively recent phenomenon, criminal justice and criminology have also become more international – meaning that policy and program efforts are increasingly international in nature as well as criminological research. It is becoming less and less acceptable to have a theory of crime that has not been tested with samples from different countries and cultures, or to have a policy that ignores the inherent diversity of almost all nations.

Results for criminological research indicate that most general theories of crime are fairly good at explaining crime and deviance across national contexts and with diverse samples. However, there are often minor cultural contingencies in the specifics behind theoretical explanations of crime which deserve more scrutiny. It is also clear that crime rates vary across nations, indicating the need to theorize about why there is such disparity in levels of crime across national boundaries.

Criminal justice policies and practices also extend across borders. INTERPOL, the ICC, and international research collaborations are becoming increasingly common and will likely continue to grow as the world continues to become more interdependent. Currently, there are now international sections of both the Academy of Criminal Justice Sciences and the American Society of Criminology, as well as major criminological

Table 12.1 The Geneva Conventions

Convention	Name	First Adopted	Revised	Main Purpose
First Geneva Convention	For the Amelioration of the Condition of the Wounded and Sick in Armed Forces in the Field	1864	1906; 1929; 1949	Provides for: 1) the immunity from capture and destruction of all establishments for the treatment of wounded and sick soldiers; 2) the impartial reception and treatment of all combatants; 3) the protection of civilians providing aid to the wounded; and 4) the recognition of the Red Cross symbol as a means of identifying persons and equipment covered by the agreement.
Second Geneva Convention	For the Amelioration of the Condition of Wounded, Sick and Shipwrecked Members of Armed Forces at Sea	1949		Major provisions: requires all parties to protect and care for the wounded, sick, and shipwrecked; protect religious and medical personnel serving on a combat ship; hospital ships cannot be used for any military purpose, and owing to their humanitarian mission, they cannot be attacked or captured.
Third Geneva Convention	Relative to the Treatment of Prisoners of War	1929	1949	Major provisions: states that prisoners of war are the responsibility of the state, not the persons who capture them, and that they may not be transferred to a state that is not party to the Convention; state that prisoners of war must be treated humanely without any adverse discrimination and that their medical needs must be met.
Fourth Geneva Convention	Relative to the Protection of Civilian Persons in Time of War	1949		Members of armed forces who have laid down their arms, and combatants who are hors de combat (out of the fight) due to wounds, detention, or any other cause shall in all circumstances be treated humanely, with the following prohibitions: 1) violence to life and person, in particular murder of all kinds, mutilation, cruel treatment and torture; 2) taking of hostages; 3) outrages upon personal dignity, in particular humiliating and degrading treatment; 4) the passing of sentences and the carrying out of executions without previous judgment pronounced by a regularly constituted court, affording all the judicial guarantees which are recognized as indispensable by civilized peoples.

Table 12.2 The Nuremberg Codes

Ten points of the Nuremberg Code

1. Required is the voluntary, well-informed, understanding consent of the human subject in a full legal capacity.

2. The experiment should aim at positive results for society that cannot be procured in some other way.

3. It should be based on previous knowledge (e.g., an expectation derived from animal experiments) that justifies the experiment.

4. The experiment should be set up in a way that avoids unnecessary physical and mental suffering and injuries.

5. It should not be conducted when there is any reason to believe that it implies a risk of death or disabling injury.

6. The risks of the experiment should be in proportion to (that is, not exceed) the expected humanitarian benefits.

7. Preparations and facilities must be provided that adequately protect the subjects against the experiment's risks.

8. The staff who conduct or take part in the experiment must be fully trained and scientifically qualified.

9. The human subjects must be free to immediately quit the experiment at any point when they feel physically or mentally unable to go on.

10. Likewise, the medical staff must stop the experiment at any point when they observe that continuation would be dangerous.

conferences on almost all continents that are regularly attended by individuals from across the world. International criminology appears to be becoming just criminology itself. The international part is a permanent fixture in most theorizing and programming, with little evidence that this will change.

Notes

1 Hartjen, 2008: xiii.
2 Kohn, 1987.
3 Nelken, 2002.
4 Howard, Newman, & Pridemore, 2000.
5 Sheptycki, 2005: 79.
6 Christie, 1970.
7 Nelken, 2000.
8 Travers, 2008; see also Nelken, 2002.
9 Esping-Andersen, 1990: 18.
10 Esping-Andersen, 1999: 34.
11 Esping-Andersen, 1990, 1999.
12 Saint-Arnaud & Bernard, 2003.
13 Esping-Andersen, 1990.
14 Esping-Andersen, 1990: 26.
15 See also Saint-Arnaud & Bernard, 2003.
16 See also Cavadino & Dignan, 2006; Lappi-Seppälä, 2007.
17 See also Saint-Arnaud & Bernard, 2003.

18 Bonoli, 1997.
19 House et al., 2004.
20 Hofstede, 2001.
21 Esping-Andersen, 1990.
22 House et al., 2004.
23 Hofstede, 1980.
24 Inglehart & Baker, 2000.
25 Cattell, 1950.
26 Cavadino & Dignan, 2006.
27 Hall & Soskice, 2001.
28 House et al., 2004; see also Cavadino & Dignan, 2006.
29 House et al., 2004.
30 Gannon & Pillai, 2013: 249.
31 House et al., 2004.
32 Gannon & Pillai, 2013.
33 House et al., 2004.
34 Gannon & Pillai, 2013.
35 Gannon & Pillai, 2013: 368.
36 Gannon & Pillai, 2013: 523.
37 House et al., 2004.
38 Gannon & Pillai, 2013.
39 Neapolitan, 1994.
40 House et al., 2004.
41 Gannon & Pillai, 2013.
42 House et al., 2004.
43 See Posick, 2013; Rocque et al., 2015.
44 Durkheim, 1951 [1897].
45 See Travers, 2008.
46 Bjarnason, Sigurdardottir, & Thorlindsson, 1999.
47 For example, Jensen & Brownfield, 1986.
48 Bennett, 1991.
49 Kennedy & Forde, 1990.
50 Hartjen & Priyadarsini, 2003.
51 Fenwick, 1983.
52 Kobayashi et al., 1988.
53 Hartjen & Kethineni, 1996.
54 Arnett & Jensen, 1994.
55 Messner & Rosenfeld, 1997.
56 Chamlin & Cochran, 2007.
57 Baron, 2004.
58 Bao, Haas, & Yijun, 2004.
59 Mazerolle & Piquero, 1998.
60 Botchkovar, Tittle, & Antonaccio, 2009.
61 Junger-Tas et al., 2012.
62 Junger & Marshall, 1997.
63 Sampson, 2012.
64 Mazerolle, Wickes, & McBroom, 2010.
65 Rebellon, Straus, & Medeiros, 2008.
66 Gottfredson & Hirschi, 1990.
67 Tittle & Botchkovar, 2005.
68 Vazsonyi et al., 2001.
69 Junger-Tas et al., 2010.
70 Junger-Tas et al., 2012.
71 Bennett, 1991.
72 See Hartjen, 2008.
73 Vazsonyi et al., 2001.
74 Botchkovar et al., 2009.
75 New York Times, 2012.

76 See www.forbes.com/sites/meghancasserly/2012/02/02/
    sex-and-the-super-bowl-indianapolis-spotlight-teen-sex-trafficking/#5965f4234c61.
77 See www.missingkids.org/1in6.
78 UNODC, 2009.
79 Personal interview with David Pyrooz, August 16, 2016.
80 See Marshall, 2010.
81 INTERPOL, 2014.
82 INTERPOL, 1956.
83 See www.icc-cpi.int/about/how-the-court-works/Pages/default.aspx#organization.
84 See https://ihl-databases.icrc.org/applic/ihl/ihl.nsf/States.
    xsp?xp_viewStates=XPages_NORMStatesParties&xp_treatySelected=375.
85 See Rafter, Posick, & Rocque, 2016.
86 Weindling, 2001.

Further reading

Gould, L. A. & Pate, M. (2016). *State fragility around the world: Fractured justice and fierce reprisal.* Boca Raton, FL: CRC Press.

Hartjen, C. A. (2008). *Youth, crime, and justice: A global inquiry.* New Brunswick, NJ: Rutgers University Press.

Junger-Tas, J., Marshall, I., Enzmann, D., Killias, M., Steketee, M., & Gruszczynska, B. (2010). *Juvenile delinquency in Europe and beyond: Results of the second International Self-Report Delinquency study.* Berlin, Germany: Springer.

Nelken, D. (2011). *Comparative criminal justice and globalization.* Surrey, UK: Ashgate Publishing.

Sheptycki, J. & Wardak, A. (2012). *Transnational and comparative criminology.* New York: Routledge.

13 Theory and various crime types

Introduction   166
Theory   166
Recent developments   167
The case of "Pharmabro" Martin Shkreli and white-collar crime   174
Summary   174

Introduction

Criminological theories, as we have discussed, may either be general or crime specific. General theories are intended to be applied to any type of crime, while crime-specific theories hone in on explaining one specific crime type (or small groups of crime). Both approaches, as evidenced by earlier chapters in this book, have achieved some support. In this chapter, new and emerging crime types ("new" and "emerging" meaning we have only recently tried to theorize about and explain these types of crimes in a systematic way, although many have been around since the dawn of man) will be discussed and theoretical approaches that have been taken to examine these types of crimes, either general, specific, or a little of both, will be introduced. Certainly not all relevant and important crimes can be included, but they are some of the most pressing areas which have gained theoretical traction in the past decade or so.

Theory

Many of the theories discussed up until this point are considered *general* theories of crime. General theories of criminal behavior claim to explain all crime at all times (for the most part, no theorist has claimed that one theory can account for all the reasons that a person would commit a crime). This is what makes these theories general. Recently, general theories have been put to the test of explaining types of crime that have traditionally received scant attention from criminologists. Can self-control perspectives explain cybercrime? Terrorism? What are all the strains that lead to crime and can new theories be included in the framework of general strain theory? These questions are now being explored.

Along with general theories, there are *specific* theories. These perspectives imply that general theories cannot account for certain types of crime and that new, or different, theoretical approaches must be applied for the explanation of certain crimes. Can general theories of crime explain why certain people become serial killers? Do general theories extend to females or transgender individuals? Perhaps not, and new perspectives need to be brought forth to explain the behavior of certain groups of individuals.

This chapter discusses some extensions of general theories of crime to explain recent crime types that have gained traction in criminology. In addition, this chapter includes discussions on theories that have been designed to address specific types of crime. In doing so, contemporary theoretical efforts are brought to the fore and emerging criminological interests are covered – both of which are often overlooked.

Recent developments

Cybercrime

I keenly (and very fondly) remember playing early computer games on floppy disks (the real flimsy disks) in grade school. Two-dimensional games such as Oregon Trail, Number Munchers, and Where in the World is Carmen Santiago consumed my computer lab free time in the early grades. Fast forward to my junior year in high school and one would see the pandemonium that would become known as Y2K. Today, I type this book on a powerful (by today's standards) laptop, which connects to my smaller portable tablet, all of which, of course, is accessible by a pocket-sized mega-computer known as a "smartphone." In under 35 years, I have seen enormous changes in the tech sphere – and the advancement does not appear to be linear but exponential. In a few years' time the technology boasted about in this paragraph will seem like a distant past and, certainly, readers will have a good laugh.

With computer technology changing and becoming increasingly sophisticated, more opportunities to commit a host of online crime are emerging. Cybercrime, narrowly defined here as crime committed with the assistance of a computer, is becoming a focus of criminologists and policy-makers alike. The looming question at this point is whether or not we can adequately explain cybercrime and why people fall victim to this costly and harmful activity.

Paving the way on this research are two cybercrime scholars who have used several criminological theories to explain cybercrime. Thomas Holt of Michigan State University and Adam Bossler of Georgia Southern University have teamed up with others to examine cybercrime and attempt to explain why people become involved with the crime and what increases the likelihood of victimization. Using routine activity theory, they find that spending time online is related to risk of victimization (more time online, more exposure to victimization) and that engaging in risky behaviors online increases the risk of victimization.[1]

In two subsequent studies, Bossler, Holt, and colleagues examine social learning and self-control as predictors of cybercrime. First, using a comprehensive social learning model that incorporates individual social learning concepts and macro-level structural concepts, Holt, Burress, and Bossler find that individuals learn cyber deviance from others and that learning mechanisms account for differences in cybercrime by males and females as well as Whites and minorities.[2] In a second study, Holt, Bossler, and May find that low self-control is positively related to cyber deviance among juveniles and so too is associating with deviant peers. The two also sometimes interact when predicting cyber deviance, suggesting the importance of comprehensive models and modeling relationships in cybercrime research.[3]

Taken together, these studies speak to the ability of criminological theories to explain cybercrime – a fairly new, and increasingly important, crime type in contemporary society.

Terrorism

Along with the cyber world, the international world is becoming more important as the world "becomes smaller." Interestingly, terrorism is often covered by fields other than criminology, including political science, psychology, and economics.[4] Slowly, criminology is answering the call to become more involved in the study of terrorism. A cadre of scholars is now applying criminological theories to explain terrorism, with varying success. In any case, the efforts are illuminating what appears to work and not work in the study of terrorism, pointing a light to future research efforts to explain the phenomenon.

The limited amount of criminological research on terrorism has mainly utilized a routine activity and rational choice framework. William Pridemore and Joshua Freilich tested whether strict laws protecting abortion clinics deterred or emboldened criminals who strike terror into abortion providers. They found that there was no impact one way or another due to the laws.[5] Gary LaFree and colleagues found contrary results to those by Pridemore and Freilich when considering political violence in Northern Ireland. They saw some deterrent effects of law enforcement operations (only one initiative) but found strong support for the backlash hypothesis in that antiterrorism interventions *increased* subsequent violence.[6]

Other traditional theories have been applied to terrorism as well. Using a large database from 101 countries over the years 1981 to 2010, Susan Fahey and Gary LaFree find that socially disorganized areas (unstable states) are more likely to experience terrorism even after adjusting for several covariates. In addition, both Ronald Akers and Robert Agnew have extended their general theories of crime to explain terrorism. Akers, along with his co-author Adam Silverman, posits that terrorism can be explained by the social psychological process of associating with others who motivate and reward terroristic behavior.[7] For Agnew, terrorism is most likely when people experience "collective strains" which he describes as high in magnitude (especially when civilians are affected), perceived to be unjust, and when the violence is inflicted by the powerful against the less powerful.[8] Given the concern over groups like Al-Qaeda and ISIS and domestic terrorism in the US, France, and the United Kingdom, theoretical and empirical work on explaining and responding to terrorism will continue to grow and may, hopefully, affect policy at the highest levels.

Genocide

The year is 1940, the place is Russia. Josef Stalin ordered his secret police to murder Polish military, law enforcement, and intellectuals who stood in opposition to his regime. Stalin's executioner, who carried out the dirty work, would shoot his victims through the back of the skull one by one – up to 250 a day. The bodies were then taken to the forest of Katyn on the western edge of Russia where the ground was soft enough to dig mass graves. The executioner would kill his victims in a basement and bury them in the forest. In the end, about 22,000 Poles were killed, making "The Katyn Forest Massacre" one of the most prominent (and one of the least known) genocides of the twentieth century.[9]

The late criminologist Nicole Rafter called genocide the "crime of all crimes." Indeed, there might be no more insidious crime than the systematic torture, rape, and murder of a specific group of people. The United Nations defines genocide as "acts committed with intent to destroy a national, ethnical, racial or religious group, as such."[10] Important in this definition is the phrase "intent to destroy." Sometimes this means, quite literally, to destroy through murder, but it may also entail the systematic destruction of a culture through the decimation of a group of people's way of life (often termed cultural genocide). Along with the killing that is equated with genocide (think of Nazi Germany, the

Rwanda conflict between Hutus and Tutsis, and the Armenia genocides), these mass incidents also include rape, slavery, and torture. Recently, scholars have turned their attention toward explaining genocide using frameworks provided by criminological theories.

In their 2009 book, *Darfur and the crime of genocide,* John Hagan and Wenona Rymond-Richmond describe the crimes in the Darfur region of the Sudan (on the West side of the country neighboring Chad) as the product of race and racial hatred.[11] The Sudanese government promoted race-based killing by highlighting differences between Arabic-speaking nomadic herders and non-Arab African farmers. In this way, the government enabled the Janjaweed (Arab herders in Sudan) to attack farming villages in Darfur. Hagan and Rymond-Richmond particularly note how the government used language to dehumanize Sudanese farmers – likely making their murderous quests easier to complete. No one laments the death of a "cockroach."

Nicole Rafter's 2016 book, *The crime of all crime: A criminology of genocide,* examined in depth eight genocides from 1900 to 2000. While acknowledging differences among these genocides, her effort was to draw similarities between the genocides. An underlying theme she uncovered was the process of splitting. "Splitting," according to Rafter, is "a psychological process that takes place in the minds of perpetrators, starts with moral disengagement, moves through a shutdown of the capacity to feel empathy, and ends with objectification of the victims. Once victims seem like objects rather than other humans," she continues, "it is relatively easy to torture and kill them."[12] This criminological approach to understanding genocide is not unlike techniques of neutralization discussed earlier in this book. However, in the case of genocide, these techniques are promoted and promulgated widely, influencing whole groups of people who are then "freed" to commit heinous crimes. Such a mechanism may be *essential* for one to commit these crimes, as such inhumane treatment of others is antithetical to human behavior.

Most recently, research in Rwanda, using a massive dataset on incidents of genocide, has shed light on the extent of the atrocities as well as theoretical understanding of genocide.[13] Sociologists Hollie Nyseth Brehm and Christopher Uggen, along with Jean-Damascéne Gasanabo from the Research and Documentation Center on Genocide, Rwandan National Commission for the Fight Against Genocide, examined the Rwandan genocide to see if patterns of violence were similar to what is generally found for street crimes. Interestingly, they found many substantial differences suggesting new ways of examining crimes of genocide. Chief among these differences is that those involved with the Rwandan genocide as perpetrators of violence were significantly older – around the age of 34 – when compared to violent street criminals who are in their late teens. This suggests that some crimes may need a little more specificity in their explanations.

Mass shootings

On June 12, 2016, 29-year-old Omar Mateen walked into Pulse, a gay-friendly nightclub in Orlando, Florida, and shot 102 people. He injured 53 and killed 49 before he was shot and killed by a police officer. Before his death, Mateen swore allegiance to the Islamic State of Iraq and the Levant (ISIL). In the investigations to follow there was no substantiating evidence to suggest that Mateen had any real ties to ISIL; nor did he have any previous dealings with gay nightclubs or websites (as some suggested). What is certain is that Mateen's actions were those of terror and mass murder.

Mateen had shown many signs of psychological distress. He had tried to get many jobs in law enforcement but each time he ran into trouble after making inappropriate comments about shooting people. His ex-wife had commented that Mateen was abusive and psychotically disturbed. She also claimed that he was a frequent steroid user which was confirmed by post-mortem toxicology examinations. His father gave a similar account of his erratic and sometimes violent behavior. Those who knew him also said he harbored a lot of hatred toward those of other races, ethnicities, and sexual orientation (although there are several informal accounts of him frequenting bars and picking up men).

It is likely that we will never know the exact reason for this act of terror, like so many other similar incidents. Some put the blame on society and others on the individual. Perhaps the answer is a little bit of both. What is likely is that research into this area will continue and increase in the upcoming years. Mass atrocities, including terrorism, genocide, and mass murder, are receiving more attention in the media and raising questions as to why people commit such heinous crimes. This is a call for criminologists to answer.

In *The will to kill*, Northeastern University scholars James Alan Fox and Jack Levin, along with Indiana University-Purdue University Indiana scholar Kenna Quinet, attempt to shed light on some of the issues around lethal violence. When considering mass murders specifically, they argue that these killers often buck the trend that we see with street criminals. Contrary to the common media perception that mass murderers "snap" or "go postal," the actual mass murderer is often calculating and plans their attack days or even months ahead of time. They also target specific people in their murderous pursuits (often those who they believe harmed them in the past).

So why would someone commit mass murder like Seung-Hui Cho in 2007 when he shot and killed 32 people at Virginia Tech, or Charles Whitman who, in 1966, sat atop a tower on the campus of the University of Texas at Austin and killed 14 people (he also killed his wife and his mother before going on his shooting rampage)? Fox, Levin, and Quinet suggest that it is complicated to understand all the causes for sure (if we did know, it would be much easier to address this type of violence). However, they do suggest that when considering people who do "snap" and spontaneously kill large groups of people there might be neurological factors that are present which contribute to their breakdown. In fact, this may have influenced Whitman to take part in his attack. Known as an even-tempered man with an IQ in the upper 130s, he went through a dramatic change later in life. He wrote before his attack:

> I do not quite understand what it is that compels me to type this letter. Perhaps it is to leave some vague reason for the actions I have recently performed. I do not really understand myself these days. I am supposed to be an average reasonable and intelligent young man. However, lately (I cannot recall when it started) I have been a victim of many unusual and irrational thoughts.[14]

Given his strange feelings and change in behavior, he explicitly requested an autopsy following his death and asked that his brain be carefully examined. After being killed by police, Whitman was taken to a medical examiner for the autopsy where the doctor removed a small brain tumor which was likely pushing against his amygdala, thereby possibly inhibiting emotion regulation.

Other types of crime may call for other theoretical approaches. Mass murder that is related to street gangs and terrorist cells probably contains a component of social learning or social psychology which explains the transmission of violent attitudes and motivations from one member to another. Regular street crime is likely influenced by many biological, psychological, and social factors that require interdisciplinary investigation. In any case, Fox, Levin, and Quinet suggest that general theories may be limited in the way they can precisely explain specific types of violence, including mass murder.

Hate crime

Shifting demographics in the US and abroad have led to a widespread feeling that hate crime is on the rise. It is challenging to determine whether or not this feeling is justified given the numbers because, while hate crime *may* be rising, the reporting and detection of hate crime is *certainly* rising. However, the sense that the frequency and intensity of hate crime is rising may also be supported. Two national non-profit organizations, the Southern Poverty Law Center (SPLC) and the Anti-Defamation League (ADL), in the United States report that hate crime has risen in recent years and has experienced a significant spike following the election of President Donald Trump. Although tracking hate crime is difficult, the FBI did report a rise of about 6.5 percent from 2014 to 2015 and a proportion of this rise is due to crime against those who are, or who are perceived to be, Muslim. According to the Bureau of Justice Statistics, an average of 250,000 hate crimes are recorded each year (from 2004 to 2015). Some have attributed rising hate crime to the ascendance of the far right in the United States and in other countries. It is likely that a closer eye will be kept on these issues over coming years.[15]

Relatedly, there are those who blame violent crime on recent immigrants and believe that crime is increasing due to illegal (and even legal) immigration. This image persists, even though crime is generally decreasing and is currently at historical lows. A massive research study was recently conducted by criminologists Graham Ousey and Charis Kubrin which found that immigration has no effect on violent crime. In fact, the relationship may be negative (but this finding was negligible in their study).[16] Regardless of the exact effect size, the results of this study challenge the theoretical propositions of early social disorganization theories which suggest that increased immigration (and areas populated by immigrants) leads to social disorganization and high crime rates. In fact, there may be something even crime preventive about immigration into some areas.[17] As Ousey and Kubrin note in their paper, the theoretical linkages between crime and immigration are not well understood and need much more attention in the future.

Rural crime

If you think back to most of the original theories covered in this book, the focus was on urban crime and delinquency. This made sense, as urban centers were growing and rural areas were decreasing in population numbers (also remember that many theorists were actually from rural areas, like Shaw, McKay, and Sutherland). Rural crime just was not a major focus of early criminology. People were leaving the agricultural life in droves and moving to the city which then became a melting pot of ideas and cultures.

Recently, some theorists have brought back attention to rural issues in crime and violence. This effort has been led by Ohio State criminologist Joseph Donnermeyer and West Virginia University criminologist Walter DeKeseredy. While applauding the recent work on understanding crime in rural areas, Donnermeyer and DeKeseredy are discouraged by the lack of a critical theoretical focus in these efforts.

Donnermeyer and DeKeseredy are interested in establishing and working toward a critical rural criminology. One model that they adapt in their book *Rural criminology* begins with the feminist/male peer support model.[18] This model begins with the assertion that society is dominated by male patriarchy and that when there are threats to masculinity violence is not too far behind. Much of this violence is supported, or at least condoned, by male peers. When relationships crumble it is seen as a threat to male masculinity, leading to separation and divorce or sexual/physical assault.

Donnermeyer and DeKeseredy take this model and discuss how a focus on rural males can further this perspective. Rural areas have been going through considerable social change over the past several decades. This is evident in the loss of family farms and the decline of industry in rural settings such as sawmills and coalmines. This has forced women in rural areas to take on more responsibilities outside the home, including working more hours and often more than one job. Since male patriarchy and the "traditional family" is generally ingrained in many rural communities, males have reduced self-worth from not being able to provide support to their families and the independence of women is a threat to masculinity. To control women, males will abuse their counterparts to ensure that their worth and family expectations are upheld. While not an entirely new theory of rural crime, this model does incorporate rural-specific causal factors in the etiology of delinquent and criminal behavior.

Does crime and violence in rural areas need new theories for explanation? Joseph Donnermeyer helps me understand via an interview. "A new theory will require recognition of two essential sociological assumptions that the theory of social disorganization in its present form has not taken seriously," he begins.

> First, there are multiple forms of social organization and forms of collective efficacy in existence at the same place, whether this place is a small rural village or the neighborhoods of large cities. Second, individuals simultaneously participate in these multiple networks.[19]

These forms of organization and the roles in which people participate may vary from rural, to suburban, to urban contexts, which is essential for Donnermeyer to understand. He admits that much needs to be done in this area but says that criminology is up to the task and has an important voice in the matter.

Global warming and violence

In 2011, Texas suffered a major drought that left Texas not only dry but at increased risk for wildfires and other catastrophes. Due to the water shortage, agricultural production was down by over $7.5 billion, the cattle business lost over $3.2 billion, and cotton business chalked up a $2.2 billion loss. Water scarcity is not only a US issue, but also a global issue. It is the cause of many deaths, wars, and the current refugee crisis. It is now clear that drought, along with other "natural disasters," is related to global climate change. Therefore, one of the greatest contemporary concerns of criminologists and natural scientists alike is the impact of widespread climate change upon the environment as well as violence.[20]

The earth is warming at a rate in which the past two years were the hottest on record. This has severe implications for crime and violence around the world. In their book *Crime, violence, and global warming*, criminologists John Crank and Linda Jacoby discuss two major theoretical models that can help explain crime and violence related to global climate change.[21] The first was previously presented by Homer-Dixon in 1999. Homer-Dixon hypothesized that changes in the environment lead to resource scarcity. For example, forest depletion results from extensive logging, fish stock is decreased from over-fishing, and rising temperatures result in severe drought which itself leads to a reduction in food crops as well as economic productivity. This scarcity leads to increased migration/refugees, strain, and inequality as individuals look for other areas to prosper. Homer-Dixon argues that these effects increase state crime, terrorism, ethnic conflict, and human trafficking.[22]

The second model discussed by Crank and Jacoby was originally proposed by criminologist and strain theorist Robert Agnew. Unsurprisingly, the basis of Agnew's approach to explaining crime through climate change is the role of strain. Where Homer-Dixon focused largely on macro-level crimes (e.g., terrorism, trafficking, ethnic conflict), Agnew discusses how climate change leads to crime through several strains. The major strains outlined by Agnew include: (1) resource scarcity; (2) social conflict; (3) weakened state controls; (4) first versus third world conflict; and (5) poverty. In other words, climate change increases strain and opportunities for crime, while decreasing social control and social support leading to higher levels of individual, group, state, and corporate crime.[23]

The problem of climate change is a serious one and perhaps one that criminology can help address. I caught up with John Crank and he agrees. "Criminology is engaged," he acknowledges, "but not to the degree that it could be. A central challenge faces all the social sciences – how do we take this problem from the physical sciences and translate it into a human science problem?" The theoretical models proposed by Homer-Dixon and

Agnew are a good start, but there is much room for this type of criminology going into the future. One important way is more interdisciplinary work. "We need much more sophisticated planning, across a lot of the human sciences – urban planning, political science, criminology and security, public administration, and the like," states Crank before getting more to the point. "Otherwise, we will have an unremitting disaster on our hands, one that we will not recover from."[24]

Organized and white-collar crime

Street crime has long been the focus of criminologists. Recently, there has been a concerted effort to include white-collar crime in criminology. White-collar crime includes offenses such as anti-trust violations, money laundering, and insider trading as well as many more damaging activities. Following dips in the American economy, a more focused effort to identify and punish white-collar criminals appeared to take hold in the US. This was especially the case around the housing crisis in 2008.

Although there has been a resurgence (of sorts but, for many, still too little) of research and attention to white-collar crime, the term was defined and discussed almost a century ago by none other than Edwin Sutherland. Sutherland wanted to expand the exploration of criminal behavior beyond the street and poor urban neighborhoods into the world of society's elites. He was dismayed that the primary focus up until his writings (in the late 1930s and early 1940s) had concentrated almost solely on the lower class and neglected the activities of the middle and upper classes. Therefore, he focused on "crime in relation to business."[25] He believed that white-collar crime was, in fact, a violation of law and it was fundamentally different from lower-class crime. Theoretically, he believed that any explanation of crime must account for the crimes of both the lower class and the upper class. Specifically, he believed that causes of crime linked to poverty failed to do this and were not good explanations of crime (even lower-class crime which was the focus of poverty-based theories). Of course, he incorporated his differential association theory into the explanation of crime whereby white-collar criminals *learn* the ways and motivations for committing white-collar crime from close family and peers (such as co-workers). He also incorporated some concepts from social disorganization theory in that many businesses are not organized around responding to white-collar crime because they are focused on profits and not on opposing certain behavior.

Two recent theoretical approaches have built upon Sutherland's pioneering work to further explain white-collar crime. In 1985, criminologist Michael Benson published his research on white-collar criminals. After interviewing individuals involved in white-collar crime, he noticed a common theme – the denial of guilt or what he called "denying the guilty mind."[26] Most of his participants used one of two strategies to put their minds at ease prior to or after the crime. First, many downplayed the seriousness of their crime. Since white-collar crimes often do not target a specific victim and because they do not cause immediate physical harm, white-collar criminals believed that they had not done something as serious as street criminals. Second, many stated that they were not blameworthy. Many criminals said that they were not aware of the rules or that the rules of business were so complicated that what they did should not be considered a crime. Benson believes that these strategies are easy to accept for people who otherwise lead an upstanding life and who are middle-class members of society. Being able to put their mind at ease, they are more likely to become involved in criminal business activities and justify it later.

A second perspective is offered by criminologists Neal Shover and Andy Hochstetler. In their 2006 book *Choosing white-collar crime*, they suggest that white-collar crime may best be described through a combination of routine activity theory and control theory.[27] Shover and Hochstetler believe that white-collar crime is a rational choice and people will engage in white-collar crime when the benefits outweigh the costs. They refer to white-collar crime as a "lure." Certain people see this lure and are attracted to it. If there is no capable guardianship or much oversight, many will "take the bait" and engage in white-collar crime. Not all people do (and some do not even see the lure in the first place). These individuals are those with high self-control and with stakes in conformity, such as a family they don't want to let down or a good relationship with their customers. Importantly, Shover and Hochstetler urge criminologists to examine those control factors that differ between upper- and lower-class individuals such as a job, family, school, and social supports which lead to different types of crime.

The case of "Pharmabro" Martin Shkreli and white-collar crime

Martin Shkreli was the CEO of an American pharmaceutical company, Turing, in 2015. Turing was developing a variety of drugs for issues associated with depression and hypertension when it acquired the drug Daraprim – an anti-malarial and anti-parasitic drug often used by those who have been diagnosed with the AIDS virus. At the time that Shkreli and Turing acquired Daraprim, the drug cost about $13.50 a pill for consumers. The company raised its price several hundred-fold to $750, essentially making the drug too costly for those who desperately needed it. While this shocked the American conscience – and led to widespread hatred of Shkreli and derogatory names of the man, not least of which was "pharmabro" – it was not illegal. But this put Shkreli on the map.

Following the drug price fiasco, Shkreli was found to be involved in a Ponzi-like scheme that violated the trust of investors in two of his previous companies: MSMB Capital Management and Retrophin. This *is* illegal. Like Bernie Madoff and Martha Stewart before him, Shkreli had misled investors to profit himself and his company – an antitrust and securities fraud violation. Currently out of jail on bail, Shkreli awaits his fate. He is no longer the CEO of Turing.

Shkreli certainly exemplifies the white-collar violations and crimes that occur among the elite in the US. The ability of those in positions of power to violate the trust of those who rely on them is a powerful force that not only de-legitimizes the business industry but costs the US billions of dollars annually.[28] For Shkreli, he hasn't remained quiet on the outside. He recently forked out over $2 million for a rare copy of the Wu-Tang Clan album *Once Upon a Time in Shaolin* and has made offers to Kanye West to be the sole owner of his album *The Life of Pablo* – which has not been accepted by West or his affiliates.[29] Along with being an exemplar of white-collar crime, he seems to also be the poster boy for sociologist Thorstein Veblen's "conspicuous consumption" concept.

Summary

A lot of work remains to be done on theorizing about contemporary crime issues and global problems. Tests of crime-specific theories are only beginning to be conducted and evidence on the ability of general theories to generalize is mixed. Criminology is finding its voice in many fields of research. It is also broadening its horizons to study many different outcomes of interest. In the coming years, given the global climate, it is likely that the field will delve deeper into issues around cybercrime, mass atrocities, hate crime, and rural crime. Criminology will also likely include work that is international in scope (as discussed in Chapter 12).

It is also unlikely that the disagreements between general theories of crime and specific theories of crime will be resolved any time soon. Or maybe this is something of a false dichotomy. For instance, Robert Agnew has offered criminology his general strain theory that is intended to explain the bulk of all crime but he has also reframed it to account for crime that arises from climate change. Therefore, the theory is still a general theory of crime, but it has been expanded to account for all different types of stressors that lead to crime. One thing is certain: as the world changes, so too will explanations of the phenomena that exist in society. Criminology, like other fields of study, will have to adapt and continue to put to task theories of behavior as the world changes.

Notes

1 Holt & Bossler, 2008; see also Pratt, Holtfreter, & Reisig, 2010.
2 Holt, Burruss, & Bossler, 2010.
3 Holt, Bossler, & May, 2012.
4 Freilich & LaFree, 2015.
5 Pridemore & Freilich, 2007.
6 LaFree, Dugan, & Korte, 2009.
7 Akers & Silverman, 2004.
8 Agnew, 2010.
9 Rafter, 2016.
10 See Kunz, 1949; Rafter, 2016.
11 Hagan & Rymond-Richmond, 2009.
12 Rafter, 2016: 22.
13 see also Brehm (2017), Brehm et al. (2016).
14 Whitman, 1966.
15 See www.usatoday.com/story/news/2017/07/09/kkk-racist-rants-religious-vandalism-us-vs-them-mentality-escalates-leaving-dark-corners-interne/418100001/.
16 Ousey & Kubrin, 2017.
17 See, e.g., Ewing, Martinez, & Rumbaut, 2015.
18 Donnermeyer & DeKeseredy, 2013.
19 Personal interview with Joseph Donnermeyer, December 23, 2016.
20 See Crank & Jacoby, 2015.
21 Crank & Jacoby, 2015.
22 Homer-Dixon, 1999.
23 Agnew, 2012.
24 Personal Interview with John Crank, January 4, 2016.
25 Sutherland, 1940: 1.
26 Benson, 1985.
27 Shover & Hochstetler, 2006.
28 GFS, 2016.
29 See www.bloomberg.com/features/2015-martin-shkreli-wu-tang-clan-album/.

Further reading

Crank, J. P. & Jacoby, L. S. (2015). *Crime, violence, and global warming*. New York: Routledge.
Donnermeyer, J. F. & DeKeseredy, W. (2013). *Rural criminology* (Vol. 3). New York: Routledge.
Fox, J. A., Levin, J. A., & Quinet, K. (2011). *The will to kill: Making sense of senseless murder*. London: Pearson Higher Education.
Holt, T. J., Bossler, A. M., & Seigfried-Spellar, K. C. (2015). *Cybercrime and digital forensics: An introduction*. New York: Routledge.
Levin, J. & McDevitt, J. (2002). *Hate crimes revisited: America's war against those who are different*. Cambridge, MA: Basic Books.
Rafter, N. (2016). *The crime of all crimes: Toward a criminology of genocide*. New York: New York University Press.

14　Crime and victimization

Criminology and victimology	177
Strain	181
Social interaction	181
Subcultural theories	182
Self- and social control	184
Biosocial victimology	187
Summary	188

It should be obvious that this book is about explaining criminal offending. However, it is difficult to understand offending apart from victimization. Unless you are talking about truly victimless crimes (which is a debatable idea in and of itself) there is at least one victim for every crime. In addition, good empirical research has shown that there is a strong link between victims and offenders.[1] In other words, offenders are often victims and vice versa. This chapter will explore how we measure offending and victimization, and the linkages between the two. We will also explore how criminological theory is useful in understanding exposure to victimization.

Taking a rather different approach than previous chapters, in this chapter I review current criminological and victimological literature as well as the overlap between offenders and victims. I begin by reviewing the main tenets of criminology and victimology as distinct fields of study that, when brought together, provide valuable insight into understanding violence holistically. Next, I present contemporary research on the relationship between offending and victimization as well as recent work on explaining the victim–offender overlap before concluding with some implications for the future study of victims and offenders.

Criminology and victimology

Criminology as a specific field of study is relatively new when compared to older physical sciences such as astronomy and chemistry. However, as we have discussed, the scientific study of criminals dates back to at least the 1800s. Victimology has a much shorter history as a scientific field of study. In its earliest days, it was still considered a branch of criminology[2] and has remained largely couched within criminology today.

An understanding of the victim–offender overlap requires revisiting the early work of Hans von Hentig and Benjamin Mendelsohn, the "Founding Fathers" of victimology. In 1948, von Hentig wrote a seminal book on the victim–offender relationship entitled *The criminal and his victim*. This was an early look into the offender and victim relationship that would focus future research on the subject. In this book, von Hentig suggested that the criminal and victim are related in such a way that the victim "molds" the criminal and shapes the outcome of events.[3] A victim might place him- or herself in a risky situation or behave in a way that increases the likelihood of becoming a victim. For instance, a victim might carry around large sums of money, making them attractive to robbers and thieves. Victims may themselves be offenders who abuse their children or other individuals who then become victims of retaliatory violence. The victim may also be dishonest like the oft cited victims of con games who themselves engage in deviant behavior with the "con man." Von Hentig saw these relationships between offender and victimizer as complex and dubbed the situation the "doer–sufferer entanglement." It should be noted that the bulk of von Hentig's theorizing about the similarity between victims and offenders is contrary to his typologies. For example, young and elderly females, typical victims in von Hentig's typologies, are not his typical offenders who tend to be swindlers and act wantonly.

Mendelsohn, a defense lawyer, keenly noted in 1976 that there were relationships among his clients (the "offenders") and their "victims." More often than not, he believed that the victims were not entirely blameless (which helped prove his case as a defense attorney). For instance, he found that many "crimes of passion" could have been prevented if the victim had not provoked the attacks of the offender. He saw offending and victimization as an intimate partnership that required the interrelated acts of two (or more) people. Thus, he named this relationship the "penal couple."[4] He also viewed the causes of victimization as diverse, stating that victim-producing phenomena are "by nature biological, psychological, sociological, mechanical, ecological, etc."[5] He continued that victimology must "adapt specific methods to every facet of each phenomenon" in an effort to address the causes of victimization and seek out solutions to stop people being victimized.[6] Mendelsohn's work was second to none in helping to develop a scientific field of study committed to victims' issues. It has also continued to influence the direction of research today. However, counter to Mendelsohn's hope for a separate study of victims, research has revealed the importance of studying offenders and victims together.

Returning to the work of von Hentig, in 1940, he wrote "Remarks on the interaction of perpetrator and victim," in which he laid out the importance of understanding the interaction between victims and offenders. He closes this article by cautioning against the separation of offenders and victims and states that if we do that there will remain a "potential perpetrator without a victim and a potential victim without a partner to whom he or she could turn to be victimized."[7] This is again a reminder of the inherent coupling of those involved with violence.

While von Hentig's work was certainly victim-centered, and he urged people to think specifically about victim issues, he did not suggest a separate domain to study victims (and cautioned against such separation). It was Benjamin Mendelsohn who advocated a separate study of victims or "victimology." In the first volume and first issue of the journal *Victimology*, Mendelsohn laid out the foundation for his vision for victimology in his article

"Victimology and contemporary society's trends." In the first sentence he stated, "the essential goal of victimology is fewer victims in all sectors of society."[8] He acknowledged that research which could be considered victimological had been going on for decades but that these efforts had not gone "beyond secondary questions."[9] In other words, an in-depth and scientific study of victims had yet to come to fruition. Thus, this article is among the first to set the foundation for a separate study of victims using scientific methods.

A few years after the publication of "Victimology and contemporary society's trends," Egypt-born victimologist Ezzat Fattah reviewed the state of victimology and concluded that it "is slowly coming of age" and that it is "one of the most promising branches of criminology."[10] In the preface to the most recent edition of Andrew Karmen's popular textbook *Crime victims: An introduction to victimology,* he described the progression of the book from its earliest days (*c.* 1980), when "it was difficult to locate reliable social science data or even well-formed speculation" about victims' issues, to the most recent editions which now deal with sorting through the large volumes of literature on victimization and victims' issues.[11] It appears that Fattah was correct when he stated that victimology was becoming a popular and successful offshoot of criminology.

Victimology can now hold its own against criminology with its copious amounts of data and writing on victim-specific issues. But what are we to gain by segregating these two fields of study? At least in the study of violence it is far better to integrate the insights from criminology and victimology than to view them separately. While this integrated approach is increasingly being utilized, Farrall and Calverley caution that it is still typical to view offending and victimization separately and that academics need to continue to identify commonalities between victims and offenders.[12] Others note in addition that the two fields fail to communicate with one another, limiting the potential of a combined approach for theory and policy.[13]

The image of the criminal, or offender, has changed over the years. Perhaps the most dramatic shift in the perception of the offender occurred in the early 1900s. Prior to the twentieth century, criminals were often viewed as inferior human beings, lacking morals or sanity. Early theorists such as Lombroso considered criminals "throwbacks" to earlier human beings. In other words, they were characterized more as primitive man than as modern-day human beings.[14] This perception shifted in the early 1900s with the advent of the Chicago School where criminals were viewed as normal people who were influenced by their environment toward offending.[15] While drastically different in their explanations of crime, both views saw criminals as generally poor, minority, and male.

The image of the victim has also been debated and has changed over time. Nils Christie portrayed the "ideal victim" as a middle-aged white woman on her way to commit good deeds in the community.[16] Here, the typical victim is blameless and vulnerable to the violent experience. The attacker of the ideal victim is a large male who randomly accosts the female stranger. This picture of the ideal victim is often portrayed in TV and most of the top news stories.[17] Others, such as Mendelsohn and von Hentig, have categorized typical victims into several categories such as the elderly, children, females, depressed, and mentally defective in an effort to describe the biological, psychological, and social factors associated with victims. In reality, this is far from the true nature of violence and the most victimized person (and contrary to some of their own insights).[18]

Research shows that the victim as a meek old lady is not the typical case. In fact, research reveals that offenders and victims share characteristics and neither category is dominated by middle-aged white females. Quite to the contrary of Christie's ideal victim, the typical victim is young, black, unmarried, and male: the same characteristics found in the typical offender.[19] This is an important empirical observation that has led the Office of Juvenile Justice and Delinquency Prevention (OJJDP) to suggest that an accurate picture of juvenile offending and victimization risk is integral to a strategy to decrease violence.[20] This is more in line with a public health approach to violence prevention and intervention as opposed to a suppression- or enforcement-based response to violence.

The similarities between offenders and victims became apparent in self-report surveys of victimization which gained popularity in the 1970s. The National Crime Survey (NCS) was one of the first scientifically rigorous self-report methods to capture victimization. The information garnered by this survey directed the theoretical development of victimization theories. Analysis of the NCS revealed that age, sex, race, and marital status were key demographic correlates of victimization. Young black males who were unmarried were found to be at most risk of victimization.[21] Lifestyle and routine activity theories were formulated based on these findings. These theoretical approaches suggested that young and unmarried individuals often spend time outside the home, placing themselves and their property at risk of victimization. In his review of research, Richard Sparks concluded that "there is abundant evidence that criminal victimization is not uniformly or randomly distributed among individuals within the population as a whole."[22] He found, as had other researchers, regardless of which survey was employed, that young minority males are at greatest risk of victimization (Figure 14.1).

Recent research has continued to show the importance of demographic variables in relation to victimization. For example, males are more likely to be victimized even when controlling for other strong correlates of offending and victimization such as self-control[23] and family and peer contexts.[24] Younger individuals are more likely to be victimized than older individuals even after controlling for low self-control, lifestyles, and offending history.[25] A later section of this chapter discusses in greater detail explanations of offending and victimization but it is important to note here that many demographic predictors of violence are shared among offenders and victims, and that these are often related to their violent experiences.

Several perspectives link prior victimization to later offending and vice versa. This has led some researchers to argue that "violence begets violence."[26] Cathy Spatz Widom, one of the most prominent researchers on the effect of childhood trauma on later delinquency, calls the link between childhood maltreatment and later offending the "cycle of violence."[27] Regardless of the term used by researchers, considerable evidence exists for a cycle whereby victimization, including trauma and vicarious victimization, leads to offending.

The cycle of violence is evident in abused children who grow up and become abusers themselves. To be sure, most individuals who are abused as children do not grow up to become offenders.[28] However, being abused as a child increases the *likelihood* of offending in adolescence and adulthood when compared to those who report no abuse. In addition, many adult offenders report being abused as children. Abuse, neglect, and other traumatic events experienced by children often lead to behavioral problems as

Victim–Offender Overlap

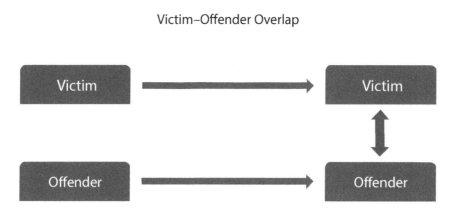

Figure 14.1 The victim–offender overlap

Source: Adapted from Shaffer (2003).

well as a host of other negative consequences such as school dropout, teen pregnancy, learning difficulties, and obesity later in life.[29] Sexually abused children are more likely to become abusers as adults and are more likely to suffer from other health-related problems such as depression, suicide, and sexual promiscuity.[30] Harsh physical punishment experienced by children is linked to later deviance and intimate partner violence,[31] and research has uncovered that it is not only direct victimization that is related to deviant outcomes but witnessing violence or receiving traumatic news that is also associated with future offending.[32] Research shows that there may be specific gendered pathways for abused children where males are more likely to channel their emotions outward (harm others) while females are more likely to channel their emotion inward (harm oneself).[33] Regardless of the pathway, research shows that there is a cycle of violence, whether it is harming others or receiving harm, which needs further untangling if there are to be better programs and policies to counter this perpetuation.

Violence does not have to be experienced only in childhood for it to impact later delinquency. For example, Chang and colleagues found that repeat victimization in later life is related to delinquency net controls for other risk factors such as drug and alcohol use.[34] Interestingly, they found that repeat victimization experienced by seniors in high school led to delinquency even among youth who were previously non-delinquent.[35] This finding suggests that, contrary to many learning and control theories, victimization itself, regardless of timing in the life-course, can influence delinquent behavior (Figure 14.2).

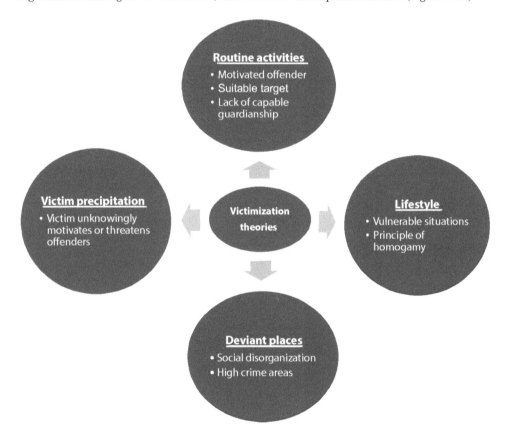

Figure 14.2 Theories of victimization

Source: Adapted from Frailing & Harper (2016).

Strain

Experienced, vicarious, and anticipated strains are implicated as causes of offending and victimization, and are used to account for the cycle of violence.[36] General Strain Theory, as originally posited by Agnew, proposed that strain produces negative emotions, such as anger, which lead to delinquent behavior.[37] The magnitude of the strain is related to the outcome in that the greater the strain, the more likely anger will be produced resulting in offending. One of the greatest strains is being the victim of violence. A test of this assumption showed that prior victimization was strongly related to delinquency. Anticipated and vicarious victimization were also shown to be related to delinquency.[38]

The effect of emotions in the link between victimization and offending is stressed by other researchers as well. For example, Manasse and Ganem investigate the path from strain (victimization) to offending through negative affect. They find that victimization is related to offending largely through depression. This effect is greater in males than in females, suggesting that males who are victimized are likely to offend when the victimization is followed by negative (depressive) affect.[39] Similarly, using anger as a mediating variable, Maschi and colleagues found that negative affect (anger) mediated the link between trauma and offending.[40] In line with this scientific evidence, Herman states that "feelings of rage and murderous revenge fantasies are normal responses to abusive treatment."[41] This statement is illustrative of the influence of negative emotions in the cycle of violence. Negative emotions, such as depression and anger, may be powerful concepts in linking traumatic events and abuse to offending. The current literature on strain and offending/victimization provides impressive support for the reciprocity of violence implicit in the victim–offender overlap.

Social interaction

While Agnew's strain theory is perhaps the most widely used theory to explain victimization's impact upon later offending, Felson offers a similar theory that attempts to explain the situational and interactional exchange between victim and offender.[42] Felson's social interactionist theory (SI) states that interplay between the victim and offender is responsible for the escalation of violent behavior. Some individuals experience stress due to everyday experiences which lead them to violate norms and social rules that range from being mildly rude to being physically aggressive. Aggressive behavior is a mechanism for controlling the behavior of others in order to cope with stress or achieve "justice." Important to SI is the reciprocal relationship between the original and subsequent aggressor. As one person acts aggressively toward another person, this person experiences distress and copes by becoming aggressive toward the original culprit. This situation of escalation and retaliation is what produces violent encounters and perpetuates successive violent encounters.

SI has not been widely tested or utilized in studies of offending and victimization. The studies that do incorporate SI show some support for its major tenets. Schreck and his collaborators used SI as a theoretical foundation for investigating the link between early puberty and victimization.[43] Their results indicated that early puberty introduced distress into the lives of girls and boys who developed earlier than their classmates. In fact, distress fully mediated the relationship between early puberty and victimization in females and partially mediated the effect of early puberty on victimization for males. First, this suggests that SI offers a useful tool in understanding the link between distress and victimization. Second, SI may be able to account for differences between genders in outcomes by explicating the emotional response to distress for boys and for girls.

Apel and Burrows argue that offending is a form of self-help – that is, a coping mechanism for emotions as a result of prior victimization. Joining gangs, carrying weapons, and acting aggressively are ways to "protect" oneself from future victimization.[44] Despite the perception that gangs and acting violently may protect against victimization, research indicates otherwise. In fact, victimization increases as involvement within the gang increases. Often, central members are more likely to be victimized than gang associates, while non-gang members have the lowest likelihood of victimization. Although youth often join gangs for protection, and even report feeling safer in gangs, there is little evidence that gang members experience less victimization.[45] This calls into question the protective function of delinquent groups.

Subcultural theories

Some of the first empirical efforts to explain the relationship between offenders and victims came from macro-level theories; in particular, subcultural theories. During his research on homicide, Marvin Wolfgang found an overlap between homicide victims and their murderers. The murderers in his sample often reported being victimized in the past. In addition, the victims who were killed were found to have had prior contact with the police for criminal behavior antecedent to their murder. He was led to describe this as the "victim–offender relationship."[46] Singer expanded this discussion by arguing that part of the overlap exists due to the fact that youth are in their peak offending years during adolescence, and youth are more likely to associate with one another during these years as well. Therefore, it is logical that, based on interaction during these years alone, youth will end up victimizing one another in reciprocal fashion. However, he also suggested that there is evidence that victims and offenders share similar characteristics other than age, such as race, school dropout rate, employment status, relationship status, and offending history. Furthermore, individuals within a subculture of violence espouse retaliatory behavior and share in a normative belief that violence is an appropriate response to being victimized. This leads to alternating roles between aggressor and defender.[47]

The subcultural perspective views offending and victimization as part of the larger concept of a subculture of violence. Elijah Anderson, in his influential 1999 book *Code of the street*, describes a cycle of violence in the inner city where youth subscribe to certain levels of violence to obtain respect and status from their peers. Central to what he calls "campaigning for respect" is the need to retaliate when disrespected or victimized in order to uphold status and maintain social order.[48] The problem with this strategy to attain or maintain respect is readily apparent: if victimizing someone increases respect on the streets, and victimization is to be met with revenge, then the campaign for respect will perpetuate the endless need to victimize one another.

Interestingly, despite the perpetuation inherent in Anderson's portrayal of acting tough and campaigning for respect, he concluded that adopting a street code would ultimately increase one's safety. However, he provided little empirical evidence to support this view. Eric Stewart and his co-authors tested whether the adoption of a street code protects against violent victimization. They found convincing evidence that adopting a street code actually increased victimization even when controlling for neighborhood disorganization.[49] This runs contrary to Anderson's claim that street codes are a protective factor for individuals living in disorganized communities. David Harding further illuminated the issues faced by youth living in inner-city communities in his work *Living the drama* and added some richness to the quantitative data provided by others. Similar to Stewart and colleagues, Harding collected substantive data which illustrated that life on the streets is characterized by repetitive offending and victimization. Using the terminology of his participants, Harding refers to such violence as "drama." Drama exists predominantly in poor communities where conflicted relationships between individuals are a normal part of everyday life. Drama is often created when youth victimize others in order to gain respect, protect their image of toughness, and defend their territory.[50]

Harding argues that disadvantaged neighborhoods are more likely to experience an overlap of offending and victimization. Through qualitative interviews, he found that individuals in disadvantaged communities are expected, and even encouraged, to victimize others to gain respect, enter into physical confrontation if neighborhood peers are involved in conflicts, and respond to any personal victimization with retaliation. Males interviewed in low poverty areas did not experience such encouragement to act violently. Recent quantitative analysis supports Harding's finding that context matters. A series of recent studies finds that offending increases victimization in disadvantaged communities but has no effect in low poverty areas. These authors theorize that the culture of disadvantaged areas is substantively different from non-disadvantaged areas. That is, in disadvantaged communities youth are expected to retaliate for being victimized while their counterparts in non-poverty areas have few problems avoiding trouble by either ignoring conflicts or dealing with them through non-violent means.[51]

Not all scholars hypothesize, or even find, that the overlap is more pronounced in disadvantaged neighborhoods. On the contrary, Zhang and colleagues hypothesize that deviant lifestyles – including crime – will lead to victimization only in low crime neighborhoods. They believe that offending will be fully mediated in high crime neighborhoods by other variables such as proximity to crime and social disorder which will account for the majority of victimization. In low crime neighborhoods, deviant lifestyles will account for much of the association with victimization because there are few other factors to link to victimization. The results of their study were that while they did find support for the hypothesis that deviant lifestyles lead to victimization to a greater extent in low crime neighborhoods the relationship was not statistically significant and may be due to chance alone.[52] Other studies find that victimization is a more powerful predictor of offending in contexts that are less violent perhaps due to crowding-out effects of multiple criminogenic factors experienced by individuals in disorganized areas.[53]

Several other researchers have argued that toughness and retaliation are valued on the streets. Almost half a century ago, pioneering gang researcher Walter Miller suggested that toughness is one of the main tenets of street culture. Toughness, he says, is "the model for the 'tough-guy' – hard, fearless, undemonstrative, skilled in physical combat."[54] Evidence of a desire for toughness on the streets is supported by the qualitative research of Tyler and Johnson, who interviewed 40 homeless males and females and found that the majority of them reported being both offenders and victims. To a large extent, this overlap was due to a cycle of retaliation for past victimization experiences. Like Miller's toughness, these authors found that "invincibility" – the need to appear tough and not someone to be messed with – is a key characteristic that homeless youth believe they must acquire if they are to survive the perils of the streets. The belief that one is invincible allows a person to place him- or herself in situations that are risky with little fear of physical harm.[55]

Retaliation, particularly among males, is not only seen in urban areas and it is not only a contemporary phenomenon. In fact, Boehm suggests that retaliation has been prevalent throughout human history based on our closest ancestors: the apes. In systems where there exists a hierarchy based on physical dominance, retaliation and "settling the score" is always one option for individuals who are victimized – thus making individuals vulnerable to re-victimization.[56] Anthropologist Jared Diamond argues that vengeance is innate in human nature and "among the strongest human emotions."[57] Diamond uses the clans of the New Guinea Highlands to illustrate vengeance through revenge killings. Clans who have members killed by rival clans will pursue those responsible for the murder and seek justice through vengeance (i.e., murder). The jury is still out on whether humans are naturally peaceful and cooperative or whether they are violent and selfish. The best evidence appears to suggest that we are a little bit of both. Criminology is uniquely positioned to address part of this issue by paying careful attention to the similarities and differences inherent in the victim–offender overlap and the cycle of violence.

Self- and social control

Recently, individual-level theories of crime and victimization have become increasingly popular and subjected to empirical investigation. In one of the pioneering studies that extended criminological theory to account for victimization, criminologist Christopher Schreck called upon low self-control theory to explain victimization.[58] He concluded that low self-control makes individuals more vulnerable to victimization. Controlling for other variables, self-control remained a direct and significant predictor of victimization. Interestingly, self-control accounted for a proportion of the gap between male and female victimization. Self-control remains a robust explanatory variable for victimization in other research[59] and has also been implicated as a conditioning variable in the path to delinquency.[60] Impulsivity, one dimension of self-control, has even been used to explain victimization in the form of online victimization whereby impulsive shoppers fail to put into place the proper safeguards when buying online.[61] This evidence indicates the importance of individual-level (non-situational) factors in the explanation of both offending and victimization (Figure 14.3).

Self-control has not been the only control theory to be extended to explain victimization. Piquero and Hickman use Charles Tittle's control-balance theory to explain

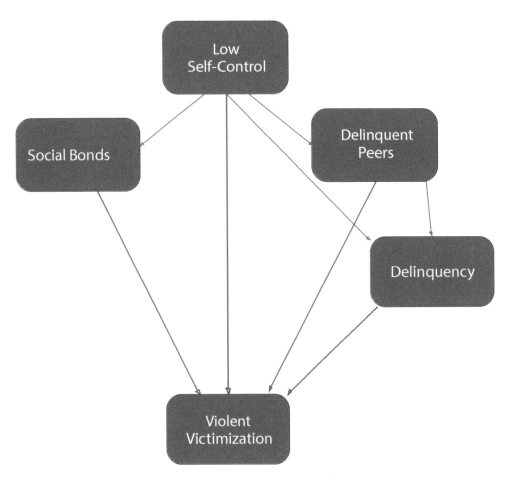

Figure 14.3 Extension of low self-control to explain victimization

Source: Figure adapted from Schreck, Stewart, & Fisher (2006).

victimization.[62] Originally, the theory suggests that offending is a mechanism to establish balance between control deficits and surpluses. Those who feel that they have little control (i.e., power, status, prestige) are likely to use violence to gain control. Individuals who have control surpluses may offend because they feel they have impunity from the law or retaliation. Acknowledging the victim–offender overlap, Piquero and Hickman argue that the same reasons a person may offend to gain control may expose them to victimization. They find that this hypothesis is supported by their data: both control surpluses and control deficits are significantly related to victimization. Although the authors cannot explain exactly why such deficits lead to victimization, they speculate that those with control deficits may be vulnerable to crime and easy to take advantage of while those with control surpluses seek out exciting or risky activities that place them at risk of victimization.

Individual-level characteristics and lifestyles should not be viewed in isolation. Schreck and colleagues show that individuals with low self-control are unlikely to change their lifestyles regardless of their victimization experiences, leading to repeat victimization.[63] Research on routine activities should incorporate measures at the individual level to better understand what type of person may or may not change their lifestyle following victimization. This integration of levels strengthens the explanatory power of frameworks accounting for a victim–offender overlap. If victims, particularly those with low self-control, are likely to continue their risky lifestyles they are also more likely to continue to associate with delinquent peers in unsupervised areas that are conducive to participation in delinquent activity.

From a social control perspective, family and other types of social bonds are implicated as insulators from crime and, recently, victimization. Originally, Hirschi proposed a theory of crime which posited that social bonds between individuals and society restrained people from engaging in crime. Theorists have considered social bonding in the link to victimization. Esbensen and colleagues found that several family context variables such as lack of family involvement, parental monitoring, and attachment to parents were predicative of victimization.[64] Schreck and Fisher similarly found that family climate insulated individuals from victimization. In two cross-national studies, along with my co-authors Michael Rocque and Laurie Gould (respectively), we found that family bonding protected against victimization and that this effect was especially pronounced in countries which valued the family institution and that victimization predicted offending especially in societies that were more individualistic as compared to family/societally oriented.[65] Social bonding, particularly to family, may be an important protective factor for both violent offending and victimization.[66]

Life-course or longitudinal research allows for a unique perspective on the victim–offender overlap by providing a picture of violence over time. University of New Hampshire victimologist David Finkelhor is one of several advocates for this perspective on offending and victimization. He suggests that victimization varies over the life-course and cross-sectional studies often miss the dynamic nature of violence. For example, while the most common victim is a young black male who is involved with crime and delinquency, the victimization of the physically weak is prevalent as well but mostly among children and the elderly. Thus, the nature of victimization may change over time and research must identify these characteristics using data collected longitudinally.[67]

Life-course research sheds light on the impact of bonds on offending and victimization over time. Victimologist Leah Daigle and her collaborators used a longitudinal sample of individuals, revealing that some social bonds are related to desistance from offending and victimization. Employment status (i.e., having a job) was related to increased victimization contrary to social bonding theory but in line with lifestyles/routine activity theory which predicts that time away from the home is positively related to victimization. Marriage, a predictor of desistance from offending, was also found to be a predictor of desistance from victimization.[68] This research supports the importance of studying changes in bonds over time to account for increases and decreases in individual victimization.

Longitudinal research also reveals interesting relationships between desistance and persistence in offending and victimization. Farrall and Calverley find a relationship between offenders and victims (that offenders have higher victimization rates than those in the general population) but also find that desisting from offending does not necessarily mean "desisting" from victimization. In their sample, offenders who stopped committing crime did not experience a drop in victimization, leading the authors to claim that "once an offender, always a victim."[69] One reason may be that crime desisters are still involved in lifestyles that promote victimization such as drinking in pubs and associating with offenders. Farrall and Calverley suggest that offending and victimization both cut off an individual from pro-social opportunities and that individuals involved in violence are often "socially caged" in areas with high rates of violence which are hard to escape.

Unconventional "family" bonds may also serve as a protective factor for youth at elevated risk of victimization. Homeless youth are one group at elevated risk of victimization given their social context.[70] McCarthy and colleagues conducted a study of homeless youth and found that those who developed strong bonds with other homeless individuals (called "street families") accumulated important social capital such as trust and physical protection which insulated them from violence. An excerpt from an interview with a homeless youth illustrates this street family bond:

Interviewer: You mentioned a street family. What is a street family?
Youth: Um, well, it's a bunch of friends that stick together. Like, they watch each other's back for you.
Interviewer: Why is it important to be part of a street family?
Youth: You wouldn't get beat up for being on the street.[71]

Viewed along with the interviews presented by Tyler and Johnson, the bonds among youth on the streets can work as a protective factor against victimization (and here an example of theft victimization), as suggested in the excerpt above, or push youth toward crime, as the following quote suggests:

> Well, one time me and my friend gave this dude a half-ounce it was like $140 [and] he decided not to pay. So we [later went to this man's apartment and] broke the window and got his TV [and] sold his TV for $140.[72]

These qualitative interviews illuminate the statistics produced by quantitative analysis on offending and victimization. Homeless youth, just as youth living in homes, experience a wide variety of violent experiences where they are both offenders and victims. It is also illustrative of the overlap between property and violent crime, since many offenders steal goods to support a drug addiction or criminal lifestyle.

Control theory argues that bonds and self-control are important mediating mechanisms in the link between offending and victimization. For example, Hirschi claims that the link between parental abuse/neglect and subsequent delinquency is mediated by social bonds. That is, abuse and neglect by parents dissolves important bonds between the parent and child, and it is the depletion of these relationships that leads to delinquency.[73] Gottfredson and Hirschi similarly argue that poor parenting fails to instill self-control in the child and it is this lack of self-control, and not the abuse itself, that is related to delinquency.[74] Although there is some theoretical support for these arguments, the evidence for the mediation of social bonds in the link between parental abuse and offending is equivocal.[75]

Biosocial victimology

Recently, biosocial explanations for delinquent behavior and vulnerability to violence have been proffered by researchers. Early puberty, as already discussed in this chapter, is one biological factor that is implicated in the link between offending and victimization. Moffitt's developmental theory of adolescent-limited and life-course-persistent offending argues that biological maturation (i.e., puberty) happens prior to social maturity (i.e., having a job and other adult responsibilities), creating a "maturity gap" that is filled by engaging in adult-like behaviors including drug use, property offending, and violence. Moffitt also suggests that early maturity has social costs. For example, pro-social youth tend to avoid individuals who display aggressive or delinquent behavior, leaving these youth to associate with other delinquents. The life-course-persistent offender is disadvantaged by early maturity which effects social relations across early adulthood.[76]

Researchers have implicated early maturity as a mechanism to explain victimization as well. Using longitudinal data, a study by Dana Haynie and Alex Piquero found that early puberty is associated with victimization for both boys and girls.[77] They also found that there are both direct and indirect effects of early puberty on victimization that vary by gender. Results showed that early puberty interacted with peer networks in the case of boys but not girls. Boys who had more female friends were less likely to be victimized. Peer networks did not mediate any effect for girls. The authors believe that a biosocial interaction may be prevalent in boys because they are more likely to associate with delinquent peers than are females and that "there is something unique about early maturity [...] that opens opportunities for victimization experiences."[78]

A proliferating biosocial literature indicates that genetic explanations for violent behavior are similar to those for victimization. For example, the dopamine receptor D2 protein (DRD2) has been found to be associated with offending[79] and victimization.[80] Biosocial criminologist Matt DeLisi and colleagues found that the DRD2 gene interacts with having a criminal father, using a sample of African American females from the National Longitudinal Study of Adolescent to Adult Health (Add Health). Interestingly, alone, neither factor predicted delinquency, but having both the DRD2 polymorphism and a criminal father significantly predicted current and future delinquency.[81]

Research on the DRD2 polymorphism also finds a link to victimization. Florida State University biosocial criminologist Kevin Beaver and his colleagues found that the DRD2 gene interacted with the delinquent peers factor to heighten the risk of victimization.[82] This interaction was only found in low-risk environments (i.e., in individuals who did not associate with delinquent peers) and not among high-risk environments, suggesting that genes may be "overshadowed" by environmental factors.[83] Another study by Beaver and others using data from Add Health found that DRD2 decreased resiliency to victimization and increased victimization experiences. They also found that another gene, 5-HTTLPR, was associated with increased resiliency in the short and long term.[84]

Another polymorphism, the monoamine oxidase A (MAOA) enzyme, has been shown to be a protective factor against delinquency. In their landmark study, Caspi and colleagues investigated the "violence begets violence" concept by studying a group of males from birth to adulthood. The authors did find evidence that maltreatment in childhood increased the chances of violence in adulthood but found that this relationship was mediated by levels of MAOA. Maltreated children who had high levels of the MAOA enzyme were less likely than those who had low levels of the enzyme to grow up and abuse others. This implies that genes may be an important yet largely overlooked factor in understanding the victim–offender overlap. To be sure, genetic research shows much promise in explaining both offending and victimization, and thus far has supported the notion that offending and victimization share common sources.[85]

Summary

While criminology and victimology are sometimes seen as two different fields of study with their own questions that need answering and issues to be addressed, it appears that there is much to gain by seeing the two areas of study as intimately linked. The research base now is quite clear: victimization increases offending (and vice versa) and similar individuals are caught up in violence as both victims and offenders. Surely crime prevention and intervention programs would be wise to note this observation.

As the field of criminology advances, the role of victims in violent behavior and the long-term impact of victimization on individuals will continue to be researched. There now seems to be a concerted focus on the role which early trauma, abuse, and neglect have on the development and ultimate life outcomes of those who experience these aversive issues early in the life-course. Along with advancing technology and research methods, the theoretical and empirical bases for victimization are likely to see much growth and refinement over the coming years.

Notes

1 See Posick, 2017.
2 Fattah, 1979.
3 Von Hentig, 1948: 348.
4 Mendelsohn, 1956: 99.
5 Mendelsohn, 1976: 24.
6 Mendelsohn, 1976: 24.
7 Von Hentig, 1940: 309.
8 Mendelsohn, 1976: 8.
9 Mendelsohn, 1976: 10.
10 Fattah, 1979: 198.
11 Karmen, 2009: xxiii.
12 Farrall & Calverley, 2006; see also Esbensen & Huizinga, 1991.
13 Stewart, Elifson, & Sterk, 2004.
14 Rafter, Posick, & Rocque, 2016.
15 Lilly, Cullen, & Ball, 2011.
16 Christie, 1986.
17 Loeber, Kalb, & Huizinga, 2001.
18 Mendelsohn, 1956; von Hentig, 1948.
19 Lauritsen, Sampson, & Laub, 1991; Lauritsen & Laub, 2007.
20 Loeber, Kalb, & Huizinga, 2001.
21 Hindelang, 1976; Hindelang, Gottfredson, & Garofalo, 1978.
22 Sparks, 1982: 96.
23 Schreck, 1999.
24 Esbensen, Huizinga, & Menard, 1999; Schreck & Fisher, 2004.
25 Stewart, Elifson, & Sterk, 2004.
26 Curtis, 1963.
27 Widom, 1989.
28 Fagan, 1991.
29 Burke et al., 2011; Lansford et al., 2007.
30 Paolucci, Genuis, & Violato, 2001.

31 Swinford et al., 2000.
32 Agnew, 2002; Eitle & Turner, 2002.
33 Herman, 1992; Stewart, Livingston, & Dennison, 2008.
34 Chang, Chen, & Brownson, 2003.
35 See also Mersky,Topitzes, & Reynolds, 2011.
36 Agnew, 1992, 2002.
37 Agnew, 1985, 1992.
38 Agnew, 2002.
39 Manasse & Ganem, 2009.
40 Maschi, Bradley, & Morgan, 2008.
41 Herman, 1992: 104.
42 Felson, 1992.
43 Schreck et al., 2007.
44 Apel & Burrows, 2011.
45 Katz et al., 2011; Melde, Taylor, & Esbensen, 2009; Thornberry et al., 2003.
46 Wolfgang, 1957: 1.
47 Singer, 1981; see also Singer, 1986.
48 Anderson, 2000: 68–69.
49 Stewart, Schreck, & Simons, 2006; See also Brezina et al., 2004.
50 Harding, 2010.
51 Berg & Loeber, 2011; Berg et al., 2012.
52 Zhang, Welte, & Wieczorek, 2001.
53 Posick & Zimmerman, 2015.
54 Miller, 1958: 9.
55 Tyler & Johnson, 2004.
56 Boehm, 2011.
57 Diamond (2008), quoted in Karstedt, 2011: 5.
58 Schreck, 1999.
59 Schreck, Fisher, & Miller, 2004.
60 Hay & Evans, 2006.
61 Reisig, Pratt, & Holtfreter, 2009.
62 Piquero & Hickman, 2003.
63 Schreck, Stewart, & Fisher, 2006.
64 Esbensen, Huizinga, & Menard, 1999.
65 Posick & Gould, 2015; Posick & Rocque, 2015.
66 Schreck & Fisher, 2004.
67 Finkelhor, 1995; See also Finkelhor & Kendall-Tackett, 1997.
68 Daigle, Beaver, & Hartman, 2008.
69 Farrall & Calverley, 2006: 158.
70 Hiday et al., 2001.
71 McCarthy, Hagan, & Martin, 2002: 849
72 Tyler & Johnson, 2004: 438.
73 Hirschi, 1995.
74 Gottfredson & Hirschi, 1990.
75 See Rebellon & Van Gundy, 2005.
76 Moffitt, 1993.
77 Haynie & Piquero, 2006.
78 Haynie & Piquero, 2006: 25.
79 DeLisi et al., 2009a.
80 Beaver et al., 2007, 2009b, 2011.
81 DeLisi et al., 2009b.
82 Beaver et al., 2007.
83 Beaver et al., 2007: 635.
84 Beaver et al., 2011.
85 Caspi et al., 2002.

Further reading

Peled, E., Jaffe, P. G., & Edleson, J. L. (1994). *Ending the cycle of violence: Community responses to children of battered women.* Thousand Oaks, CA: Sage.

Rothe, D. L. & Kauzlarich, D. (2014). *Towards a victimology of state crime.* New York: Routledge.

Schafer, S. (1968). *The victim and his criminal: A study in functional responsibility.* New York: Random House.

Vanfraechem, I., Fernández, D. B., & Aertsen, I. (2015). *Victims and restorative justice.* New York: Routledge.

Von Hentig, H. (1948). *The criminal and his victim: Studies in the sociobiology of crime.* New Haven, CT: Yale University Press.

Online resource: www.oxfordbibliographies.com/view/document/obo-9780195396607/obo-9780195 396607-0220.xml.

The future of criminological theory

Developmental and life-course criminology	192
Biosocial criminology	192
Mass murder, terrorism, and genocide	193
Cybercrime	195
Crimes of the powerful and green criminology	195
Evaluation of theory and crime prevention	196
Conclusion	199

Readers of this book have traveled from the earliest theories of criminal behavior through the theories born out of the Enlightenment all the way up until the most contemporary theories integrating insights from biology, evolutionary psychology, chemistry, and sociology (among others). These theories have been thoroughly tested through empirical methods and some, but not all, have stood the test of time – however long or short that may be. The theories have also shed light on programs and policies in the US and abroad, and have even influenced the laws on the books. This history is rich, interesting, and exciting. Now the question is: "Where do we go from here?"

The exact future of criminology is anyone's guess, but there is reason to believe that we will continue to see important developments in criminological research and theory far into the future. This final chapter discusses what may become of criminology moving forward and some promising areas of theoretical development that we can all look forward to. I do not pretend to know the future, nor do I intend to lay out my own plan for the field, but extrapolating from recent developments I do lay out what is likely, in my estimation, to take place in the upcoming years. Hopefully this chapter can guide others to pick up where things have left off and continue to develop the field of theoretical criminology.

There are several areas that are likely to continue to grow and develop into the near future, but I wish to only discuss at any length a handful of these: (1) developments on change throughout the life-course, including the process of maturation and desistance; (2) expansion of biosocial criminology incorporating insight from several hard sciences such as chemistry and genetics; (3) new theoretical developments of mass murder such as terrorism, mass shootings, and genocide; (4) continued development in cybercrime; (5) growing interest in crimes of the powerful; and (6) the increase in the use of randomized controlled trials and quasi-experimental methods for evaluating theory and policy.

Developmental and life-course criminology

Recall for a moment the early work of the Gluecks in the mid-twentieth century. Their study, which followed boys in Massachusetts across their early lives, together with the follow-up interviews conducted by Sampson and Laub, represents one of the most comprehensive studies across participants' life-courses. Later longitudinal studies, including the Montreal Longitudinal and Experimental Study (MLES),[1] The Pathways to Desistance Study, and the National Longitudinal Study of Adolescenct to Adult Health study have also attempted to monitor individuals at different points in their lives to better understand continuity and changes in offending as well as the factors influencing criminal behavior at different life-stages. The bulk of research using these types of datasets shows that, indeed, there are changes across the span of a person's life and that the variables related to crime may change as well – or at least the relative importance of certain variables may change (in line with Agnew's developmental theory).

One of these developmental perspectives has been put forward by Michael Rocque and was discussed earlier in the book. From his perspective, maturation is a key component of desistance and deserves careful consideration from criminologists and prevention programs. This was a major concern of the Gluecks in the 1950s, but it took a few decades for the focus on maturation to come back around. With more longitudinal data becoming available to researchers, a stronger focus on biological, psychological, and social factors impacting desistance appears to be on the horizon.

This may coincide, as will be discussed next, with the advances being seen in biosocial criminology. People mature at different ages, to different extents, and are more influenced by certain maturational factors at different points in life. It is likely that maturation is dependent on both genetic predisposition and social environments, which interact in complex ways. As criminology moves further into a multidisciplinary arena, it will become increasingly pertinent to explore these issues.

Biosocial criminology

As we have seen, biosocial criminology has experienced an expansion as of late and biosocial work is appearing in major journals across several fields of study. We can trace these contemporary efforts to pioneers such as Anthony Walsh and Lee Ellis, who brought the evolutionary perspective to the fore of criminology, to John Paul Wright in Cincinnati, who was responsible for training Kevin Beaver who has, subsequently, trained a new cadre of biosocial criminologists at Florida State University. Today, there is a biosocial criminology association, a biopsychosocial criminology section of the American Society of Criminology that was recently approved, several courses being taught across the United States on biosocial criminology (including one at my institution taught by me), and several criminologists who claim biosocial criminology as one of their areas of expertise.

The current foundation for biosocial criminology is strong and appears to offer a building ground for future biosocial research on a variety of important topics. One of these factors is how the environment and biology work together (or not) in producing outcomes. Because DNA (and our genomes) are incredibly similar at the molecular level, there must be processes by which DNA is manipulated to produce the diversity we see in the world; and there are. Transcription factors and epigenetic tags are mechanisms that regulate the expression of DNA. So, even though DNA and genomes are remarkably similar across people (and actually our genomes are similar to other mammals), the way in which our genes are used is very different. Regulation is often, but not always, the result of environmental input, meaning that a biosocial approach is integral to the study of crime and victimization. This is a very new area of research which needs much more investigation.

It may be possible to better understand all of these issues as biological and environmental data become more widely available to researchers. For most of the history of biosocial research, the bulk of studies have used samples of monozygotic and/or dizygotic twins or considered one or a few candidate genes and their role in certain behaviors. However, genome sequencing has decreased substantially in costs over recent years. Therefore, entire genomes are increasingly being used in criminological research (Figure 15.1).

Mass murder, terrorism, and genocide

Not only is the general public becoming more interested in mass murder events but researchers are as well. The attack on the World Trade Center in New York on September 11, 2001 brought the issues of terrorism and mass murder to the fore of American politics. Up until then, much of the terrorism and incidents of mass violence had seemed

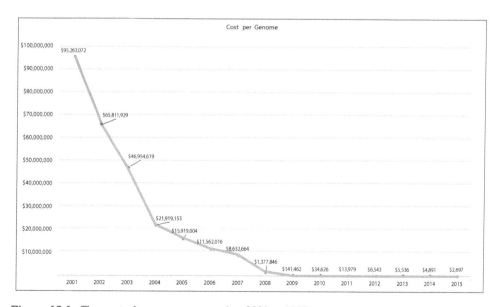

Figure 15.1. The cost of genome sequencing 2001 to 2015

to be distant, if tragic, issues. All of a sudden, mass atrocities struck home for many people and scholars began to explore and take seriously these issues of violence.[a] Along with this, international incidents have begun to seem less distant and research on atrocities such as the Rwandan genocide, the Norwegian youth camp shooting on the Island of Utoya, and the terrorism being experienced in Syria – particularly Aleppo – have become front and center in criminology of late.

Other mass murder events have hit close to home, in areas thought to be relatively insulated from mass killing, terror events: the United States and the United Kingdom. The Orlando mass killing event was described in Chapter 13 but other terroristic, hate-based incidents have happened since. For example, on May 26, 2017 in Portland, Oregon, Jeremy Christian provoked two females with an anti-Muslim tirade. When Christian was confronted by three men, he stabbed them with a knife – killing two and severely injuring one.[2] In the United Kingdom, two major incidents have occurred as this book was being completed. The first was an attack at an Ariana Grande concert in Manchester, UK. A suicide bomber detonated a bomb at Grande's concert killing 22 people and injuring about 60 more.[3] Only weeks later, an attack on citizens took place around London Bridge. Men drove a van into random citizens who then exited the vehicle wielding knives. The terrorists ended up killing 8 people and injuring 48.[4] The terrorist group ISIS claimed responsibility for both crimes in the UK and promised more attacks in the future.

Interestingly, terrorism has been somewhat ignored in criminology, attracting more interest from political scientists and international scholars. This appears to be changing of late, especially with the work of a handful of prominent criminologists. As data become available and more criminologists are exposed to the study of terrorism, this seems like a prime area of future research.

Terrorist attacks are not the only mass killing events of interest to the public and criminologists alike, as incidents of genocide are too. Recently, the work of Ohio State criminologist Hollie Nyseth Brehm has expanded what the field understands about genocide; its causes and effects. Her work, discussed in Chapter 13, is leading the field in theorizing about why certain individuals become engaged in genocidal behavior and how to prevent mass atrocities. I was very interested in this area of research and where it might be going, so I decided that the best idea would be to talk to Dr. Brehm herself.

I asked her what criminology's role is in studying genocide and how we address concerns. "Right now, the genocide in Darfur is still ongoing," she reminded me.

> Civilians who oppose the al-Assad regime in Syria have been living an absolute nightmare in Aleppo as their government has been systematically bombing neighborhoods. And the government of Myanmar is killing and displacing the Rohingya people, who are a minority group that is effectively stateless.

At this point it was obvious that the issues we tended to hear much about years ago are still problematic today.

Brehm continued,

> To me, this means that as we address the harms of genocide, we must be aware of (and strive to understand) the practical implications of our scholarship. This involves

---

a. This is certainly not to suggest that these issues were of no concern or interest to criminologists in the past and it would be inaccurate to say that there was no research in these areas prior to 9/11 in the US. However, it is difficult to deny that research on terrorism, genocide, and mass atrocities proliferated in the US after 9/11.

keeping an eye toward how research on the causes of genocide or on how societies rebuild in its aftermath can be used to inform policy-makers, those working with governmental and nongovernmental organizations, and other applied pursuits.

She is clear: this work has only just begun.

Cybercrime

It is undeniable that the past 20 years have witnessed an explosion in the technology sphere. In my lifetime, I received the first Nintendo Entertainment System as a gift two years after it hit the marketplace, bought an "advanced" computer with a Pentium processor and six gigs of storage on the hard drive, and recently have kept updating my Samsung Galaxy and statistical software packages capable of analyzing millions of cases with thousands of lines of code. Technology is everywhere and permeates almost all facets of our lives. At times it has made life easier and more enjoyable, and at others it has complicated our lives immeasurably and exposed us to extreme harm. For these reasons, criminology will continue to examine crimes that are facilitated by the use of computers.

Recent figures show that the number of internet users worldwide exceeds 2.5 billion and, as countries continue to develop and expand their technology, this number is expected to increase.[5] As cybercrime is a worldwide problem, the costs, too, are global in nature and total in the billions. This total increases as one also incorporates how much is spent on crime prevention tools such as antivirus software and firewall security.[6] Certainly, cybercrime is a modern-day issue in need of understanding and prevention. It is also a problem that has a long, international reach and requires coordinated global efforts to address.

Theorizing about and researching cybercrime is also on the rise. While many top-tier criminology publishers have not yet published much on cybercrime, this may be changing. A study by cybercrime expert Adam Bossler showed that publications on cybercrime are increasing and even finding their way into the most prestigious criminology journals. He speculates that this is likely to continue.[7] Together with the research discussed in Chapter 13, there is good reason to believe that more theories will be applied to cybercrime and, perhaps, specific theories will be developed to explain cybercrime.

Crimes of the powerful and green criminology

In 2016, Wells Fargo Bank was legally required to pay $185 million in fines and to settle restitution to customers at $5 million. Why? For five years, the bank had been opening fraudulent bank and credit card accounts without their customers knowing it. This resulted in customers being saddled with credit card late fees and interest for purchases on credit cards that they had no idea were opened in their name. This was done so that employees could reach productivity goals to receive bonuses and raises.[8]

The Wells Fargo fiasco is far from the only major white-collar incident in recent years. Citizens have been outraged by a litany of unethical practices in big business and almost everyone has been touched by the effects of these crimes over the past decade. Currently, there is unease in the United States, as the President and his staff are at present under investigation for engaging in unlawful behaviors at the highest level of government. Citizens, to say the least, are very concerned about white-collar crime and the crimes of the powerful. They demand to know why these behaviors are taking place and how best to respond.

In 2014, author Elizabeth Kolbert released her book *The sixth extinction* which received widespread acclaim and a 2015 Pulitzer Prize for General Non-fiction. Kolbert carefully and passionately documents the extinction of major species across the globe and estimates that as much as half of the current flora and fauna will disappear by the end of the twenty-first century.[9] This bleak vision of the future has struck a chord with many – and the dark prophecy is one shared by many green criminologists. With major concerns over the changing climate, resource depletion in vulnerable areas throughout the world, and disappearing biodiversity, academics and the public alike are increasing their attention to these issues. This appears especially acute, since the United States has pulled out of the Paris Climate Accord and, along with other nations, is in the process of scaling back major environmental protection laws and policies.

Evaluation of theory and crime prevention

As the United States and other nations move into the future, and as government funding for violence prevention and intervention waxes and wanes, there will likely be more efforts to merge research with policy. In fact, past director of the National Institute of Justice, the research arm of the Department of Justice, John Laub, advocated "translational research."[10] For Laub, research is most useful when it is relevant and practical in the real world, and today, for the most part, we know a lot about what works broadly for crime prevention.[11] This is evidenced by databases such as *Crime solutions* and *Blueprints for healthy youth development*, which now have a considerable knowledge base and set of programs that have been thoroughly researched. This is not to say that more cannot be learned, and even the best programs do not work for everyone, all the time. More needs to be done.

Randomized controlled trials (RCTs) are considered by many to be the "gold-standard" of crime prevention evaluation. RCTs randomly assign individuals to a treatment group (receives intervention) and a control group (does not receive treatment). The random assignments allow researchers to account for any differences between individuals so that only intervention varies among groups. Thus, any change observed is due to treatment and not to individual differences (this is a simplistic explanation of RCTs and they have their own limitations as well).

Many researchers have conducted RCTs, increasing our understanding of many theoretically driven crime prevention and intervention strategies. Several RCTs have been performed on police interventions at crime hotspots[12] and the use of foot patrol to police neighborhoods[13] – both of which were shown to be quite successful. RCTs have also been used to examine intervention programs such as cognitive behavioral therapy. One RCT, for example, found that CBT could reduce the symptoms of post-traumatic stress disorder following exposure to violence[14] while another concluded that home visits from nurses improved long-term outcomes for mothers and children.[15]

However, RCTs are not always possible to examine criminological theories. Often that would require randomly assigning an individual to harm someone or be harmed by someone – unethical and disturbing to say the least. Fortunately there are some methods, often called quasi-experimental methods, that come close to an RCT, which may be used in their place. One tool is propensity score matching (PSM) which uses statistical methods to match people on similar characteristics with the only significant difference among groups being whatever is the "intervention." PSM has been used to examine the role of gangs on risk of victimization,[16] age of onset of substance abuse on incarceration,[17] and the impact of offending on victimization.[18]

Importantly, we still know little about how to implement best practice programs on a wide scale across diverse populations – something researchers call "scaling up." RCTs and quasi-experiments enable practitioners to adopt practices that are effective but it becomes challenging when those efforts are brought to larger jurisdictions. Recently, researchers have made use of computer simulation models to approximate the effects when taking best practices to scale. Implementation is the key to successfully bringing best practices to unique jurisdictions and statistical models can guide these efforts.[19] The future of criminology may be to evaluate and add empirical research to efforts that seek to scale up crime prevention efforts for maximum effect.

On the side of biosocial criminology, new methods are allowing for an even more in-depth investigation of the role of biology in behavior. First, researchers are now able to use entire genomes to map molecular differences to uncover potential genetic contributions to disorders and behaviors. Genome-wide association studies (GWAS) have been used to clarify genetic explanations of antisocial behavior with some success. One study found that genes related to brain functioning were also related to antisocial behavior,[20] while another found associations between immune system genes and antisocial behavior.[21] Second, epigenetic methylation patterns are now being explored in terms of their relation to antisocial behavior. DNA methylation has been linked to antisocial behavior in adult females[22] and MAOA promoter methylation has been found in offender populations.[23] One prevention strategy to interrupt the intergenerational transmission of violence alluded to here has been proffered by recent Stockholm Prize in Criminology recipient Richard Tremblay. He suggests that by focusing on girls with problem behaviors and pregnant mothers, chronic violence often encountered in boys and men can be prevented (Figure 15.2). Such developmental interventions are likely to lead the way to successfully addressing antisocial behavior in the future.

Criminological theory is unlikely to stop there. Criminologists themselves are expanding their intellectual territory to include various social ills and individual maladies. This

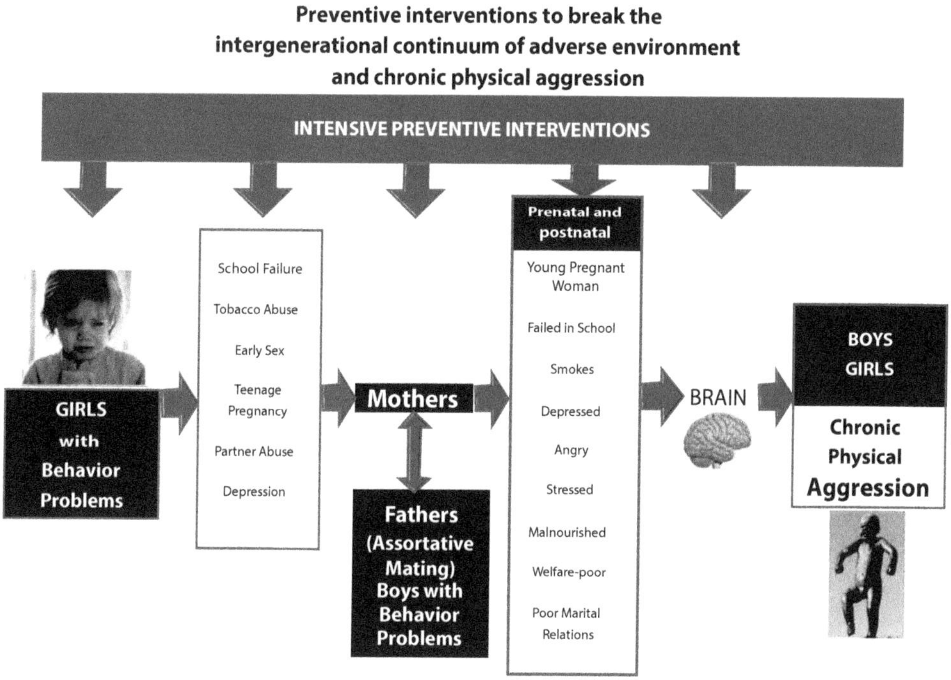

Preventive interventions to break the intergenerational continuum of adverse environment and chronic physical aggression

Figure 15.2 Intergenerational transmission of criminality: explanations and prevention

is evident in a 2017 article by William & Mary criminologist Graham Ousey. He urges criminologists to explore the various social problems that coincide with high crime and violence rates, including infant mortality and sexually transmitted infections. In talking with Ousey he states,

> As social scientists, I think most criminologists have broader concerns than crime. And what should trouble us is that many of the factors that we know are strongly associated with crime – concentrated disadvantage, racial isolation and discrimination – do not just influence crime rates. They influence a host of deleterious outcomes that we, as a society, should seek to minimize.

It is evident in his words that there is a constellation of factors that plague small segments of society. He continues,

> Beyond that, studying these other outcomes could help us to understand crime. We certainly have evidence to indicate that exposure to poor nutrition or environmental toxins is stratified by race and by class; and these outcomes also may affect health outcomes, which in turn may influence criminal offending.[24]

There is reason to believe that more expansive work will be coming out of criminology, investigating areas that have traditionally been outside of criminology.

This is further reflected in many conversations I have had with the editors of major criminological journals. Echoing some of the thoughts discussed in this chapter, Mike Maxfield, editor of the *Journal of Research in Crime and Delinquency*, told me that he has seen:

> environmental criminology become more mainstream. A growing number of such papers have been published in the field's top journals. Biosocial criminology is another developing area, but such work is uneven. Developmental and life-course criminology has continued to grow. I think the criminology of place is the most important theoretical development. This is partly because it has been generally embraced without the rancorous debate that has accompanied biosocial, and the criminal career debate. It has a lot in common with environmental criminology, which has focused on place for many years.[25]

Eric Baumer, co-editor of *Criminology*, is a little unsure of the future of criminology but tells me,

> [T]he large cohort of outstanding scholars who entered the field between approximately the mid-1970s and mid-1980s have recently, or will soon, retire. Coupled with the major growth we've seen over the past decade or so in new criminology PhDs, I think this means that we have a relatively large concentration of young scholars who will play a major role in defining where we go from here. I think it's too early to tell right now.[26]

Not everyone views this emergence of new scholars producing recent work in a positive light. Simon Cole, co-editor of *Theoretical Criminology*, says,

> I feel that we are seeing the results of increased pressure to publish, so junior scholars and students are really jamming out manuscripts rather than working on them till they are excellent. Also, surprisingly, we've seen an increase in what I call "half-assed" revisions. Really fast turnaround on revise and resubmits, rather than really trying to improve the piece. Again, I think we're seeing the pressure to publish a lot and quickly.[27]

While some of these issues are beyond the scope of this book, it is worth noting the exciting new ground waiting to be broken by young, ambitious scholars, along with Cole's warning about the "monetization" of publishing in academia which promotes quantity over quality.

Conclusion

Throughout this book, my intention has been to introduce the history of the field of criminology, explore the various theories of the origins of criminal behavior as well as its escalation and desistance in the lives of individuals, and the development of policy related to theories of crime across history. That history has been tortuous but incredibly interesting. I have also attempted to focus on the contemporary work on criminological theory. Hopefully this sheds light on the otherwise neglected work going on right before our eyes. In the end, perhaps this volume itself can act as a version of history for future criminologists to expand upon.

I am not sure where the field will go from here. I hope others are as excited as I am to see where it will go.[28] This chapter has hypothesized about where the field may go in the future, but there are certainly different avenues through which to travel. Regardless, it is sure to be an enjoyable ride.

Notes

1 Tremblay et al., 2003.
2 See https://www.nytimes.com/2017/05/27/us/portland-train-attack-muslim-rant.html.
3 See www.aljazeera.com/news/2017/05/uk-police-confirmed-fatalities-manchester-concert-170522230211269.html.
4 See www.theguardian.com/uk-news/2017/jun/07/london-bridge-attack-last-of-eight-victims-identified-as-xavier-thomas.
5 Holt & Bossler, 2016.
6 Anderson et al., 2013.
7 Bossler, 2017.
8 See www.cnbc.com/2017/05/12/wells-fargo-fake-account-scandal-may-be-bigger-than-thought.html.
9 Kolbert, 2014.
10 Laub & Frisch, 2011.
11 Elliott & Fagan, 2017.
12 Braga, 2005.
13 Ratcliffe et al., 2011.
14 Stein et al., 2003.
15 Olds et al., 1997.
16 DeLisi et al., 2009a.
17 Slade et al., 2008.
18 Posick, 2017.
19 Sullivan, Welsh, & Ilchi, 2017.
20 Tielbeek et al., 2012.
21 Salvatore et al., 2015.
22 Beach et al., 2011.
23 Checknita et al. 2015.
24 Personal interview with Graham Ousey, June 30, 2017.
25 Personal interview with Michael Maxfield, January 31, 2017.
26 Personal Interview with Eric Baumer January 30, 2017.
27 Personal interview with Simon Cole, December 19, 2016.
28 Loeber and Welsh (2012) produced an entire volume on this very topic and it is recommended reading to all.

Further reading

Bottomley, A. K. (1979). *Criminology in focus: Past trends and future prospects.* London: Martin Robertson.

Fattah, E. A. (1997). *Criminology: Past, present and future: A critical overview.* New York: Springer.

Loeber, R. & Welsh, B. C. (2012). *The future of criminology.* New York: Oxford University Press.

Nelken, D. (1994). *The futures of criminology.* London: Sage.

Appendices

Appendix I Important criminological works, 1700 to the present day

1700s

1764 Beccaria: Tratto dei delitti e delle pene (*Essay on crimes and punishment*)
1765 Bentham: An introduction to the principles of morals and legislation
1793 Godwin: Political justice
1797 Kant: Foundations of the metaphysics of morals and philosophy of law

1800s

1806 Pinel: A treatise on insanity
1810 Gall: Les fonctions du cerveau
1824 Calwell: Elements of phrenology
1845 Engels: The condition of the working class in England
1868 Marx: Das Kapital
1876 Lombroso: L'uomo delinquente (*Criminal man*)
1877 Dugdale: The Jukes: A study in crime, pauperism, disease, and heredity
1893 Durkheim: Division of labor in society
1897 Ellis: The criminal

1900s

1912 Goddard: The Kallikak family: A study in the heredity of feeblemindedness
1915 Healy: The individual delinquent
1923 Burgess: "The study of the delinquent as a person"
1925 Park, Burgess, & McKenzie: The city
1927 Thrasher: The gang
1927 Freud: Civilization and its discontents
1930 Glueck & Glueck: Criminal careers
1931 Hooton: Crime and the man

1934 Sutherland: Principles of criminology

1939 Hooton: The American criminal

1942 Shaw & McKay: Juvenile delinquency and urban areas: A study of delinquents in relation to differential characteristics of local communities

1947 Friedlander: The psychoanalytical approach to juvenile delinquency

1949 Sheldon et al.: Varieties of delinquent youth

1949 Sutherland: White collar crime

1950 Glueck & Glueck: Unraveling juvenile delinquency

1951 Lemert: Social pathology

1955 Cleckley: The mask of sanity

1955 Cohen: Delinquent boys

1956 Garfinkel: "Conditions of successful degradation ceremonies"

1957 Sykes & Matza: "Techniques of neutralization: A theory of delinquency"

1957 Merton: Social theory and social structure

1960 Cloward & Ohlin: Delinquency and opportunity

1961 Matza & Sykes: "Juvenile delinquency and subterranean values"

1963 Becker: Outsiders: Studies in the sociology of deviance

1964 Eysenck: Crime and personality

1968 Becker: "Crime and punishment: An economic approach"

1968 Mischel: Personality and assessment

1969 Blumer: Symbolic interactionism

1969 Hirschi: Causes of delinquency

1970 Hare: Psychopathy: Theory and research

1971 Skinner: Beyond freedom and dignity

1972 Wolfgang: Delinquency in a birth cohort

1973 Schur: Radical nonintervention

1973 Akers: Deviant behavior: A social learning approach

1974 Taylor, Walton, & Young: Critical criminology

1975 Adler: Sisters in crime: The rise of the new female criminal

1975 Simon: Women and crime

1976 Yochelson & Samenow: The criminal personality

1977 Bandura: Social learning theory

1977 Chesney-Lind: "Judicial paternalism and the female status offender: Training women to know their place"

1977 Foucault: Discipline and punish

1979 Jeffrey: Biology and crime

1981 Greenberg: Crime and capitalism

1981 Goffman: Forms of talk

1982 Ellis: Genetics and criminal behavior

1983 Hirschi & Gottfredson: "Age and the explanation of crime"

1984 Samenow: Inside the criminal mind

1985 Wilson & Herrnstein: Crime and human nature

1986 Cornish & Clarke: "Rational choice theory"

1986 Felson: "Routine activities, social controls, rational decisions and criminal outcomes"

1986 Messerschmidt: Capitalism, patriarchy, and crime: Toward a socialist feminist criminology

1987 Thornberry (interactional theory): "Toward an interactional theory of delinquency"

1989 Braithwaite (reintegrative shaming theory): *Crime, shame, and reintegration*

1989 Sampson & Groves: "Community structure and crime: Testing social disorganization theory"

1989 Chesney-Lind: "Girl's crime and woman's place: Toward a feminist model of female delinquency"

1990 Gottfredson & Hirschi: A general theory of crime

1990 Rafter: "The social construction of crime and crime control"

1991 Pepinsky & Quinney: Criminology as peacemaking

1992 Agnew: "Foundation for a general strain theory of crime and delinquency"

1993 Moffitt: "Adolescence-limited and life-course-persistent antisocial behavior: A developmental taxonomy"

1993 Messerschmidt: Masculinities and crime: Critique and reconceptualization of theory

1993 Sampson & Laub (life-course/pathways): Crime in the making: Pathways and turning points through life

1994 Anderson: Code of the street

1994 Messner & Rosenfeld: Crime and the American dream

1995 Hirschi & Gottfredson: "Control theory and the life-course perspective"

1995 Ferrell & Sanders: Cultural criminology

1995 Tittle (control balance theory): Control balance: Toward a general theory of deviance

1995 Simpson & Ellis: "Doing gender: Sorting out the caste and crime conundrum"

1997 Messerschmidt: Crime as structured action: Gender, race, and class

1997 Agnew: "Stability and change in crime over the life course: A strain theory explanation"

1997 Rafter: Creating born criminals

1997 Ellis & Walsh: "Gene-based evolutionary theories in criminology"

1997 Bandura: Self-efficacy: The exercise of control

1998 Ferrell, Hayward, & J. Young: Cultural criminology

1999 Bandura: Moral disengagement theory

1999 Chesney-Lind: Female gangs in America

2000s

2000 Walsh: "Behavior genetics and anomie/strain theory"

2001 Surette & Otto: "The media's role in the definition of crime"

2001 Messner & Rosenfeld: An institutional-anomie theory of crime

2002 Rowe: Biology and crime

2003 Kubrin & Weitzer: "New directions in social disorganization theory"

2003 Warner: "The role of attenuated culture in social disorganization theory"

2004 Chesney-Lind: Girls, women, and crime

2005 Lombroso: Criminal man (new translation)

2005 Farrington: The Integrated Cognitive Antisocial Potential (ICAP) theory

2005 Topalli: "When being good is bad: An expansion of neutralization theory"

2006 Ward, Stafford, & Gray: Rational choice, deterrence, and theoretical integration

2006 Rutter: Genes and behavior: Nature–nurture interplay explained

2008 Rafter: The criminal brain: Understanding the biological theories of crime

2009 Walsh & Beaver: Biosocial criminology: New directions in theory and research

2009 Beaver: Biosocial criminology: A primer

2013 Raine: The anatomy of violence: The biological roots of crime

Appendix II Important world events, 1700 to the present day

1700s

1755 William Cullen invents the first artificial refrigeration machine.

1760 Industrial Revolution begins in England.

1764 James Hargreaves invents the spinning jenny.

1769 James Watt patents the first steam-engine.

1776 US Declaration of Independence.

1783 Claude de Jouffroy builds the first steamboat.

1787 US Constitution signed.

1789 George Washington is unanimously elected as the first president of the United States in a vote by state elector.

1789 French Revolution begins – First Republic established.

1791 First ten amendments to the Constitution, known as the Bill of Rights, are ratified.

1793 Eli Whitney invents the modern cotton gin.

1796 Edward Jenner discovers the first successful vaccine, the smallpox vaccine.

1799 Louis-Nicolas Robert invents the first paper machine.

1800s

1800 Napoleon conquers Italy, and firmly establishes himself as First Consul in France.

1801 Thomas Jefferson is inaugurated as the third president in Washington, DC.

1803 The US negotiates Louisiana Purchase from France.

1804 Hanaoka Seishū creates tsūsensan, the first modern general anesthetic.

1810 Nicolas Appert invents the canning process for food.

1815 Napoleon Bonaparte is defeated at the Battle of Waterloo, ending the Napoleonic era of European history.

1820 Missouri Compromise.

1822 Charles Babbage, considered the "father of the computer," begins building the first programmable mechanical computer.

1823 U.S. Monroe Doctrine warns European nations not to interfere in Western Hemisphere.

1836 Samuel Morse invents Morse code.

1849 California gold-rush begins.

1849 Elizabeth Blackwell is the first woman to receive a medical degree (Geneva Medical College in Geneva, New York).

1859 Gaston Planté invents the lead acid battery, the first rechargeable battery.

1864 General Sherman's Atlanta campaign and "march to the sea."

1865 The Thirteenth Amendment abolishes slavery in the United States.

1867 Alfred Novel invents dynamite.

1870 Franco-Prussian War (to 1871) – Napoleon III surrenders at Sedan.

1876 Alexander Graham Bell is granted a patent for the telephone.

1879 Thomas Edison invents electric light.

1886 Karl Benz invents the first petrol- or gasoline-powered automobile.

1895 The Lumière Brothers invent the cinematograph.

1895 German physicist, Wilhelm Roentgen, discovers X-rays.

1900s

1903 Orville and Wilbur Wright fly the first manually controlled, motorized aircraft in Kitty Hawk, North Carolina.

1905 Albert Einstein announces theory of relativity.

1907 First successful human blood transfusion using Landsteiner's ABO blood-typing technique.

1914 World War I begins.

1918 World War I ends.

1919 The Nineteenth Amendment guarantees all American women the right to vote.

1928 Alexander Fleming discovers that penicillin exudes antibiotic substances.

1931 Ernst Ruska invents the electron microscope.

1933 FM radio is patented by inventor Edwin H. Armstrong.

1933 The Holocaust begins.

1935 First vaccine for yellow fever.

1939 Hitler invades Poland; World War II begins.

1941 Japanese attack Pearl Harbor, forcing the US into war.

1945 Atomic bombs dropped on Hiroshima and Nagasaki.

1945 World War II ends.

1945 The Holocaust ends.

1945 First vaccine for influenza.

1950 Korean War begins.

1953 Korean War ends.

1955 Vietnam War begins.

1964 First vaccine for measles.

1967 First vaccine for mumps.

1969 Neil Armstrong becomes the first person to walk on the moon.

1970 The pocket calculator is invented in Japan.

1975 Vietnam War ends.

1977 First vaccine for pneumonia.

1977 Raymond Vahan Damadian invents MRI.

1978 First test-tube baby is born in the UK.

1981 AIDS is identified.

1983 HIV, the virus that causes AIDS, is identified

1984 Motorola invents the first commercially available cell phone, the DynaTAC 8000X.

1985 Alec Jeffreys invents DNA profiling.

1989 Fall of communism in Eastern Europe.

1990 Sir Tim Berners-Lee introduces The World Wide Web to the public.

1990 The fMRI technique is invented by a group at Bell Laboratories led by Seiji Ogawa.

1991 The Persian Gulf War.

1993 MOSAIC, the first popular web browser, is introduced.

1995 DVD is an optical disc storage format, invented and developed by Philips, Sony, Toshiba, and Panasonic. DVDs offer higher storage capacity than compact disks while having the same dimensions.

1996 USB interface launched by Compaq, DEC, IBM, Intel, Microsoft, NEC, and Nortel.

1996 Dolly the sheep becomes the first mammal cloned from an adult cell (dies in 2003).

1999 European Union introduces the euro as the new currency.

2000s

2001 US military commence the first attack in the War on Terrorism on the Taliban and Al-Qaeda in Afghanistan.

2002 Angolan Civil War ends (began in 1975).

2003 Saddam Hussein is captured.

2005 Hurricane Katrina strikes Gulf Coast (largest and third strongest to make landfall in the US).

2007 The first iPhone is released.

2008 Barack Obama is elected as the forty-fourth president, making him the first African American president in the history of the United States.

2009 The World Health Organization deems the H1N1 virus (swine flu) a global pandemic.

2009 President Obama closes all secret prisons and detention camps run by the CIA.

2011 Al-Qaeda leader Osama bin Laden is killed by US Special Forces.

2014 The Islamic State of Iraq and Syria (ISIS) emerges.

2014 Ebola outbreak in Western Africa.

2015 The US Supreme Court rules that same-sex couples have the fundamental right to marry.

2015 All US military combat roles now open to women.

2015 Paris terrorist attacks coordinated by ISIS.

2015 The US and Cuba re-establish diplomatic relations and reopen embassies.

2016 Michael Phelps wins his twenty-second gold medal, breaking a 2,168-year-old record for individual Olympic titles.

2016 Hillary Clinton becomes the first woman to be nominated by a major party for the US presidency.

2016 Britain decides to withdraw from the European Union.

References

Adler, F. (1975). *Sisters in crime: The rise of the new female criminal*. New York: McGraw-Hill.

Agnew, R. (1985). A revised strain theory of delinquency. *Social Forces, 64*(1), 151–167.

Agnew, R. (1992). Foundation for a general strain theory of crime and delinquency. *Criminology, 30*(1), 47–88.

Agnew, R. (2001). Building on the foundation of general strain theory: Specifying the types of strain most likely to lead to crime and delinquency. *Journal of Research in Crime and Delinquency, 38*(4), 319–361.

Agnew, R. (2002). Experienced, vicarious, and anticipated strain: An exploratory study on physical victimization and delinquency. *Justice Quarterly, 19*(4), 603–632.

Agnew, R. (2005). *Why do criminals offend? A general theory of crime and delinquency*. Los Angeles, CA: Roxbury.

Agnew, R. (2010). A general strain theory of terrorism. *Theoretical Criminology, 14*(2), 131–153.

Agnew, R. (2011). *Toward a unified criminology: Integrating assumptions about crime, people and society*. New York: New York University Press.

Agnew, R. (2012). Dire forecast: A theoretical model of the impact of climate change on crime. *Theoretical Criminology, 16*(1), 21–42.

Agnew, R. (2014). Social concern and crime: Moving beyond the assumption of simple self-interest. *Criminology, 52*(1), 1–32.

Agnew, R. (2016). A theory of crime resistance and susceptibility. *Criminology, 54*(2), 181–211.

Agnew, R., Brezina, T., Wright, J. P., & Cullen, F. T. (2002). Strain, personality traits, and delinquency: Extending general strain theory. *Criminology, 40*(1), 43–72.

Akers, R. L. (1968). Problems in the sociology of deviance: Social definitions and behavior. *Social Forces, 46*(4), 455–465.

Akers, R. L. (2002). A social learning theory of crime. *Criminological Theories: Bringing the Past to the Future*, 135–144.

Akers, R. L. & Silverman, A. (2004). Toward a social learning model of violence and terrorism. In Zahn, M. A., Brownstein, H. H., & Jackson, S. L. (eds.) *Violence: From theory to research* (pp. 19–30). Cincinnati, OH: LexusNexus-Anderson Publishing.

Alexander, M. (2012). *The new Jim Crow: Mass incarceration in the age of colorblindness*. New York: The New Press.

Allen, D. S. (2009). *The world of Prometheus: The politics of punishing in democratic Athens*. Princeton, NJ: Princeton University Press.

Anderson, E. (2000). *Code of the street: Decency, violence, and the moral life of the inner city*. New York: WW Norton & Company.

Anderson, R., Barton, C., Böhme, R., Clayton, R., Van Eeten, M. J., Levi, M., Moore, T., & Savage, S. (2013). Measuring the cost of cybercrime. In Böhme, R. (ed.) *The economics of information security and privacy* (pp. 265–300). New York: Springer Berlin Heidelberg.

Apel, R. & Burrows, J. D. (2011). Adolescent victimization and violent self-help. *Youth Violence and Juvenile Justice, 9,* 112–133.

Arnett, J. J. & Jensen, L. A. (1994). Socialization and risk behavior in two countries: Denmark and the United States. *Youth and Society, 26,* 3–22.

Aseltine Jr, R. H., Gore, S., & Gordon, J. (2000). Life stress, anger and anxiety, and delinquency: An empirical test of general strain theory. *Journal of Health and Social Behavior, 41*(3), 256–275.

Ball, M. (2014). Queer criminology, critique, and the "art of not being governed". *Critical Criminology, 22*(1), 21–34.

Bandura, A. (1977). *Social learning theory.* Englewood Cliffs, NJ: Prentice Hall.

Bandura, A. (1986). *Social foundations of thought and action: A social cognitive theory.* New York: Prentice-Hall.

Bao, W-N., Haas, A., & Yijun, P. (2004). Life strain, negative emotions, and delinquency: An empirical test of general strain theory in the People's Republic of China. *International Journal of Offender Therapy and Comparative Criminology, 48,* 281–297.

Barnes, J. C. & Boutwell, B. B. (2012). On the relationship of past to future involvement in crime and delinquency: A behavior genetic analysis. *Journal of Criminal Justice, 40*(1), 94–102.

Barnes, J. C., Beaver, K. M., & Boutwell, B. B. (2011). Examining the genetic underpinnings to Moffitt's developmental taxonomy: A behavioral genetic analysis. *Criminology, 49*(4), 923–954.

Barnes, J. C., Boutwell, B. B., & Beaver, K. M. (2014). Genetic and nonshared environmental factors predict handgun ownership in early adulthood. *Death Studies, 38*(3), 156–164.

Baron, S. W. (2004). General strain, street youth and crime: A test of Agnew's revised theory. *Criminology, 42,* 457–483.

Beach, S. R., Brody, G. H., Todorov, A. A., Gunter, T. D., & Philibert, R. A. (2011). Methylation at 5HTT mediates the impact of child sex abuse on women's antisocial behavior: An examination of the Iowa adoptee sample. *Psychosomatic Medicine, 73*(1), 83–87.

Beaver, K. M. & Wright, J. P. (2011). The association between county-level IQ and county-level crime rates. *Intelligence, 39*(1), 22–26.

Beaver, K. M., Barnes, J. C., Schwartz, J. A., & Boutwell, B. B. (2015). Enlisting in the military: The influential role of genetic factors. *Sage Open, 5*(2), 2158244015573352.

Beaver, K. M., Gibson, C. L., Jennings, W. G., & Ward, J. T. (2009a). A gene X environment interaction between DRD2 and religiosity in the prediction of adolescent delinquent involvement in a sample of males. *Biodemography and Social Biology, 55*(1), 71–81.

Beaver, K. M., Mancini, C., DeLisi, M., & Vaughn, M. G. (2011). Resiliency to victimization: The role of genetic factors. *Journal of Interpersonal Violence, 26*(5), 874–898.

Beaver, K. M., Vaughn, M. G., DeLisi, M., & Higgins, G. E. (2010). The biosocial correlates of neuropsychological deficits: Results from the National Longitudinal Study of Adolescent Health. *International Journal of Offender Therapy and Comparative Criminology, 54*(6), 878–894.

Beaver, K. M., Wright, J. P., DeLisi, M., & Vaughn, M. G. (2008). Genetic influences on the stability of low self-control: Results from a longitudinal sample of twins. *Journal of Criminal Justice, 36*(6), 478–485.

Beaver, K. M., Schutt, J. E., Boutwell, B. B., Ratchford, M., Roberts, K., & Barnes, J. C. (2009b). Genetic and environmental influences on levels of self-control and delinquent peer affiliation: Results from a longitudinal sample of adolescent twins. *Criminal Justice and Behavior, 36*(1), 41–60.

Beaver, K. M., Wright, J. P., DeLisi, M., Daigle, L. E., Swatt, M. L., & Gibson, C. L. (2007). Evidence of a gene x environment interaction in the creation of victimization: Results from a longitudinal sample of adolescents. *International Journal of Offender Therapy and Comparative Criminology, 51,* 620–645.

Beccaria, C. ([1764]2009). *On crimes and punishments and other writings.* Toronto, Canada: University of Toronto Press.

Becker, G. S. (1968). Crime and punishment: An economic approach. In Fielding, G. G., Clarke, A., & Witt, R. (eds.) *The economic dimensions of crime* (pp. 13–68). London: Palgrave Macmillan.

Bellair, P. E. (1997). Social interaction and community crime: Examining the importance of neighbor networks. *Criminology, 35*(4), 677–704.

Bennett, R. (1991). Routine activities: A cross-national assessment of a criminological perspective. *Social Forces, 70,* 147–163.

Benson, M. L. (1985). Denying the guilty mind: Accounting for involvement in a white-collar crime. *Criminology, 23*(4), 583–607.

Bentham, J. ([1789]1988). *The principles of morals and legislation.* Amherst, NY: Prometheus Books.

Berg, M. T. & Loeber, R. (2011). Examining the neighborhood context of the violent offending–victimization relationship: A prospective investigation. *Journal of Quantitative Criminology, 27*(4), 427–451.

Berg, M. T., Stewart, E. A., Schreck, C. J., & Simons, R. L. (2012). The victim–offender overlap in context: Examining the role of neighborhood street culture. *Criminology, 50*(2), 359–390.

Bergen, S. E., Gardner, C. O., & Kendler, K. S. (2007). Age-related changes in heritability of behavioral phenotypes over adolescence and young adulthood: A meta-analysis. *Twin Research and Human Genetics, 10*(3), 423–433.

Bersani, B. E., Laub, J. H., & Nieuwbeerta, P. (2009). Marriage and desistance from crime in the Netherlands: Do gender and socio-historical context matter? *Journal of Quantitative Criminology, 25*(1), 3–24.

Best, J. (1997). Victimization and the victim industry. *Society, 34*(4), 9–17.

Bjarnason, T., Sigurdardottir, T. J., & Thorlindsson, T. (1999). Human agency, capable guardians, and structural constraints: A lifestyle approach to the study of violent victimization. *Journal of Youth and Adolescence, 28,* 105–119.

Blackwell, B. S. & Cruze, J. (forthcoming). Intersectionality and crime. *International encyclopedia of the social and behavioural sciences.*

Boehm, C. (2011). Retaliatory violence in human prehistory. *British Journal of Criminology, 51,* 518–534.

Boman IV, J. H., Stogner, J. M., Miller, B. L., Griffin III, O. H., & Krohn, M. D. (2012). On the operational validity of perceptual peer delinquency: Exploring projection and elements contained in perceptions. *Journal of Research in Crime and Delinquency, 49*(4), 601–621.

Bonger, W. A. ([1905]1969). *Criminality and economic conditions.* Boston, MA: Little, Brown.

Bonoli, G. (1997). Classifying welfare states: A two-dimension approach. *Journal of Social Policy, 26*(3), 351–372.

Bossler, A. M. (2017). Cybercrime research at the crossroads: Where the field currently stands and innovative strategies to move forward. In Holt, T. J. *Cybercrime through an interdisciplinary lens.* New York: Routledge.

Bossler, A. M. & Holt, T. J. (2009). On-line activities, guardianship, and malware infection: An examination of routine activities theory. *International Journal of Cyber Criminology, 3*(1), 400–420.

Botchkovar, E. V., Tittle, C. R., & Antonaccio, O. (2009). General strain theory: Additional evidence using cross-cultural data. *Criminology, 47,* 131–176.

Botchkovar, E., Marshall, I. H., Rocque, M., & Posick, C. (2015). The importance of parenting in the development of self-control in boys and girls: Results from a multinational study of youth. *Journal of Criminal Justice, 43*(2), 133–141.

Bouffard, L. A. & Muftic, L. R. (2006). The "rural mystique": Social disorganization and violence beyond urban communities. *Western Criminology Review, 7*(3), 56–66.

Boutwell, B. B., Beaver, K. M., & Barnes, J. C. (2014). The association of parent-reported lead exposure with language skills and externalizing behavioral problems in children. *Journal of Geography & Natural Disasters, 4*(2), 2167–0587.

Boutwell, B. B., Barnes, J. C., Beaver, K. M., Haynes, R. D., Nedelec, J. L., & Gibson, C. L. (2015). A unified crime theory: The evolutionary taxonomy. *Aggression and Violent Behavior, 25,* 343–353.

Boutwell, B. B., Nelson, E. J., Emo, B., Vaughn, M. G., Schootman, M., Rosenfeld, R., & Lewis, R. (2016). The intersection of aggregate-level lead exposure and crime. *Environmental Research, 148,* 79–85.

Braga, A. A. (2005). Hot spots policing and crime prevention: A systematic review of randomized controlled trials. *Journal of Experimental Criminology, 1*(3), 317–342.

Braga, A. A. & Weisburd, D. L. (2012). The effects of focused deterrence strategies on crime: A systematic review and meta-analysis of the empirical evidence. *Journal of Research in Crime and Delinquency, 49*(3), 323–358.

Braga, A. A., Papachristos, A. V., & Hureau, D. M. (2014). The effects of hot spots policing on crime: An updated systematic review and meta-analysis. *Justice Quarterly, 31*(4), 633–663.

Braithwaite, J. (1989). *Crime, shame and reintegration.* Cambridge, MA: Cambridge University Press.

Braithwaite, J. (1993). Shame and modernity. *The British Journal of Criminology, 33*(1), 1–18.

Brantingham, P. J. & Brantingham, P. L. (1981). *Environmental criminology.* Beverly Hills, CA: Sage.

Brantingham, P. & Brantingham, P. (1995). Criminality of place. *European Journal on Criminal Policy and Research, 3*(3), 5–26.

Brantingham, P. L. & Brantingham, P. J. (2004). Computer simulation as a tool for environmental criminologists. *Security Journal, 17*(1), 21–30.

Breasted, J. H. (2003). *Ancient time or a history of the early world* (Part 1). Grand Rapids, MI: Kessinger Publishing.

Brehm, H. N. (2017). Subnational determinants of killing in Rwanda. *Criminology, 55*(1), 5–31.

Brehm, H. N., Uggen, C., & Gasanabo, J. D. (2016). Age, gender, and the crime of crimes: Toward a life-course theory of genocide participation. *Criminology, 54*(4), 713–743.

Brezina, T., Agnew, R., Cullen, F. T., & Wright, J. P. (2004). The code of the street: A quantitative assessment of Elijah Anderson's subculture of violence thesis and its contribution to youth violence research. *Youth Violence and Juvenile Justice, 2,* 303–328.

Briggs, C. S., Sundt, J. L., & Castellano, T. C. (2003). The effect of supermaximum security prisons on aggregate levels of institutional violence. *Criminology, 41*(4), 1341–1376.

Britt, C. L. (2000). Social context and racial disparities in punishment decisions. *Justice Quarterly, 17*(4), 707–732.

Britt, C. L. (2001). Health consequences of criminal victimization. *International Review of Victimology, 8*(1), 63–73.

Brody, G. H., Murry, V. M., Gerrard, M., Gibbons, F. X., McNair, L., Brown, A. C., Wills, T. A., Molgaard, M., Spoth, R. L., Luo, Z., & Chen, Y. F. (2006). The strong African American families program: Prevention of youths' high-risk behavior and a test of a model of change. *Journal of Family Psychology, 20*(1), 1–11.

Broidy, L. M. (2001). A test of general strain theory. *Criminology, 39*(1), 9–36.

Brunson, R. K. (2007). "Police don't like black people": African-American young men's accumulated police experiences. *Criminology & Public Policy, 6*(1), 71–101.

Burke, N. J., Hellman, J. L., Scott, B. G., Weems, C. F., & Carrion, V. G. (2011). The impact of adverse childhood experiences on an urban pediatric population. *Child Abuse & Neglect, 35,* 408–413.

Bursik, R. J. (1988). Social disorganization and theories of crime and delinquency: Problems and prospects. *Criminology, 26*(4), 519–552.

Bursik, R. J. & Grasmick, H. G. (1993). *Neighborhoods & crime.* Lanham, MD: Lexington Books.

Burt, C. H. & Simons, R. L. (2014). Pulling back the curtain on heritability studies: Biosocial criminology in the postgenomic era. *Criminology, 52*(2), 223–262.

Burt, C. H., Simons, R. L., & Simons, L. G. (2006). A longitudinal test of the effects of parenting and the stability of self-control: Negative evidence for the general theory of crime. *Criminology, 44*(2), 353–396.

Button, D. M. (2016). Understanding the effects of victimization: Applying general strain theory to the experiences of LGBQ youth. *Deviant Behavior, 37*(5), 537–556.

Byrd, A. L. & Manuck, S. B. (2014). MAOA, childhood maltreatment, and antisocial behavior: Meta-analysis of a gene–environment interaction. *Biological Psychiatry, 75*(1), 9–17.

Campbell, A. (1999). Staying alive: Evolution, culture, and women's intrasexual aggression. *Behavioral and Brain Sciences, 22*(2), 203–214.

Campbell, A. (2013). *A mind of her own: The evolutionary psychology of women.* Oxford: Oxford University Press.

Caplan, J. M. & Kennedy, L. W. (2011). *Risk terrain modeling compendium.* Newark, NJ: Rutgers Center on Public Security.

Carey, N. (2012). *The epigenetics revolution: How modern biology is rewriting our understanding of genetics, disease, and inheritance.* New York: Columbia University Press.

Caspi, A., McClay, J., Moffitt, T. E., Mill, J., Martin, J., Craig, I. W., Taylor, A., & Poulton, R. (2002). Role of genotype in the cycle of violence in maltreated children. *Science, 297*(5582), 851–854.

Caspi, A., Sugden, K., Moffitt, T. E., Taylor, A., Craig, I. W., Harrington, H., McClay, J., Mill, J., Martin, J., Braithwaite, A., & Poulton, R. (2003). Influence of life stress on depression: Moderation by a polymorphism in the 5-HTT gene. *Science, 301*(5631), 386–389.

Cattell, R. (1950). The principal culture patterns discoverable in the syntax dimensions of existing nations. *Journal of Social Psychology, 32,* 215–253.

Caulkins, J. P., Kilmer, B., & Kleiman, M. A. (2016). *Marijuana legalization: What everyone needs to know.* New York: Oxford University Press.

Cavadino, M. & Dignan, J. (2006). *Penal systems: A comparative approach.* Thousand Oaks, CA: Sage.

Chabris, C. F., Lee, J. J., Cesarini, D., Benjamin, D. J., & Laibson, D. I. (2015). The fourth law of behavior genetics. *Current Directions in Psychological Science, 24*(4), 304–312.

Chamlin, M. B. & Cochran, J. K. (2007). An evaluation of the assumptions that underlie institutional anomie theory. *Theoretical Criminology, 11,* 39–61.

Chang, J. J., Chen, J. J., & Brownson, R. C. (2003). The role of repeat victimization in adolescent delinquent behavior and recidivism. *Journal of Adolescent Health, 32,* 272–280.

Chappell, A. & Piquero, A. (2004). Applying social learning theory to police misconduct. *Deviant Behavior, 25*(2), 89–108.

Checknita, D., Maussion, G., Labonté, B., Comai, S., Tremblay, R. E., Vitaro, F., Turecki, N., Bertazzo, A., Gobbi, G., Cote, G., & Turecki, G. (2015). Monoamine oxidase: A gene promoter methylation and transcriptional downregulation in an offender population with antisocial personality disorder. *The British Journal of Psychiatry, 206*(3), 216–222.

Chesney-Lind, M. (1989). Girls' crime and woman's place: Toward a feminist model of female delinquency. *NPPA Journal, 35*(1), 5–29.

Chesney-Lind, M. (2006). Patriarchy, crime, and justice: Feminist criminology in an era of backlash. *Feminist Criminology, 1*(1), 6–26.

Chisholm, H. (1911). Lavater, Johann Kaspar. *Encyclopædia Britannica* (11th edn). New York: Cambridge University Press.

Christian, L. M., Galley, J. D., Hade, E. M., Schoppe-Sullivan, S., Dush, C. K., & Bailey, M. T. (2015). Gut microbiome composition is associated with temperament during early childhood. *Brain, Behavior, and Immunity, 45,* 118–127.

Christie, N. (1970). Comparative criminology. *Canadian Journal of Corrections, 12,* 40–46.

Christie, N. (1986). The ideal victim. In Fattah, E. A. (Ed.) *From crime policy to victim policy* (pp. 17–30). London: Macmillan.

Clarke, R. V. (1999). Hot products: Understanding, anticipating and reducing demand for stolen goods. *Police Research Series.* Paper 112. Home Office, Policing and Reducing Crime Unit, Research, Development and Statistics Directorate.

Clarke, R. V. & Cornish, D. B. (1985). Modeling offenders' decisions: A framework for research and policy. *Crime and Justice,* 147–185.

Clear, T. R. & Frost, N. A. (2015). *The punishment imperative: The rise and failure of mass incarceration in America.* New York: New York University Press.

Cloward, R. & Ohlin, L. (1960). *Delinquency and opportunity. A theory of delinquent gangs.* New York: The Free Press.

Cohen, A. K. (1955). *Delinquent boys: The culture of the gang.* New York: The Free Press.

Cohen, L. E. & Felson, M. (1979). Social change and crime rate trends: A routine activity approach. *American Sociological Review, 44*(4), 588–608.

Cohen, L. E., Kluegel, J. R., & Land, K. C. (1981). Social inequality and predatory criminal victimization: An exposition and test of a formal theory. *American Sociological Review, 46*(5), 505–524.

Conley, D. & Fletcher, J. (2017). *The genome factor: What the social genomics revolution reveals about ourselves, our history, and the future.* Princeton, NJ: Princeton University Press.

Costello, B. J. & Vowell, P. R. (1999). Testing control theory and differential association: A reanalysis of the Richmond Youth Project data. *Criminology, 37*(4), 815–842.

Cowles, E. L. & Castellano, T. C. (1996). Substance abuse programming in adult correctional boot camps: A national overview. In MacKenzie, D. L. & Herbert, E. E. (Eds.) *Correctional boot camps: A tough intermediate sanction* (pp. 207–232). Washington, DC: US Department of Justice.

Crank, J. P. & Jacoby, L. S. (2015). *Crime, violence, and global warming.* New York: Routledge.

Cryan, J. F. & Dinan, T. G. (2015). More than a gut feeling: The microbiota regulates neurodevelopment and behavior. *Neuropsychopharmacology, 40*(1), 241–242.

Cullen, F. T. (1994). Social support as an organizing concept for criminology: Presidential address to the Academy of Criminal Justice Sciences. *Justice Quarterly, 11*(4), 527–559.

Cullen, K. (1997). The Comish. *Boston Globe Magazine,* May 25.

Currie, E. (1997). Market, crime and community: Toward a mid-range theory of post-industrial violence. *Theoretical Criminology, 1*(2), 147–172.

Curtis, G. C. (1963). Violence breeds violence – perhaps? *American Journal of Psychiatry, 120,* 386–387.

Cusson, M. & Pinsonneault, P. (1986). The decision to give up crime. In Cornish, D. B. & Clarke, R. V. (Eds.) *The reasoning criminal: Rational choice perspectives on offending* (pp. 72–82). New York: Springer.

Dadds, M. R., Moul, C., Hawes, D. J., Mendoza Diaz, A., & Brennan, J. (2015). Individual differences in childhood behavior disorders associated with epigenetic modulation of the cortisol receptor gene. *Child Development, 86*(5), 1311–1320.

Daigle, L. E., Beaver, K. M., & Hartman, J. L. (2008). A life-course approach to the study of victimization and offending behaviors. *Victims & Offenders, 3,* 365–390.

Daly, K. & Chesney-Lind, M. (1988). Feminism and criminology. *Justice Quarterly, 5*(4), 497–538.

Darwin, C. ([1859]1968). *The origin of species.* London: Penguin.

Dawkins, R. (2009). *The greatest show on earth: The evidence for evolution.* New York: Simon and Schuster.

De Coster, S. & Kort-Butler, L. (2006). How general is general strain theory? Assessing determinacy and indeterminacy across life domains. *Journal of Research in Crime and Delinquency, 43*(4), 297–325.

De Haan, W. & Vos, J. (2003). A crying shame: The over-rationalized conception of man in the rational choice perspective. *Theoretical Criminology, 7*(1), 29–54.

DeKeseredy, W. S. & Schwartz, M. D. (2017). Days of whine and poses. *The British Journal of Criminology, 57*(3), 742–745.

DeLisi, M. (2009). Psychopathy is the unified theory of crime. *Youth Violence and Juvenile Justice, 7*(3), 256–273.

DeLisi, M. (2013). *Revisiting Lombroso.* In Cullen, F. T. & Wilcox, P. (Eds.) *The Oxford handbook of criminological theory* (pp. 5–21). Oxford: Oxford University Press.

DeLisi, M. (2016). *Psychopathy as unified theory of crime.* Basingstoke: Palgrave Macmillan.

DeLisi, M., Barnes, J. C., Beaver, K. M., & Gibson, C. L. (2009a). Delinquent gangs and adolescent victimization revisited: A propensity score matching approach. *Criminal Justice and Behavior, 36*(8), 808–823.

DeLisi, M., Beaver, K. M., Vaughn, M. G., & Wright, J. P. (2009b). All in the family: Gene × environment interaction between DRD2 and criminal father is associated with five antisocial phenotypes. *Criminal Justice and Behavior, 36*(11), 1187–1197.

DeLisi, M., Wright, J. P., Vaughn, M. G., & Beaver, K. M. (2010). Nature and nurture by definition means both: A response to Males. *Journal of Adolescent Research, 25*(1), 24–30.

Della Porta, G. (1586). De humana physiognomonia. *"Maximum Caput"* [digital image]. Available at: www.italianways.com/giovanni-battista-della-portas-de-humana-physiognomonia/.

De Morgan, E. (1903) *The Love Potion: A witch with a black cat familiar at her feet.* Public Domain.

Demuth, S. & Steffensmeier, D. (2004). The impact of gender and race-ethnicity in the pretrial release process. *Social Problems, 51*(2), 222–242.

Diamond, J. (2008). Vengeance is ours. *The New Yorker,* April 21.

DiCristina, B. (2012). *The birth of criminology: Readings from the eighteenth and nineteenth centuries.* Frederick, MD: Wolters Kluwer.

Donnermeyer, J. F. & DeKeseredy, W. (2013). *Rural criminology.* New York: Routledge.

Douglas, K., Chan, G., Gelernter, J., Arias, A. J., Anton, R. F., Poling, J., Farrer, L., & Kranzler, H. R. (2011). 5-HTTLPR as a potential moderator of the effects of adverse childhood experiences on risk of antisocial personality disorder. *Psychiatric Genetics, 21*(5), 240-248.

Du Bois, W. E. B. (1899). *The Philadelphia negro: A social study.* Philadelphia, PA: Pennsylvania University Press.

Dugdale, R. (1877). *The Jukes: A study in crime, pauperism, disease and heredity.* New York: G. P. Putnam's Sons.

Durkheim, E. ([1897]1951). *Suicide: A study in sociology* (J. A. Spaulding & G. Simpson, trans.). Glencoe, IL: The Free Press.

Durkheim, E. ([1895]1982). *The rules of the sociological method and selected texts on sociology and its method.* New York: The Free Press.

Dyson, R. W. (2001). *The pilgrim city: Social and political ideas in the writings of St. Augustine of Hippo.* Rochester, NY: Boydell & Brewer.

Einstadter, W. J. & Henry, S. (2006). *Criminological theory: An analysis of its underlying assumptions.* New York: Rowman & Littlefield.

Eitle, D. & Turner, R. J. (2002). Exposure to community violence and young adult crime: The effects of witnessing violence, traumatic victimization, and other stressful life events. *Journal of Research in Crime and Delinquency, 39,* 214–237.

Elliott, D. & Fagan, A. (2017). *The prevention of crime.* Malden, MA: John Wiley & Sons.

Ellis, L. (1982). Genetics and criminal behavior evidence through the end of the 1970s. *Criminology, 20*(1), 43–66.

Ellis, L. (1988). Criminal behavior and r/K selection: An extension of gene-based evolutionary theory. *Personality and Individual Differences, 9*(4), 697–708.

Ennett, S. T., Rosenbaum, D. P., Flewelling, R. L., Bieler, G. S., Ringwalt, C. L., & Bailey, S. L. (1994). Long-term evaluation of drug abuse resistance education. *Addictive Behaviors, 19*(2), 113–125.

Erez, E., Adelman, M., & Gregory, C. (2009). Intersections of immigration and domestic violence: Voices of battered immigrant women. *Feminist Criminology, 4*(1), 32–56.

Esbensen, F. A. & Huizinga, D. (1991). Juvenile victimization and delinquency. *Youth and Society, 23*, 202–228.

Esbensen, F. A. & Osgood, D. W. (1999). Gang Resistance Education and Training (GREAT): Results from the national evaluation. *Journal of Research in Crime and Delinquency, 36*(2), 194–225.

Esbensen, F. A., Huizinga, D., & Menard, S. (1999). Family context and criminal victimization in adolescence. *Youth & Society, 31*, 168–198.

Esbensen, F. A., Osgood, D. W., Taylor, T. J., Peterson, D., & Freng, A. (2001). How great is GREAT? Results from a longitudinal quasi-experimental design. *Criminology & Public Policy, 1*(1), 87–118.

Esping-Andersen, G. (1990). *The three worlds of welfare capitalism.* Princeton, NJ: Princeton University Press.

Esping-Andersen, G. (1999). *Social foundations of postindustrial economies.* Oxford: Oxford University Press.

Ewing, W. A., Martínez, D. E., & Rumbaut, R. G. (2015). The *criminalization of immigration in the United States.* Washington, DC: American Immigration Council Special Report, July.

Fagan, A. (1991). The gender cycle of violence: Comparing the effects of child abuse and neglect on criminal offending for males and females. *Violence and Victims, 16*, 457–474.

Fahey, S., & LaFree, G. (2015). Does country-level social disorganization increase terrorist attacks? *Terrorism and Political Violence, 27*(1), 81–111.

Farrall, S. & Calverley, A. (2006). *Understanding desistance from crime: Theoretical directions in resettlement and rehabilitation.* Maidenhead: Open University Press.

Farrington, D. P. (2003). Developmental and life-course criminology: Key theoretical and empirical issues – The 2002 Sutherland Award address. *Criminology, 41*(2), 221–225.

Farrington, D. P. & Welsh, B. C. (2008). *Saving children from a life of crime: Early risk factors and effective interventions.* New York: Oxford University Press.

Farrington, K. (1996). *Dark justice: A history of punishment and torture.* New York: Reed International Books.

Fattah, E. A. (1979). Some recent theoretical developments in victimology. *Victimology, 4*, 198–213.

Feeley, M. M. & Simon, J. (1992). The new penology: Notes on the emerging strategy of corrections and its implications. *Criminology, 30*(4), 449–474.

Felson, R. B. (1992). "Kick 'em when they're down": Explanations of the relationship between stress and interpersonal aggression and violence. *The Sociological Quarterly, 33*, 1–16.

Fenwick, C. R. (1983). The juvenile delinquency problem in Japan: Application of a role relationship model. *International Journal of Comparative and Applied Criminal Justice, 7*, 119–128.

Ficks, C. A. & Waldman, I. D. (2014). Candidate genes for aggression and antisocial behavior: A meta-analysis of association studies of the 5HTTLPR and MAOA-uVNTR. *Behavior Genetics, 44*(5), 427–444.

Fine, P., Victora, C. G., Rothman, K. J., Moore, P. S., Chang, Y., Curtis, V., & Roberts, I. (2013). John Snow's legacy: Epidemiology without borders. *The Lancet, 381*(9874), 1302–1311.

Finkelhor, D. (1995). The victimization of children: A developmental perspective. *American Journal of Orthopsychiatry, 65*, 177–193.

Finkelhor, D. & Kendall-Tackett, K. (1997). In Cicchetti, D. & Toth, S. L. (Eds.) *Developmental perspectives on trauma: Theory, research, and intervention.* Rochester symposium on developmental psychology (Vol. 8., pp. 1–32). Rochester, NY: University of Rochester Press.

Fishbein, D. H. (1990). Biological perspectives in criminology. *Criminology, 28*, 27–72.

Fox, J. A., Levin, J. A., & Quinet, K. (2011). *The will to kill: Making sense of senseless murder.* London: Pearson Higher Education.

Frailing, K. & Harper, D. W. (2016). *Fundamentals of criminology: New dimensions.* Durham, NC: Carolina Academic Press.

Fraser, S. (2008). *The bell curve wars: Race, intelligence, and the future of America*. New York: Basic Books.

Freilich, J. D. & LaFree, G. (2015). Criminology theory and terrorism: Introduction to the special issue. *Terrorism and Political Violence, 27*(1), 1–8.

Gajos, J. M., Fagan, A. A., & Beaver, K. M. (2016). Use of genetically informed evidence-based prevention science to understand and prevent crime and related behavioral disorders. *Criminology & Public Policy, 15*(3), 683–701.

Gannon, M. J. & Pillai, R. (2013). *Understanding global cultures: Metaphorical journeys through 31 nations, continents, and diversity*. Los Angeles, CA: Sage.

Garfinkel, H. (1956). Conditions of successful degradation ceremonies. *American Journal of Sociology, 61*(5), 420–424.

Gato, W. E., Posick, C., Williams, A., & Mays, C. (forthcoming). Examining the link between the human microbiome and antisocial behavior: Why criminologists should care about biochemistry, too. *Deviant Behavior*.

Genius, S. J. (2008). Toxic causes of mental illness are overlooked. *Neurotoxicology, 29*, 1147–1149.

GFS. (2016). Global Fraud Study: Report to the nations on occupational fraud and abuse. Available at /www.acfe.com/rttn2016.aspx.

Giordano, P. C., Cernkovich, S. A., & Rudolph, J. L. (2002). Gender, crime, and desistance: Toward a theory of cognitive transformation. *American Journal of Sociology, 107*(4), 990–1064.

Glenn, A. L. & Raine, A. (2014). *Psychopathy: An introduction to biological findings and their implications*. New York: New York University Press.

Glenn, A. L., Lochman, J. E., Dishion, T., Powell, N. P., Boxmeyer, C., & Qu, L. (2017). Oxytocin receptor gene variant interacts with intervention delivery format in predicting intervention outcomes for youth with conduct problems. *Prevention Science*. doi: 10.1007/s11121-017-0777-1.

Glueck, S. & Glueck, E. T. (1930). *500 criminal careers*. New York: Alfred A. Knopf.

Glueck, S. & Glueck, E. T. (1934a). *One thousand juvenile delinquents*. Cambridge, MA: Harvard University Press.

Glueck, S. & Glueck, E. T. (1934b). *Five hundred delinquent women*. New York: Alfred A. Knopf.

Glueck, S. & Glueck, E. (1950). *Unraveling juvenile delinquency*. New York: Commonwealth Fund.

Glueck, S. & Glueck, E. (1957). *Physique and delinquency*. New York: Harper and Brothers.

Goffman, E. (1963). *Stigma: Notes on the management of spoiled identity*. New York: Simon & Schuster.

Goodlad, J. K., Marcus, D. K., & Fulton, J. J. (2013). Lead and attention-deficit/hyperactivity disorder (ADHD) symptoms: A meta-analysis. *Clinical Psychology Review, 33*(3), 417–425.

Goring, C. (1913). *The English convict*. Montclair, NJ: Patterson-Smith.

Gottfredson, M. & Hirschi, T. (1986). The true value of lambda would appear to be zero: An essay on career criminals, criminal careers, selective incapacitation, cohort studies, and related topics. *Criminology, 24*(2), 213–234.

Gottfredson, M. R. & Hirschi, T. (1990). *A general theory of crime*. Stanford, CA: Stanford University Press.

Grandjean, P. & Landrigan, P. J. (2014). Neurobehavioral effects of developmental toxicity. *The Lancet Neurology, 13*, 330–338.

Grasmick, H. G., Tittle, C. R., Bursik Jr, R. J., & Arneklev, B. J. (1993). Testing the core empirical implications of Gottfredson and Hirschi's general theory of crime. *Journal of Research in Crime and Delinquency, 30*(1), 5–29.

Hagan, J. (1993). The social embeddedness of crime and unemployment. *Criminology, 31*(4), 465–491.

Hagan, J. & Rymond-Richmond, W. (2009). *Darfur and the crime of genocide*. New York: Cambridge University Press.

Hall, P. & Soskice, D. (2001). An introduction to varieties of capitalism. In Hall, P. & Soskice, D. (Eds.) *Varieties of capitalism: The institutional foundations of comparative advantage*. Oxford: Oxford University Press.

Harcourt, B. E. (2009). *Illusion of order: The false promise of broken windows policing*. Cambridge, MA: Harvard University Press.

Harding, D. (2010). *Living the drama: Community, conflict, and culture among inner-city boys*. Chicago, IL: University of Chicago Press.

Harris, J. R. (2009). *The nurture assumption: Why children turn out the way they do*. New York: Simon & Schuster.

Hartjen, C. A. (2008). *Youth, crime, and justice: A global inquiry*. New Brunswick, NJ: Rutgers University Press.

Hartjen, C. A. & Kethineni, S. (1996). *Comparative delinquency: India and the United States*. New York: Garland Press.

Hartjen, C. A. & Priyadarsini, S. (2003). Gender, peers, and delinquency. *Youth & Society, 34,* 387–414.

Hartmann, J. L. & Sundt, J. L. (2011). The rise of feminist criminology: Freda Adler. In Cullen, F. T., Jonson, C. L., Myer, A. J., & Adler, F. *The origins of American criminology: Advances in criminological theory* (pp. 205–220). New Brunswick, NJ: Transaction Publishers.

Hay, C. & Evans, M. M. (2006). Violent victimization and involvement in delinquency: Examining predictions from general strain theory. *Journal of Criminal Justice, 34,* 261–274.

Hay, C. & Forrest, W. (2006). The development of self-control: Examining self-control theory's stability thesis. *Criminology, 44*(4), 739–774.

Haynie, D. L. (2001). Delinquent peers revisited: Does network structure matter? *American Journal of Sociology, 106*(4), 1013–1057.

Haynie, D. L. (2002). Friendship networks and delinquency: The relative nature of peer delinquency. *Journal of Quantitative Criminology, 18*(2), 99–134.

Haynie, D. L. & Piquero, A. R. (2006). Pubertal development and physical victimization in adolescence. *Journal of Research in Crime and Delinquency, 43*(1), 3–35.

Hayward, K., Maruna, S., & Mooney, J. (Eds.). (2010). *Fifty key thinkers in criminology*. New York: Routledge.

Heimer, K. & De Coster, S. (1999). The gendering of violent delinquency. *Criminology, 37*(2), 277–318.

Henson, B., Wilcox, P., Reyns, B. W., & Cullen, F. T. (2010). Gender, adolescent lifestyles, and violent victimization: Implications for routine activity theory. *Victims & Offenders, 5*(4), 303–328.

Herman, J. L. (1992). *Trauma and recovery*. New York: Basic Books.

Herrnstein, R. & Murray, C. (1994). *The bell curve*. New York: Simon & Schuster.

Hibbeln, J. R., Davis, J. M., Steer, C., Emmett, P., Rogers, I., Williams, C., & Golding, J. (2007). Maternal seafood consumption in pregnancy and neurodevelopmental outcomes in childhood (ALSPAC study): An observational cohort study. *The Lancet, 369*(9561), 578–585.

Hibbert, C. (1963). *The roots of evil: A social history of crime and punishment*. London: Weidenfeld & Nicolson.

Hiday, V. A., Swanson, J. W., Swartz, M. S., Borum, R., & Wagner, H. R. (2001). Victimization: A link between mental illness and violence? *International Journal of Law and Psychiatry, 24,* 559–572.

Higgins, B. R. & Hunt, J. (2016). Collective efficacy: Taking action to improve neighborhoods. National Institute of Justice, No. 277.

Hindelang, M. J. (1976). *Criminal victimization in eight American cities: A descriptive analysis of common theft and assault*. Cambridge, MA: Ballinger.

Hindelang, M. J., Gottfredson, M. R., & Garofalo, J. (1978). *Victims of personal crime: An empirical foundation for a theory of personal victimization*. Cambridge, MA: Ballinger.

Hipp, J. R. & Kubrin, C. E. (2017). From bad to worse: How changing inequality in nearby areas impacts local crime. *RSF: The Russell Sage Foundation Journal of the Social Sciences, 3*(2), 129–151.

Hirschi, T. (1969). *Causes of delinquency*. New Brunswick, NJ: Transaction Publishers.

Hirschi, T. (1986). On the compatibility of rational choice and social control theories of crime. In Cornish, D. B. & Clarke, R. V. (Eds.) *The reasoning criminal: Rational choice perspectives on offending* (pp. 105–118). New Brunswick, NJ: Transaction Publishers.

Hirschi, T. (1995). The family. In Wilson, J. Q. & Petersilia, J. (Eds.) *Crime*. San Francisco, CA: ICS Press.

Hirschi, T. (2004). Self-control and crime. In Baumeister, R. F. & Vohs, K. D. (Eds.) *The handbook of self-regulation: Theory, research and applications* (pp. 537–552). New York: Guilford Press.

Hirschi, T. (2011). *The craft of criminology: Selected papers*. New Brunswick, NJ: Transaction Publishers.

Hobbes, T. ([1651]2006). *Leviathan*. New York: Continuum International Publishing Group.

Hoeve, M., Stams, G. J. J., van der Put, C. E., Dubas, J. S., van der Laan, P. H., & Gerris, J. R. (2012). A meta-analysis of attachment to parents and delinquency. *Journal of Abnormal Child Psychology, 40*(5), 771–785.

Hoffmann, J. P. & Cerbone, F. G. (1999). Stressful life events and delinquency escalation in early adolescence. *Criminology, 37*(2), 343–374.

Hofmann, S. G., Asnaani, A., Vonk, I. J., Sawyer, A. T., & Fang, A. (2012). The efficacy of cognitive behavioral therapy: A review of meta-analyses. *Cognitive Therapy and Research, 36*(5), 427–440.

Hofstede, G. (1980). *Culture's consequences: International differences in work-related values*. Beverly Hills, CA: Sage.

Hofstede, G. H. (2001). *Culture's consequences: Comparing values, behaviors, institutions, and organizations across nations*. Thousand Oaks, CA: Sage.

Holmes, A. J., Hollinshead, M. O., O'Keefe, T. M., Petrov, V. I., Fariello, G. R., Wald, L. L., Fischl, B., Rosen, B.R., Mair, R.W., Roffman, J.L., & Smoller, J. W. (2015). Brain Genomics Superstruct Project initial data release with structural, functional, and behavioral measures. *Scientific Data, 2*(150031).

Holt, T. J. & Bossler, A. M. (2008). Examining the applicability of lifestyle-routine activities theory for cybercrime victimization. *Deviant Behavior, 30*(1), 1–25.

Holt, T. J. & Bossler, A. M. (2016). *Cybercrime in progress: Theory and prevention of technology-enabled offenses*. London: Routledge.

Holt, T. J., Bossler, A. M., & May, D. C. (2012). Low self-control, deviant peer associations, and juvenile cyberdeviance. *American Journal of Criminal Justice, 37*(3), 378–395.

Holt, T. J., Burruss, G. W., & Bossler, A. M. (2010). Social learning and cyber-deviance: Examining the importance of a full social learning model in the virtual world. *Journal of Crime and Justice, 33*(2), 31–61.

Homer-Dixon, T. F. (1999). *Environment, scarcity, and conflict*. Princeton, NJ: Princeton University Press.

Hopkins, M. (1647). *The discovery of witches*. Public Domain.

House, R. J., Hanges, P. J., Javidan, M., Dorfman, P. W., & Gupta, V. (2004). *Culture, leadership, and organizations: The GLOBE study of 62 societies*. Thousand Oaks, CA: Sage.

Howard, G. J., Newman, G., & Pridemore, W. A. (2000). Theory, method, and data in comparative criminology. In *Measurement and analysis of crime and justice* (vol. 4) of Criminal Justice. Washington, DC: National Institute of Justice, Office of Justice Programs, U.S. Department of Justice.

Huff, C. R. & Scarpitti, F. R. (2011). The origins and development of containment theory: Walter C. Reckless and Simon Dinitz. In Cullen, F. T., Jonson, C. L., Myer, A. J., & Adler, F (Eds.) *The origins of American criminology* (pp. 277–294). New Brunswick, NJ: Transaction Publishers.

Husak, D. N. (2002). *Legalize this! The case for decriminalizing drugs*. New York: Verso.

Hutcheson, F. (1755). *A system of moral philosophy*. London: Millar.

Hutchings, A. & Hayes, H. (2008). Routine activity theory and phishing victimisation: Who gets caught in the net. *Current Issues in Criminal Justice, 20*, 433–451.

Inglehart, R. & Baker, W. E. (2000). Modernization, cultural change, and the persistence of traditional values. *American Sociological Review, 65*, 19–51.

INTERPOL. (1956). Constitution of the international criminal police organization – INTERPOL. Available at www.interpol.int/About-INTERPOL/Legal-materials/The-Constitution.

INTERPOL. (2014). *Annual report*. Available at www.interpol.int/News-and-media/Publications2/Annual-reports2.

Ishikawa, S. S., Raine, A., Lencz, T., Bihrle, S., & Lacasse, L. (2001). Autonomic stress reactivity and executive functions in successful and unsuccessful criminal psychopaths from the community. *Journal of Abnormal Psychology, 110*(3), 423–432.

Israel, J. I. (2001). *Radical enlightenment: Philosophy and the making of modernity 1650–1750*. New York: Oxford University Press.

Jackson, D. B. (2016). The link between poor quality nutrition and childhood antisocial behavior: A genetically informative analysis. *Journal of Criminal Justice, 44*, 13–20.

Jackson, D. B. & Vaughn, M. G. (2016). Household food insecurity during childhood and adolescent misconduct. *Preventive Medicine, 96*, 113–117.

Jackson, D. B., Vaughn, M. G., & Salas-Wright, C. P. (2017). Poor nutrition and bullying behaviors: A comparison of deviant and non-deviant youth. *Journal of Adolescence, 57*, 69–73.

Jacobs, B. A. (2010). Deterrence and deterrability. *Criminology, 48*(2), 417–441.

Jeffery, C. R. (1979). *Biology and crime*. Beverly Hills, CA: Sage.

Jeffery, C. R. (1993). Biological perspectives. *Journal of Criminal Justice Education, 4*(2), 291–306.

Jencks, C. (1992). *Rethinking social policy: Race, poverty, and the underclass*. Cambridge, MA: Harvard University Press.

Jennings, W. G. & Reingle, J. M. (2012). On the number and shape of developmental/life-course violence, aggression, and delinquency trajectories: A state-of-the-art review. *Journal of Criminal Justice, 40*(6), 472–489.

Jensen, G. F. & Brownfield, D. (1986). Gender, lifestyles, and victimization: Beyond routine activity. *Violence and Victims, 1*, 85–99.

Junger, M. & Marshall, I. M. (1997). The interethnic generalizability of social control theory: An empirical test. *Journal of Research in Crime and Delinquency, 34*, 79–112.

Junger-Tas, J., Marshall, I., Enzmann, D., Killias, M., Steketee, M., & Gruszczynska, B. (2010). *Juvenile delinquency in Europe and beyond: Results of the second International Self-Report Delinquency Study.* Berlin: Springer.

Junger-Tas, J., Marshall, I. H., Enzmann, D., Killias, M., Steketee, M., & Gruszczynska, B. (2012). *The many faces of youth crime.* New York: Springer.

Karmen, A. (2009). *Crime victims: An introduction to victimology.* Belmont, CA: Wadsworth Cengage Learning.

Karr, C.J., & Rauh, V.A. (2014). Pesticides. In Landrigan, P. J. & Etzel, R. A. (Eds.) *Textbook of children's environmental health* (pp. 296–302). New York: Oxford University Press.

Karstedt, S. (2011). Handle with care: Emotions, crime and justice. In Karstedt, S., Loader, I., & Strang, H. (Eds.) *Emotions, crime and justice.* Portland, OR: Hart Publishing.

Katz, C. M., Webb, V. J., Fox, K., & Shaffer, J. N. (2011). Understanding the relationship between violent victimization and gang membership. *Journal of Criminal Justice, 39*(1), 48–59.

Katz, J. (1988). *Seductions of crime: Moral and sensual attractions in doing evil.* New York: Basic Books.

Katz, R. S. (2000). Explaining girls' and women's crime and desistance in the context of their victimization experiences: A developmental test of revised strain theory and the life course perspective. *Violence against Women, 6*(6), 633–660.

Kaylen, M. T. & Pridemore, W. A. (2011). A reassessment of the association between social disorganization and youth violence in rural areas. *Social Science Quarterly, 92*(4), 978–1001.

Kaylen, M. T. & Pridemore, W. A. (2013). Social disorganization and crime in rural communities: The first direct test of the systemic model. *British Journal of Criminology, 53*(5), 905–923.

Kempf, K. L. (1993). The empirical status of Hirschi's control theory. In Adler, F. & Laufer, W. S. (Eds.) *New directions in criminological theory: Advances in criminological theory* (pp. 143–185). New Brunswick, NJ: Transaction Publishers.

Kennedy, L. W. & Forde, D. R. (1990). Routine activities and crime: An analysis of victimization in Canada. *Criminology, 28*, 137–152.

Kerlinger, F. N., & Lee, H. B. (2000). *Foundations of behavioral research.* Stamford: Wadsworth.

Kirk, G. S. (1954). *Heraclitus: The cosmic fragments.* Cambridge: Cambridge University Press.

Kirk, G. S., Raven, J. E., & Schofield, M. (1983). *The pre-Socratic philosophers: A critical history with a selection of texts.* Cambridge: Cambridge University Press.

Kleiman, M. A., Kilmer, B., & Fisher, D. T. (2014). Theory and evidence on the swift-certain-fair approach to enforcing conditions of community supervision. *Federal Probation, 78*, 71–75.

Kobayashi, J., Nishimura, H., Takahashi, Y., Tozaki, Y., & Suzuki, S. (1988). Relations of school life and peers at the time of arrest to subsequent delinquency. *Reports of the National Research Institute of Police Science, 29*, 15–26.

Kodera, S. (2015). Giambattista della Porta. *The Stanford encyclopedia of philosophy* (summer), Zalta, E. N. (Ed.). Available at https://plato.stanford.edu/archives/sum2015/entries/della-porta/.

Kohn, M. L. (1987). Cross-national research as an analytic strategy: American Sociological Association, 1987 presidential address. *American Sociological Review, 52*(6), 713–731.

Kolbert, E. (2014). *The sixth extinction: An unnatural history.* New York: Bloomsbury.

Kornhauser, R. R. (1978). *Social sources of delinquency: An appraisal of analytic models.* Chicago, IL: University of Chicago Press.

Krohn, M. D. (1974). An investigation of the effect of parental and peer associations on marijuana use: An empirical test of differential association theory. In *Crime and delinquency: Dimensions of deviance* (pp. 75–89). New York: Praeger.

Kubrin, C. E. & Weitzer, R. (2003). New directions in social disorganization theory. *Journal of Research in Crime and Delinquency, 40*(4), 374–402.

Kunz, J. L. (1949). The United Nations Convention on Genocide. *The American Journal of International Law, 43*(4), 738–746.

LaFree, G. (1998). *Losing legitimacy: Street crime and the decline of social institutions in America.* Boulder, CO: Westview Press.

LaFree, G., Dugan, L., & Korte, R. (2009). The impact of British counterterrorist strategies on political violence in Northern Ireland: Comparing deterrence and backlash models. *Criminology, 47*(1), 17–45.

LaGrange, T. C. & Silverman, R. A. (1999). Low self-control and opportunity: Testing the general theory of crime as an explanation for gender differences in delinquency. *Criminology, 37*(1), 41–72.

Lansford, J. E., Miller-Johnson, S., Berlin, L. J., Dodge, K. A., Bates, J. E., & Pettit, G. S. (2007). Early physical abuse and later violent delinquency: A prospective longitudinal study. *Child Maltreatment, 12*, 233–245.

Lappi-Seppälä, T. (2007). Penal policy and prisoner rates in Scandinavia: Cross-comparative perspectives on penal severity. In Nuotio, K. (Ed.) *Festschrift in Honour of Raimo Lahti. Publications of the faculty of law* (pp. 265–306). University of Helsinki, Helsinki University Print.

Laub, J. H. (2006). Edwin H. Sutherland and the Michael-Adler Report: Searching for the soul of criminology seventy years later. *Criminology, 44*(2), 235–258.

Laub, J. & Frisch, N. E. (2011). Translational criminology. In Blomberg, T. G., Brancale, J. M., Beaver, K. M., & Bales, W. D. (Eds.) *Advancing criminology and criminal justice policy*. New York, NY: Routledge.

Laub, J. H. & Sampson, R. J. (2003). *Shared beginnings, divergent lives*. Cambridge, MA: Harvard University Press.

Lauritsen, J. L. & Laub, J. H. (2007). Understanding the link between victimization and offending: New reflections on an old idea. *Crime Prevention Studies, 12*, 55–76.

Lauritsen, J. L., Sampson, R. J., & Laub, J. H. (1991). The link between offending and victimization among adolescents. *Criminology, 29*, 265–292.

Lavater, J. C. & Holcroft, T. T. (1878). *Essays on physiognomy, also one hundred physiognomical rules, and a memoir of the author*. London: William Tegg and Co.

Lee, D. (1987). *Plato: The republic*. London: Penguin Books.

Lee, S. H. & La Serre, C. B. (2015). Gut microbiome–brain communications regulate host physiology and behavior. *Journal of Nutrition and Health Food Science 3*(2), 1–12.

Lemert, E. M. (1951). *Social pathology: A systematic approach to the theory of sociopathic behavior*. New York: McGraw-Hill.

Lemert, E. M. (1972). *Human deviance, social problems, and social control*. Englewood Cliffs, NJ: Prentice-Hall.

Lilly, R. J., Cullen, F. T., & Ball, R. A. (2011). *Criminological theory: Context and consequences*. Thousand Oaks, CA: Sage.

Lin, N. (1986). Conceptualizing social support. In Lin, N., Dean, A., & Ensel, W. M. (Eds.) *Social support, life events, and depression* (pp. 17–30). Orlando, FL: Academic Press.

Loeber, R. & Welsh, B. C. (Eds.). (2012). *The future of criminology*. New York: Oxford University Press.

Loeber, R., Kalb, L., & Huizinga, D. (2001). Juvenile delinquency and serious injury victimization. *Juvenile Justice Bulletin, 8*, 1–8.

Lombroso, C. & Ferrero, G. (1895). *The female offender*. New York: D. Appleton.

Lombroso, C., Gibson, M., & Rafter, N. H. (2006). *Criminal man*. Durham, NC: Duke University Press.

Love, J. M., Chazan-Cohen, R., Raikes, H., & Brooks-Gunn, J. (2013). What makes a difference: Early Head Start evaluation findings in a developmental context. *Monographs of the Society for Research in Child Development, 78*(1), vii–viii.

Lynch, M. J. & Stretesky, P. (2001). Toxic crimes: Examining corporate victimization of the general public employing medical and epidemiological evidence. *Critical Criminology, 10*(3), 153–172.

Lynch, M. J., & Stretesky, P. B. (2016). *Exploring green criminology: Toward a green criminological revolution*. New York, NY: Routledge.

MacDonald, H. (2017). *The war on cops: How the new attack on law and order makes everyone less safe*. New York, NY: Encounter Books.

Mackay, C. S. (2009). *The hammer of witches: A complete translation of the Malleus Maleficarum*. Cambridge: Cambridge University Press.

Maier, S. L., Mannes, S., & Koppenhofer, E. L. (2017). The implications of marijuana decriminalization and legalization on crime in the United States. *Contemporary Drug Problems*. doi: 0091450917708790.

Manasse, M. E. & Ganem, N. M. (2009). Victimization as a cause of delinquency: The role of depression and gender. *Journal of Criminal Justice, 37*, 371–378.

Mangum, G. L. (1983). Legislative history in the interpretation of law: An illustrative case study. *BYU Law Review, 2*, 281–304.

Marshall, I. H. (2010). "Pourquoi pas?" versus "absolutely not!" Cross-national differences in access to schools and pupils for survey research. *European Journal on Criminal Policy and Research, 16*(2), 89–109.

Martinez, R., Stowell, J. I., & Lee, M. T. (2010). Immigration and crime in an era of transformation: A longitudinal analysis of homicides in San Diego neighborhoods, 1980–2000. *Criminology, 48*(3), 797–829.

Maruna, S. (2001). *Making good: How ex-convicts reform and rebuild their lives*. Washington, DC: American Psychological Association.

Maschi, T., Bradley, C. A., & Morgen, K. (2008). Unraveling the link between trauma and delinquency: The mediating role of negative affect and delinquent peer exposure. *Youth and Violence and Juvenile Justice, 6,* 136–157.

Mason, L. H., Harp, J. P., & Han, D. Y. (2014). Pb neurotoxicity: Neuropsychological effects of lead toxicity. *BioMedical Research International,* 1–8.

Matsueda, R. L. (1982). Testing control theory and differential association: A causal modeling approach. *American Sociological Review, 47*(4), 489–504.

Matsueda, R. L. & Anderson, K. (1998). The dynamics of delinquent peers and delinquent behavior. *Criminology, 36*(2), 269–308.

Matsueda, R. L. & Heimer, K. (1987). Race, family structure, and delinquency: A test of differential association and social control theories. *American Sociological Review, 52*(6), 826–840.

Matza, D. (1964). *Delinquency and drift.* New Brunswick, NJ: Transaction Publishers.

Mazerolle, P. & Maahs, J. (2000). General strain and delinquency: An alternative examination of conditioning influences. *Justice Quarterly, 17*(4), 753–778.

Mazerolle, P. & Piquero, A. (1997). Violent responses to strain: An examination of conditioning influences. *Violence and Victims, 12*(4), 323–343.

Mazerolle, P. & Piquero, A. (1998). Linking exposure to strain with anger: An investigation of deviant adaptations. *Journal of Criminal Justice, 26,* 195–211.

Mazerolle, L., Wickes, R., & McBroom, J. (2010). Community variations in violence: The role of social ties and collective efficacy in comparative context. *Journal of Research in Crime and Delinquency, 47,* 3–30.

Mazerolle, P., Burton, V. S., Cullen, F. T., Evans, T. D., & Payne, G. L. (2000). Strain, anger, and delinquent adaptations specifying general strain theory. *Journal of Criminal Justice, 28*(2), 89–101.

McCart, M. R., Priester, P. E., Davies, W. H., & Azen, R. (2006). Differential effectiveness of behavioral parent-training and cognitive-behavioral therapy for antisocial youth: A meta-analysis. *Journal of Abnormal Child Psychology, 34*(4), 525–541.

McCarthy, B., Hagan, J., & Martin, M. J. (2002). In and out of harm's way: Violent victimization and the social capital of fictive street families. *Criminology, 40,* 831–866.

McCarthy, R. J., Rabenhorst, M. M., Milner, J. S., Travis, W. J., & Collins, P. S. (2014). What difference does a day make? Examining temporal variations in partner maltreatment. *Journal of Family Psychology, 28*(3), 421–428.

McClelland, G. H. & Judd, C. M. (1993). Statistical difficulties of detecting interactions and moderator effects. *Psychological Bulletin, 114*(2), 376–390.

McNeeley, S. (2015). Lifestyle-routine activities and crime events. *Journal of Contemporary Criminal Justice, 31*(1), 30–52.

Melde, C., Taylor, T. J., & Esbensen, F. (2009). "I got your back": An examination of the protective function of gang membership in adolescence. *Criminology, 47,* 565–594.

Melossi, D. (2010). Thorsten Sellin (1896–1994). In Hayward, K., Maruna, S., & Mooney, J. (Eds.) *Fifty key thinkers in criminology* (pp. 76–82). New York: Routledge.

Mendelsohn, B. (1956). A new branch of bio-psychological science: La victimology. *Revue Internationale de Criminologie et de Police Technique, 10,* 782–789.

Mendelsohn, B. (1976). Victimology and contemporary society's trends. *Victimology, 1,* 8–28.

Mersky, J. P., Topitzes, J., & Reynolds, A. J. (2011). Unsafe at any age: Linking childhood and adolescent maltreatment to delinquency and crime. *Journal of Research in Crime and Delinquency, 49*(2), 295–318.

Merton, R. K. (1938). Social structure and anomie. *American Sociological Review, 3*(5), 672–682.

Messerschmidt, J. W. (1993). *Masculinities and crime: Critique and reconceptualization of theory.* Lanham, MD: Rowman & Littlefield.

Messner, S. F. & Rosenfeld, R. (1997). Political restraint of the market and levels of criminal homicide: A cross-national application of institutional-anomie theory. *Social Forces, 75,* 1393–1416.

Messner, S. F. & Rosenfeld, R. (2008). *Crime and the American dream* (4th edn). Belmont, CA: Cengage Learning.

Messner, S. F. & Rosenfeld, R. (2012). *Crime and the American dream* (5th edn). Belmont, CA: Cengage Learning.

Michael, J. & Adler, M. J. (1933). *Crime, law and social science.* New York: Harcourt, Brace.

Miethe, T. D. & Meier, R. F. (1994). *Crime and its social context: Toward an integrated theory of offenders, victims, and situations.* Albany, NY: State University of New York Press.

Miller, B. L., Boman, J. H., & Stogner, J. (2013). Examining the measurement of novel drug perceptions: Salvia divinorum, gender, and peer substance use. *Substance Use & Misuse, 48*(1–2), 65–72.

Miller, W. B. (1958). Lower class culture as a generating milieu of gang delinquency. *Journal of Social Issues, 14*(3), 5–19.

Moffitt, T. E. (1993). Adolescence-limited and life-course-persistent antisocial behavior: A developmental taxonomy. *Psychological Review, 100*(4), 674–701.

Moffitt, T. E. & Beckley, A. (2015). Abandon twin research? Embrace epigenetic research? Premature advice for criminologists. *Criminology, 53*(1), 121–126.

Mohhai, P., Lantz, P. M., Morenoff, H., House, J. S., & Mero, R. P. (2009). Racial and socioeconomic disparities in residential proximity to polluting industrial facilities: Evidence from the Americans' Changing Lives Study. *American Journal of Public Health, 99*, S649–S656.

Molteni, R., Barnard, R. J., Ying, Z., Roberts, C. K., & Gomez-Pinilla, F. (2002). A high-fat, refined sugar diet reduces hippocampal brain-derived neurotrophic factor, neuronal plasticity, and learning. *Neuroscience, 112*(4), 803–814.

Monte, A. A., Zane, R. D., & Heard, K. J. (2015). The implications of marijuana legalization in Colorado. *JAMA, 313*(3), 241–242.

Montesquieu, Charles de Secondat, Baron de. (1748). *The spirit of laws*. La Brede, France.

Moon, B. & Morash, M. (2017). Gender and general strain theory: A comparison of strains, mediating, and moderating effects explaining three types of delinquency. *Youth & Society, 49*(4), 484–504.

Muraven, M. & Baumeister, R. F. (2000). Self-regulation and depletion of limited resources: Does self-control resemble a muscle? *Psychological Bulletin, 126*(2), 247–259.

Murphy, D. S. & Robinson, M. B. (2008). The Maximizer: Clarifying Merton's theories of anomie and strain. *Theoretical Criminology, 12*(4), 501–521.

Myers, T. A., Maibach, E., Peters, E., & Leiserowitz, A. (2015). Simple messages help set the record straight about scientific agreement on human-caused climate change: The results of two experiments. *PloS One, 10*(3), e0120985.

Nagin, D. S. & Pogarsky, G. (2001). Integrating celerity, impulsivity, and extralegal sanction threats into a model of general deterrence: Theory and evidence. *Criminology, 39*(4), 865–892.

Navarro, J. N. & Jasinski, J. L. (2012). Going cyber: Using routine activities theory to predict cyberbullying experiences. *Sociological Spectrum, 32*(1), 81–94.

Neapolitan, J. L. (1994). Cross-national variation in homicides: The case of Latin America. *International Criminal Justice Review, 4*, 4–22.

Needleman, H. L. & Gatsonis, C. A. (1990). Low-level lead exposure and the IQ of children: A meta-analysis of modern studies. *JAMA, 263*(5), 673–678.

Nelken, D. (2000). Just comparing. In Nelken, D. (Ed.) *Contrasting criminal justice: Getting from here to there*. Aldershot: Ashgate.

Nelken, D. (2002). Comparing criminal justice. In Maguire, M., Morgan, R., & Reiner, R. (Eds.) *The Oxford handbook of criminology* (3rd edn, pp. 175–202). Oxford: Oxford University Press.

New York Times. (2012). *Live coverage: Super Bowl XLVI*.

Newman, O. (1972). *Defensible space*. New York: Macmillan.

Newman, O. (1996). *Creating defensible space*. US Department of Housing and Urban Development. Office of Policy Development and Research.

Ngo, F. T., Paternoster, R., Cullen, F. T., & Mackenzie, D. L. (2011). Life domains and crime: A test of Agnew's general theory of crime and delinquency. *Journal of Criminal Justice, 39*(4), 302–311.

Nye, F. I. (1958). *Family relationships and delinquent behavior*. Westport, CT: Greenwood Press.

Nye, F. I. & Short, J. F. (1957). Scaling delinquent behavior. *American Sociological Review, 22*(3), 326–331.

Olds, D. L. (2006). The nurse–family partnership: An evidence-based preventive intervention. *Infant Mental Health Journal, 27*(1), 5–25.

Olds, D. L., Eckenrode, J., Henderson, C. R., Kitzman, H., Powers, J., Cole, R., Sidora, K., Morris, P., Pettitt, L. M., & Luckey, D. (1997). Long-term effects of home visitation on maternal life course and child abuse and neglect: Fifteen-year follow-up of a randomized trial. *JAMA, 278*(8), 637–643.

Osgood, D. W. & Anderson, A. L. (2004). Unstructured socializing and rates of delinquency. *Criminology, 42*(3), 519–550.

Osgood, D. W. & Chambers, J. M. (2000). Social disorganization outside the metropolis: An analysis of rural youth violence. *Criminology, 38*(1), 81–116.

Ousey, G. C. (2017). Crime is not the only problem: Examining why violence & adverse health outcomes co-vary across large US counties. *Journal of Criminal Justice, 50*, 29–41.

Ousey, G. C. & Kubrin, C. E. (2017). Immigration and crime: Assessing a contentious issue. *Annual Review of Criminology.* Online First.

Ousey, G. C., Wilcox, P., & Schreck, C. J. (2015). Violent victimization, confluence of risks and the nature of criminal behavior: Testing main and interactive effects from Agnew's extension of General Strain Theory. *Journal of Criminal Justice, 43*(2), 164–173.

Paliwal, A., Cabrera, N., Dougherty, J., & Klofas, J. (2016). Comparison of cities' homicide rates over time: 2015 data. Center for Public Safety Initiatives. Working Paper 2016–07. Available at www. rit.edu/cla/criminaljustice/cpsi.

Paolucci, E. O., Genuis, M. L., & Violato, C. (2001). A meta-analysis of the published research of the effects of child sexual abuse. *The Journal of Psychology, 135*, 17–36.

Park, R. E. (1936). Succession, an ecological concept. *American Sociological Review, 1*(2), 171–179.

Park, R. E. & Burgess, E. W. (1925). *The city.* Chicago, IL: University of Chicago Press.

Passas, N. (2000). Global anomie, dysnomie, and economic crime: Hidden consequences of neoliberalism and globalization in Russia and around the world. *Social Justice, 27*(2), 16–44.

Paternoster, R. (1989). Decisions to participate in and desist from four types of common delinquency: Deterrence and the rational choice perspective. *Law and Society Review, 23*(1), 7–40.

Paternoster, R. & Bushway, S. (2009). Desistance and the "feared self": Toward an identity theory of criminal desistance. *The Journal of Criminal Law and Criminology, 99*(4), 1103–1156.

Paternoster, R. & Iovanni, L. (1989). The labeling perspective and delinquency: An elaboration of the theory and an assessment of the evidence. *Justice Quarterly, 6*(3), 359–394.

Pepinsky, H. E. (1978). Communist anarchism as an alternative to the rule of criminal law. *Contemporary Crises, 2*, 315–334.

Petrosino, A., Turpin-Petrosino, C., & Guckenburg, S. (2010). Formal system processing of juveniles: Effects on delinquency. *Campbell Systematic Reviews, 1*, 1–88.

Pfohl, S. J. (1994). *Images of deviance and social control: A sociological history.* New York: McGraw-Hill.

Piquero, A. R. (2011). Understanding the development of antisocial behavior: Terrie Moffitt. In Cullen, F. T., Jonson, C. L., Myer, A. J., & Adler, F. (Eds.) *The origins of American criminology* (pp. 397–408). New Brunswick, NJ: Transaction Publishers.

Piquero, A. R. & Hickman, M. (2003). Extending Tittle's control balance theory to account for victimization. *Criminal Justice and Behavior, 30*, 282–301.

Piquero, N. L. & Sealock, M. D. (2004). Gender and general strain theory: A preliminary test of Broidy and Agnew's gender/GST hypotheses. *Justice Quarterly, 21*(1), 125–158.

Piquero, N. & Sealock, M. D. (2010). Race, crime, and general strain theory. *Youth Violence and Juvenile Justice, 8*(3), 170–186.

Polderman, T. J., Benyamin, B., De Leeuw, C. A., Sullivan, P. F., Van Bochoven, A., Visscher, P. M., & Posthuma, D. (2015). Meta-analysis of the heritability of human traits based on fifty years of twin studies. *Nature Genetics, 47*(7), 702–709.

Popper, K. R. (1959). *The logic of scientific discovery.* London: Hutchinson.

Portnoy, J. & Farrington, D. P. (2015). Resting heart rate and antisocial behavior: An updated systematic review and meta-analysis. *Aggression and Violent Behavior, 22*, 33–45.

Portnoy, J., Raine, A., Chen, F. R., Pardini, D., Loeber, R., & Jennings, J. R. (2014). Heart rate and antisocial behavior: The mediating role of impulsive sensation seeking. *Criminology, 52*(2), 292–311.

Posick, C. (2013). The overlap between offending and victimization among adolescents: Results from the second International Self-Report Delinquency study. *Journal of Contemporary Criminal Justice, 29*(1), 106–124.

Posick, C. (2017). Reappraising the impact of offending on victimization: A propensity score matching approach. *International Journal of Offender Therapy and Comparative Criminology.* Online First.

Posick, C. & Gould, L. A. (2015). On the general relationship between victimization and offending: Examining cultural contingencies. *Journal of Criminal Justice, 43*(3), 195–204.

Posick, C. & Rocque, M. (2015). Family matters: A cross-national examination of family bonding and victimization. *European Journal of Criminology, 12*(1), 51–69.

Posick, C. & Zimmerman, G. M. (2015). Person-in-context: Insights on contextual variation in the victim–offender overlap across schools. *Journal of Interpersonal Violence, 30*(8), 1432–1455.

Posick, C., Farrell, A., & Swatt, M. L. (2013). Do boys fight and girls cut? A general strain theory approach to gender and deviance. *Deviant Behavior, 34*(9), 685–705.

Posick, C., Rocque, M., & Rafter, N. (2014). More than a feeling: integrating empathy into the study of lawmaking, lawbreaking, and reactions to lawbreaking. *International Journal of Offender Therapy and Comparative Criminology, 58*(1), 5–26.

Pratt, T. C. (2016). A self-control/life-course theory of criminal behavior. *European Journal of Criminology, 13*(1), 129–146.

Pratt, T. C., Holtfreter, K., & Reisig, M. D. (2010). Routine online activity and internet fraud targeting: Extending the generality of routine activity theory. *Journal of Research in Crime and Delinquency, 47*(3), 267–296.

Pratt, T. C., Cullen, F. T., Blevins, K. R., Daigle, L. E., & Madensen, T. D. (2008). The empirical status of deterrence theory: A meta-analysis. In Cullen, F. T., Wright, J. P., & Blevins, K. R. *Taking stock: The status of criminological theory* (pp. 367–396). New Brunswick, NJ: Transaction Publishers.

Pratt, T. C., Cullen, F. T., Sellers, C. S., Thomas Winfree Jr, L., Madensen, T. D., Daigle, L. E., Fearn, N. E., & Gau, J. M. (2010). The empirical status of social learning theory: A meta-analysis. *Justice Quarterly, 27*(6), 765–802.

Pridemore, W. A. & Freilich, J. D. (2007). The impact of state laws protecting abortion clinics and reproductive rights on crimes against abortion providers: Deterrence, backlash, or neither? *Law and Human Behavior, 31*(6), 611–627.

Pyrooz, D. C., Sweeten, G., & Piquero, A. R. (2013). Continuity and change in gang membership and gang embeddedness. *Journal of Research in Crime and Delinquency, 50*(2), 239–271.

Quinney, R. (1991). The way of peace: On crime, suffering, and service. In Pepinsky, H. E. & Quinney, R. (Eds.) *Criminology as peacemaking* (pp. 3–13). Bloomington, IN: Indiana University Press.

Quinney, R. (1993). A life of crime: Criminology and public policy as peacemaking. *Journal of Crime and Justice, 16*(2), 3–9.

Rafter, N. H. (1990). The social construction of crime and crime control. *Journal of Research in Crime and Delinquency, 27*(4), 376–389.

Rafter, N. H., & Heidensohn, F. (1995). *International feminist perspectives in criminology: Engendering a discipline.* Buckingham, UK: Open University Press.

Rafter, N. (2004). Earnest A. Hooton and the biological tradition in American criminology. *Criminology, 42*(3), 735–772.

Rafter, N. (2007). Somatotyping, antimodernism, and the production of criminological knowledge. *Criminology, 45*(4), 805–833.

Rafter, N. (2008). Criminology's darkest hour: Biocriminology in Nazi Germany. *Australian & New Zealand Journal of Criminology, 41*(2), 287–306.

Rafter, N. (2010). Silence and memory in criminology – The American Society of Criminology 2009 Sutherland Address. *Criminology, 48*(2), 339–355.

Rafter, N. (2016). *The crime of all crimes: Toward a criminology of genocide.* New York: New York University Press.

Rafter, N., Posick, C., & Rocque, M. (2016). *The criminal brain: Understanding biological theories of crime.* New York: New York University Press.

Raine, A. (1993). *The psychopathology of crime: Criminal behavior as a clinical disorder.* San Diego, CA: The Free Press.

Raine, A. (2013). *The anatomy of violence: The biological roots of crime.* New York: Random House.

Raine, A., Mellingen, K., Liu, J., Venables, P., & Mednick, S. A. (2003). Effects of environmental enrichment at ages 3–5 years on schizotypal personality and antisocial behavior at ages 17 and 23 years. *American Journal of Psychiatry, 160*(9), 1627–1635.

Ratcliffe, J. H., Taniguchi, T., Groff, E. R., & Wood, J. D. (2011). The Philadelphia foot patrol experiment: A randomized controlled trial of police patrol effectiveness in violent crime hotspots. *Criminology, 49*(3), 795–831.

Rautiainen, M. R., Paunio, T., Repo-Tiihonen, E., Virkkunen, M., Ollila, H. M., Sulkava, S., Jolanki, O., Palotie, A., & Tiihonen, J. (2016). Genome-wide association study of antisocial personality disorder. *Translational Psychiatry, 6*(9), e883.

Rebellon, C. J. & Van Gundy, K. (2005). Can control theory explain the link between parental physical abuse and delinquency: A longitudinal analysis. *Journal of Research in Crime and Delinquency, 42,* 247–274.

Rebellon, C., Straus, M., & Medeiros, R. (2008). Self-control in global perspective: An empirical assessment of Gottfredson and Hirschi's general theory within and across 32 national settings. *European Journal of Criminology, 5,* 331–362.

Reckless, W. C., Dinitz, S., & Murray, E. (1956). Self concept as an insulator against delinquency. *American Sociological Review, 21*(6), 744–746.

Regan, R. J. & Baumgarth, W. P. (2002). *On law, morality, and politics.* Indianapolis, IN: Hackett Publishing.

Reisig, M. D., Pratt, T. C., & Holtfreter, K. (2009). Perceived risk of internet theft victimization: Examining the effects of social vulnerability and financial impulsivity. *Criminal Justice and Behavior, 36,* 369–384.

Reiss, A. J. (1951). Delinquency as the failure of personal and social controls. *American Sociological Review, 16*(2), 196–207.

Reyes, J. W. (2015). Lead exposure and behavior: Effects on antisocial and risky behavior among children and adolescents. *Economic Inquiry, 53*(3), 1580–1605.

Rissel, C., Donovan, B., Yeung, A., de Visser, R. O., Grulich, A., Simpson, J. M., & Richters, J. (2017). Decriminalization of sex work is not associated with more men paying for sex: Results from the second Australian study of health and relationships. *Sexuality Research and Social Policy, 14*(1), 1–6.

Ritchie, S. (2016). *Intelligence: All that matters.* Abingdon, Oxon: Teach Yourself Books.

Ritzer, G. & Goodman, D. J. (2004). *Classical sociological theory.* New York: McGraw-Hill.

Rocque, M. (2015). The lost concept: The (re)emerging link between maturation and desistance from crime. *Criminology and Criminal Justice, 15*(3), 340–360.

Rocque, M. (2017). *Desistance from crime: New advances in theory and research.* New York: Palgrave Macmillan.

Rocque, M. & Posick, C. (2017). Paradigm shift or normal science? The future of (biosocial) criminology. *Theoretical Criminology, 21*(3), 288–303.

Rocque, M. & Snellings, Q. (2017). The new disciplinology: Research, theory, and remaining puzzles on the school-to-prison pipeline. *Journal of Criminal Justice.* Online First.

Rocque, M., Posick, C., & Felix, S. (2015). The role of the brain in urban violent offending: Integrating biology with structural theories of "the streets". *Criminal Justice Studies, 28*(1), 84–103.

Rocque, M., Posick, C., & Paternoster, R. (2016). Identities through time: An exploration of identity change as a cause of desistance. *Justice Quarterly, 33*(1), 45–72.

Rocque, M., Posick, C., & Piquero, A. R. (2016). Self-control and crime: Theory, research, and remaining puzzles. In Vohs, K. D. & Baumeister, R. F. (Eds.) *Handbook of self-regulation: Research, theory, and applications* (pp. 514–532). New York: Guilford Publications.

Rocque, M., Posick, C., & White, H. R. (2015). Growing up is hard to do: An empirical evaluation of maturation and desistance. *Journal of Developmental and Life-course Criminology, 1*(4), 350–384.

Rocque, M., Posick, C., & Zimmerman, G. M. (2013). Measuring up: Assessing the measurement properties of two self-control scales. *Deviant Behavior, 34*(7), 534–556.

Rocque, M., Welsh, B. C., & Raine, A. (2012). Biosocial criminology and modern crime prevention. *Journal of Criminal Justice, 40*(4), 306–312.

Rocque, M., Posick, C., Marshall, I. H., & Piquero, A. R. (2015). A comparative, cross-cultural criminal career analysis. *European Journal of Criminology, 12*(4), 400–419.

Rosenbaum, D. P., Flewelling, R. L., Bailey, S. L., Ringwalt, C. L., & Wilkinson, D. L. (1994). Cops in the classroom: A longitudinal evaluation of Drug Abuse Resistance Education (DARE). *Journal of Research in Crime and Delinquency, 31*(1), 3–31.

Ross, D. & Brown, L. (2009). *Aristotle: The Nicomachean ethics.* New York: Oxford University Press.

Rushton, J. P. & Bogaert, A. F. (1988). Race versus social class differences in sexual behavior: A follow-up test of the rK dimension. *Journal of Research in Personality, 22*(3), 259–272.

Sabra, A. I. (1989). The optics of Ibn al-Haytham. Books I–II–III: On direct vision. English translation and commentary (2 vols), Studies of the Warburg Institute, vol. 40. London: The Warburg Institute, University of London.

Sabra, A. I. (2007). The "Commentary" that saved the text. The hazardous journey of Ibn al-Haytham's Arabic optics. *Early Science and Medicine, 12*(2), 117–133.

Saint-Arnaud, S. & Bernard, P. (2003). Convergence or resilience? A hierarchical cluster analysis of the welfare regimes in advanced countries. *Current Sociology, 51,* 499–527.

Salvatore, J. E., Edwards, A. C., McClintick, J. N., Bigdeli, T. B., Adkins, A., Aliev, F., Edenberg, H.J., Foroud, T., Hesselbrock, V., Kramer, J., & Nurnberger, J. I. (2015). Genome-wide association data suggest ABCB1 and immune-related gene sets may be involved in adult antisocial behavior. *Translational Psychiatry, 5*(4), e558.

Sampson, R. J. (2011). Communities and crime revisited: Intellectual trajectory of a Chicago School education. In Cullen, F. T., Jonson, C. L., Myer, A. J., & Adler, F. (Eds.) *The origins of American criminology* (Vol. 16). New Brunswick, NJ: Transaction Publishers.

Sampson, R. J. (2012). *Great American city: Chicago and the enduring neighborhood effect.* Chicago, IL: University of Chicago Press.

Sampson, R. J. & Castellano, T. C. (1982). Economic inequality and personal victimisation: An areal perspective. *The British Journal of Criminology, 22*(4), 363–385.

Sampson, R. J. & Groves, W. B. (1989). Community structure and crime: Testing social-disorganization theory. *American Journal of Sociology, 94*(4), 774–802.

Sampson, R. J. & Laub, J. H. (1993). *Crime in the making: Pathways and turning points through life.* Cambridge, MA: Harvard University Press.

Sampson, R. J. & Laub, J. H. (1997a). A life-course theory of cumulative disadvantage and the stability of delinquency. In Thornberry, T. P. (Ed.) *Developmental theories of crime and delinquency* (pp. 133–161). New Brunswick, NJ: Transaction Publishers.

Sampson, R. J. & Laub, J. H. (1997b). Unraveling the social context of physique and delinquency. In Raine, A., Brennan, P. A., Farrington, D. P., & Mednick, S. A. (Eds.) *Biosocial bases of violence* (pp. 175–188). New York: Plenum Press.

Sampson, R. J. & Walsh, A. (2015). The Concentric Zone Model. Available at: www.umsl.edu/~keelr/200/socdisor.html.

Sampson, R. J. & Wooldredge, J. D. (1987). Linking the micro- and macro-level dimensions of lifestyle-routine activity and opportunity models of predatory victimization. *Journal of Quantitative Criminology, 3*(4), 371–393.

Sampson, R. J., Castellano, T. C., & Laub, J. H. (1981). Analysis of national crime victimization survey data to study serious delinquent behavior. *Monograph Five. Juvenile criminal behavior and its relation to neighborhood characteristics.* Albany, NY: Criminal Justice Research Center.

Sampson, R. J., Raudenbush, S. W., & Earls, F. (1997). Neighborhoods and violent crime: A multilevel study of collective efficacy. *Science, 277*(5328), 918–924.

Schafer, K. A., Wu, W-H., & Colgan, D. G. (2017). Unexpected mutations after CRISPR-Cas9 editing in vivo. *Nature Methods, 14*(6), 547–548.

Schiff, S. (2015). *The Witches: Salem, 1692.* London: Hachette.

Schild, W. (1981). Penal law as a phenomenon of the history of ideas. In Hinkeldey, C. (Ed.) *Criminal justice through the ages: From divine judgment to modern German legislation.* (pp. 30–45). Rothenburg, Germany: Mittelalterliches Kriminalmuseam.

Schreck, C. J. (1999). Criminal victimization and low self-control: An extension and test of a general theory of crime. *Justice Quarterly, 16*, 633–654.

Schreck, C. J. & Fisher, B. S. (2004). Specifying the influence of family and peers on violent victimization: Extending routine activities and lifestyle theories. *Journal of Interpersonal Violence, 19*, 1021–1041.

Schreck, C. J., Fisher, B. S., & Miller, J. M. (2004). The social context of violent victimization: A study of the delinquent peer effect. *Justice Quarterly, 21*, 23–47.

Schreck, C. J., Stewart, E. A., & Fisher, B. S. (2006). Self-control, victimization, and their influence on risky lifestyles: A longitudinal analysis using panel data. *Journal of Quantitative Criminology, 22*, 319–340.

Schreck, C. J., Burek, M. W., Stewart, E. A., & Miller, J. M. (2007). Distress and violent victimization among young adolescents: Early puberty and the social interactionist explanation. *Journal of Research in Crime and Delinquency, 44*, 381–406.

Schur, E. M. (1973). *Radical nonintervention: Rethinking the delinquency problem.* Englewood Cliffs, NJ: Prentice-Hall.

Schwalbe, C. S., Gearing, R. E., MacKenzie, M. J., Brewer, K. B., & Ibrahim, R. (2012). A meta-analysis of experimental studies of diversion programs for juvenile offenders. *Clinical Psychology Review, 32*(1), 26–33.

Schwartz, J. (1994). Low-level lead exposure and children's IQ: A meta-analysis and search for a threshold. *Environmental Research, 65*(1), 42–55.

Sellin, T. (1938). Culture conflict and crime. *American Journal of Sociology, 44*(1), 97–103.

Shaffer, J. N. (2003). *The victim–offender overlap: Specifying the role of peer groups.* Doctoral dissertation, Pennsylvania State University. Available at: www.ncjrs.gov/pdffiles1/nij/grants/205126.pdf.

Sharkey, P. (2013). *Stuck in place: Urban neighborhoods and the end of progress toward racial equality.* Chicago, IL: University of Chicago Press.

Shaw, C. R. & McKay, H. D. (1942). *Juvenile delinquency and urban areas.* Chicago, IL: University of Chicago Press.

Sheldon, W. H. (1940). *The varieties of human physique.* Oxford: Harper.

Sheldon, W. H. (1942). *The varieties of human physique* (2nd edn). Oxford: Harper.

Sheptycki, J. W. E. (2005). Relativism, transnationalisation and comparative criminology. In Sheptycki, J. W. E. & Wardak, A. *Transnational and comparative criminology.* New York: Routledge Cavendish.

Sherman, L. W. (1993). Defiance, deterrence, and irrelevance: A theory of the criminal sanction. *Journal of Research in Crime and Delinquency, 30*(4), 445–473.

Sherman, L. W., Gartin, P. R., & Buerger, M. E. (1989). Hot spots of predatory crime: Routine activities and the criminology of place. *Criminology, 27*(1), 27–56.

Shermer, M. (2015). *The moral arc.* New York: Henry Holt.

Shover, N. & Hochstetler, A. (2006). *Choosing white-collar crime.* New York: Cambridge University Press.

Sigfusdottir, I. D., Farkas, G., & Silver, E. (2004). The role of depressed mood and anger in the relationship between family conflict and delinquent behavior. *Journal of Youth and Adolescence, 33*(6), 509–522.

Simmel, G. (1903). *The metropolis and mental life.* London: The Free Press.

Simmel, G. (1907). *The philosophy of money.* London: Routledge & Kegan Paul.

Simon, R. J. (1975). *Women and crime.* Lexington, MA: Lexington Books.

Simons, R. L., Chen, Y. F., Stewart, E. A., & Brody, G. H. (2003). Incidents of discrimination and risk for delinquency: A longitudinal test of strain theory with an African American sample. *Justice Quarterly, 20*(4), 827–854.

Simpson, S. & Geis, G. (2008). The undeveloped concept of opportunity. In Goode, E. (Ed.) *Out of control: Assessing the general theory of crime* (pp. 49–60). Stanford, CA: Stanford University Press.

Singer, D. (1950). *Giordano Bruno: His life and thought, with annotated translation of his work – on the infinite universe and worlds.* Tulsa, OK: Schuman.

Singer, S. I. (1981). Homogeneous victim–offender populations: A review and some research implications. *Journal of Criminal Law and Criminology, 72,* 779–788.

Singer, S. I. (1986). Victims of serious violence and their criminal behavior: Subcultural theory and beyond. *Violence and Victims, 1,* 61–70.

Singer, S. I. (2014). *America's safest city: Delinquency and modernity in suburbia.* New York: New York University Press.

Skardhamar, T. (2009). Reconsidering the theory on adolescent-limited and life-course persistent anti-social behaviour. *The British Journal of Criminology, 49*(6), 863–878.

Skardhamar, T., Savolainen, J., Aase, K. N., & Lyngstad, T. H. (2015). Does marriage reduce crime? In Tonry, M. (Ed.) *Crime & justice: A review of research* (Vol. 44, pp. 385–557). Chicago, IL: University of Chicago Press.

Skinner, B. F. (1957). *Verbal behavior.* Englewood Cliffs, NJ: Prentice Hall.

Slade, E. P., Stuart, E. A., Salkever, D. S., Karakus, M., Green, K. M., & Ialongo, N. (2008). Impacts of age of onset of substance use disorders on risk of adult incarceration among disadvantaged urban youth: A propensity score matching approach. *Drug and Alcohol Dependence, 95*(1), 1–13.

Slocum, L. A., Simpson, S. S., & Smith, D. A. (2005). Strained lives and crime: Examining intra-individual variation in strain and offending in a sample of incarcerated women. *Criminology, 43*(4), 1067–1110.

Slutkin, G. (2013). Violence is a contagious disease. In *Contagion of violence, forum on global violence prevention, workshop summary. Institute of Medicine and National Research Council* (pp. 94–111). Washington, DC: The National Academies Press.

Sparks, R. F. (1982). *Research on victims of crime: Accomplishments, issues, and new directions.* U.S. Department of Health and Human Services, Public Health Service, Alcohol, Drug Abuse, and Mental Health Administration, National Institute of Mental Health, Center for Studies of Crime and Delinquency.

Spurzheim, J. (1815). *The physiognomical system of Drs. Gall and Spurzheim.* London: Baldwin, Cradock, and Joy.

Stafford, M. C. & Warr, M. (1993). A reconceptualization of general and specific deterrence. *Journal of Research in Crime and Delinquency, 30*(2), 123–135.

Stark, R. (1987). Deviant places: A theory of the ecology of crime. *Criminology, 25*(4), 893–910.

Steffensmeier, D., Allan, E., & Streifel, C. (1989). Development and female crime: A cross-national test of alternative explanations. *Social Forces, 68*(1), 262–283.

Stein, B. D., Jaycox, L. H., Kataoka, S. H., Wong, M., Tu, W., Elliott, M. N., & Fink, A. (2003). A mental health intervention for schoolchildren exposed to violence: A randomized controlled trial. *JAMA, 290*(5), 603–611.

Steinberg, L. (2014). *Age of opportunity: Lessons from the new science of adolescence*. Boston, MA: Houghton Mifflin Harcourt.

Steinberg, L., Cauffman, E., Woolard, J., Graham, S., & Banich, M. (2009). Are adolescents less mature than adults? Minors' access to abortion, the juvenile death penalty, and the alleged APA "flip-flop." *American Psychologist, 64*(7), 583–594.

Stewart, A., Livingston, M., & Dennison, S. (2008). Transitions and turning points: Examining the links between child maltreatment and juvenile offending. *Child Abuse & Neglect, 32*, 51–66.

Stewart, E. A., Elifson, K. W., & Sterk, C. E. (2004). Integrating the general theory of crime into an explanation of violent victimization among female offenders. *Justice Quarterly, 21*, 159–181.

Stewart, E. A., Schreck, C. J., & Simons, R. L. (2006). "I ain't gonna let no one disrespect me": Does the code of the street reduce or increase violent victimization among African American adolescents? *Journal of Research in Crime and Delinquency, 43*, 427–458.

Stowell, J. I., Messner, S. F., McGeever, K. F., & Raffalovich, L. E. (2009). Immigration and the recent violent crime drop in the United States: A pooled, cross-sectional time-series analysis of metropolitan areas. *Criminology, 47*(3), 889–928.

Stretesky, P. B. (2003). The distribution of air lead levels across US counties: Implications for the production of racial inequality. *Sociological Spectrum, 23*(1), 91–118.

Subhas, N. & Chandra, A. (2004). *Baltimore City Police Athletic League assessment study*. Baltimore, MD: Center for Adolescent Health – Johns Hopkins Bloomberg School of Public Health.

Sullivan, C. J., Welsh, B. C., & Ilchi, O. S. (2017). Modeling the scaling up of early crime prevention. *Criminology & Public Policy, 16*(2), 457–485.

Sutherland, E. H. (1934). *Principals of criminology*. Philadelphia, PA: Lippincott.

Sutherland, E. H. (1940). White-collar criminality. *American Sociological Review, 5*(1), 1–12.

Swinford, S. P., DeMaris, A., Cernkovich, S. A., & Giordano, P. C. (2000). Harsh physical discipline in childhood and violence in later romantic involvements: The mediating role of problem behaviors. *Journal of Marriage and Family, 62*, 508–519.

Sykes, G. M. & Matza, D. (1957). Techniques of neutralization: A theory of delinquency. *American Sociological Review, 22*(6), 664–670.

Szasz, T. (1970). *The manufacture of madness*. New York: Dell.

Tannenbaum, F. (1938). *Crime and the community*. Boston, MA: Ginn.

Tappan, P. W. (1960). *Crime, justice and correction* (Vol. 1221). New York: McGraw-Hill.

Tarde, G. ([1903]1980). *The laws of imitation*. New York: H. Holt.

Taylor, R. B. (2001). *Breaking away from broken windows: Baltimore neighborhoods and the nationwide fight against crime, grime, fear, and decline*. Boulder, CO: Westview Press.

Thornberry, T. P., Krohn, M. D., Lizotte, A. J., Smith, C. A., & Tobin, K. (2003). *Gangs and delinquency in developmental perspective*. Cambridge, MA: Cambridge University Press.

Thrasher, F. M. (1927). *The gang: A study of 1,313 gangs in Chicago*. Chicago, IL: University of Chicago Press.

Tielbeek, J. J., Medland, S. E., Benyamin, B., Byrne, E. M., Heath, A. C., Madden, P. A., Martin, N. G., Wray, N. R., & Verweij, K. J. (2012). Unraveling the genetic etiology of adult antisocial behavior: A genome-wide association study. *PloS One, 7*(10), e45086.

Tittle, C. R. (1995). *Control balance: Toward a general theory of deviance*. Boulder, CO: Westview Press.

Tittle, C. R. & Botchkovar, E. V. (2005). Self-control, criminal motivation and deterrence: An investigation using Russian respondents. *Criminology, 43*, 307–354.

Tittle, C. R., Ward, D. A., & Grasmick, H. G. (2003). Gender, age, and crime/deviance: A challenge to self-control theory. *Journal of Research in Crime and Delinquency, 40*(4), 426–453.

Toby, J. (1957). Social disorganization and stake in conformity: Complementary factors in the predatory behavior of hoodlums. *Journal of Criminal Law and Criminology, 48*(1), 12–17.

Tomlinson, S. (2005). *Head masters: Phrenology, secular education, and nineteenth-century social thought*. Tuscaloosa, AL: University of Alabama Press.

Tonry, M. (1995). *Malign neglect: Race, crime, and punishment in America*. New York: Oxford University Press.

Travers, M. (2008). Understanding comparison in criminal justice research: An interpretive perspective. *International Criminal Justice Review, 18*, 389–405.

Tremblay, R. E. (2010). Developmental origins of disruptive behaviour problems: The "original sin" hypothesis, epigenetics and their consequences for prevention. *Journal of Child Psychology and Psychiatry, 51*(4), 341–367.

Tremblay, R. E., Vitaro, F., Nagin, D., Pagani, L., & Seguin, J. R. (2003). The Montreal longitudinal and experimental study. In Thornberry, T. P. & Krohn, M. D. (Eds.) *Taking stock of delinquency* (pp. 205–254). New York: Springer.

Tsigos, C. & Chrousos, G. P. (2002). Hypothalamic–pituitary–adrenal axis, neuroendocrine factors and stress. *Journal of Psychosomatic Research, 53*(4), 865–871.

Tsouna, V. (1998). *The epistemology of the Cyrenaic school*. New York: Cambridge University Press.

Turk, A. (1969). *Criminality and legal order*. Chicago, IL: Rand McNally.

Tyler, K. & Johnson, K. (2004). Victims and offenders: Accounts of paybacks, invulnerability and financial gain among homeless youth. *Deviant Behavior, 25*, 427–449.

Uggen, C. (1999). Ex-offenders and the conformist alternative: A job quality model of work and crime. *Social Problems, 46*(1), 127–151.

Uggen, C. (2000). Work as a turning point in the life course of criminals: A duration model of age, employment, and recidivism. *American Sociological Review, 65*(4), 529–546.

Uggen, C., Manza, J., & Thompson, M. (2006). Citizenship, democracy, and the civic reintegration of criminal offenders. *The Annals of the American Academy of Political and Social Science, 605*(1), 281–310.

UNODC. (2009). United Nations Office on Drugs and Crime. Global report on trafficking in persons. Available at www.unodc.org/documents/Global_Report_on_TIP.pdf.

Ursell, L. K., Metcalf, J. L., Parfrey, L. W., & Knight, R. (2012). Defining the human microbiome. *Nutrition Reviews, 70*(suppl.1), S38–S44.

Vargas, E. V., Latour, B., Karsenti, B., Aït-Touati, F., & Salmon, L. (2008). The debate between Tarde and Durkheim. *Environment and Planning D: Society and Space, 26*(5), 761–777.

Vaske, J. C. (2017). Using biosocial criminology to understand and improve treatment outcomes. *Criminal Justice and Behavior*. Online First.

Vaske, J., Galyean, K., & Cullen, F. T. (2011). Toward a biosocial theory of offender rehabilitation: Why does cognitive-behavioral therapy work? *Journal of Criminal Justice, 39*(1), 90–102.

Vaughn, M. G. (2016). Policy implications of biosocial criminology. *Criminology & Public Policy, 15*(3), 703–710.

Vazsonyi, A. T. & Crosswhite, J. M. (2004). A test of Gottfredson and Hirschi's general theory of crime in African American adolescents. *Journal of Research in Crime and Delinquency, 41*(4), 407–432.

Vazsonyi, A., Pickering, L., Junger, M., & Hessing, D. (2001). An empirical test of a general theory of crime: A four-nation comparative study of self-control and the prediction of deviance. *Journal of Research in Crime and Delinquency, 38*, 91–131.

Vlastos, G. (1991). *Socrates, ironist and moral philosopher* (Vol. 50). Cornell, NY: Cornell University Press.

Vold, G. B. (1958). *Theoretical criminology*. Oxford: Oxford University Press.

Von Hentig, H. (1940). Remarks on the interaction of perpetrator and victim. *Journal of Criminal Law and Criminology, 31*, 303–309.

Von Hentig, H. (1948). *The criminal & his victim: Studies in the sociobiology of crime*. New Haven, CT: Yale University Press.

Walsh, A. A. (1972). The American tour of Dr. Spurzheim. *Journal of the History of Medicine and Allied Sciences, 27*(2), 187–205.

Walsh, A. (2009). Criminal behavior from heritability to epigenetics: How genetics clarifies the role of the environment. *Biosocial criminology: New directions in theory and research*, 29–49.

Walsh, A. & Vaske, J. C. (2015). *Feminist criminology through a biosocial lens*. Durham, NC: Carolina Academic Press.

Walsh, A. & Yun, I. (2014). Epigenetics and allostasis implications for criminology. *Criminal Justice Review, 39*(4), 411–431.

Walsh, A., Johnson, H., & Bolen, J. D. (2012). Drugs, crime, and the epigenetics of hedonic allostasis. *Journal of Contemporary Criminal Justice, 28*(3), 314–328.

Warner, B. D. (2003). The role of attenuated culture in social disorganization theory. *Criminology*, *41*(1), 73–98.

Warr, M. (1996). Organization and instigation in delinquent groups. *Criminology*, *34*(1), 11–37.

Warr, M. (2002). *Companions in crime: The social aspects of criminal conduct*. New York: Cambridge University Press.

Watson, B., Watson, A., Siskind, V., Fleiter, J., & Soole, D. (2015). Profiling high-range speeding offenders: Investigating criminal history, personal characteristics, traffic offences, and crash history. *Accident Analysis & Prevention*, *74*, 87–96.

Weaver, B. & McNeill, F. (2011). *Giving up crime: Directions for policy*. Glasgow: Scottish Centre for Crime & Justice Research. Available at www.sccjr.ac.uk/publications/giving-up-crime-directions-for-policy/.

Weindling, P. (2001). The origins of informed consent: The international scientific commission on medical war crimes, and the Nuremberg code. *Bulletin of the History of Medicine*, *75*(1), 37–71.

Weinhold, B. (2006). Epigenetics: The science of change. Environmental health perspectives. *Neuroscience*, *7*, 847–854.

Weir, H. & Orrick, E. (2013). The most prolific female scholars in elite criminology and criminal justice journals, 2000–2010. *Journal of Criminal Justice Education*, *24*(3), 273–289.

Weisburd, D. & Britt, C. (2007). *Statistics in criminal justice*. New York: Springer.

Weisburd, D., Groff, E. R., & Yang, S. M. (2012). *The criminology of place: Street segments and our understanding of the crime problem*. New York: Oxford University Press.

Weisburd, D., Bushway, S., Lum, C., & Yang, S. M. (2004). Trajectories of crime at places: A longitudinal study of street segments in the city of Seattle. *Criminology*, *42*(2), 283–322.

Wells, J., Armstrong, T., Boisvert, D., Lewis, R., Gangitano, D., & Hughes-Stramm, S. (2017). Stress, genes, and generalizability across gender: Effects of MAOA and stress sensitivity on crime and delinquency. *Criminology*. *55*(3), 548–574.

Welsh, A. & Lavoie, J. A. (2012). Risky eBusiness: An examination of risk-taking, online disclosiveness, and cyberstalking victimization. *Cyberpsychology: Journal of Psychosocial Research on Cyberspace*, *6*(1), 1–12.

Whitman, Charles. (1966). "Whitman Letter." The Whitman Archives. *Austin American-Statesman*, July 31.

Widom, C. S. (1989). The cycle of violence. *Science*, *244*, 160–166.

Wieck, D. (1978). Anarchist justice. *Nomos*, *19*, 215–236.

Wikström, P-O. H. (2006). Individuals, settings, and acts of crime: Situational mechanisms and the explanation of crime. In Wikström, P-O. H. & Sampson, R. J. *The explanation of crime: Contexts, mechanisms and development* (pp. 61–107). New York: Cambridge University Press.

Wilson, E. O. (1975). *Sociobiology*. Cambridge, MA: Harvard University Press.

Wilson, J. Q. & Herrnstein, R. J. (1998). *Crime and human nature: The definitive study of the causes of crime*. New York: The Free Press.

Wilson, J. Q. & Kelling, G. L. (1982). The police and neighborhood safety: Broken windows. *Atlantic Monthly*, *127*(2).

Wittebrood, K. & Nieuwbeerta, P. (2000). Criminal victimization during one's life course: The effects of previous victimization and patterns of routine activities. *Journal of Research in Crime and Delinquency*, *37*(1), 91–122.

Wolfgang, M. E. (1957). Victim precipitated criminal homicide. *Criminal Law, Criminology, and Police Science*, *48*, 1–11.

Wolfgang, M. E., Figlio, R. M., & Sellin, T. (1972). *Delinquency in a birth cohort*. Chicago, IL: University of Chicago Press.

Wolfgang, M. E., Thornberry, T. P., & Figlio, R. M. (1987). *From boy to man, from delinquency to crime*. Chicago, IL: University of Chicago Press.

Wong, J. S., Bouchard, J., Gravel, J., Bouchard, M., & Morselli, C. (2016). Can at-risk youth be diverted from crime? A meta-analysis of restorative diversion programs. *Criminal Justice and Behavior*, *43*(10), 1310–1329.

Woods, J. B. (2014). Queer contestations and the future of a critical "queer" criminology. *Critical Criminology*, *22*(1), 5–19.

Woolf, A. (2000). Witchcraft or mycotoxin? The Salem witch trials. *Journal of Toxicology: Clinical Toxicology*, *38*(4), 457–460.

Wright, J. P., Beaver, K. M., DeLisi, M., Vaughn, M. G., Boisvert, D., & Vaske, J. (2008). Lombroso's legacy: The miseducation of criminologists. *Journal of Criminal Justice Education, 19*(3), 325–338.

Xu, Z., Hu, Q., & Zhang, C. (2013). Why computer talents become computer hackers. *Communications of the ACM, 56*(4), 64–74.

Yar, M. (2010). Cesare Beccaria (1738–94). In Hayward, K., Maruna, S., & Mooney, J. (Eds.) *Fifty key thinkers in criminology* (pp. 3–7). New York: Routledge.

Young, J. (1979). Left idealism, reformism and beyond: From new criminology to Marxism. In Fine, B., Kinsey, R., Lea, J., Picciotto, S., & Young, J. (Eds.) *Capitalism and the rule of law* (pp. 13–28). London: Hutchinson.

Young, J. (1987). The tasks facing a realist criminology. *Contemporary Crises, 11*(4), 337–356.

Zaibert, L. (2016). *Punishment and retribution.* New York: Routledge.

Zhang, L., Welte, J. W., & Wieczorek, W. F. (2001). Deviant lifestyle and crime victimization. *Journal of Criminal Justice, 29*, 133–143.

Zimmerman, G. M. (2010). Impulsivity, offending, and the neighborhood: Investigating the person–context nexus. *Journal of Quantitative Criminology, 26*(3), 301–332.

Zimmerman, G. M. & Messner, S. F. (2011). Neighborhood context and nonlinear peer effects on adolescent violent crime. *Criminology, 49*(3), 873–903.

Zimmerman, G. M. & Posick, C. (2016). Risk factors for and behavioral consequences of direct versus indirect exposure to violence. *American Journal of Public Health, 106*(1), 178–188.

Cases cited

Buck vs. Bell, 274 U.S. 200, 47 S. Ct. 584, 71 L. Ed. 1000 (1927).

People vs. Williams (Cal S. Ct. April 11, 1988).

Roper vs. Simmons, 543 U.S. 551, 125 S. Ct. 1183, 161 L. Ed. 2d 1 (2005).

Personal interviews

Agnew, Robert, December 30, 2016.

Baumer, Eric, January 30, 2017.

Brehm, Hollie, December 19, 2016.

Boman, John, July 25, 2017.

Cole, Simon, December 19, 2016.

Crank, John, January 4, 2017.

Donnermeyer, Joseph, December 23, 2016.

Leverentz, Andrea, January 21, 2017.

Lynch, Michael, April 21, 2016.

Maruna, Shadd, December 12, 2016.

Maxfield, Michael, January 31, 2017.

Ousey, Graham, June 30, 2017.

Pratt, Travis, February 28, 2016.

Ritchie, Stuart, October 9, 2016.

Robinson, Matthew, July 13, 2016.

Singer, Simon, January 29, 2016.

Vaughn, Michael, January 9, 2017.

Warner, Barbara, October 12, 2016.

Index

action research 7
Adler, Freda 85–6
age-graded theory of informal social control 124–6
Agnew, Robert 5, 60–1, 63–5, 126–7, 168, 172–5, 181
Akers, Ron 69–72, 76, 168
Alhazen 5–6
allostatic load 140–1
American Dream 56–8, 61–2, 65
Ammons, Latoya 21–2
Anderson, Elijah 45, 182
anomie 57–59
applied research 7
Aristotle 15, 27

Bandura, Albert72–3
Baumer, Eric 198
Bayout, Abdelmalek 35–6
Beccaria, Cesare 28, 106–10, 118
Becker, Gary 110
Benson, Michael 173
Bentham, Jeremy 106–7, 109–10, 112, 118
biology 9–10
biocriminology 25–6; empirical support for 36–7; and evolution 29, 32; and genetics 30–2, 34–8; and heredity 29–31, 33–7; and intelligence 30, 33; origins of 26–32; and public policy 37–8; recent developments in 32–5

biosocial criminology 10, 26, 30, 90, 135–6, 146–7; empirical support for 143–4; ethical considerations of 145–7; future directions in 144–5, 192–3, 197; and the gut 142–3; origins of 136–7; and physical abuse 142; and physiology 34, 136; policy implications of 145–6; recent developments in 137–43; and victimization 187–8
Boman, John 75
Bonger, Willem 81
Boutwell, Brian 137
Bossler, Adam 167, 195
Boston Marathon Bombing 7374
Brain Genomics Superstruct Project 34
Braithwaite, John 84, 91
Brantingham, Patricia and Paul 46–7, 53
Brehm, Hollie Nyseth 169, 194–5
broken windows theory 53
Brown, Michael 114–5
Buck, Carrie 35–6
Burgess, Ernest42–5
Bursick, Robert 47, 51
Bushway, Shawn 107, 126

Cambridge-Somerville Youth Program 132
Campbell, Anne 86

Causation 7–8
Chesney-Lind, Meda 86
Chicago Area Project 44, 52
Chicago School 9, 41–6, 69, 178
child maltreatment 160, 179–80, 187–8
classical theories 1, 106–9, 112
Cloward, Richard 59, 62, 75
Code of Hammurabi 14–15
cognitive behavioral therapy 37–8, 196
Cohen, Albert K. 59, 75
cognitive landscapes 48
Cohen, Lawrence E. 110–2
Cole, Simon 198–9
collective efficacy 47–8, 157, 172
comparative criminology 149–52, 161–3; future directions in 159–60; origins of 154–5; policy implications of 160–1; recent developments in 155–9
Comprehensive Employment and Training Act of 1973 65
concentric zone model 43, 45
conflict 10, 78–9
consensus 10
constructivism 4
containment theory 95
context 2, 42, 100
constitutional theories 31
control theories 10, 45–46, 94–5, 104, 157–9, 173; empirical support for 102;

origins of 95–97; policy implications of 103–104; recent developments in 97–10; and victimization 185–186

correlation 7

Crank, John 172–3

crime: as a social construction 4–5, 9; definitions of 5, 9, 14

criminal law 5, 14–5

criminology: definition of 9; as a field of study 11; future of 191–2, 198–9; as a science 2; of place 46–7, 53, 198

critical criminology 78–80, 90–1; origins of 80

Cullen, Francis 61

cultural deviance theories 6

culture 151–4

Currie, Elliott 85

cybercrime 167–8, 195

data 5–6

decriminalization 5, 91

defensible space 46–7, 52–3

degradation ceremonies 83

Dekeseredy, Walter 171

Delisi, Matt 138, 187

della Porta, Giambatta 26–8

demonology 14, 17–8, 20–2; empirical support for 22

Descartes, Rene 20

desistance 84, 123–32

deterrence theory 107, 118–9; empirical support for 116–7; origins of 107–9; policy implications of 117–8; recent developments in 112–3; role of fear 113

developmental theories 121–2, 133; empirical support for 130–1; future of 192; origins of 122–3; policy implications of 131–2; recent developments in 123–9

differential association 45, 69, 74, 76, 173; recent developments in 70–3; origins of 69–70

Dinitz, Simon 95–6

diversion programs 91

Donnermeyer, Joseph 171–2

Du Bois, W.E.B. 41–3

Dugdale, Richard 29–30

Durkheim, Emile 42, 57–8, 61, 70, 154–5

empiricism 3, 12, 14

Enlightenment 1, 6, 13, 15, 20, 25–6, 28, 106–8

environmental exposure to toxins 141

epigenetics 139–140, 144–145

epistemology 4

Esping-Andersen, Gøsta 151–152

exorcism 14, 21

experiments 5

eugenics 27, 30–2, 37

evil, 14–5, 17, 23

evolution 137–8

facts 11–2

Farrington, David 127–8

Fattah, Ezzat 178

Felson, Marcus 110–2

Felson, Richard 181

feminist criminology 80, 85–7, 89; empirical support for, 89–90

Ferguson effect 114–5

Fox, James Alan 170

free will 15

Gall, Franz Joseph 28

Gannon, Martin J. 152–4

gangs 43–5, 59, 73, 82, 129–30, 160, 182

gene-by-environment interactions 136, 139

general strain theory 60–61 156–7, 174–5, 181

Geneva Conventions 161, **162**

genocide 168–9, 194–5

Giordano, Peggy 125–6

global warming and violence 172–1

globalization 152

Glueck, Sheldon and Eleanor 26, 31–2, 122–3, 127–8, 192

Goddard, Henry 30

Goffman, Erving 83

Goring, Charles 29

Gottfredson, Michael 98–9, 104, 132, 186

Grasmick, Harold 47, 51

Great Recession 143

green criminology 80, 87–8; empirical support for 89; future of 196

Groves, Casey 47

Guided Group Interaction 76

Hagan, John 169

Harding, David 182–3

hate crime 170–1

Haynie, Dana 73, 187

Head Start 65

Hegel, G.W.F. 80–1

Henting, Hans von 177–8

Hernnstein, Richard J. 33

Hipp, John 50–1

Hirschi, Travis 6, 46, 97–102, 104, 132,185–6

Hobbes, Thomas 6, 16, 107–8

Hochstetler, Andy 173–4

Holt, Thomas 167

Homer-Dixon, Thomas 172–3

hotspots 114

Hume, David 107–8

Hutcheson 106–8

Hypotheses 5–6

ideal victim 178

imitation 70, 72–4

immigration 40, 44, 52, 56–7, 171

institutional anomie theory 9, 61–2, 156

integrated cognitive antisocial potential theory 127

International Criminal Court 160–1

international criminology see comparative criminology

International Self-Report Delinquency studies 158–9

INTERPOL 160–1

intersectionality 80, 86–8

Jacoby, Linda 172

Jeffrey, C. Ray 136–7

Kant, Immanuel 20

Katz, Jack, 44

Kelling, George L. 53

Kempf, Kimberly 102

Kluegel, James 112
Kornhauser, Ruth 46, 48–9, 75
Kraft, Randy 101–2
Kubrin, Charis 50–1, 171

labeling theory 78–80, 82–3;
    empirical support for 89,
    92; policy implications of
    90–1; recent developments
    in 84
LaFree, Gary 115, 168
Land, Kenneth 112
Laub, John 32, 84, 124–6, 192,
    196
Lavater, Johann Kaspar 27–8
jeft realism 84–5
legal cynicism 51
Lemert, Edwin 83
Levin, Jack 170
lex talionis 14–16
lifestyle and routine activities
    theory 112
lifestyles theory 110, 112
Locke, John 16, 20, 107
Lombroso, Cesare 26, 28–9,
    32, 68, 85, 178
Lynch, Michael J. 87

MAOA gene 139, 144, 187
marijuana 5
Maruna, Shadd 2, 130
Marx, Karl 79–81
Marxist criminology 80–2, 85;
    policy implications of 90–1
masculinity 86
mass shootings 169–70, 193–4
Mateen, Omar 169–70
maturation 123, 192
Matza, David 96–7, 123
Maxfield, Mike 198
McKay, Henry 44–9, 53
McNeill, Fergus 131–32
Mendelsohn, Benjamin
    177–178
Merton, Robert K. 58–9, 61
Messerschmidt 86
Messner, Steven 9, 62, 65, 156
Michael-Adler Report 68–9
Mitchell, Tonya 63
Mobilization for Youth 65
Moffitt, Terrie 36, 123–4,
    130–1, 137, 187

Montesquieu 106–8
Morality 15
Murphy, Dan 62–3

National Crime Survey 110, 179
naturalistic perspectives on
    crime 19–20
nature vs. nurture debate 9–10
neutralization theory 96–7,
    169
Newman, Oscar 46–7, 52–3
Nuremberg Codes 161, **163**
nutrition 141–2
Nye, F. Ivan 96

objectivism 1–2
Ohlin, Lloyd 59, 61–62, 75
opportunity structure theory 59
Oregon Social Learning
    Center 76
Ousey, Graham 171, 198

Park, Robert 42–5
Parmenides, 4
Passas, Nikos 62
Paternoster, Raymond
    107, 126
patriarchy 80, 86, 171–2
peacemaking criminology
    84, 91
phenomenology 8
phrenology 26, 28
physiognomy 26–8
Pillai, Rajnandini 152–4
Plato 14
pluralism 10
positivism 4, 14, 20, 25, 68, 150
postmodernism 4
Prett, Travis 100–1
program evaluation 7
psychopathy 8, 101–2, 138–9
Pyrooz, David 160

queer criminology 80, 88
Quinet, Kenna 170
Quinney, Richard 71, 84, 91

racism 27, 41
radical non-intervention 82, 90
Rafter, Nicole 32, 37, 145, 168–9
Raine, Adrian 33–4, 101–2,
    138, 145

randomized controlled trials
    196–7
rational choice theory 107,
    118–9, 168; empirical
    support for 115; origins
    of 107–109; recent
    developments in 110–112
Reckless, Walter 95–6
rehabilitation 15–6, 11
Reiss Jr., Albert 95
religion and crime 10–1,
    16, 25; monotheistic
    perspectives, 17–19; pagan
    perspectives, 16–17
restorative justice 15, 17, 79,
    84, 90–1
retribution 14–5
rK theory 32–3, 137–8
Robinson, Matthew 62–3
Rochester, NY 49–50
Rocque, Michael 102–3,
    127–9, 145, 192
Rosenfeld, Richard 9, 62, 65,
    115, 156
routine activities theory
    110–2, 155, 158–9, 167–8,
    173; empirical support for
    115–116; and
modern technology 116;
    policy implications of 117
rural crime 171–2
Rymond-Richmond, Wenona
    169

St. Augustine of Hippo 16
St. Thomas Aquinas 16
Sampson, Robert 32, 42, 47–8,
    51, 53, 84, 124–6, 192
Schkreli, Martin 174
science: and controversy 10–1;
    definition of 4
scientific method 5–7, 10, 14,
    25, 29
scientific revolution 11
Schur, Edwin 82, 90
self-concept 95–6
self-control 8, 14–5, 22,
    51, 98–104, 157–9, 167;
    and upbringing 15; and
    victimization 179, 184–6
self-report surveys 95
Sellin, Thorsten 81–82

sex trafficking 159
Shaw, Clifford 44–9, 52–3
Shover, Neal 173–4
Simmel, George 42
Simon, Rita 86
Singer, Simon 53, 99–100
situational action theory 100
Skinner, B.F. 71
Slutkin, Gary 114
Smith, Adam 107, 109
Snow, John 114
social bonding theory 5–8
social capital 124, 186
social disorganization theory 9, 41, 45, 158, 171, 173; empirical support for 50–1; origins of 41–5; policy implications of 52–3; and race 48, 51; recent developments in 45–9; in rural areas 52; and spillover effects 51
social interactionist theory 181–2
social learning theory 10, 15, 69, 71–4, 155, 159, 167, 170; criticisms of 75; and delinquent peers 73–4, 158; empirical support for 74–5; policy implications of 75

specific theories of crime 166–7, 174–5; recent developments in 167–4
spuriousness 7–8
Spurzheim, Johann, 28
Stafford, Mark 107, 113
stakes in conformity 96, 98
Stark, Rodney 47
stigma, 83
strain theories, 6, 8, 10, 15, 46, 56–7, 156–7, 159; conditioning factors in 64; and emotions 63–4; empirical support for 63–5; and gender 60, 64; and modes of adaptation 58–9; origins of 57–60; policy implications of 64–6; recent developments in 60–2; and victimization 181
subcultural theories 59–60, 182–3
subjectivism 4, 8
Sutherland, Edwin 44–5, 69–70, 75–6, 173
Sykes, Gresham 96–9

Tannenbaum, Frank 82
Tarde, Gabriel 69–70, 72
tautology 8
terrorism 168, 193–4

theory 4–5; and assumptions of human behavior 9; elements of 7–8; macro-level 8–9; micro-level 8–9; proving of 8, 11–2; testability of 4–5, 10, 14
Thrasher, Frederick 44
Tittle, Charles 99, 157, 184–5
Toby, Jackson 96, 98
Turner, Brock Allen 88–9

Vaughn, Michael 146
victimology 176–80, 188

"War on Poverty" 65–6
Warr, Mark 73, 107, 113
Warner, Barbara 48–49
Weaver, Beth 131–2
Weitzer, Ronald 50–1
white-collar crime 173–4, 195
Wikstrom, Per-Olaf 100
Williams, Abigail 20–1
Williams III, Stanley "Tookie" 129–30
Wilson, Edward O. 136–7
Wilson, James, Q. 33, 53
Wilson, William Julius 48
witchcraft 17–23, 108
Wolfgang, Marvin 82, 123, 182

Young, Jock 84